Balkan Essays

Hubert Butler

Balkan Essays

With a Foreword by
Chris Agee

Edited by Chris and Jacob Agee

Nov 21
Natalie, this journey has
been fun and enlightening,
and, thankfully i see no
end in sight.

The Irish Pages Press
2016

Balkan Essays
is first published in hardback
by The Irish Pages Press
on 26 September 2016.

The Irish Pages Press
129 Ormeau Road
Belfast BT7 1SH
Ireland

www.irishpages.org

The Irish Pages Press gratefully acknowledges
the generous support and assistance of The Lilliput Press, Dublin.

Designed and composed in Brioni Text Std by Fraktura, Zaprešić, Croatia

Printed in Croatia by Denona, Zagreb

ISBN: 978-09935532-0-2

Contents

Notes on Sources

Essays

"Escape From the Ant-hill": *Trbelin Times* No 1 (September 1973). First collected in *Escape From the Anthill.*

"Mr Pfeffer of Sarajevo": *Nonplus* (Dublin), Winter 1960. First collected in *Escape from the Anthill.*

"In Dalmatia": unpublished typescript, 1937. First collected in *In the Land of Nod.*

"The Last Izmerenje": *The Irish Press*, 28 February 1947. First collected in *Escape From the Anthill.*

"Nazor, Oroshatz and the Von Berks," 1947. First collected in *The Children of Drancy.*

"A Trial": unpublished typescript, 1947.

"Yugoslavia: The Cultural Background," 1947. First collected in *Grandmother and Wolfe Tone.*

"Father Chok and Compulsory Conversion," 1947. First collected in *Grandmother and Wolfe Tone.*

"Yugoslav Papers: The Church and Its Opponents," 1947. First collected in *Grandmother and Wolfe Tone.*

"Report on Yugoslavia": typescript of report to the War Resisters International conference at Shrewsbury, England, in August 1947. First collected in *In the Land of Nod.*

"Memorandum on the Struggle Between Communism and Christianity": typescript of address delivered at War Resisters International council meeting at Haarlem, The Netherlands, 1 August 1949. First collected in *In the Land of Nod.*

"The Compulsory Conversion Campaign of 1941: I-III": preamble, with episcopal documents translated from the Croatian. *The Church of Ireland Gazette* 15, 29 December 1950 and 5 January 1951.

"A Visit to Lepoglava": original typescript of an essay published in *Church of Ireland Gazette*, 20 April 1951. First collected in *In the Land of Nod.*

"The Invader Wore Slippers": *The Bell*, November 1950. First collected in *Escape From the Anthill*.

"Ireland and Croatia": unpublished manuscript. Iriney Georgevitch's statement, made in 1948, was published in the July-August 1969 edition of *Svobodnoye Slovo* (*Free Word*), a Carpatho-Russian monthly, published in Newark, New Jersey, USA. First collected in *In the Land of Nod*.

"The Sub-Prefect Should Have Held His Tongue": *The Twentieth Century*, June 1956. First collected in *Escape From the Anthill*.

"The Artukovitch File": Section I appeared in *New Blackfriars* (Journal of Oxford Dominicans), February 1971, under title "What(ever) Became of Artukovitch? Reflections on a Croatian Crusade." First collected in *Escape From the Anthill*.

"Artukovitch: A Postscript": unpublished typescript, 1966.

"Cardinal Seper and the Ulster of Yugoslavia I-II": Section I appeared in *Grille: The Irish Christian Left* No 2 (Autumn 1968) under the title "A Sordid Chapter of Church History and Cardinal Seper."

"James Bouchier: An Irishman in Bulgaria," 1948. First collected in *Grandmother and Wolfe Tone*.

"Croatia, Gaj, Etc": unpublished handwritten manuscript, late 1940s.

"In Serbian Macedonia": unpublished typescript, 1930s.

"The Barriers": *The Bell*, July 1941. First collected in *Grandmother and Wolfe Tone*.

"The Two Languages," 1943. First collected in *Granmother and Wolfe Tone*.

"Fiume, Shusak, and the Nugents," 1947. First collected in *The Children of Drancy*.

"Maria Pasquinelli and the Dissolution of the Ego": A shorter version of this was published in *The Dublin Magazine* in 1947, under the title "Istria and Maria Pasquinelli." Butler wrote a brief addendum, placing Pasquinelli's story in a broader historical context. First collected in *In the Land of Nod*.

"The Russian Consul": BBC Radio, The Third Programme, 17 October 1947, under the title "A Journey to Split." First collected in *The Children of Drancy*.

"Some Encounters: Zagreb 1946," 1946. First collected in *Grandmother and Wolfe Tone*.

"Two Faces of Postwar Yugoslavia: Belgrade and Split," 1948. First collected in *Grandmother and Wolfe Tone*.

"In Europe's Debatable Lands": *The Irish Times* 26, 27, 28, 29, 30, 31 March 1951; *Irish Pages*, Vol 1, No 1 (Summer 2002).

"Trieste": *Peace News*, 20 November 1953. First collected in *The Appleman and the Poet*.

"Yugoslavia Today": *Peace News*, 5 August 1955. First collected in *The Appleman and the Poet*.

"Tito's Marxist Heretic": *Peace News*, 21 November 1958. First collected in *The Appleman and the Poet*.

"Return to Hellas": *The Twentieth Century*, January 1961. First collected in *Escape From the Anthill*.

"The Final Solution": *The Irish Times*, 3-6 June 1963. First collected in *Grandmother and Wolfe Tone.*

"Rebecca West in Yugoslavia": *The Irish Times*, 17 September 1977; the uncut version. First collected in *The Appleman and the Poet.*

"A Three Day Nation: Alexei Gierowski and Carpatho-Russia," 1990. First collected in *In the Land of Nod.*

Afterword

Brodsky, Joseph. "Appendix." *In the Land of Nod.* By Hubert Butler. Dublin: The Lilliput Press, 1996.

In memory of

Vojka Đikić
(1932 – 2016)

Poet, editor, translator, Sarajevan

Hearer and heartener

A Rare Tolerance of Disagreeable Truths

*I have always thought that compared with the question of how
we behave, what we believe is of little importance.*

Hubert Butler, 1990

I

In "The Artukovitch File" – his masterpiece of ethical forensics, and
one of the suite of magisterial Yugoslav essays gathered together here
for the first time – Hubert Butler recounts an incident in Rome in March
1942. The French Cardinal Tisserant, a member of the Curia, has an
audience with Rušinović, the representative at the Vatican of the Quisling "Independent State of Croatia," established by the Croat Separatist
Leader Pavelić and his Ustaše movement in April 1941, under the patronage of Nazi Germany and Fascist Italy, after the Axis invasion of
royal Yugoslavia.

Over the intervening year, Tisserant had got wind of the vast massacres of Serbian Orthodox Christians unleased by that genocidal regime, aided and abetted by a part of the Catholic Church, including
many if not most of the higher clergy, in what is now Croatia and
Bosnia. He denounces Rušinović in direct, undiplomatic language:

> I know for sure that even the Franciscans of Bosnia-Herze-
> govina behaved atrociously. Father Simitch, with a revolver

in his hand, led an armed gang and destroyed Orthodox
Churches. No civilized and cultured man, let alone a priest,
can behave like that... The Germans helped you kill all the
priests and you got rid of 350,000 Serbs, before you set up
the Croatian Orthodox Church. What right have you to accuse others and keep telling us that you are the guardians of
culture and the faith? In the war with the Turks the Serbs
did just as much for Catholicism as you did and perhaps more.
But it was the Croats, all the same, who got the title of *Antemurale Christianitatis*. ("The Artukovitch File")

As careful readers of *Balkan Essays* will soon discern, the selection
of this incident and its explosive quotation is quintessential Butler.
But not simply for the classic bull-eye's of this ethical marksman, or
even the profound historical implication thereby adumbrated – here
clearly, but also incrementally elsewhere across these essays, as if some
overall image from a jigsaw puzzle was slowly emerging, even when
left only partly assembled.

Butler has also spotted, in the figure of Tisserant, an "independent
spirit" – and in an unlikely place, the Roman Curia, and in an unlucky
time, when across the Adriatic "the most bloodthirsty religio-racial
crusade in history, far surpassing anything achieved by Cromwell and
the Spanish Inquisitors" ("The Artukovitch File"), had just spent its fury
in the mayhem of the NDH (the Croatian acronym for the Ustaše state).
Tisserant, says Butler in an aside, "had a rare tolerance of disagreeable
truths," attributing, implicitly, his honesty *and* truth-telling to this trait.

For the aficionado of Butler's oeuvre, the phrase will have the immediate ring not only of ethical admiration, but proxy self-description.
The English author Christopher Hitchens said something similar of
George Orwell, that "a power of facing unpleasant facts" was central
to this writer's work on twentieth-century totalitarianism – which,
Balkan Essays makes clear again, must comprehend not just communism and ideological fascism, but genocidal nationalism (or sectarianism) of all stripes, since in our age too this is again, revived, "the

new passionate racialism – the disease" ("Maria Pasquinelli and the Dissolution of the Ego") of our twenty-first century.

Butler's five previous volumes of essays abound in figures, like Tisserant, who, in some way, large or small – historical, cultural, intellectual, and/or creative – embody an "independent spirit." In this collection too, there is a characteristic focus on the single personality through whose lens or microcosm a larger historical picture is glimpsed. In addition to the innate interest of their persons, lives and informing times, to each of these figures is attached one or more of Butler's characteristic, highly atmospheric preoccupations: Mr Pfeffer (the collapse of empire, the death of liberalism); Vladimir Nazor (artists and revolution, the writer as independent spirit, the legacies of imperialism); Father Chok (personality under totalitarian pressure, sectarian crime); James Bourchier (the commitment to truth-seeking, truth-telling); Ljudevit Gaj (national and cultural independence); Miroslav Djilas (the eclipse of old South Slav culture, the rise of modernity); Hannah Arendt (twentieth-century bureaucratic crime); Rebecca West (the promise of the Succession States); and Alexei Gierowski (the treatment of small peoples by great powers).

What Butler says of Father Chok – who had first-hand experience of the massacres of the Ustaše-inspired campaign to convert the Orthodox Serbs of Croatia and Bosnia to Catholicism, welcomed initially and ecstatically by the Catholic hierarchy within the NDH – might be said, too quickly, of the writer himself: "he was more interested in personalities than in generalizations" ("Father Chok and Compulsory Conversion"). But that would be facile: Butler is, innately, interested in both personalities *and* generalizations. It is precisely his ability to mesh seamlessly the two that gives his writing such tensile strength and well-woven style.

His generalizations, however, are generally not of the sweeping, "pseudo-cosmic" variety; rather, they are most often expressed in the distilled, summative, conclusive, and brilliant aperçus that approach a kind of wisdom in human affairs and are the unmissable hallmark of this most subtle, compact and ironical of writers. How much he can cover in a paragraph, or even a sentence! – and how carefully the reader must attend to his swift concatenation of images and allusions within the momentum of his prose.

In comparison to the focus on individuals so congenial to Butler's writerly genius, Cardinal Tisserant would appear a bit player in this book's grand accumulative narrative on the genocidal NDH, and the Catholic Church's "collaborationist" support and appeasement of it – and, yes, very conscious connivance with it, "sometimes by their active complicity, sometimes by their silence" ("Appendix", p. 560). Yet, like certain small but important characters in Shakespeare – or like the Russian Consul and Maria Pasquinelli in two of these essays – Tisserant's rôle points to something much greater because his own active involvement proves to be much larger. What that "something" is, it transpires, is close, in several historical senses, to the heart of Butler's critique of the wartime role of the Catholic hierarchy and, in particular, of Archbishop Alojzije (Alosius) Stepinac.

That this writer's depth, breadth and even height of Balkan knowledge and experience are incontrovertible – to say nothing of the patterning of thought applied to both, for coming on sixty years – can, with this volume, hardly be gainsaid. Most fair-minded readers, I daresay, would tend to agree after reading even a few of the major Yugoslav essays, whatever they might think of his general outlook or specific conclusions.

The extraordinary accumulation of telling detail, laced within incisive insights and vivid distillations, is particularly impressive vis-à-vis the region's interwar, wartime and immediate post-war periods. He knew the Yugoslav lands exceedingly well and spoke their predominant language fluently. It is abundantly clear that, in particular, he was a great lover of Croatia, especially Dalmatia. In retrospect, there is also the small matter that he proved – by the standard of final output – to be one of the finest Irish literary intellects of the twentieth century.

I also used "height" in the phrase "height of Balkan knowledge and experience" because, in fact, a great deal of what Butler brings to every essay is nearly invisible, nearly wholly unsaid. But not, thereby, absent – because *assumed*. This element of his prose is like the lower contour lines supporting the peaks of his paragraphs, the ridges of his sentences. Because he is a highly sophisticated and subtle prose stylist, he does not "picnic at each cross-roads" ("The Two Languages") – does not feel obliged to describe the processes by which he reached those peaks and ridges, like a mathematician presenting final formulae, who omits the trail of all prior calculations.

You can, however, "work out" his underlying headwork by reading across his writings at length. The headwork left out in one essay – so as not to dawdle at the cross-roads – appears in another. Butler is the most self-referential, self-intertextual of writers because he assumes full equality with his readers and, therefore, makes no allowances for, or concessions to, what they might wish or need in the form of background assistance. He presents his literary algebra full and finished – and, if necessary, you must catch up on your own with his uphill calculations.

Nothing could illustrate this better than Butler's extensive writings on Archbishop Stepinac – the undoubted centrepiece of this volume. Surprisingly, there is no single essay dedicated either to the Archbishop and/or to the wider collaboration of the Catholic Church, despite his declared post-war intention to make "a study of the Christian crisis in Yugoslavia" ("Appendix", p. 550). It might thus be thought that Stepinac is used simply, though persistently, as a prop for illustrative purposes vis-à-vis his great theme in Part One of *Balkan Essays*, the corruption of contemporary Christianity; but that would be to misunderstand the capacious interlacings and revelatory divagations of his style.

In fact, apart from such single individuals, almost all of the essays in the six volumes lack a single exclusive focus; his final literary head-and-handiwork is always inescapably multi-faceted and polyphonic. Rather, we are expected to follow his reflections on a compromised prelate across a range of texts whose cumulative effect is that of a jigsaw puzzle slowly assembled. If the danger in this procedure is that some pieces are missed even by the attentive reader – and here is where Tisserant re-enters – the reward is a distinct superaddition of ethical power owing to the repeated literary brilliance of his singular portrait of "the extraordinary alliance of religion and crime" ("The Invader Wore Slippers") that was the NDH.

In the two allusions to Tisserant cited above, Butler neglects a revelatory fact which he knew and so assumed, but includes only in a third allusion: that the Cardinal was the Curial Secretary of the Sacred Congregation of the Eastern Church, that is to say, the Vatican official responsible for those Uniat churches, among others, that maintain the Eastern Orthodox rite but adhere to the papacy.

As such, the soon-to-be-outspoken Tisserant was directly and personally connected with the conversion campaign in Croatia, having written a letter of Curial endorsement to Archbishop Stepinac in July 1941 ("The Compulsory Conversion Campaign of 1941: I-III"), not long after its commencement. In other words, when Tisserant spoke to Rušinović, he himself (*and by extension the Curia*) was to a degree on the ethical hook for a catastrophic conversion campaign that had led to hundreds of thousands of deaths. Butler adds that it was probably only Cardinals Tisserant and Montini (the future Pope Paul VI) who "appear to have fully grasped what was happening in Croatia" ("The Artukovitch File").

What is the promised historical significance of all this?

That certain high echelons of the Vatican were aware of "the gigantic massacre of 1941... linked to Paveltitch's conversion campaign" ("The Compulsory Conversion Campaign of 1941: I-III") has long been known, or at least suspected – if never definitively, with primary documentation, established. That those same echelons, knowing what they did, did or said nothing further, so as to check or publicize "the rule of violence" and "this inroad of fanatical barbarians into the purely ecclesiastical domain of conversion" ("The Compulsory Conversion Campaign of 1941: I-III"), follows swiftly as the damning corollary.

Nothing new, in short, in the idea that the Vatican likely knew and remained silent about "the Croatian crusade" in the NDH. That powerless micro-state, with its history of sympathies, was, after all, surrounded by Fascist Italy in an era of totalitarian war. When, indeed, was there not something amiss in the Curia – or in any state institution?

Although I have read, re-read, studied and loved the work of Hubert Butler for over thirty nears, it is only when I compiled *Balkan Essays* that I began to appreciate the emphasis that Butler places on the concurrent role – subordinate, of course, to that of the Roman Catholic Church, led by Stepinac – of the Uniat (Greek Catholic) Church in Croatia (see "Father Chok and Compulsory Conversion;" "The Compulsory Conversion Campaign of 1941: I-III") in the compulsory conversion campaign of 1941. This, it now seems to me, is a function of that dimension of assumed knowledge in Butler's writing that avoids dawdling at the crossroads.

It was rather late in the day, in fact, that I finally appreciated the ecclesiastical stature of that undoubted supporter of the Ustaše regime, Dr Šimrak, "editor of the leading Catholic daily" ("Appendix", p.545), and unquestionably (as Butler makes plain) Stepinac's closest colleague in the formal "regulation" and "supervision" of the conversion campaign. I had long assumed that he was simply a mid-ranking Monsignor in the Roman Catholic structure, but he was actually first Apostolic Administrator, then Bishop, of the Eparchy of Križevci, effectively the Uniat Chruch for all "Greek Catholics" in interwar Yugoslavia – and so of course part of Tisserant's Congregation of the Eastern Church.

It transpires that Stepinac and Šimrak were not merely standard ecclesiastical colleagues on a trying religious mission, but the respective heads of two distinct Churches within the Catholic communion, which were thereby allied and engaged in the joint enterprise of a "crusade against the heretic and the schismatic" ("Cardinal Seper and the Ulster of Yugoslavia: I-II"). That rather fine readjustment of perspectives may well have been why Tisserant knew more about the massacres than his colleagues in the Curia – especially given the long and violent history of religious conflicts, in the Western and Catholic political interest, between the Uniats and Orthodox in Eastern and Central Europe since the sixteenth century. So the Croatian massacres must be seen, in part at least, as a three-way sectarian conflict, no doubt primed by the shared liturgical intimacy of two of the parties.

Once registered, the degree to which Butler concerns himself with the role of the Uniats apropos the fate of European Orthodoxy is quite noticeable. He spends roughly a fifth of his "Introduction" to *Escape from the Anthill* on this topic, specifically remarking that it is "the historical background" to the Croatian events he describes and singling out Dr Šimrak for "his notable part" in the forcible conversion campaign. In his last essay, "A Three-Day Nation," he returns to the theme in a still-ampler vein, even illustrating the obscure religious connection between the Orthodox see of Sremski-Karlovac (once in Austria-Hungary, now in Vojvodina, Serbia) and the short-lived nation of Carpatho-Russia. Part of the overall unique importance of this book generally for the Balkans lies in the lapidary filigree of such detail – heavily erased by Communism – but now slipping further from living memory in the aftermath of the second Yugoslavia.

The gigantic Croatian massacres of 1941 – authoritatively documented by Slavko Goldstein in *1941: The Year That Keeps Returning* (2007) – easily constitute one of the ten largest genocides of the twentieth century. To Goldstein's masterly mix of personal memoir and first-hand political history, Butler has now brought to the table many further key pieces of the catastrophic jigsaw that was the NDH.

It is up to the reader to take the time to assemble them into the patterns that will surely emerge if the effort is honest – and if the mind is kept open to Hubert Butler's long campaign of truth-facing and truth-telling.

II

Not only is Butler a superb prose stylist, he is also one of those rare writers, like George Orwell or Alexander Solzhenitsyn or Albert Camus, for whom the source of his inspiration is what might be termed "the ethical imagination." His palette is narrow yet profound: he writes out of a compact but interrelated set of preoccupations that over the course of his life he elaborated into a unique terrain of historical, cultural, religious, and philosophical reflection. A true son of the New

Testament and the classics, of the Reformation and the Enlightenment, he writes with a modern dissident sensibility that is profoundly at odds with the civilizational grain of our centripetal age. The crux of his worldview is the championing of the small-scale over the colossal, the parish over "the global village," the solitary spirit over the metropolitan "centres of culture" – the ant, in short, over the anthill. He is, in fact, an "artistic philosopher" of the various meshed forms of human relations – local, regional, national, continental, global: arguing from the start that our age's human energy and focus must be shifted back to the first two of those adjectives, whose vitality sustains the health of the rest.

Having come to maturity when the Russian, Ottoman, and Austro-Hungarian empires disintegrated and the British world *imperium* began to unravel in Ireland, Butler was deeply alert to the complex, ambiguous, and pan-European phenomena often blithely described by that single rubric "nationalism." Furthermore as a member of the Protestant minority, and steeped in the religious history of the island, where since the seventeenth century the great schism of Western Christendom has contended and coexisted, he had an intuitive feel for the complexities of the Yugoslav confluence of Islam, Orthodoxy, and Catholicism. Of the bifocal Irish-Yugoslav parallel, which he often elaborates, he remarks: "So even when these essays appear to be about Russia or Greece or Spain or Yugoslavia, they are really about Ireland" ("Introduction" to *Escape from the Anthill*). In his lexicon, *nationalism* was a positive and inclusive concept, the love of one's country and *all* its inhabitants – defined thus when speaking of an early Irish nationalist: "He would have said that a country belongs to the people who were born in it and intend to die there and who make its welfare their chief concern." It was *racialism* – the decay of nationalism into chauvinism and exclusiveness – that he saw as the grave and abiding danger. Perhaps no modern writer has enunciated this essential distinction with greater subtlety – and certainly no other modern Irish writer has handled notions of nation, nationalism, national culture and temperament, with such well-grounded and magisterial precision.

Style, of course, follows intellect. The strange virtuosity of Butler's deepens with scrutiny. Because he is such a lambent stylist, he carries you along, and it is easy to begin to take for granted the intelligence and incandescent sturdiness that suffuses his work. There is about all his writing a highly crafted digressive or meandering air – that proves anything *but* on closer inspection. It abounds with leaps of thought whose logic is unstated, as in a vibrant and quick-witted conversation. Holding together this lapidary discursiveness is the glue of the ethical imagination. Speaking through others, often by quotation, is one of his hallmarks, and in a passage he quotes from Chekhov we glimpse his own literary finesse: "The best of [writers] describe life as it is, but in such a way that every line is penetrated, as it were, with a juice, with the consciousness of an aim. Apart from life as it is, you feel that other life as it ought to be and it bewitches you." Like an image emerging from quick atmospheric strokes, this orchestration of ethical intent gives his essays, however discursive, the exactitude of master drawings.

So what is Butler "at" with the interlacings of his style? Overall it balances the imaginative and the conceptual, the language and sensibility of a poet with the discernments of a philosopher-cum-social-thinker. Virtually every page is studded with aphoristic remarks and many leap out with an Emersonian freshness.

Yet he had equally the gift of rendering a concept with a striking image, so that it partakes of both the metaphorical energy and the memorability of poetic speech:

> Yet, as I read the newspaper files in Zagreb, I felt that it was not the human disaster but the damage done to honoured words and thoughts that was most irreparable. The letter and the spirit had been wrested violently apart and a whole vocabulary of Christian goodness had blown inside out like an umbrella in a thunderstorm. ("The Invader Wore Slippers")

> In that way charity and humanity, where they were only superficial, could be skinned away like paint under a blowtorch. ("The Invader Wore Slippers")

All this raises an intriguing question: in what genre is Butler writing? Reading him at length one has the curious sensation of experiencing more or less the same generic mode whatever the topic or published format – as if his oeuvre were the single unfolding of a scroll. Yet it is difficult to label it. Neither "essayist" (too vague) nor "belles-lettres" (too insipid) does justice to his talent. In his Foreward to *In the Land of Nod* the Scots journalist Neal Ascherson comes closer, pinpointing a "specialized sort of writer, very rare in our islands": "Butler was what in Central Europe they call a *feuilleton* writer. The word has misleading echoes of leafy lightness and even weightlessness. But for a century and a half it has meant a special kind of intellectual journalism, witty and often angry, elegant but piercing, and revealing great learning lightly borne, interested in the 'epiphanies' which make currents of social and political change visible through the lens of some small accident or absurdity" (Ascherson, epigraph, p. 303). Still, even this does not seem right as an overall description. Actually, I think the best way to view Butler is as a writer of *parables*. Not, of course, parable in antiquity's sense, a form rooted in the mentality of oral tradition, but a modern descendant, realized in the richer noetics of the literate mind, in the telling of a *story*, through which he is able nonetheless to achieve a kindred *wisdom*. Setting down Butler is thus often curiously like having heard, in modern guise, a distant echo of biblical provenance.

III

Nearly two decades ago I ventured the following critical assessment:

> Hubert Butler, the last late scion of the Irish Literary Revival, is surely one of the great essayists in English of the twentieth century. Only over the past decade, however, have his essays been collected and published, in Ireland, first with *Escape from the Anthill* (1985), then *The Children of Drancy* (1988), *Grandmother and Wolfe Tone* (1990), and *In the Land of Nod* (1996). The original appearance of his writings was confined

almost completely to Irish periodicals, many of them obscure.
For this reason his corpus of a hundred or so essays, including
magisterial pieces on the Balkans and *Mitteleuropa*, has only
recently come before a large readership in the English-speaking world, quickly mustering acclaim. Equally astonishing
is that, despite the historical importance of his writing on
the Balkans (he spoke fluently what used to be called Ser-
bo-Croat, having studied in Zagreb in the mid-1930s), until
recently none of it had ever appeared in translation in the
lands of the former Yugoslavia.

Since then, the "happy few" of Butler admirers, both readers and writers, have grown considerably.

A fifth volume of essays, *The Appleman and the Poet*, was published
by The Lilliput Press in 2014. The editor of those five Lilliput collec-
tions, Antony Farrell, who single-handedly brought Butler to prominence, signed off that last volume with these words: "It is a huge cause
for joy in now knowing that his spirit and work endures, and will
continue to inhabit and to nurture our minds." Seldom can an octoge-
narian writer of such stature have received such celebrated recognition
for writing published in book form so late in his life. Butler, it can be
said truly, did most things differently.

Now *Balkan Essays* arrives. It includes 37 essays, written between
1937 and 1990, amongst them some of Butler's greatest work. Just over
three-quarters of the book has appeared in those five previous col-
lections, but the remainder has never previously been collected. An
Appendix to this English edition gathers his further voluminous correspondence on the Stepinac controversy. For the first time, the extraordinary body of Butler's Balkan work – written over a half century
– is brought together in a single volume. A simultaneous edition in
Croatian, *Balkanski eseji*, has been published by Fraktura, in Zaprešić.

A number of the essays here – notably "Mr Pfeffer of Sarajevo," "The
Last Izmerenje," "The Sub-Prefect Should Have Held His Tongue," and
"The Artukovitch File" – appeared in his first collection and have often
been numbered amongst his best. But I think it would be fair to say

that his Balkan work has been eclipsed somewhat by the better-known or closer-to-home territories of his Irish, literary and other European essays that constitute the bulk of the other volumes.

Spanning five decades, the Yugoslav work is not, however, some "Ruritanian" spur to a more central Irish track. On the contrary, the Croatian genocide is firmly at the centre of his corpus; it is not so much a limb as a backbone. To read the Balkan essays in roughly chronological order, as here, is to become aware of the fugal skill with which he broaches and elaborates the matter of the genocide. Themes are introduced and outlined; later they are embellished and extended. He begins by writing of his Balkan time in the thirties, his postwar visits, and the wartime genocide; then "the Nuncio controversy" in Ireland intervenes; then he interlaces both perspectives; what emerges in the later essays is something more universal, transcending the particulars of either country.

The difficulty was that, scattered through the five previous volumes, the pattern of the Balkan work, second nature to the author, was lost on the reader not intent on unravelling it. Even when laid out in chronological order the titles have an occasional and even strange air to the English ear, and so do not quite do justice to the crafted and supple orchestration that they embody. And this general feeling of alienness on the part of his mainly Western readers was heavily reinforced by the comparative absence of cultural intercourse between the English-speaking and South Slavonic linguistic zones until the fall of Communism.

That now seems set to change. Since Butler's death, there have been important French and English selected editions, most recently two 2012 volumes edited by the leading Irish novelist John Banville. In late 2000, the well-attended Hubert Butler Centenary Celebration in Kilkenny more than lived up to its celebratory aspiration vis-à-vis his life and work; three years later, the first book dedicated to his achievement, *Unfinished Ireland: Essays on Hubert Butler*, assembled the outstanding addresses delivered at the Centenary – becoming, *faute de mieux*, the foundation stone for future scholarship on a unique life and oeuvre.

Then, in early 2016, Johnny Gogan's *Hubert Butler: Witness to the*

Future premiered at the Dublin International Film Festival. In this remarkable documentary by one of Ireland's most innovative film-makers, Butler's life and work are brought to the big screen for the first time. The film follows his writer's journey from an Anglo-Irish childhood and study at Oxford; through his time in Stalinist Russia (where he worked as a teacher in 1932), interwar Yugoslavia, and Nazi Germany (where he helped expedite the escape of Jews in 1938-39); to his later life as a market gardener, writer and public intellectual at Maidenhall, Bennettsbridge, Co Kilkenny, where his family had lived for a century and a half. A particular focus of the film is his time in interwar Yugoslavia and his subsequent writing on the NDH.

So it seems likely that both *Balkan Essays* and *Balkanski eseji* are bound, in some way or other, to enter the fray in post-communist Croatia over the possible canonization of Archbishop Stepinac. The first stage of this process, beatification, was begun by the Church in 1981. In 1998, Stepinac – who had been elevated to cardinal in 1952 after his trial and imprisonment for collaboration – was declared a martyr at the hands of communist persecution and beatified by Pope John Paul II in front of a crowd of 500,000 in Marija Bistrica, central Croatia.

A contrary view, still widely held in Croatia, albeit somewhat silently, is that, as Butler puts it, "Mgr Stepinac's martyrdom had been deliberately courted" and that "there is something callous in this engineering of sympathy... towards a sectarian end" ("Ireland and Croatia"). Judge for yourself, reader, in the following pages.

In this epic struggle between hagiography and historiography – "of supreme importance for all thinking Christians" ("A Visit to Lepoglava") – Butler's posthumous voice may prove an especially tough foe, for his arguments were well-tempered by the intensely contemporaneous controversy that engulfed him in 1950s Ireland. "The Stepinac legend," he writes already in 1949, "is not dwindling, it is growing" ("Memorandum on the Struggle Between Communism and Christianity").

Nonetheless, against the continuing "fairy tale" of much Stepinac hagiography and Church kitsch, *Balkan Essays* has real strengths. First and foremost, Butler was neither a foreign Communist, nor a home-grown Partisan, but an independent spirit writing out of a clearly Christian ethic; a more improbable "fellow-traveller" there could not be. Secondly, he knew the Croatia of the day (from the mid-thirties to the mid-forties) in a way that most partisans of Stepinac today cannot have experienced with any sophisticated adult perspective.

Finally, a superb linguist, he had worked in the archives of the church papers, all in Croatian, published during the Occupation. In several essays in "Part One: The Yugoslav Suite," his careful citing of chapter-and-verse from those deeply incriminating papers is, more or less, unanswerable. (Incidentally, where are those church newspapers now? Still in the Zagreb Municipal and University Libraries? Destroyed, or transferred elsewhere? Surely there must be copies in the Vatican archives...)

Whether any of the Croatian hierarchy takes any ethical account of *Balkan Essays* remains, of course, to be seen – but perhaps this is beside the point. What seems possible is that the Vatican *might* – especially through The Stepinac Commission, comprised of Catholic and Orthodox prelates from the Balkans, established by Pope Francis in 2016 to report to him on the proposed canonization. You cannot, of course, make mistakes with future saints.

On the evidence of this book, Stepinac must seem to most open-minded readers far from "that great hero of Auschwitz, the Polish Franciscan Father Kolbe" ("The Artukovitch File"). "Many will say," writes Butler of the conversion campaign, "that these [church] missives had at worst the embarrassed connivance of the bishops, but though the concentration camps were full with men who opposed Pavelitch's New Order, there is no record of a bishop going there for violent opposition to the Poglavnik's intervention in ecclesiastical affairs" ("Father Chok and Compulsory Conversion"). And so it was that Father Rihar – who refused to celebrate the first anniversary of the NDH with a *Te Deum* – became the only known Catholic Croat cleric (along with seven Slovene priests) to pay with his life for open opposition to Pavelić. Would he not be a better candidate for Croatian martyrdom?

As an Argentine, Pope Francis will be familiar, perhaps very familiar, with the many Nazis and Ustaše, including Eichmann and Pavelić,
who spent spells in his homeland – soon to experience its own ruthless
massacres. It may be that His Holiness might take a dim view of a
prelate of whom it could *factually* be said: "Surely it must be one of the
biggest blows that fate has dealt him that both Pavelitch and Sharitch
speak well of him? " ("The Sub-Prefect Should Have Held His Tongue").

IV

Awarded a Travelling Scholarship to Yugoslavia by the School of Slavonic Studies in London, Butler lived in the country for three years,
from 1934 to 1937. "I think I was first attracted there," he wrote in 1979,
"by the fact that it attained its independence at the same time as we
did in Ireland and had to confront similar problems of diverse religions,
culture, loyalties."

Although he took seriously the adjective "travelling" and spent
much of the time crisscrossing Croatia, Bosnia, Serbia, Macedonia and
Montenegro, his main base was Zagreb, where he taught English for
the Anglo-Yugoslav Society and had a wide circle of friends and ac-
quaintances, including several notable literary and ecclesiastical figures, such as the Orthodox Bishop of Dalmatia, Dr Đorđević, and the
editor of the liberal paper *Nova Europa*, Dr Milan Ćurčin. In his wonderful evocations of royal Yugoslavia – "In Dalmatia," "The Last Izmerenje" and "In Serbian Macedonia" – part of the pleasure of the reading
lies in the feeling of sharing his own excitements as he learns about
new lands and peoples.

In no essay, however, does he give us a fuller picture of what exact
combination of circumstance and inner-life led him, at the age of 34,
with his wife, to plump for such a long sojourn in the new state of
Yugoslavia. But it is not hard to glean with some certainty that this
decision was of piece with his lived trajectory since mid-adolescence.
In 1916, returning from boarding school in England, he passed through

the smoking ruins of Dublin in the aftermath of the Easter uprising against British rule and concluded, against all claims of familial background, that he was an Irish republican. That early decision, like the one to stay put in his ancestral place in Kilkenny, would shape decisively the entire course of his life and intellect.

Unlike many or most nationalists at the time, Butler from an early stage did not view the Irish War of Independence in primarily insular terms. The freedom of Ireland was inextricably bound up with a wider pan-European phenomenon, the disintegration of empires and the emergence of what in the interwar period were known as the Succession States; a dozen small nations, he wrote (in his great credo, the Epilogue to "Mr Pfeffer of Sarajevo"), "formed at the same time (1919-1921), and under the influence of much the same ideas." From this perspective, which he never abandoned, indeed never ceased refining, the ideals of the Easter Rising were but a spiritual stone's throw from those that brought forth the new states in the East. Pearse in Dublin was cognate with Princip in Sarajevo.

In retrospect, he had consciously become, early on, what might now be called "a succession state intellectual." On the very first page of *Balkan Essays*, he recalls that too-brief post-Versailles moment, "the rise of the Succession States," so reminiscent of 1848 or 1968:

> I was at Oxford then and there was springtime in the air. There were Serbs, Croats and Czechs, there were Irish too, all rejoicing in their new-found freedom. We all had minority problems and I was surprised that Ireland, least scarred by war, did not identify herself with the other small new states more warmly, share experiences and take the lead for which she was qualified. ("Introduction" to *Escape from the Anthill*)

Nearly sixty years later, the glow of that moment is still undimmed as he quotes Rebecca West, offering her as one of those "who lived through that springtime and can never forget it" ("Rebecca West in Yugoslavia"); the newly liberated peoples, she writes, "were all like young men stretching themselves at the open window in the early morning after a long sleep ("Rebecca West in Yugoslavia")."

A page later, he is on to West's account of Yugoslavia's epic three-day resistance to Hitler, which electrified Europe: "The news that Hitler had been defied by Yugoslavia travelled like sunshine over the countries that he had devoured and humiliated, promising Spring."

Yet – tellingly for "the Aeschylean tragedy" of Stepinac ("Introduction" to *Escape from the Anthill*) related in this book by Butler – is there any record of any Croatian prelate voicing any such feeling in April 1941? Surely the supreme danger of the rampant militarism and racialism of a Nazi Germany *bordering* on Yugoslavia would have been apparent, well before invasion, to any perceptive non-sympathsizer, or true opponent?

But before Yugoslavia there was, for Butler, Russia also. Like many of his post-war, post-imperial, post-Versailles generation, Butler became interested in the new revolutionary Soviet state and, in particular, the Russian language, which he studied in the early twenties. By 1930, Russia had become enough of an intellectual focus (of distinctly non-communist hue) to prompt him to attempt spending his honeymoon there. He tried to enter through Latvia, but was turned back. The honeymoon was spent among Letts, Russians and Jews on the coast of the new state, resulting in one of the greatest of all his essays, "Riga Strand in 1930," where his extraordinary and moving intimations of the coming Holocaust are atmospherically palpable.

In the early thirties, he published two book translations from the Russian – one of which Joseph Brodsky would praise as the finest ever translation of Chekhov's *The Cherry Orchard* ("On Hubert Butler," Joseph Brodsky). Yet it would be forty years before his third book, a complex work of immense scholarship on the Irish Saints, was published by an obscure local press.

Until the publication of *The Appleman and the Poet*, very little was known of how he managed his amazing sojourn in Leningrad at the height of the Red Terror. The five re-discovered essays, describing his teaching at a specialist Soviet language school, as well as his travels around the city and region, fill in the picture exquisitely adumbrated in another of his finest essays, "Peter's Window."

All in all, by 1934, he had become something of a Slavist, with intimate experience of the one succession state of undoubted world-historical importance – the USSR. It is not hard to see how his experience of the wider Slav world, along with that perception of certain problems in common with Ireland, might have "first attracted" him to Yugoslavia – especially as he had already travelled in Greece in the late twenties, a visit touched upon in the first sentence of "Return to Hellas."

Within a quarter century, all but one of the free small succession states had been extinguished by Hitler and Stalin: "Of the dozen states which were created from fragments of empires a score of years (Russian, British, Turkish, French, Dutch), ours alone [Ireland] is intact ("The Two Languages"). But if these states had been first menaced, then consumed, by the new totalitarian great powers, they were also decisively weakened by their own internal conflicts. Everywhere in his work Butler alludes to the fault-lines of "race, religion, language, and the political use that can be made of them" that quickly overwhelmed the humane and republican "nationalism" of a shared homeland, and decayed into the catastrophic "racialism" so poignantly described in the Epilogue to "Mr Pffefer of Sarajevo."

For Butler, the foremost of these fault-lines – because it binds all the rest – is the problem of minorities and so of minority rights. As he is fond of remarking, the imperial power invariably manipulated, and often privileged, minorities to further its own control. But when the imperial power withdrew, the privileged or protected minority of whatever stripe (like his own Anglo-Irish class) suddenly became vulnerable to the liberated majority. Here the unseasonable Partition of Ireland is his tragic background exemplar.

As the interwar transfer of populations in the Tyrol, the Baltics, the Balkans and the Aegean quickly illustrated, the subsequent opportunity for the great powers to exploit these older divisions gave them new opportunities to use small subject peoples as "guinea pigs" ("The Invader Wore Slippers"). On both imperial and post-imperial manipulation, Butler is an implacable and deeply persistent foe of the endlessly cynical imperialism of *all* Great Powers – never over the course of his writing career (1930-1990) wavering in his localist belief "that small nations have been less likely to be corrupt than large ones" ("A Three-Day Nation: Alexei Gierowski and Carpatho-Russia") – his deeply-felt inheritance from 1919 and "the self-determination of peoples."

When Butler returned to Tito's Yugoslavia in the late forties and early fifties, his desire to undertake "a study of the Christian crisis in Yugoslavia" was surely inseparable from the flip-side of a second preoccupation, still more important to his commitment to the small nation – and the obverse to that gloomy religious bust of Stepinac. The other side of his politico-religious coin was clearly this: what "vicious circle of hate and extermination" ("A Trial") had been unleashed on Yugoslavia by the new invader? "The jackboot was worn by the Croats themselves and used so vigorously against the schismatic Serbs that the Germans and Italians, who established the little state, were amazed" ("The Invader Wore Slippers"). How exactly had the invader incited such a perversion of piety? No wonder that for Butler, the aghast small-state intellectual, "Pavelitch's Croatia deserves the closest study" ("The Invader Wore Slippers").

How had that promise of the small succession states been so utterly perverted across Europe? How had the Yugoslav ideal of Strossmayer – the "ancient dream of harmony between four neighbouring and kindred peoples" ("Introduction" to *Escape from the Anthill*) – or the "gentle and generous Croatian nationalism" of Ljudevit Gaj, so swiftly morphed to "a warped and terrible phenomenon, savage and remorseless to those within its power" ("Croatia, Gaj, Etc."), which "for four years made Croatia the model for all satellite states in German Europe" ("The Invader Wore Slippers")?

V

Even with no one essay on Stepinac alone, Butler's *J'accuse*, his shrewd and meticulous portrait of a compromised prelate, belongs to one of his quintessential modes: the aforementioned focus on the single personality through which a wider historical, cultural and/or ethical picture is adumbrated. Most of these figures in other volumes – such as Anton Chekhov, Boucher de Perthes, Ernst Renan, and Carl von Ossietzky – are drawn from Butler's eclectic pantheon of intellectual heroes, and in his hands they become universal parables for the struggle of the independent spirit against the conformist tide of history, culture or scholarship.

Only in the writing on Stepinac does this pattern vary decisively. The figure of the Archbishop is Butler's great parable for something at odds with the cussedness he extols in his heroes – not something more complex, necessarily, but something more opaque, fluid, unsettling, elusive. The Monsignor's is a parable about a breakdown in the ethical machinery connected to the absence of that independence of spirit.

Butler does not simply lay charges at the door of the Archbishop. With the forensic eye for inner detail that characterizes all his writing on personality, he is interested in something more important, more exemplary of a social process, than simple moral condemnation. Butler avoids any sense of anathematizing the character of Stepinac, whose courage, piety and personal kindliness he often emphasizes. Moreover, there is no suggestion that the Monsignor belongs to the same moral universe as actual war criminals like Pavelić, Artuković and Eichmann.

Nonetheless, Butler does not shirk from making a decisive comparison with them in the matter of *the process of behaviour*. For Butler, Stepinac is another avatar of the Organization Man, subset Ecclesiastical. In a period of Alice-in-Wonderland values, institutional order itself, in a sense, is the problem. "The Organization Man's fatal respect for orderliness" ("The Final Solution") becomes integral to the vastness of the criminal enterprise. In bureaucratic cases like Eichmann and Artuković, who were dutiful cogs in the momentum of the state, the role of the figure of the Organization Man is now well-understood. But what I think Butler saw in the figure of Stepinac – what he saw first-hand in the church newspapers in the Municipal and University Libraries in Zagreb in 1947 and 1950 – is a less obvious form of the phenomenon, a corollary of the first, though perhaps no less essential to that breakdown in the ethical machinery: *the Organization Man in proximity to crime.*

These two faces of the Organization Man are so entwined as to suggest the continuum of human nature itself. If Eichmann and Artuković are instances of what Hannah Arendt called "the banality of evil," then Butler on Stepinac concerns what I would call "the gentility of evil"... so long as we understand the word "evil" as a moral evaluation of consequences and not an explanation of its metaphysical provenance.

VI

If Butler's monumental *J'accuse* is amendable to no single essay, how can his multi-faceted portrait of Stepinac be described in the round? I think the best way is to sort the numerous jigsaw pieces into their various types of content and shape – *viz.*, the assessment of character; the frame of a public profile; the textual evidence; the indirect proofs; the sociology of totalitarian occupation; the Šimrak question; and, flowing from all of the above, the summative conclusions. Then the puzzle to be assembled assembles itself more swiftly.

Right from the beginning – more at the beginning, as the early newspaper correspondence suggests – Butler is at pains to distinguish the person from the actions. Stepinac is "modest as well as brave" ("The Sub-Prefect Should Have Held His Tongue"); he has shown "courage and humanity" ("The Sub-Prefect Should Have Held His Tongue"); he acted "in all sincerity" ("Appendix", p.535). I think what Butler means to convey is a scrupulous Christian charity, so that there is no trace of crude character assassination that might cloud the essential focus on the *actual actions* of the Archbishop. A thought dawns, novel in its obvious, even priestly, wisdom: there is no easy transit from being a "good person" to doing the right thing.

But soon enough it becomes clear that Butler's praise almost always carries a barb. "We see how Stepinac, a brave and merciful though very simple man, was hopelessly compromised by his official connection with the state" ("The Artukovitch File"); he made "a grave error of judgment at a time when such errors have terrible consequences and are terribly requited" ("Appendix," p 536); he and his bishops "may have been kindly men but they had released something they could not control" ("Cardinal Seper and the Ulster of Yugoslavia: I-II").

Cumulatively, Butler's sympathies for this "unhappy man" ("Appendix," p.535) begin to feel a little like the final twist of the ethical knife. To be a "good man," we see, is insufficient in a period of totalitarian war, where "human nature is reduced to its simplest terms" ("The Invader Wore Slippers"). Stepinac was by far the biggest ecclesiastical fish in the NDH: he had considerable control of the Church and, like all of us, should be judged by his actions and their consequences, as well his intentions. In the end, Butler is more interested in what Stepinac did than in what he believed he did, or in his immediate personal, evenly saintly, aura.

Like the squared edges of the jigsaw, Butler sketches a number of cameos of "the Stepinac story." The story runs, in sum, as follows. Stepinac fought for Austria-Hungary but switched armies at the conclusion of the war, to the Yugoslav Legion on the Allied side. A few days after Butler arrived in Yugoslavia, news reached the country of the Ustaše assassination of King Alexander, ordered by Pavelić and carried out in Marseilles. The country was plunged into well-organized mourning and the body lay in state briefly at a Zagreb railway station, where Butler noticed that two Catholic bishops, Bishop Bauer and his young Auxiliary Stepinac, prayed over the body.

In his subsequent years in the country, Butler observed that Stepinac – made an archbishop at only 39 – had a visible role in two public controversies of a sectarian nature: the King's concordat with the Vatican (associated in the public mind with a commercial treaty with

Fascist Italy), and Catholic opposition to the building of an Orthodox cathedral in Zagreb.

Then, on the coattails of the German and Italian invaders, the Ustaše swept to power:

> The same young priest who had stood beside the coffin of his murdered king, reappeared before his countryman as Archbishop at the right hand of the king's assassin, helpless in the face of Pavelitch's resolve to exterminate the Orthodox by expulsion, massacre or forced conversion. Unhappy but icily correct, Stepinac considered himself to be the servant of a power that is higher than the king or his murderer, and one that has rules for every occasion. His conscience was clear. ("Author's Proem")

Within three weeks, the Archbishop had issued two ecclesiastical circulars commending the NDH to all his clergy, and urging them to further "the protection and promotion" of the state ("Appendix," p.551). He then ordered all Catholic churches to ring a *Te Deum* to welcome the new regime and, in particular, its Poglavnik (Leader). During the war, Stepinac also had a formal association with the Ustaše Parliament whose state was recognized only by the Axis powers, which, in Butler's view, makes him guilty of treason in a time of war ("Appendix," p.530), given the existence a legal Yugoslav government in exile. He was also Military Vicar to the Croatian Home Guard, most of which eventually was placed under the control of the regime.

Stepinac, with the rest of the hierarchy, supported the NDH to the end, even as Tito's Partisans closed in and the Allies overran the Axis Powers to which the regime remained fanatically loyal. Whereupon he attempted to express a new ecclesiastical loyalty to the victors – only to be rebuffed and placed on trial by Tito, when he refused to be withdrawn to the Vatican. In short, he had served three contradictory states, and attempted to toady up to a fourth.

The rest is history – or more precisely, hagiography. Butler concludes that Stepinac is a prime example of militant and political ecclesiasti-

cism that must, almost always, be "militarist Christianity" ("Memorandum on the Struggle Between Communism and Christianity"). In
the end, Stepinac stands for the principle of a state-controlled church
("Report on Yugoslavia"), and the forcible conversion campaign was
fundamentally pre-communist and inter-Christian ("Author's Proem").

Within his template of the public figure, Butler piles up the textual
evidence for his case that Stepinac and his bishops were, in effect, not
so much collaborators in the usual political sense as totally compromised "collaborationists" in their religious, moral and practical support
for an utterly criminal regime and its ruthless Leader, "one the vilest
of the war criminals" ("Report on Yugoslavia").

From the essay on Father Chok; through "Yugoslav Papers: The
Church and Its Opponents" and "Report on Yugoslavia"; to "Memorandum on the Struggle Between Communism and Christianity" and the
high drama of documentation in "The Compulsory Conversion Campaign of 1941: I-III" – there is a mounting, scrupulous, just, precise and
highly researched description of Church connivance, spiritual collaboration and outright Ustaše idolatry that had taken over much of the
Catholic ecclesiastical structure on Stepinac's watch. The several texts
cited at length speak for themselves. It is for the reader to assemble the
final complicated picture and decide whether Butler's ethical *J'accuse*
proves, more or less, irrefutable.

In particular, the essay on Father Chok should be read closely in
tandem with the astonishing account of Butler's personal conversation
with the imprisoned Archbishop, "A Visit to Lepoglava." In the latter,
Stepinac denies that *forcible* conversion was ever formally endorsed by
the Church or himself (likely true, in a narrowly bureaucratic-textu-
al-theological sense). In the latter, Butler quotes from a diocesan leaflet
(found by himself in the archives at the Municipal Library) from a pious
bishop urging Serb villagers to convert or (threateningly in the context
of the times) face the loss of their "homes," "husbandry" and (many
might have intuited) life itself.

It is impossible, in good historiographical faith, to square the circle
of the clerical legalism of the Archbishop's comment in prison with
the glimpsed actualities of the quoted document. Either Stepinac was

utterly naïve about what was happening outside his Palace, especially due to his rosy faith in the Leader ("The Compulsory Conversion Campaign of 1941: I-III"); or he had no real control over a host of extremist Ustaše-supporting priests and bishops; or "the violence of the times was being used for the purposes of proselytism" ("The Sub-Prefect Should Have Held His Tongue") in a process of connivance and evasion (of fundamental opposition) aiming to alter the ethno-religious composition of not only Croatia, but Bosnia ("The Compulsory Conversion Campaign of 1941: I-III"). Such sophistical ecclesiastical self-exculpation is simply not the stuff of saints like Father Kolbe or Edmund Rice, let alone Pope Francis' namesake.

The indirect proofs for most of the higher clergy's gushing embrace of the Leader and his confessional fascism are, if anything, even more clear-cut. Throughout these essays they fly like sparks from Butler's ethical anvil.

The hysterical adulation for the Poglavnik that poured forth, without opposition, from all the Catholic press, large and small. An ode by the Archbishop of Bosnia praising Pavelić's measures against Serbs and Jews and published with a photograph of Pavelić in a leading paper on Christmas Day. No sign of reprimand or sanction from the Archbishop for such excesses amongst his flock, "our peaceful Croatian people" ("The Compulsory Conversion Campaign of 1941: I-III"). No request for Christian mercy extended to the defeated or to the minorities in his circulars welcoming the NDH. The still more incredible exoneration of the NDH as well as praise for the convicted regicide Pavelić in his infamous letter of "protest" concerning the massacres. The use of the language of "Aryan" and "non-Aryan," "Leader" and "concentration camp," *et cetera*, in his official correspondence.

And so on – and on. The reader can assemble the rest of the tricky pieces.

In 1941: *The Year That Keeps Returning*, Goldstein describes how the more naïve, respectable and/or genteel members or supporters of the regime believed at first that the New Order should and could be implemented with some sort reference to the due process of laws and trials

– even if the black tome of the legal code was itself, literally, half cut-and-paste from its Nazi cousin. These "liberal Ustaše," as they might be called, soon learnt the error of their ways as the unregulated chaos and rapid wildfire of the massacres overtook parts of the country – and some themselves became victims. Although Stepinac himself was never a member of the movement – more, seemingly, from the interwar "Frankist" tradition – it is easy enough to analogize him loosely to the ecclesiastical equivalent of those early liberal Ustaše sympathsizers who, though shocked, did not foreswear, for whatever reasons, the initial allegiance.

In "The Invader Wore Slippers," Butler produces a bijoux sociology of Occupation, precipitating the main catalysts: the patriotic, the pious, and the respectable. His description of Croatia in these terms is one of the most memorable lines of the book: "When an incendiary sets a match to respectability, it smoulders malodorously, but piety, like patriotism, goes off like a rocket." Stepinac is clearly a blend of all three of those precipitates; but "genteel" respectability, ironically, may have been the one that misled him most in his imagined ability to influence Pavelić, "a professional man of respectable standing, the writer of a couple of books, the editor of newspapers in Austria and Berlin" ("Report on Yugoslavia"). The latter's "horrible blend of sophistication and savagery" was well-hidden by the genteel façade of his extreme devoutness. No rockets appeared to be in the vicinity.

I have often wondered why, of all the questions Butler might have asked Stepinac in prison at Lepoglava, it was this one he chose for the few minutes available:

> I said I had read a letter he had written to Pavelitch... But why, when he wished to regulate this campaign, had he chosen as one of his two collaborators Mgr. Shimrak, Apostolic administrator of the Greek Catholic (Uniate) Church? Mgr Shimrak's enthusiasm for the disgraceful conversion campaign had been well known and publicly expressed. I had myself looked up his published address in his diocesan magazine...

In his diocesan manifesto, Šimrak argues *in 1942* that the already ethically bankrupt conversion campaign is legal in light of rulings by the Holy See, the Congregation of the Eastern Churches (Tisserant again: "The Compulsory Conversion Campaign of 1941: I-III") *and* the NDH. We can only conclude that Butler sees in the Church's bad faith an egregious disconnect between word and deed – between the desire by the Bishops Conference led by the Archbishop to regulate the bloody (but waning) conversion campaign in their resolution of *November 1941*, and Stepinac's appointment of one of its most enthusiastic, active and "outspoken" advocates to the committee of three (including himself) supervising it *after* the major initial massacres of the first six months after April 1941 ("The Compulsory Conversion Campaign of 1941: I-III").

Either Stepinac is highly naïve about his Uniat colleague, or he is in personal sympathy with the more militant-ecclesiastical, Ustaše-inspired approach of Šimrak. The thought dawns that the delegation of part of the now-bloody responsibility (when it was too late to withdraw *his and his bishops'* initial enthusiastic support) to the leader of another autonomous sister Church with a history of such conversions might have been a good way of still having your cake and eating it, while expanding the responsibility for what Tisserant, for instance, would later denounce *to the regime's representative.*

Especially telling in this regard is the passage, in the Chok essay, on the cooperation between the Roman Catholics and Uniats over the ruined, often burnt and looted, dioceses of the Orthodox. The picture is of Šimrak and Stepinac working hand-in-glove on the conversion commission ("Father Chok and Compulsory Conversion"); the former acting aggressively in the field, the latter orchestrating and overseeing at the bureaucratic centre, whilst perhaps absolving himself in his own eyes through distance from the actuality, as well as continuing obedience to his belovéd, rule-bound "ecclesiastical fabric." The Archbishop, Butler remarks, "seems to have had a curious detachment from the laws of cause and effect" ("Yugoslav Papers: The Church and Its Opponents"), possibly because he believed that Church belonged to a power above such historical laws.

Butler offers this general summation, one amongst many in these pages:

> Roughly speaking one may say that the bishops were enthusiastic about the Quisling Pavelitch himself and saw in his advent an admirable opportunity of extending the domain of the Catholic church but were horrified when they found by what brutal methods the campaign was to be conducted. It was then too late for them to withdraw their support. No one was excommunicated... ("Appendix," p.562)

Šimrak, Butler notes several times, was made Bishop of Križevci, in 1942, after his appointment to the conversion commission.

VII

Balkan Essays, of course, is not merely about the Balkans *then*. It is also, in numerous and subtle ways, about the Balkans *now*. His three essays on the frontiers of Slav and Latin culture ("Fiume, Sushak and the Nugents," "Maria Pasquinelli and the Dissolution of the Ego," "Trieste") have a long-term prophetic feel, as Brodsky remarks ("On Hubert Butler," Joseph Brodsky); as does the foreseen disintegration of Tito's Yugoslavia, where the Dayton Accords could be said to be described a half-century *avant la letter*: "When Yugoslavia comes to be reorganized, facts will be so cogent and clamorous and innumerable that they will just be used as seasonings to the theoretic puddings made by the powers" ("The Two Languages"). And of which "black infidel" ("Nazor, Oroshatz and the Von Berks") would this be more true – the "Catholic" Ustaše, or the so-called "Islamic" State, both clad completely in black – when he writes in 1947: "There are numbers of broken and frustrated people with no great love of life or expectations from it, who look forward to Armageddon with almost religious excitement" ("The Russian Consul").

Those wedded to cultural exclusivity in the Balkans, and indeed in

Ireland and elsewhere, might read with extreme benefit "Report on Yugoslavia," "The Barriers," and "The Two Languages," where together the case is made that "there is no such thing as a pure national culture" and "except through collaboration there is no future for the small national state" ("Yugoslavia: The Cultural Background"). The alternative is "a bitter recoil into self-sufficiency, pedantry, mythology and linguistics" ("The Barriers"). All of which seems a breath of clarity and sanity into the current hothouse of ethno-religious tensions across the former Yugoslavia.

Unsurpassed in this collection, those latter two essays, written during neutral Ireland's Emergency (1939-1946), flow from his nobly steadfast formation as a succession state intellectual. They are *tours de force* of conceptual subtlety, the prescient fruit of a *sui generis* life and oeuvre. In the first, he parses why "a distinctive culture cannot exist without cultural intercourse" ("The Barriers") and how the post-imperial barriers designed to foster cultural self-sufficiency ended in just the opposite. In the other, with its wonderful mix of classical imagery and modern apperception, he reflects on what actually binds together governments, states, nations and peoples, especially small ones.

Is Butler also a Balkan writer? If the question is judged by knowledge, experience, content, thought and love, then perhaps yes. If determined by ethnicity, religion, language and native culture, then probably not.

Yet English, now, is the established *lingua franca* between the several languages of the Balkans as a whole – so a *Yes* is not quite as improbable as it might at first seem. Whatever the determination – like the prose of Conrad, Nabokov or Berlin in reverse, all great writers from the Slavonic world – it can be said that *Balkan Essays* joins Rebecca West's *Black Lamb and Grey Falcon* (1941) and Ann Bridge's *Illyrian Spring* (1935) – among others, and however assessed – as major works that belong now as much to the new Balkans as to the global English language.

Chris Agee
Croatia, August 2016

Hubert Marshal Butler: A Chronology

1900	Born 23 October at Maidenhall, Bennettsbridge, Co Kilkenny to George and Rita Butler
1909-12	Bigshotte Rayles Prep School, England
1912-18	Charterhouse, England, on a mathematics scholarship
1919	Matriculates at St John's College, Oxford, as Senior Classical Scholar
1922	Graduates from Oxford
1922-26	Recruited by Sir Horace Plunkett as a librarian for the Irish County Libraries and works in Ballymena, Coleraine and Portstewart
1927	Teaches several months in Alexandria, Egypt, having travelled through Italy
1928-29	Travels in Greece, Switzerland, Austria and Germany
1930	Marries Susan Margaret (Peggy) Guthrie in June and honeymoons in Latvia, having been refused entry to the Soviet Union
1931-32	His translation of Leonid Leonev's novel *The Thief* published in London; teaches several months in Leningrad at the height of the Red Terror
1934	His translation of Chekhov's *The Cherry Orchard* produced at the Old Vic and published in London
1934-37	Awarded a Travelling Scholarship to Yugoslavia by the School of Slavonic Studies in London; is based in Zagreb,

	Belgrade and Dubrovnik; travels extensively in Croatia, Serbia, Bosnia, Macedonia and Montenegro
1935	Peggy returns to Ireland for the birth of their daughter, Julia
1938-39	Works with the Quakers in Vienna expediting the escape of Jews after the *Anschluss*
1941	Inherits Maidenhall upon the death of his father, and returns with his family; it will remain his home for the next half-century
1944	Revives the Kilkenny Archaeological Society
1947 & 50	Visits to Yugoslavia; investigates the wartime genocide under the Quisling Ustaše regime in Croatia
1952	The "Papal Nuncio Incident" at a public meeting in Dublin; censured by various civic bodies for his stance on the ecclesiastical role in the Croatian genocide; is forced to resign from the Kilkenny Archaeological Society
1954	Organizes the first Kilkenny Debate
1955	Stands for Kilkenny County Council with the aim of offering "a minority voice"; is heavily defeated
1956	Visits China with an Irish cultural delegation and returns to the Soviet Union
1961-62	Travels in the American South during the Civil Rights Movement
1967	Founds the Butler Society with Lord Dunboyne and George Butler and begins his annual editorship of *The Journal of the Butler Society*
1972	*Ten Thousand Saints: A Study in Irish and European Origins* published by The Wellbrook Press, Kilkenny
1985	*Escape From the Anthill*, published by The Lilliput Press
1986	American-Irish Literary Award
1988	*The Children of Drancy*, published by The Lilliput Press
1989	Irish Book Award, Silver Medal for Literature
1990	*Grandmother and Wolfe Tone*, published by The Lilliput

Press; *The Sub-Prefect Should Have Held His Tongue, and Other Essays*, published by Penguin

1991   Died 5 January in Kilkenny

1994   *L'envahisseur est venue en pantoufles*, published by Anatolia Editions, France

1996   *In The Land of Nod*, published by The Lilliput Press; *Independent Spirit* published by Farrar, Straus and Giroux, USA

2000   The Hubert Butler Centenary Celebration, Kilkenny, 20-22 October

2014   *The Appleman and the Poet*, published by The Lilliput Press

2016   *Balkan Essays*, published by The Irish Pages Press, Belfast; *Balkanski eseji*, translated and published by Fraktura, Zagreb

Note on Croatian Names

Butler's English spelling of Croatian names is maintained throughout this book. Until recent decades, a common convention was to substitute the Slavonic diacritics with the equivalent English sounds (e.g., "Pavelić" becomes "Pavelitch"). However, with all other editorial texts and footnotes here, the diacritics follow standard contemporary usage in Croatian/Bosnian/Serbian (widely considered a single language, despite considerable dialectical and national variations).

PART ONE
The Yugoslav Suite

"The twentieth century produced the greatest hopes for mankind, but it buried most of them. It became the graveyard of great ideals. It taught us that ideals are most often a seductive chimera and that doubt is not a fatal weakness but a necessary defence against fatal beliefs."

Slavko Goldstein

1941: The Year That Keeps Returning

(Novi Liber, 2007)

"Butler, then, is both a profound sceptic and a profound optimist. That is perhaps the special flavour of the brandy-cask, a mingling of realistic acumen with high hopes. He is a buoyant and inspiriting writer because, as he said of Chekhov, "his faith is so soberly expressed as to be proof against disillusionment." Consciously, he brought a blend of humanism and realism, clarity and hope, into a century where the ethical imagination has been tested by historical complexity much greater than that faced by writers in the stable Europe of the nineteenth century."

Chris Agee

"Poteen in a Brandy-Cask:

The Ethical Imagination of Hubert Butler"

(The Yale Review, 1998)

Author's Proem

(from the "Introduction" to Escape from the Anthill)

Men and women are surely more important than the systems in which they imprison themselves. Yet it is not easy to disentangle ourselves and to commit ourselves unreservedly to personal relations. Organized religion cannot liberate us for it is a system too, and there is nothing more bitter than the conflict of two religious systems, as I have found both in my own country and the foreign country I know best, Yugoslavia.

Three years after I returned from Russia I went to teach in Zagreb in the Anglo-American-Yugoslav Society. It had been founded by my friend, Dr Milan Churchin, the editor of *Nova Evropa*, the leading liberal journal of Central Europe, and by Dr Georgievitch, the Orthodox Bishop of Dalmatia. I also had a small scholarship from the School of Slavonic Studies in London.

Yugoslavia had been born in 1918 after the defeat of Austria-Hungary and the rise of the Succession States. For the southern Slavs it was the fulfilment of an ancient dream of harmony between four neighbouring and kindred peoples. I was at Oxford then and there was springtime in the air. There were Serbs, Croats and Czechs, there were Irish too, all rejoicing in their new-found freedom. We all had minority problems and I was surprised that Ireland, least scarred by war, did not identify herself with the other small new states more warmly, share experiences and take the lead for which she was qualified. The Croats knew about Ulster and some of them talked of Croatia, ruefully, as "the

Ulster of Yugoslavia." This needed a readjustment of roles, but one knew
what they meant. They were Catholics and to them Zagreb, the Croatian capital, was "a little Vienna." They wondered how they would fare
in union with the more primitive Serbian Orthodox, who had fought
for freedom while they had mostly fought for Austria-Hungary.

The day we arrived in Zagreb, 9 October 1934, news had just come
that King Alexander, a Serb, had, with Barthou the French Foreign
Minister, been assassinated in Marseilles by agents of the separatist
Croat leader, Pavelitch. Zagreb was plunged in well-organized mourning with portraits of the king surrounded by black crape in the
shop-windows and black bows on the funnels of the railway engines.
Two days later the king's body arrived from Split, where it had been
shipped from Marseilles on its way to Belgrade. It lay for a couple of
hours, surrounded by pot-plants, in the first class waiting-room at the
station, where it was visited by mile-long processions. One of those
who prayed beside the royal coffin was Archbishop Bauer, the Catholic
Primate, accompanied by his Auxiliary Monsignor Stepinac.

During our time in Yugoslavia the shadow of the assassination hung
over the whole country. Hitler had come to power in Germany and
Jewish refugees were flocking to the Dalmatian coast. In Italy and
Hungary, Pavelitch and his helper, Artukovitch, were training the army
of the Croat rebels, who were, in 1941, to sweep into Yugoslavia with
the Nazis and proclaim the Independent State of Croatia.

And yet my recollections are of peace and beauty. There was almost
no traffic in Yelachitch Trg, the central square. Fat amethyst pigeons
strutted through the market stalls looking for pickings and panicking
when the church bells rang. The scent of mimosa and wood-smoke,
holy candles and freshly tanned leather drowned the faint whiff of
petrol. On Sunday, we walked up Slijeme Mountain, where wild cyclamen and hellebore grew through the beech woods. In our room I rooted
oleander cuttings in bottles between the double windows. And when
my pupils were on holiday I wrote down the story of Mr Pfeffer.

Zagreb, in the thirties, was a very cultivated little town; it had an
opera house and theatres, and there were still remnants of an

Austrianized aristocracy in the leafy suburbs. Dalmatia was Italianate and Belgrade was still largely Turkish in character. When one went south and penetrated to Montenegro, one seemed to pass from our cruel, complicated century to an earlier one, just as cruel, where each man was responsible to his neighbours for his crimes and where organized twentieth-century barbarity had not yet emerged. Possibly in "The Last Izmerenje" I have idealized what I saw. To know what Montenegro was really like you must read Djilas's superb autobiography, *Land Without Justice* (1958).

The war came and Yugoslavia was carved up by Germany and her allies. Croatia, which had not resisted the Nazis, was rewarded with her Independent State under the rule of Pavelitch, King Alexander's convicted murderer.

Then in Zagreb an Aeschylean tragedy was enacted. The same young priest who had stood beside the coffin of his murdered king, reappeared before his countrymen as Archbishop at the right hand of his king's assassin, helpless in the face of Pavelitch's resolve to exterminate the Orthodox by expulsion, massacre or forced conversion. Unhappy but icily correct, Stepinac considered himself to be the servant of a power that is higher than the king or his murderer, and one that has rules for every occasion. His conscience was clear.

Violence came a second time to the city. Caring neither for king nor priest nor pope nor assassin, the Communists swept in, resolved to make all things new. I have written about this period in my two pieces, "The Sub-Prefect Should Have Held His Tongue" and "The Artukovitch File," yet I would like here to recall the historical background to the events I have described. There are three great sources of power and influence in Eastern and Central Europe: Roman Catholicism, Byzantine Orthodoxy and Communism. Orthodoxy, which broke away from Rome five centuries before the Protestant Reformation, was once, with its Patriarch magnificently enthroned at Constantinople, the rival of Rome in power and splendour. Now the Orthodox Church is a shadow of its former self. With Saint Sophia a secular museum, the Patriarch lives on sufferance from the Turks in a small quarter of Istanbul. Since the Russian Revolution the other Patriarchs over whom he reigns as *primus inter pares* are weak and scattered. Communist Moscow threatens them from the East and the Catholic powers from the West. Those Russian Orthodox who survived beyond the borders of Tsarist Russia and later the Soviet State, have had to fight for their faith and culture against the politico-religious scheming of Austria-Hungary and her successors, Czechoslovakia and Poland.

A powerful instrument in this little-known struggle is the Uniat* Church, devised by King Sigismund III of Poland and the Pope in the sixteenth century to attract the peasants of the eastern border-lands away from Orthodoxy. The Orthodox received into this Church retained their ritual and their married clergy but Rome, not Moscow, became the focus of their obedience.

This Uniat Church has been used many times in our century by the Western Powers for political purposes. At the beginning of the war in 1914, when the Austrians were advancing against the Russian Ukraine, a detailed memorandum about its occupation was formulated by the Uniat Archbishop, Count Szepticky of Lemberg in Austrian Galicia. Apart from the military and juridical arrangements, the Orthodox Church in the new Protectorate was to be detached from the Moscow Patriarchate and subjected to Szepticky himself, as Uniat Metropolitan. Prayers for the Tsar were to be forbidden and prayers for the Emperor substituted. The Muscovite saints were to be eliminated from the calendar. The new Prince of the Ukraine was to be Archduke Wilhelm,

---

* The historical term *Uniat* or *Uniate* is applied to those Eastern Catholic churches which were previously part of Eastern or Oriental Orthodox churches or the Assyrian Church of the East. These 23 churches are *sui juris* in full communion with the pope of Rome and make up the Catholic Church together with the Western or Latin Church, which uses the Latin liturgical rites, among which the Roman Rite is the most widespread. Although Eastern Catholics are full members of the larger Catholic Church, they share the rites, traditions and canon law of the three other branches of Eastern Christianity – the Eastern Orthodox, the Oriental Orthodox and the Assyrian Church of the East. The term *Greek Catholic* refers exclusively to those Uniats of the Easter Orthodox rite. (Editors)

who had changed his name to Vasily, learnt Ukrainian and wore an embroidered Ukrainian tunic. But the Russians struck back, occupied Lemberg, arrested the Archbishop and published the Memorandum in the Petrograd papers. Soon after this the Revolution occurred.

In the Second World War the Uniat Church was active in Croatia; in 1941-2 Dr Shimrak, the Uniat Bishop, played a notable part in the campaign for the conversion of the Orthodox.

For many years the Czechs and Slovaks used the Uniats to secure and, if possible, extend their eastern frontier, where Carpatho-Russian Orthodox were settled along the Ukrainian border. They revived for themselves the old Austro-Hungarian dream of a vast Ukrainian protectorate and for this purpose rechristened Carpatho-Russia "Carpatho-Ukraine" and supported the Uniats against the Orthodox. The story of this often violent struggle has been told month by month in *Svobodnoye Slovo (Free Word)*, the organ of the many *émigré* Carpatho-Russian Orthodox in the USA.

In Europe it is now only in Greece that a free Orthodox Church survives. When in 1964 there was a friendly meeting in the Holy Land between the Pope and the titular head of the Orthodox Church (the Patriarch in Constantinople), Chrysostom, the Primate of Greece, and his bishops refused to participate and even asked for the dissolution of the Uniat Church. The world was shocked that when all Christendom is craving for unity the Primate of Greece could be so intransigent, yet it is intelligible enough. The Greeks are the countrymen of Aesop, who wrote so many fables about small animals to whom large ones made friendly overtures. It is natural for them to dread the Uniat embrace.

Should we involve ourselves with complex happenings in far countries? Sometimes we have to, but we misinterpret them at our peril.

On May Day 1949 a crowd of 150,000, said to be the largest ever seen in Dublin, assembled in O'Connell Street to protest against the imprisonment of Archbishop Stepinac of Yugoslavia and a Hungarian Cardinal, Mindszenty. There were bands, speeches, telegrams, women fainted and a young man, wrongly suspected of distributing Communist leaflets, was struck on the head and taken to hospital.

In America there were even greater demonstrations and many thought that with so righteous a cause, and Russia still weak after the Nazi invasion, the moment for a third world war had arrived.

I know nothing about Cardinal Mindszenty but I knew that the struggle in which Stepinac was involved was totally misconceived. It was a pre-Communist and inter-Christian one. As in Ireland, race and religion go together, Catholic Croat confronted Orthodox Serb and Hitler's war had triggered off a massacre of the Orthodox by the Catholics. Hugh Seton-Watson, the well-known historian of Central Europe, wrote in 1945: "The Communists saved Yugoslavia from a bloody civil war on racial lines, which would have been inevitable, if Mihailovitch (the Serbian Orthodox general) had come to power."* This is something which in Ireland we would be reluctant to believe. Who could wish a Communist solution to our own racial and religious problems?

We live and think under a nuclear cloud and stretch our brains, built for solving human problems, into thinking cosmically. If sooner or later they fail us, friend and enemy will be destroyed together. How soon can we return to being men, not human adjuncts to machines, and handle again man-sized problems? How soon can we escape from the anthill which we have built round ourselves?

(1985)

---

* Hugh Seton-Watson, *Nationalism and Communism* (London: 1945), page 90. (H.B.)

Mr Pfeffer of Sarajevo

It must have been in the late twenties that the first wave of nostalgia for imperial Austria, its glamour and its grace, swept across the theatre and the screen. Later, it invaded the study and has long given a giddy twist to many serious historical researches. For very many people, whose parents fought against the Hapsburgs, the assassinations at Sarajevo have come to mean the first great irruption of violence into a prosperous and orderly world, the signal for the decay of romance, colour and freedom, the prelude to the crude despotism of the bully and the statistician. In fact, there was never a time when it was harder to enter into the minds of those who saw the Sarajevo assassinations as the dawn of liberty.

But the record of the monuments on the Latinska Bridge in Sarajevo shows that there was no simple struggle between poetry and prose, between tradition and anarchy. There was a duel to the death between two rival ideals, one died and the other was stricken with a mortal illness.

The large Austro-Hungarian monument to the Archduke and his wife, with its crowns, columns and marble mourners, stood on the bridge for only two years. It was smashed by the Serbs in 1918 and in the presence of an archbishop a tablet was set in its place to the memory of their assassin, Gavrilo Princip, and to the dawn of Yugoslav freedom. At the same time the bones of Princip and his fellow conspirators were collected from the prison cemeteries of Czechoslovakia and lower Austria and given a splendid interment. The tablet stayed there for

twenty-four years and then it was torn down and sent to Hitler at
Berchtesgaden by one of his loyal generals. After the Germans, Italians,
Croat separatists and finally Communists held the bridge. Today Princip's romantic dreams seem scarcely more compatible with the public
aspirations of his countrymen than do the ingenious political construc-
tions of imperial Vienna. They are revered, of course, like a historic
blunderbuss in a show-case, but they are not for handling.

The real tragedy of Sarajevo was never commemorated on the bridge
and yet it was more momentous than the collapse of imperialism or
the rapid degradation of the nationalism which superseded it. All
through the empire and through Europe there were men of liberal
outlook who foresaw the fatal collision and tried in vain to prevent it.
Their failure meant the disgrace and finally the extinction of liberalism. If another commemorative monument were ever to be erected on
the bridge at Sarajevo it ought to be to Mr Leo Pfeffer, the examining
magistrate at the trial of the assassins; a liberal, he defended his creed
as stoutly as Princip and Franz Ferdinand defended theirs and his defeat, too, was symbolic.

It was not till 1934 that Mr Pfeffer, a Croat and a Catholic, brought
his manuscript account of the preliminary examination and his comments on it to my friend, Dr Churchin of Zagreb. Churchin was at that
time editor of *Nova Evropa*, the only liberal monthly of consequence
to be published in the Balkans. He printed the manuscript in instalments and asked my help in preparing an English translation. But it
was a bad time. The rise of Hitler made it hard to focus the attention
on Mr Pfeffer's scrupulous analysis of these complex distant events or
to make them interesting to others. His book is still unpublished.

Mr Pfeffer, an expert in the law of the Austro-Hungarian Empire,
tried to administer it with justice and charity. He treated the assassins
as what they were, men of honour and principle, who had acted deliberately and did not wish to shift the responsibility for their acts onto
the shoulder of others. They resisted the bullying of the police but they
were ready to co-operate with Mr Pfeffer, with the result that we have
an all but complete picture of the passage of six bombs and four

revolvers from Belgrade through the Bosnian highlands to Sarajevo, of the endless variety of men and women who handled them and hid them in cow byres and in reading rooms and under pillows and in loaves of oaten bread, till finally the Heir Apparent lay dead on an iron bed in the governor of Bosnia's palace.

When Mr Pfeffer had ordered the arrest of a student Grabezh, whom he had correctly associated with the assassination, the young man, the son of an Orthodox priest near Sarajevo, was led to him, filthy and soaking and defiant. The police had tried to force him to tell them where he had hidden the bombs he had failed to throw; they had ducked him in the river and in the town drain. Mr Pfeffer spoke to him in his usual way.

> I am the examining magistrate and I am going to call you "thou," not from any lack of respect but so that we may understand each other better. I do not consider you a common criminal, you acted from political conviction and history will decide whether you were right. But the court must prosecute you for your act. It was not with my knowledge or approval that the police tortured you. If you do not tell me where the bomb was hidden it will explode and injure some innocent person.

Grabezh promptly answered: "You are the first person who has spoken to me like a human being, so I will tell you." And half-an-hour later the bomb was found in the earth closet of a hotel belonging to Grabezh's cousin. Another chapter was added to the story of the crime and the chief of police liked Mr Pfeffer even less than before.

If it was due to Mr Pfeffer in the first place that the conspirators were detected, it is also because of him that they remain more than mere names carved in marble or woven into patriotic ballads. We know their hesitations as well as their final resolve and in them we see the reflection of an entire nation in revolt.

After the tension and the triumph of the Balkan Wars the Serbs were more proud and prickly than ever and Mr Pfeffer, a Croat, gives a good picture of the small mortifications that the non-German subjects of Franz Josef had to endure. Bosnia, which borders upon Serbia and has a mainly Serbian population had been recently annexed. It was being given railways and hospitals, but every spoonful of jam had its pill and the local Austrian officials often scraped off the jam for themselves. For example, every town had its Beamtenverein, a small club for government clerks, but though the majority of the members were Slav, there was an unwritten law that all the committee should be German. Mr Pfeffer tells how he and some friends managed once to canvass the voters so that the committee of the club was controlled by Slavs and its name altered. This triumph lasted for one month and then all the Slav committee members were transferred to posts in other towns. But the members elected more Slavs to the committee. Then the Germans all withdrew and formed a *Herrenklub* of their own.

If these lofty ways could exasperate a civil servant like Mr Pfeffer, a more violent reaction can be imagined among the Serbian patriots. When the old Emperor Franz Josef came to Sarajevo in 1910, a student called Jeracic decided to kill him. But, touched by his age and frailty, he flung his bomb at the governor of Bosnia instead, missed, and then killed himself. Jeracic became a great hero, poems were written about him, declamations were made and dozens of students, including Princip himself, swore upon his grave that he would be avenged. The excitement spread to Croatia and four attempts were made upon the life of the governor in Zagreb.

Franz Ferdinand, the Heir Apparent, was supposed to be mildly Slavophile, and to favour the creation of a trialist monarchy in which Austrians, Hungarians, and Slavs had equal rights. His views made him enemies in Vienna and Budapest but no friends in Bosnia. He was a Hapsburg and that was enough.

The circumstances of his visit to Sarajevo are so strange that Mr Pfeffer raised a doubt that has frequent echoes and has never been satisfactorily laid to rest. Was the visit a provocation? Did the Vienna

Government want some incident to occur that would give an excuse for the subjugation of Serbia? Mr Pfeffer can explain in no other way the absence of police and military from the streets (very strange when you recall that there were manoeuvres on and troops in abundance outside the town). And how was it possible for a second assassin to have another try half-an-hour after the first had failed? The photographs have survived and you can see the archducal car proceeding down an almost empty street. A small boy waves his hat from the quayside, while on the opposite pavement, Mr Pfeffer tells us, six assassins were stationed at intervals (the photographer had marked one of them with a cross), but not a single policeman. Then why ever did the royal visit take place on Vidovdan, a great day of mourning for the defeat of the Serbs by the Turks in the fourteenth century, a defeat which the Serbs had just so triumphantly reversed?

But one must not oversimplify. Of course there may have been some high official who said, "The Archduke thinks he's so popular with the Serbs, let him find out for himself!" and then cynically relaxed security measures. Baron Bolfras, for example, who accompanied the Archduke, expressed that opinion in his reminiscences. But I doubt whether respectable bureaucrats often consciously plan for assassination. I think, when they want a major blunder made, they delegate authority to some naïve and irreproachable subordinate. One can imagine some minor diplomatic personage getting fuddled by the mystique of royalty and Austria's cultural mission to the Balkans. He would specially choose Vidovdan for the visit. "We must teach Serbs and Turks to forget about these ancient quarrels," he would argue, "and to bury the hatchet. We must show them how our royalty moves freely and fearlessly among its subjects. We put our trust in Providence." Then the assassination would be deemed the violation of the most sacred trust, and the ultimatum to Belgrade would seem to have been countersigned in Heaven. They could settle down to the absorption of Serbia with the easiest of consciences.

As the days passed, the mourning for the royal couple assumed a majesty that must have made it very hard for Mr Pfeffer to keep his head. The royal corpses passed out of the hands of the doctors and the police and lay in state with a hundred tapers burning. They travelled overland and by sea to Trieste with solemn ceremonies at every halt. Finally, at midnight, they reached Vienna; with torches and muffled drums and a cavalry escort, they were brought to the Church of the Hofburg. The next day the old emperor drove up from Schonbrunn to the service while his ministers got ready for the annihilation of Serbia.

Meanwhile in Sarajevo, Mr Pfeffer looking out of his window saw a procession of boys and girls issuing from the police station with a large portrait of the Archduke draped in crape. A wave of mourning was followed by a wave of indignation against the Serbs. Their shops, hotels, reading rooms were wrecked. The police knew that provided you organize the mourning, there will always be volunteers to carry through the retribution.

Mr Pfeffer slowly pieced together the whole of the story of the assassinations. Very many Serbs in Bosnia and outside it, as well as some Croats and Moslems, were linked in the conspiracy. The individual had set himself in a big way against the state but nothing appeared to prove the complicity of the Serbian Government which the Austrian ultimatum assumed.

There was, of course, a link between the political intrigues of Belgrade and the young Bosnian rebels, but Pfeffer, after a detailed examination of all the evidence, decided that encouragement from Serbia had been unofficial and half-hearted. Captain Tankoshitch, a hero of the Balkan Wars, had indeed got the bombs for the Bosnian students, when they had come to him in Belgrade, begging his assistance. He was a member of the Black Hand*, a Serbian organization for the liberation of the Southern Slavs of the Austro-Hungarian Empire. It had

---

* There are some who now dispute Pfeffer's conclusion, e.g. Joachim Remak, an American professor, who thinks that the whole assassination was organized by Apis (of the Black Hand) in Belgrade, but I don't believe he proves his case at all. (H.B.)

seemed to him and others that the Archduke's visit and military manoeuvres in Bosnia, which, as Supreme Commander he came to supervise, were sly preliminaries to an attack on Serbia. Possibly, they
thought, a bomb or two might warn the Austrians of the resistance
they would meet, though the conspirators did not seek the approval
of the Serbian Government, which knew nothing of their schemes.
Soon after the bombs had been provided, the leaders of the Black Hand
had misgivings. Not in their wildest dreams had they thought that the
Archduke would be so carelessly guarded that the assassination might
succeed, but the young men seemed too ingenious to be trusted. Shar-
ats, a theological seminarist, was sent post haste to Sarajevo to stop
the enterprise, but the bombs were already on the way, the students
had made up their minds. They would not listen to him.

Mr Pfeffer secured abundant photographs. Alone of all the conspirators, the guerrilla Tankoshitch faces the camera with dandified composure, spruce moustachios and a chest criss-crossed with bandoliers.
We know the others only from prison photographs. There are about a
dozen university students, a village schoolmaster, a prosperous citizen
of Tuzla who had opened the first cinema, a patron of gymnastic clubs
and reading rooms. There is a peasant farmer, a very handsome old man
in the white tunic and gay woven girdle of the Bosnian highlands. His
son, a pastoral figure from the Old Testament, appears with his hands
lightly clasped. He is grave, bewildered and yet relaxed, strangely different from the tense figures of the townspeople. You can see in their
eyes that their resolution was shaped by text books, newspapers, committees, while for the peasants the tragedy of Vidovdan was the fulfilment of old legends, ancient curses. For them the Archduke must
have been a shadowy figure not easily to be distinguished from the
Turkish overlords of the past. The bombs which the students brought
them slipped into their broad girdles all too naturally.

These bombs must have changed hands twenty times on their way
to Sarajevo. Let me describe a single episode, one of many similar ones.
One June day a fortnight before the assassination, Chubrilovitch, the
young teacher of a church school near the Serbian frontier, was riding

beside the village priest to buy lambs. He had offered to help the priest ford a river swollen by the floods, but before they reached it a plough-man came out of the woods to say that two students wanted to see the schoolmaster. As soon as the priest had gone, the students, whom the ploughman had helped across the frontier, crept into the open. They explained that in their rucksacks were bombs for the murder of the Archduke. These would somehow have to be brought to Tuzla, the market town, and left with the cinema proprietor for the next stage of their journey to Sarajevo. The schoolmaster put the bombs into the panniers of his horse and took the students to the large farmhouse of his godfather, Kerovitch. The whole family came in to discuss how to get the bombs to Tuzla. One of the sons of the house had cut his hand scything; he had to go to town to see the doctor; then he remembered that their neighbour had to take out his horse and cart to fetch a trunk belonging to a brother who was leaving his school at Tuzla. When night fell they set off, skirting the village where there were military barracks, sitting at different tables whenever they stopped at taverns, till after many adventures they reached the reading-room over which the cinema proprietor had his flat.

Even so crude a summary may illustrate how the Austrian annex-ation of Bosnia had brought two worlds into violent collision; it shows that the assassination was not hatched in an anarchist cellar. In the wild barren mountains, which the Turk never completely subdued, the fierce spirit of independence, though it might exchange ballads for reading-rooms, daggers for bombs, was scantily concealed.

Princip and Chabrinovitch, the two students who actually used the weapons on Vidovdan, were reading-room rather than mountain trained. Mr Pfeffer speaks well of their courage and sincerity. When the trial was over the judge called on those prisoners who repented of their crime to stand up. They all stood up except for Princip. When interrogated, he replied that he was sorry that he had robbed some children of their parents and that he had killed the Archduchess, par-ticularly as she was a Czech, but he was not sorry he had killed the Archduke. He had intended to do so. Then Chabrinovitch, confused and ashamed, sat down again. He had changed his mind, he said; he wasn't sorry either for what he had done.

Chabrinovitch was a nineteen-year-old printer. His evidence was heard with difficulty because the cyanide, which he had tried to swallow at the moment of arrest, had burnt his lips. He was a more theatrical type than the others. He longed to be conspicuous and was so unwisely talkative that the other two students, Princip and Grabezh, had separated from him on their journey across the mountains. There had been ructions in the Chabrinovitch household the day before Vidovdan, when he had hidden the imperial standard which his father had intended to hang out of the window. He had made his preparations for immortality rather elaborately, getting photographs of himself to present to his friends, consigning his watch and his savings to his sister. After his bomb had missed he had leapt into the river with the cyanide between his teeth. But everything went wrong; the river washed off the cyanide and his terrified friends destroyed his photographs. He died in prison at the moment when Serbia had suffered her greatest defeat.

Their nationalism was of the traditional kind. Princip declared that Serbs and Croats were one people and that Yugoslavia must be united as Italy and Germany had been. They must throw out the Austrians as the Italians had done. They were quite unlike the subsidized revolutionaries of later days; indeed they were always penniless. A week or two before the assassination the director of the academy library had noticed that Princip always read on through the lunch hour; finding that he had no money for food, he offered him some. Princip refused but agreed to earn a few shillings by copying out the minutes of a committee meeting. A couple of months later, when it was discovered who had copied them, the offensive pages were solemnly erased.

Mr Pfeffer wrote his book at a time when the Croats were suffering as much from Serbian despotism as under Austria-Hungary. King Alexander's police surpassed the Austrians in brutality and a Croat might well have been tempted to regret the world of culture and learning destroyed on Vidovdan.

But in Mr Pfeffer's pages we see the empire fading naturally and inevitably as a flower. It could not be saved, but the ground might be got ready for its seeds. Mr Pfeffer and others were doing this, but most of the Austrian officials could not face the truth. Their diplomacy had become a network of lies and tricks in which they strangled as many friends as enemies. We see this happening even in Sarajevo. The Austrians were trying to conciliate the Moslems in Bosnia in order to counterbalance the Croats and Serbs, who formed the majority. Perhaps they had some pre-vision of their war-time alliance with Turkey. Their Bosnian regiments wore the fez and a hideous Turko-Viennese town hall was erected at Sarajevo. The authorities were therefore displeased when Mr Pfeffer discovered that one of the young men who waited on the quayside with a bomb for the Archduke was a Moslem. He was twice imprisoned and twice escaped with the connivance, Mr Pfeffer was convinced, of the police. He was never brought to trial or charged.

And there were fatuous, place-hunting lies as well as mean, political ones. Contrary to custom, Mr Pfeffer was not asked to be present at the examination of the bodies of the royal pair, but he was expected later to sign the official report testifying to facts he had not seen. He indignantly refused. Later he learnt that he had not been asked in because of his grey suit. In the presence of royalty, even dead royalty, a frock coat is obligatory. Also decorations were to be awarded to all those present on that solemn occasion and his rank did not qualify him for one.

The convicted students were under twenty and therefore exempted by Austrian law from hanging. But they and most of the others died after a year's imprisonment; Mr Pfeffer does not attribute this very strange fact to Austrian cruelty. TB can, perhaps, account for two out of a dozen. One of them went mad. Is it possible that these unsophisticated people simply sank under the gigantic consequences of what they had done? At times they may have had some intimation of the honour in which they would later be held, but more often they must have thought of the German and Austrian armies advancing everywhere and the Serbians hopelessly crushed. Night and day five soldiers watched over Princip in his cell at Theresienstadt, one in his room, two in the passage, two outside the window. He can never have learnt that the empire he had challenged was collapsing.

The Austrian authorities strongly disapproved of Mr Pfeffer, but he had done his work well and could not be dismissed. With ingenious malice the minister succeeded in transferring him to Tuzla, the home ground of so many of the conspirators whom he had brought to trial. When the war ended, the Tuzla town council pressed for his trial, but the brother of the schoolmaster, Chubrilovitch, who had been hanged, came to his defence and he was allowed to retire into private life.

He was universally detested and yet it was clear that he had acted in the only possible way that an Austrian official could honourably act. He had fixed the guilt clearly and categorically upon individuals who were ready to shoulder it. He had tried to dispel the clouds of dark suspicion and vague accusation from which wars arise. He had localized and isolated a crime at a time when the Austro-Hungarian Government, with the German Empire behind it, was trying to put a whole nation in the dock.

He failed; but in honouring what was generous and self-sacrificing in a young nation which claimed its rights, he upheld better than its own ministers the honour of the doomed old empire which he served.

Epilogue

The Sarajevo conspirators were Croats, Serbs and Moslems, and they aimed at a nation in which the diverse peoples of Yugoslavia should live in free and equal union. They were mostly republicans and the movement to which they belonged was not tainted with racialism till the new state was set up under the Serbian king. It was racialism, not nationalism, that undermined Yugoslav unity, but this vital distinction is seldom observed and when "petty nationalism" is attacked as the source of our troubles, the "petty nations" seldom defend themselves. Unlike monarchies, empires and Communist states, they have no trade union nor have they developed a common philosophy. They have few arguments to oppose to the universalists and imperialists, who believe that incompatibilities of language and culture are best ironed out by the kindly pressure of a dominant race. In fact, the small peoples often subscribe to this belief themselves. Frequently you will hear an Irish nationalist lamenting the collapse of Austria-Hungary and explaining that Yugoslavia and the other succession states were mere puppet contrivances of the League of Nations, rag-bags of racial oddments, doomed to disintegrate. He ignores that these states all have living languages and often a more distinctive culture, a longer history of independence than our own. And since the Succession States owed their existence to England and France, their citizens often scoffed at Ireland's independence. The Croats used to call themselves the "Ulster of Yugoslavia" because they considered the Six Counties as progressive as themselves and in equal danger of being absorbed into the peasant economy of a more primitive people.

What then is nationalism and how can it be distinguished from racialism? Thomas Davis, being only half-Irish, is probably a sounder nationalist, more immune from racialism, than Mazzini and the other Victorian apostles of the resurgent peoples. He would have said that a country belongs to the people who were born in it and intend to die there and who make its welfare their chief concern. There is no mention of "minority rights," because these were assumed. Even in Ireland not many think like that now. Read the speeches reported in the press. Where one man talks of national unity, a hundred will talk of some unity that is racial, confessional or political.

It was because nationalism lacked a philosophy that in the early twenties it began to decay and racialism took its place. The first sign of this degeneration came in 1923, when by the Treaty of Lausanne in exchange for Turks from Europe over a million Greeks were moved from the coast of Asia Minor, where they had lived for three thousand years. This ghastly crime was committed so efficiently under the auspices of the League of Nations that it won universal applause. What Churchill was later to call "the disentanglement of populations" began to seem a sensible and modern way of solving finally an ancient problem.

The old view that men should enjoy equal rights in the land of their birth began to seem hopelessly out of date, and soon Hitler and Mussolini and Stalin were eliminating causes of friction by large and admirably organised population exchanges in the Tyrol and the Baltic States. The war had hardly started, when it became obvious to all sensible Germans that, if there was ever to be world peace, all conquered peoples should either be Germanized or deported. That much-respected man, Dr Oberlander, who later became Adenauer's Minister for Refugees, said with reference to the Poles: "It is better to be harsh now than have petty warfare waged for generations." Soon the contagion of this generous realism reached the Allies, and in 1940 we find Benes writing in *The Nineteenth Century* that three million Sudeten Germans should be "amicably and under decent human conditions" expelled. When the time came they were expelled. Again, Churchill in 1944 expressed the opinion that expulsion was "the most lasting and satisfactory method" of dealing with the 7,500,000 Germans of the East. They, too, were satisfactorily expelled.

When we recall such gigantic endeavours, scientifically conducted, to sort out the old rag-bag nations of 1918 into homogenous states, how petty and parochial seem the dreams of the Sarajevo conspirators, and the poor old League of Nations with its condominiums and Free Cities and minority rights! And how more than dead are Davis and Herder and their romantic insistence on Homeland and Nationhood! One has to listen hard to catch the least echo of that extinct ideology. Yet here is one from the most improbable source of all, from Germany, which once led the world in the social science of Disentanglement. It comes from The Exiles' Charter, an appeal for Heimatrecht published on behalf of those 7,500,000 German refugees from the East.

God placed men in their homes. To drive men out of their homes spells spiritual death. We have experienced this fate. Hence we feel called upon to demand that the right to one's home be recognized as one of the basic rights given by God to man.

(1956)

In Dalmatia

The most sensational way to approach Dalmatia is from inland, for the small train that winds through an infinity of tunnels from Serbia across Bosnia and Herzegovina to Dubrovnik takes you in one March night from deep winter to mild spring. One day in Macedonia I saw a policeman and his wife laboriously cutting their way on to a main road through a seven-foot bank of snow. Our bus was stuck on the main road and we needed spades and tools, but for all the help the policeman could offer us he might have been a hundred miles away, rather than a hundred yards. Not very many hours later, and in bright sunlight, we saw Dalmatian women washing their clothes in the Adriatic, plum trees in blossom, hills covered with narcissus and wild hyacinths, mimosa and almond flowers already faded and families sitting under magnolia trees sipping wine and complaining of the weather. In the meantime, I had crossed the great barrier of Karst that separates central Yugoslavia from the Adriatic and which accounts for the extraordinary divergence in the climate. Herzegovina, which I saw by moonlight in the early morning, must be one of the most desolate and barren districts in Europe. For miles, the only houses are the ruined cottages of the workmen and engineers who built the railway; here and there a cabbage patch has been formed by collecting earth into a pocket and protecting it from the goats with boulders. The cabbages bear tiny leathery heads on tall fat stalks as high as the Herzegovinian oak trees, which the goats and the rocks have kept to the size of pot plants. Yugoslavs say that the Venetians cut down the original forests for the piles on which

Venice was built, and later rains and storms washed away the soil. It is hard to replant it, for the hot summer sun sets fire to the parched co-nifers – but to reafforest the Karst is one of the great ambitions of Yugoslavia, and in the summer schoolchildren can be seen planting and watering young spruces in the mountains near their village.

For a long way, the rail line clung to a ledge of rock that hung over a black, winding lake which dries up in the summer and is planted with maize. As we descended almost vertically towards the sea, the tunnels and twists became more frequent, and sometimes we saw the engine coming from the mouth of tunnels we had not yet entered ourselves. A final bend, and the creeks of the Ombla and the islands opposite Dubrovnik appeared, and we were dropping through myrtle, and ar-butus, yellow spurge and heather, into an almost tropical luxuriance of vegetation. This band of barren rock which runs from Fiume to Cotor separates the whole Dalmatian coast from central Yugoslavia. The barren hinterland has given the coast its unique character and history, and has forced Dalmatians to look to the sea rather than to the land for their livelihood. From these districts the Yugoslav navy recruits its best sailors, as did the Austrian navy before the war. Dubrovnik (or Ragusa), Split, Cotor, Trogir, Sibenik and Zara, not merely from Greek and Roman traditions, but also by geography, were forced to become seafaring city-states, repelling raids from the hungry hinterland and keeping their independence by intriguing alternately with one or other of their powerful, predatory neighbours, with Venice or Turkey, France, Spain or Hungary, the Serbian or Bulgarian empires. Dubrovnik alone was completely successful in this. There is no breach in the walls which surround the town; it must be, with Rhodes, the most compact and beautiful and unchanged of mediaeval cities. Till Napoleon conquered it and made it a part of the Republic of Illyria and created Marmont Duke of Ragusa, it had been governed by its own aristocratic council for a thousand years. It is true that its rector was for many centuries a Venetian, but this was a device worthy of Mr de Valera for making him a nobody. Not he but the native half-Slav, half-Latin aristocratic fam-ilies were to be the real rulers; but to prevent rivalries it was necessary to have a nominal figurehead, whom nobody could envy and everybody would distrust. Characteristically, the Republic of Ragusa offered Machiavelli a seat on its council.

On the way from Dubrovnik to Split, most ships call at the islands of Korcula and Hvar, and there is just time to race round the little towns before the steward summons one back with his bell. They are all walled against pirates; flights of narrow ramshackle stone steps run past old houses with the coats of arms of Venetian noble families over the doorways. Above the towns there is nothing but rocks and olives and hens scratching among tins. Korcula is the loveliest but Hvar has a more pretentious sea front with palm trees and local beaux and belles lined up to watch the steamer come in. They owe their prosperous appearance to sardines and rosemary from which an essence is made, and later on in the spring the tourists begin to come. In this season, most of the travellers are businessmen. There was a French agent for Bordeaux from Fiume, a Russian shipping agent and an American engineer who had been visiting his parents in Herzegovina. He was earning seven dollars a day so he had to stay not with them but at the hotel. He was shocked to find that his sisters wore "silly clothes" and he had spoilt all his four suits in the mud on his father's farm. This can only have been a stage in his social development, because the same day a Cunarder had landed in Ragusa, and its passengers had ransacked the town for "silly clothes" which, in Ragusa, it has already become profitable to fake.

We passed the island of Brac which provided Diocletian with limestone for his palace at Split, and soon along the seafront we could distinguish vast Roman walls and Corinthian columns embedded in a long line of hotels and shops and restaurants. For Diocletian's palace has been preserved by being absorbed. The greater part of the old town is squeezed between its immense ramparts. The mausoleum, except for an ugly tower for which an English architect is responsible, and a Renaissance chapel, survives almost intact as a Catholic church while round it, except for a line of columns and the narrow lean-to roof, the peristyle stands almost as it did. Diocletian, who resigned his imperial powers in Nicomedia, had this palace, as large in itself as a small garrison town, built rapidly in ten years for his old age. As at Dedinje, King Alexander's residence near Belgrade, the royal quarters must have been a modest appendage to a vast military establishment. When the barbarians captured and laid waste to Salona, the great Roman seaport a few miles away that was twice the size of modern Split, the survivors took refuge in the palace and till the Slav invasion it was never taken. They dug themselves houses out of the thick walls, and even now fragments of columns, of tablets and Roman archways can be seen buried in the walls of the squat stone houses.

As for the great city of Salona, till a few years ago not a trace of it could be seen. When the Dalmatian coast, all but Ragusa, came under Venice, Venetian officials were encouraged to carry away the masonry and build from it the palaces in Venice. Sometimes they got masonry in part-payment of their salaries. From the mountain above, the town debris slowly slid down but was held back by the city walls, and now it is on the higher level outside the ramparts that the most interesting discoveries have been made. A long line of sarcophagi stretches around the outer edge of the cemetery, each of them with a neat round hole bored in its massive lid, through which the Avars had extracted everything of value. They left only one tomb for the museum officials to rifle. Attilia Varia, a civil servant's wife, was buried with a pair of gold brooches shaped like cockles, some earrings of seed-pearls and a row of large grey marble buttons. Case after case is filled with coins and amphorae and terracotta lamps, with the mantelpiece ornaments of merchants' wives, with busts of judges and dolls' tea sets. Salona must have been a prosperous provincial town like Cardiff, with a decent theatre and amphitheatre, near enough to the capital for the merchants' daughters to go there for the season and to follow the fashions, able to afford high-quality gladiators and lions and respectable touring companies.

The amphitheatre forms one corner of the city wall, but much still remains to be excavated. Professor Bulic, the excavator, is himself buried in one of the sarcophagi beside the foundations of the Church of the Martyrs of Salona. Diocletian, who organized the last and most terrible of the Christian persecutions, saw that his native town had a liberal supply of victims for their amphitheatre. A soldier himself, he must have hated above all the spread in the army of what he no doubt considered an unmanly, disintegrating faith. Many of his victims were soldiers. Many too of the martyrs of Salona were not natives but from the East, from the Euphrates or the Nile. Was this an accident or was it an attempt to prove that Christianity was un-Roman – un-Illyrian? Soon after Diocletian's death Christianity became the religion of the Roman Empire, and his body was flung out from his mausoleum. A couple of centuries more and his birthplace, Salona, had been sacked by the barbarians. Illyria was lost to Rome.

Some generations later a pope, by birth an Illyrian, collected funds and sent a mission to help Roman citizens who still survived in the devastated land. They came back with the bones of the martyrs of Salona and there still exists in Rome an altar-piece he had painted in their honour: four Roman soldiers carrying their martyrs' crowns and four martyred high officials of the Church surround the pious organizers of the expedition.

Trogir is only a few miles from Split. It is the most perfect of all the little Venetian towns of the coast. Two years ago, Mussolini declared in a resounding oration that wherever there was a lion of St Mark's, there was Venice; wherever was Venice there was Italy. The patriotic youths of Trogir took up the challenge and one night at 1 a.m., armed with stones and mallets, they smashed all the Venetian lions in the town. One vast lion, half-disembowelled, still wags his tail upon a bastion too high and large to be easily destroyed. Two were removed in time to the safe-keeping of the museum, a third still survives in Trogir because the courtyard where it stands is always locked. This lion is the most insulting of them all, because the Bible on which he props his paw is closed; the text which the Venetian lion usually examines is one of peace, but there could be no peace with the Slavs of Dalmatia. The lion at Trogir had to be always ready to spring.

There is one town on the Dalmatian coast, Zara, that was given to

Italy by the peace treaty. But in Dalmatia, as a whole, the population is overwhelmingly Croat; at most 5 or 6 per cent are Italians. Italy can, therefore, base her claim to Dalmatia only on sentiment and history. Zara and Fiume are sufficiently expensive tributes to sentiment, for the port of Fiume, severed from its hinterland, is dead and Zara must buy its food from Yugoslavia and have its numerous officials paid from Italy. There was a rumour in Split that a result of the new friendly relations between Italy and Yugoslavia might be the return of Zara to Yugoslavia in exchange for concessions to Fiume, by which she might recover some of the shipping which has been diverted to Susak, Fiume's Yugoslav suburb. But in modern Italy glory is more important than gain and the rumour has been sceptically received.

The cruising habit has lead to the discovery of the more famous Dalmatian ports such as Split and Dubrovnik. How long will it be before Sibenik and Rab, Crkvenica, Herzegnovi and all the enchanting towns and islands that line the coast from Fiume to Montenegro become well known to tourists? Those who like hotels that are good and cheap and life that is simple and unspoilt must go now before Dalmatia becomes a second Côte d'Azure.

(1937)

The Last Izmerenje

For three days the rain had fallen steadily. When we arrived in Kotor, the top of Lovcen was invisible, and festoons of moist cloud swam across the mountains behind us. Nonetheless, there was a band to meet the boat and a great crowd, and on an iron mooring post a youth was arranging salvoes of welcome. Every now and then there was an enormous bang, and he disappeared in thick white smoke, for explosions are the Dalmatians' favourite way of celebrating great occasions, and today was a feast day in both the Catholic and Greek Churches. It was Easter Day for the Orthodox, while for the Catholics it was the feast of St Hosanna, a nun whose mummified body lies below an altar in one of the Kotor churches.

I pushed my way through the crowd, and asked the first likely person I met where the monastery of Grbalj was, and what time the "izmerenje" was to be. Nobody knew, though I had heard in Belgrade about it three hundred miles away, while here it was only half-an-hour's drive by car. It was not till I had searched the town for information that I found, at last, that I was a day too early. I was rather relieved; perhaps the next day the rain-clouds would have lifted.

In the afternoon, with two others, I made a half-hearted attempt to drive to Cetinje, but soon after we had passed the old Austrian customs house, at the frontier of Dalmatia and Montenegro, we were in dense fog and the whole panorama of Kotor Bay, which must be one of the loveliest in the world, had disappeared, and we were shivering with cold and damp. We went back; and that evening, when I was having tea in one of the old houses at Dobrota, I was told the story of the Montenegrin blood feud by a lady who had studied law and had attended the trial of Stevo Orlovich in an official capacity.

The Orlovichs and the Bauks were two families living some fifteen miles from Kotor, not in Montenegro itself, but observing the old Montenegrin customs. Two years ago the Orlovichs had made enquiries and learnt that Stjepo Bauk, whose father was dead, would let his sister accept a proposal from Stevo Orlovich. Stevo, thereupon, set out with a group of his relations to make a formal offer, carrying firearms, as was the custom, so as to celebrate the betrothal with the usual explosions. When they reached the Bauks' house, they were told that the offer was refused.

It appeared that an old uncle of the Bauks had been greatly insulted that his permission had not been asked. He had made a row, and Stjepo had given in to him. Stevo Orlovich was outraged and indignant, and whipping out his gun he fired at Stjepo Bauk and hit him in the leg. Bauk fired back and injured Orlovich – there was a scuffle and the Orlovichs took to their heels. A few days later, Stjepo Bauk's leg had to be amputated, and he died. The case was tried in the courts, and Stevo Orlovich was sentenced to three years' imprisonment.

But the Bauks were not in the least pacified by this; they held to the old Montenegrin tradition that blood should be avenged by blood, and the Orlovichs continued to feel uneasy. Near Podgorica, in Montenegro, just such a murder had taken place in 1930, and since then thirty murders have followed it in alternate families, the last one six months ago. It has been impossible for the courts to collect satisfactory evidence; though the relations of the victim in most cases knew the murderer, they would scorn to hand him over to justice. Revenge is a private, not a public, responsibility. But there was a way out, and this the Orlovichs took.

Some ten months ago, when Stevo Orlovich had had the rest of his sentence remitted for good behaviour, twenty-four "good men" of the Orlovichs called on the Bauks, and asked them to agree to the izmerenje ceremony. The Bauks refused. Five months later, the Orlovichs appealed again, and this time they were granted a day's armistice for every member of the deputation, that is to say, twenty-four. After that they came a third time, and at last the Bauks granted their request. It would be the first izmerenje celebrated in the neighbourhood for more than a generation, and it was this ceremony that I had come to Kotor to see.

"Of course," my friend said, "it won't be nearly as elaborate an affair as it used to be. In the old days the murderer had to crawl on his hands and knees and beg forgiveness; and then he must give a gun to the head of the other family as a token. And then there were the babies at the breast. Seven women of the murderer's family had to come with their seven babies in cradles, and ask the head of the family of the murdered man to be the 'kum' or godfather, and he was obliged to accept.

"That shows you what size the families were," she added. "Today, in all Dobrota, you couldn't find seven babies at the breast, far less in one family."

The birds were singing next morning at six o'clock, and the fog seemed to have lifted completely from Lovcen. It looked as if the day was to be fine. I was told to be ready on the quay at 7 a.m., and was to share a car with the two judges who had sentenced Orlovich, two local correspondents of a Belgrade paper, and one of the hundred guests invited by Orlovich. This guest was so confident that the ceremony would wait for him that we were an hour late in starting. To get out to the monastery of Grbalj you must climb up the slope of Lovcen out of the Boka, and then down again towards Budva on the open sea. Most of the district is a "polje" or flat space between the mountains, and relatively fertile; the peasant houses are placed for the most part on the rocky, barren slopes, where nothing grows except scrub or wild pomegranates and stunted oak; their farms lie below them in the polje, full of vines, fig-trees, beans and potatoes, market crops that they can sell in Kotor.

The people of Grbalj were always an enterprising community from the time of the great medieval Tsar of Serbia, Dushan; they had their own laws, and the Venetians, when they occupied the Boka and its surroundings, respected the Grbalj Statute, which was only abolished when Dalmatia was seized by Austria after the Napoleonic wars.

We soon saw the monastery perched on a hill on the left – an un-expectedly small, insignificant building, its courtyard black with moving people. The larger half was completely new.

"The old building was raided and burnt by the Montenegrins them-selves during the war," the judge told me. "They say the Austrians were using it as a store for ammunition. It was rebuilt, and they opened it again last year. There are some twelfth-century frescoes in the end of the chapel, but they're badly damaged by damp, as it was roofless for so long."

Behind us, a mile or two away, but plainly visible as it lay open on the rocky face of the mountain over against the monastery, was the cluster of houses where the Bauks and the Orlovichs lived. They were large red-tiled farmhouses two or three stories high, with big windows and several annexes. The Bauks' house was the bigger of the two.

"The Bauks have a dozen families scattered over the place," said the judge, "but the Orlovichs only have two, so I don't know how they'll pay for the dinner; you see, they must bring a hundred of their sup-porters and the Bauks must bring a hundred of theirs: the Bauks will be the hosts, but the Orlovichs must pay for it all. It may run them into a couple of thousand dinars [about £8]. If either side brings more or less than a hundred, it's a gross insult, and they'll have to start the whole business over again."

The hundred Orlovich guests were already there when we arrived; outside the wall of the churchyard a group of women and neighbours, whom neither side had invited, were leaning watching. The women, in Montenegrin fashion, had their thick black hair wound across their foreheads in heavy plaits, a black lace veil fell from behind to their shoulders.

There were two long tables stretched out in the courtyard covered with brown paper, but the Orlovichs were most of them sitting upon the wall. The six "good men" who headed the Orlovich deputation were in the vestry when we arrived, drinking Turkish coffee. One was a fat, pleasant-looking priest in a grey soutane from a neighbouring parish. Two seemed prosperous town relations in smart overcoats, clean-shaven, with gold teeth and Homburg hats; two were well-to-do farmers in full Montenegrin dress, round caps with red crowns embroidered in gold and the black bands that all Montenegrins wear in mourning for the battle of Kossovo, when the Serbians were defeated by the Turks in 1399. They had red waistcoats with heavy gold embroidery, orange sashes and blue breeches with thick white woollen stockings and string shoes. The other ninety-four Orlovichs had compromised about their clothes; they nearly all had the caps and some had either the breeches or the waistcoat, but they mostly had an ordinary Sunday coat on top of it. They all had black moustaches, and held either a heavy stick or an umbrella in their hands. I saw one or two men who had both.

One of the journalists from Kotor beckoned me into the church, and introduced me to the priest and a small dark man with terrified eyes who stood beside him.

"That's the murderer," he told me. "You are the murderer, Stevo Orlovich, aren't you?" he asked to make certain.

"Yes" – and we shook hands.

We shook hands with his brother, too, an older, solid-looking man. He, too, had received a bullet wound in the leg as he was running away from the Bauks' house. Stevo Orlovich shrank away behind the chapel walls as soon as he could; he was very slightly built, and had black bristly hair and a small Charlie Chaplin moustache; he wore a neat but worn black suit, with a fountain pen clipped in the breast pocket. He was evidently in an agony of shame and embarrassment about the ceremony he was going to have to go through. But he was sufficiently collected to make it clear that he wasn't pleased to see us.

All at once a boy began to toll the three small bells of the chapel, and five or six people went in to hear the priest celebrate the short Easter Mass according to the Greek rite. I saw the correspondent of the Belgrade *Politika* standing beside them leading the responses in a booming voice.

"Christ is risen!"

"Lord, have mercy on us!"

The priest was swinging a censer vigorously, and the whole court-yard was filled with sound and the smell of incense.

It lasted a quarter of an hour. When I came out of the church one of the Orlovichs who was sitting on the seat, cried out, "Hello, boy!" and I went and sat down beside him. He had been at the copper mines at Butte, Montana, and said that at least ten others present had been there, too. I complimented him on his gorgeous embroidered waistcoat, but he said it was nothing to what they used to have. Times were bad...

"Montenegrin mans should do like Irishmans," he said, "raise hell, holler!"

Evidently, a good deal of information about Ireland had filtered via Butte, Montana, to Grbalj, because he had a muttered conversation with his neighbour about de Valera and the Lord Mayor who had died after a seventy day hunger-strike.

"I was telling him about the Liberty Irish State," he said.

The six good men walked out of the church yard and he said:

"You see that bunch? They go fetch the otha bunch!"

But the six Orlovichs returned alone and another hour passed before down the mountain slope the procession of the Bauks, a long black line like a school crocodile, issued slowly from behind a little wood. They were a long way off still. From the terrace of the priest's house I watched them going down a small lane through an olive grove into the main road, crossing the wooden bridge over a very swift stream then climb-ing up the hill towards the monastery.

A man came out of the monastery with a big basket of bread and he was followed surprisingly by a sailor with some paper table napkins. Carafes of rakkia were planted at intervals along the table... The Or-lovichs got up and walked leisurely towards one side of the churchyard, they formed themselves in a long row, fifty abreast, two deep. In the back row towards the end I saw the murderer flatten himself against the wall. He was fingering his fountain pen nervously. His brother was beside him.

The little priest in the grey soutane came bustling out of the church.

"Take of your hats," he said, and we all did so.

Then the Bauks came in, headed by two handsome elderly priests with black beards, then four other good men.

They lined themselves opposite the Orlovichs, exactly a hundred, with their hats still firmly on, facing a hundred with bare heads. It was like Sir Roger de Coverley.

There was a long silence and then one of the Bauk "good men," a professor from Kotor, came out into the middle and in a loud voice read the sentence. This is a slightly abbreviated version of what he read:

> In the name of Christ the Saviour Who is eternal peace between men.
>
> Today, when the Ascension is near at hand, in the year of Our Lord 1937 in the monastery of the Blessed Virgin of Grbalj good men have met together and pleaded with the families of Bauk and Orlovich to lay aside their blood feud which arose in the month of February 1935.
>
> In the name of God from Whom all true justice proceeds and after long cognition, they pronounced this sentence which shall be executed on the third day of Easter, 1937, in the monastery of the Blessed Virgin of Grbalj.
>
> Seeing that God's justice fell upon the wounds of Stjepo Bauk, the son of Vuk and Stevo Orlovich, the son of Lazo, who remained alive after wounds received, and seeing that Mirko Bauk valiantly forgave the murder of his brother Stjepo and reconciled himself through God and St John with the Orlovichs, we declare this sentence:
>
> 1. That the brothers Orlovich wait with a hundred of their people on the Bauks with a hundred of theirs.
> 2. That the Orlovichs humbly, according to custom (but not carrying firearms), shall approach the Bauks who shall embrace them in this order.

> Mirko Bauk, the son of Vuk, shall kiss Stevo Orlovich, the son of Lazo.
>
> Vaso Bauk, the son of Rado, shall kiss Ilya Orlovich, the son of Lazo.

3. That at the first baptism of a child of theirs the Orlovichs shall ask Bauk to be godfather and he shall accept.

4. That from this reconciliation everlasting friendship and mutual respect for their mutual honour in word and deed shall proceed and that this blood feud shall be ended for all time.

> Each family must receive a copy of this sentence and one must be preserved in the archives of the monastery where this reconciliation was made.
>
> Drawn up by the undersigned: (Here follow the signatures of the six good men of the Bauks and the six good men of the Orlovichs.)

The professor stepped back into the Bauk ranks and put the sentence back into his leather portfolio.

Then one of the Orlovich good men cried out in a voice breaking with emotion:

"Stevo Orlovich!"

The murderer folded his arms across his breast and bending down from the waist he darted forward from the wall. He was like someone in a trance. He did not see where he was going and butted his bowed head into a man in front. It was a second before he had disentangled himself from the overcoat and was heading once more for the Bauks. Mirko Bauk, a fat young man with fair hair and moustache, all in black except for the red crown of his Montenegrin cap, stepped out and raised him up.

"Forgive me!" said Orlovich.

"I forgive you my brother's blood," Bauk answered and they kissed each other on both cheeks. I heard people sobbing behind me. Then Vaso Bauk, who was small and puny, embraced Ilya Orlovich and finally all the hundred Bauks stepped forward and shook hands and greeted the hundred Orlovichs. Then they all took their seats at the table, the Orlovichs sitting at one table, the Bauks at another. Stevo Orlovich did not appear but stayed in the monastery with his brother.

I and the four men from Kotor were preparing to go home but the Bauk professor pressed us to stay.

"The Orlovichs would like to ask you," he said, "but they have to be so humble today – it isn't the custom – so we invite you."

A table was brought out from the vestry and a red table cloth and we sat by ourselves in the other side of the courtyard.

Before we started to feed, the Bauk priest got up and began an Easter hymn... and once more the journalist's big voice filled the courtyard.

A lot of forks arrived and a platter heaped with boiled beef. Someone else explained to me that when the monastery had been rededicated last year, there had been six hundred guests and each had had a knife for himself and also a tumbler; but today it was different – it was custom. So there were no tumblers and we pushed round from mouth to mouth, first a big bottle of rakkia, then a big flask of an excellent red wine.

"Please thank you, Mister!" the journalist with the big voice said every time he gave the flask a shove in my direction.

He then muttered very rapidly into my ear a couple of verses of a poem beginning:

> My 'ome iz zy ocean
> My 'arth iz ze ship!

The meal was quite good and the platters were constantly replenished by the sailor and two men running backward and forward with white napkins held in their teeth. After the beef came boiled ham. Except at our table nobody talked very much. There seemed to be no fraternization between the Bauks and the Orlovichs. First came forgiveness, a little later, perhaps, friendship would follow.

They must have had an extraordinary capacity for keeping the

practical and the emotional side of their lives distant for on the slope
of the hill their two houses seemed only a few hundred yards apart.
Their sheep must graze the same mountains, they must use the same
tracks. How had they managed to pass two years so close without
lending things and without borrowing things?

There could be no doubt, anyway, that the quarrel had at last been
settled. The sentences of the law courts usually leave bitterness and
dissatisfaction behind but the ceremony at Grbalj, so impressive and
deeply moving, aimed at something far higher. Did it achieve it? I
thought so, but couldn't be sure. Did Mirko perhaps look a bit too
self-righteous? Does one ever feel very friendly towards people who
force on one too abject an apology or towards one's relations who watch
it? I think Stevo may go to Butte, Montana.

Most European law is based on compensation and punishment,
justice is important, but it is also impersonal. Montenegrin custom on
the other hand takes into account forgiveness which English justice
ignores, and because of that, when "izmerenje" passes away, as pass it
must, an important element of justice will have gone with it.

The journalist borrowed the copy of the sentence from the monastery archives.

"Meet me in the Café at Kotor," he said to me, "and I'll let you have
a read of it."

And we crammed in eleven of us, for some of the Orlovich friends
came too, into the car... There was some angry tooting behind us and
a lemon-coloured sports car thrust past, containing the professor and
two of the Bauk "good men."

A moment later we were on the main highway to Cetinje, negoti-
ating the hair-pin bends of that incredible road. Every now and then
we passed policemen with fixed bayonets and we dodged a charabanc
full of German tourists. Below us at Kotor a yacht lay at anchor by the
quays, a procession of soldiers was marching through the streets which
were green with acacia trees. The grimness of the mountains lay behind
us and we were in the twentieth century again.

"It's beautiful," I said to one of the judges.

"Yes," he replied, "but you should have seen it when the King and Mrs Simpson were here. The evening they arrived all the bay from Tivat to Kotor was illuminated – bonfires and petrol. It was wonderful. One of the bonfires set alight to some dry grass where there were some young trees. Not much damage done, but it made a wonderful blaze!"

By the time our car had drawn up at the Town Kafana, the izmerenje at Grbalj was like something that happened in a dream. Will there ever be another one in Montenegro? I can hardly believe it. The "good men" in the Homburg hats were getting self-conscious about it and I am convinced I heard the murderer and his brother grumbling about the journalists behind the chapel wall. I was glad he didn't know that someone had suggested bringing a film apparatus. Nowadays, too, one can always interrupt blood feuds by going to Butte, Montana.

(1947)

Nazor, Oroschatz and the Von Berks

At the beginning of a revolution artists and writers find themselves in a position of unaccustomed importance. Their support is eagerly canvassed, and it is very hard for them not to be flattered by these attentions. In Yugoslavia the writer must depend on a very small public, perhaps, owing to the differences of dialect within the country, on only a fraction of the reading public, which is not large. Even though some writers are of outstanding merit, they have very rarely been translated so that, when a writer parts with his country, he says goodbye, too, to his craft and his livelihood. Painters, sculptors and musicians are less tried by their medium, and a man like Mestrovich, with an international reputation, can choose his politics without reference to economic considerations: a writer can't.

A French writer, when asked to explain why certain artists collaborated in France, said "Collaborate? But in politics artists are just children, you know!" It would be truer to say that artists are passionate individualists and there are certain temptations to which they succumb rather easily. They will tolerate any system which gives scope to their temperament. They are restless, discontented people in modern democracies and are unusually open-minded in regard to any change.

Pavelitch and his German patrons took very great pains to conciliate the artists and writers of Croatia; a novelist, Budak, was the first President, and a number of literary papers of excellent quality were produced. I do not think the artist was much molested at the start; for example, Krleza, the best-known Croatian dramatist, lived on peacefully through the Occupation in Zagreb, though a Communist. In the early numbers of *Spremnost* there are constant flattering articles about Mestrovich and Augustinchich, the sculptors, and Nazor the poet, and the most prominent of the Croatian painters. The articles hinted, often incorrectly, that the subject of their praise was a supporter of the government. Sometimes the artist or writer responded to this flattery with an ode or a picture; sometimes he contributed something non-committal to the papers. That was good enough. The editors felt they had netted him. They did not insist on ideological conformity, his name was what they were after, and because of that these papers of the occupation have much admirable material in them.

There was a curious technique if the writer or artist did not respond at all to their advances. He suddenly found himself whipped off to prison for no reason he could understand... as suddenly he would be let out; soon after some friendly, casual person would come up and say to him, "Oh by the way, I'm getting up an exhibition (or bringing out a new number), I'd be awfully pleased, old man, if you'd let me have something." One artist told me that he was only able to resist this technique by pretending that his mind had been unhinged by prison. Very few said flatly, "No." But the painters had difficulty with paint or materials or found their inspiration drying up, the producers found the plays were quite impossible to cast. The mercurial artistic temperament was freely invoked and as it was wartime, there were often plausible excuses for doing nothing. Mestrovich, after he had been in prison for some weeks, found there was only one subject to which he could do justice at the moment. He must go to the Vatican and make some busts of the mediaeval Popes. He knew Pavelitch could not refuse so praiseworthy a suggestion. On the way there he was asked to accompany the Croatian exhibition to Venice where his sculpture was to be displayed. He did so. He then made the busts in Rome, got a visa to Switzerland through the Vatican, and never returned to Croatia.

Soon after the liberation a magazine was published in Zagreb with the intention of disconcerting the government. It published various odes and declamations, photographs, busts and pictures that had appeared under well-known names during the Occupation and in which the Ustashe* and the Germans were glorified. The editor pointed out that these people were now ardent Partisans and supporters of the government. It was, I believe, the last freely critical paper published since the liberation and it was very quickly suppressed. I do not know whether the editor was making a gesture against corruption or whether he was being just malicious. What he proved, I think, was that while the power and influence of the creative mind is acknowledged, only unrepresentative governments are prepared to subsidize it. They invite the writers and artists to compensate with their enthusiasm for the frigidity of the electorate.

But it was not only creative minds that the Ustashe tried to buy, it was also cultivated and educated minds. With the collapse of several empires in 1918 a number of men, product of the wealth and leisure of this society, found themselves deprived of the climate in which their talents developed and needed to be maintained. I suppose they were considered greenhouse plants in a society which could not afford a greenhouse, but, as it turned out, their talents, which needed artifice and privilege for their development, were missed in a thousand ways in the new states. Alexander during his dictatorship made a great use of the Russian émigrés in Belgrade, and under Pavelitch in Zagreb the remnant of the Austro-Hungarian ascendancy, which was all but moribund, began to show signs of life; they were, I think, not quite so militant, embittered and combatant as the Russians, their days of glory were further in the past, but they could not forget that Zagreb and

---

* The Ustaše (also known in English as Ustashe, Ustasha or Ustashi) were members of the "Ustaša – Hrvatski revolucionarni pokret" (Insurgents – Croatian Revolutionary Organization), a Croatian fascist, ultranationalist and terrorist organization active, in its original form, between 1929 and 1945. Founded and led by Ante Pavelić, the "Poglavnik" (Leader, *Führer*, or *Duce*), its members murdered hundreds of thousands of Serbs, Jews, Roma and anti-fascist or dissident Croats during the Independent State of Croatia (Nezavisna Država Hrvatska, or NDH), established on the territory of Yugoslavia between 1941 and 1945, in what is now mainly Croatia and Bosnia. (Editors)

Croatia had once been a great greenhouse for the forcing of their talents and that the civilization of the Croatian towns had been given an indelible stamp by the Austro-Hungarians. Probably it was the most idealistic and disinterested of them who took part in the new Croatia, the ambitious would find more scope under Hitler in Germany or Austria.

I can think of one Austro-Hungarian poet who for the first time in his life found in Pavelitch's Croatia an outlet for his remarkable gifts. As an Austrian, whose family had been connected for centuries with Croatia and Slovenia, he felt himself qualified to act as interpreter between Croat and Austrian and for three years he filled the Zagreb newspapers with remarkable poetry and prose. The new Croatia was as indulgent as it dared to the old ascendancy; its temper was romantic and pseudo-mediaeval but as all the Croatian aristocracy had disappeared or been absorbed generations earlier into the Austro-Hungarian upper classes, much compromise and connivance was essential. Poets, if they can't be anarchists, are susceptible to the romance of aristocracy, and I think it must have been this spurious pretence of aristocracy, with its bogus titles and resurrected pomps, ceremonies and traditions, that seduced for a time some of the better Croatian writers. I am told that the great poet Nazor* was induced at the beginning to write praises of the new régime, but though I found many articles in the Occupation papers praising his work, I could not find anything written by him.

After a year he had had enough and in the New Year of 1943 the Partisans sent a car to Zagreb for him to fetch him "to the woods." He was an old man in poor health, and victory for the Partisans was still

---

*Vladimir Nazor (1876-1949) was a well-known Croatian poet, writer and translator. During the Second World War, he became one of Tito's closest associates and was chosen as the President of the State Anti-Fascist Council for the National Liberation of Croatia (ZAVNOH), the governing organ of the anti-fascist movement in Croatia. After the war, he became the first President of the Presidium of the People's Republic of Croatia, one of the constituent republics of Tito's Socialist Federal Republic of Yugoslavia. (Editors)

a long way out of sight, so his courage in leaving his comfortable home in Zagreb and a devoted sister in order to undertake this arduous journey across the frozen rivers and through trackless mountains of Bosnia will not be forgotten. The Partisans on their side paid a fine tribute to his fame and to poetry in undertaking the task of transporting, often by stretcher, this distinguished old gentleman with eczema and digestive troubles. He had his reward when he became the Vice-President of the Federal Republic of Croatia and was the first to address in Zagreb the liberated citizens.

If it is true that romance and poetry disappeared under the Communist government in Yugoslavia, there was an abundance of both in the Partisan warfare. There cannot be many wartime descriptions to equal Nazor's; it is not ordinary reporting... the enchantment of the Bosnian woods in the early morning and the hallucinations that the interlacing branches and mists weave in the mind of a sick old man recall Turgenev. The hero-worship and the comradeship of the woods was the real kind; not till it was transferred to the streets and newspapers and the election platform did the metamorphosis begin. The process is, I think, inevitable. Nazor prints in his book the poems that his comrades wrote, often about Tito; they are monotonous and uninventive as the song of the blackbird but in the woods they have their own appropriateness. Tito is their Achilles, he has the head of a young lion, says Nazor, and like the heroes of Homer he is only partly real; he becomes the symbol of what men admire in each other and everything he does and says becomes charged with significance. It is not till the symbol has to appear on the election platform that some spell is broken. "Tito with us and we with Tito" they scribble on all the walls. But it is not the same. Some appalling catastrophe happens which should be explained not in terms of politics but of social psychology.

Nazor's diary has great documentary interest.˙ As an old, bourgeois poet campaigning with young revolutionaries, his elderly attempts to

---

˙ Vladimir Nazor, *Parizanska Knjiga* (1943-1944) (Zagreb: 1949). (H.B.)

share their thoughts as well as their hardships are sometimes embarrassing, but the reader gets the feeling that he is trying sincerely to interpret the virtues of the old world in which he grew up in terms of the new, and that he is trying to save a good many venerable but discredited idols from the first fury of the iconoclasts.

A staff-officer, Major Moma Djurich, looked after him and saw that he had very quiet horses and refused to allow him to carry arms. In a rebellious mood Nazor wrote him a poem:

When will you give to me, Commandant Moma,
Rifle and horse, not a broken old screw?
Did you forget how Nestor of Homer
Was older than I but a warrior too?

Did you forget how, when Doichen was dying,
They strapped on his harness? Come harness me well,
And set me on horseback! I'm weary of lying.
I too would be after the black infidel!

One day they arrived at a castle in Bosnia where Tito had his headquarters. It had been built in 1902 with turrets and battlements by a romantic landowner, Frau Isabella von Berks. She herself was of Croatian descent but her husband's family came originally from England to Austria during a time of religious persecution under James I. They had been Earls of Berkshire but had been deprived of their estates, and that may have influenced her in spending her dowry on erecting this imitation Anglo-Norman castle on the banks of the stormy river Una. Inside it was furnished with four-posters and rich canopies, with carved Gothic presses and cabinets and refectory tables, no doubt in polished pitch pine. The long gloomy passages were hung with trophies of the chase, there were mirrors in heavy gilt surrounds, and ranks of ancestors in the dining-room. The library was full of ancient tomes in lofty book-cases, German and French and Italian, but there was not a single book in the Croatian or any other Slav tongue. There was literally nothing in the whole castle, said Nazor, to indicate the country in which it was built. It was as if the owner had deliberately set out to ignore the people of whose blood she was. The castle had been ransacked by all the armies which had passed through it in the last year, Italian and German and Ustashe, as well as Moslem fugitives, and insults about the von Berks family were scribbled in Italian on the walls. Now it was the temporary headquarters of Marshal Tito and Nazor describes the speed and vigour with which water and electricity and telephones were installed by the Partisans and Tito. "May he do as well," he cried, "when they come into possession of the derelict and plundered castle which is Croatia!" Outside there was deep snow so that the burnt and deserted villages, the unburied corpses, were hidden from view, the stumps of the plantations along the Una which the Italians had cut down no longer offended, even the rocks gleamed like silver in the sunlight. On the wireless the news came through of the victories of the Partisans in the Lika, of the Russian armies by Rostov. It was easy to believe, in this castle, that the worst was past.

In the night Nazor was restless with his illness and could not sleep, so he got up and wandered round the castle. There was no one about except the two guards on watch outside the little room where Tito was still writing up his despatches. In the dining-room the bright snow outside the window made such a lovely light in the rooms that he found his way around without lighting his torch. He was looking for a ghost, the inevitable tenant of an English castle, and what ghost was he more likely to see than Isabella von Berks? If she was ever to appear it would be now, when "barbarians" were desecrating this creation of her romantic soul. There was no ghost, and he did not know which of the portraits was Isabella, but he persuaded himself that if he flashed his torch into their faces, one after the other, the proud owner would surely move in her frame, if only to turn her back on him. He had an obsession that one day he would meet her and know more about her; he would find her perhaps sitting at the head of the dining table, reproachful and indignant, waiting for him. He felt that he understood her, for he too had a nostalgia for the past. He had lived for twenty years on his

Dalmatian island in the shadow of a tower, and wherever he had moved to afterwards, conscious of being ridiculous, he had built himself a tower. He went back to bed disappointed but confident that all the same he would somehow get to know her.

The next day the doctor would not allow him to move and while Tito and his men were ranging the countryside, Nazor was confined to the castle watching from the large window the snow thudding and slipping down from the evergreens and tossed off irritably, like prema-ture flowers, from the bare and spindly twigs of the lilac. There was a slight thaw. The Una was black between its snowy banks, and the devastation on either bank was revealed. Where were the woods in which the animals, whose heads hung in the dining room, had ranged? Where was the bridge and little mill? When Isabella lived here and sat on the terrace the hills must have been clothed in greenery and filled with songbirds. (Now there is nothing but bleakness and in the distance the minarets of a mosque.) The voices of the villagers and servants must have come up to her. What a place for an old person to live and forget the past!

Every day, as they did repairs, something came to light in the castle; a muffin dish from behind the panelling, some candelabra from a hole in the wall, silver fruit dishes from the roof; but the Partisans had not time for a thorough investigation. Only Nazor had the leisure to ex-plore, but that was not the sort of research in which he was interested. He wanted to re-create the life of Isabella.

He had luck, for Lisica, the wife of the caretaker, a sly and lazy person, still lived in the castle, and she took Nazor to see Isabella's room, and showed him an old photograph of Isabella, an unpretentious looking woman in a white blouse and Edwardian *coiffeur*. Lisica told him she was tall with blue eyes, did not talk much, and as a mistress was kind but firm.

But Isabella sent him a second messenger, a Serbian in Tito's entou-rage called Tsrni, who had lived in Soviet Russia and spoke and read Russian and French, a hard, dry but prompt and resourceful man. Somewhere or other he discovered the "Stammbuch" of the von Berks, one of those monstrous, illuminated books, all gold and azure and crimson, compiled at the end of the last century to please the parvenu wives or unmarried sisters of the Austro-Hungarian nobility. He also found two packets of letters from Isabella to her son written in 1922 and 1923.

From these letters Nazor learnt that Isabella's last years had been spent in struggles and difficulties and not peacefully and romantically in the castle of Oroschatz. Her son was looking after it for her; his own house in Slavonia had been burnt by the Communists (that is what he called them but probably they were Serbian nationalists) in 1918, and she was living with a married daughter and nine grandchildren in Germany. It was the inflation time and they were in great poverty and wretchedness. But she wrote with patience and courage and an utter absence of that pride and self-dramatization which Nazor had anticipated; she seemed to have given up all her dreams about the castle, there was nothing left of all her romantic fantasies. "She had only her Croatian mother's heart," said Nazor, "the cold misty romanticism of the foreigners from the North had been purged and chastened on the day of wrath, and it had given way to our Slavonic sensitiveness, warm, plebeian, creative."

Isabella, said Nazor, was not buried here, and it was useless to look for her ghost, but if the hopes of Tito were realized and the castle was turned into a holiday home for poor children or for veterans, perhaps her kind shade would appear under the roof.

It seemed to Nazor that she had not spent her dowry in vain. "Build!" he exclaimed, as he ended this entry in his diary. "Build! Even though you do not know for whom or for what you are building!"

I had read all this with interest because I had stayed with Isabella's son, to whom the letters had been written, at his house in the village of Podgorac in Slavonia. I had come as a friend of his children's tutor, Christopher Cooper, whom I had met in Zagreb. Von Berks had been murdered early after the invasion of Yugoslavia, I suppose by the same people who had burnt his house thirty years before and whom he called, with more justification than then, "Communists." They were probably just his neighbours and employees. He and such neighbours as he considered his equals were living precariously and resentfully on the edge of the abyss into which they were shortly to plunge. If he had been told that he would be murdered and his wife and sons have to fly, and his daughter, to whom he was devoted, only save herself by marrying a village Communist, what would he have done? I think he could have done very little, except juggle a bit more with his and his wife's investments and see that his sons got a good English education.

They all of them refused to see anything inevitable about their fate; they had a personal grievance against Destiny which had permitted them, intelligent, educated, fastidious and honourable people, to be ordered about by people of low breeding and semi-barbarous culture. Yet when I read Nazor's diary it seems to me that there is nothing inevitable abut ruthlessness, that it comes from a misuse of words; that it is the business of men of education to keep words flexible and rich in significance and to keep them free of crude antitheses. Mr von Berks and most of his friends indulged freely in antitheses. There were good people and bad people, Communists and democrats, educated and uneducated, Slav and Teuton, us and them.

Mr von Berks had none of his mother's romantic nature nor was he a snob; he valued wealth and privilege for the power they conferred, not for prestige. He had been in a bank in America after the collapse of Austria-Hungary and he had a superstitious belief in science. This did not interfere with his support of the Church, which he thought exercised a stabilizing influence on those incapable of independent reflection and without scientific training. Archbishop Stepinac was an honoured guest at his table but when the parish priest came to meals this polyglot family used to joke about him in different languages and their superior education showed itself not in the power to deflect or soften the impact of cultural difference but in giving the contrast extra pungency and force, which they did with eloquence and skill. International politics entertained him, local politics hardly at all. I think that he derived his extraordinary arrogance less from his pride of birth than from scientific enlightenment and American bumptiousness.

When the Mayor's daughter in Podgorac was married Mr von Berks asked me and Christopher to the interminable banquet in the village hall. He enjoyed himself on equal terms, arguing, quarrelling, drinking in the most convivial way with his red-faced sweating neighbours. He knew all their failings, just as they knew his, but there was not a trace of real comradeship in this reciprocal knowledge. He was an individualist more than a democrat. I don't think he had any confidence such as his mother had in the glamour and prestige of his ancestors. What he admired was science and power and American nationalism which he mistook for internationalism. He regarded small nations as nonsense and was humiliated by the imputation that he now belonged to one. It was degrading to have to ask permission of Belgrade to travel through the land of the former Austro-Hungarian empire, so he had provided himself with a special stamp and ink eraser so that he could organize his own passport and travel to Budapest or Vienna without ridiculous formalities.

I think his generation, Americanized and internationalized, was less easily assimilated than even his mother's. They were of more common fibre: they could capitulate or dominate but not live on equal terms, and with the disappearance of the feudal relationship with all its vague reciprocal obligations, the stark antitheses of wealth and poverty, pretension and powerlessness, became more pronounced than ever before.

The von Berks lived in an ugly mansion at the end of the main street of Podgorac. It had been rebuilt after the Yugoslav nationalists had burnt it in 1918, as splendidly as was consistent with comfort and practical good sense. The grandeur had been laid on afterwards on the side that faced the street. At the back was a straggling garden with a large rickety greenhouse which did not look as if it were much used. Paprikas and tomatoes drying on the edge had stuck to the woodwork. There were aubergines there, some like polished ebony but most had gone a dirty brown. Obviously the von Berks took no interest in their garden.

The second day I was there the Count, a local magnate, came to lunch. I had met him at the wedding banquet and had found him a very congenial person. After we had eaten we all four walked up the street together. It was October and the broad flat fields round Podgorac were full of dried stumps of maize stalks with golden pumpkins crawling around them, some of them pale green, some frosted and rotten. Four Podolian oxen were dragging a one-furrow plough across one of the fields. The ploughman shouted at them as they reached the headland and they trudged round as if in a trance, dark-eyed and blue-grey. "How beautiful," said the Count. "Horses would do this quicker," said the steward, "oxen for harrowing."

I never learnt the Count's name or saw his house, but the fields at the eastern end of the village must have been his as he showed us his wine-cellar under a mound in the Turkish cemetery. "I won't have much wine this year, I'm afraid, as I've had lumbago and I could not go round and see that the vines were properly sprayed."

I think that, unlike the von Berks, the Count was proud to be Yugoslav. He spoke Croatian, not German, to the steward. He had been born an Austro-Hungarian citizen but remained proud of his Croat nationality. Many such had cherished the Yugoslav ideal and, when the empire collapsed in 1918, had given their support to it. The man who had earlier pioneered the Croatian revival, Lyudevit Gai, had been half-German. It often happens like that. In an empire subject peoples are shamed of their language till someone of the imperial blood urges them to value it. That was the story of Douglas Hyde and the Gaelic League, of Yeats and Synge and the Irish Literary Renaissance. They were all Anglo-Irishmen.

As elsewhere in the formerly Hungarian parts of Yugoslavia, each cottage had a strip of land behind it. In the Austro-Hungarian days the landlord ruled the village and had the right of life and death over the villagers and kept a certain routine going, which still partially survived.

At four o'clock on summer mornings the cow-boy blew a horn under the priest's window and the cows went off to their grazing. The broad street was crisscrossed with the tracks of the cows. It is very muddy in the autumn but there is space enough for the traffic to use one half of the road till the other half has time to dry.

Podgorac on my last day seemed amazingly tranquil and beautiful. Turkeys and geese strutted down the street. There were maize cobs stuck away for the winter under the tiles. There was a short, rather noisy interruption. The fire-brigade band, having got out their uniforms and instruments for the wedding, marched up and down a couple of times extra before they put them away. The second time they collided with the cows coming back from the pastures. Each cow knew its own home and made for it, but they were wildly alarmed by the drumming and trumpeting and for a few moments man and beast were helplessly interlocked.

Before I left, the Count insisted on my visiting the village school. There were little boys with books and little girls with embroidery crouched round the central stove. They must have had an imaginative teacher. He had helped them make a map of the country round Podgorac and another map of the Dravska Banovina, the province through which their river, the Drava, flows. It was constructed out of coloured matches, powdered paint and little bits of sponge dyed green for the trees. They were growing cherry trees from cherry stones and later were going to learn to graft them. The Count had given them a drawer full of oddities from his home and also an "orrery" to show the movements of the planets round the sun. And there were two large coloured posters on the wall, one to illustrate the growth of a lobster, the other the formation of a molehill. The children all looked lively and interested. I complimented the Count from my heart for what he had done for the school. I thought that, as he trotted away behind his white pony, he looked pleased.

Years later, when I heard what had happened to the von Berks, I wondered how the Count had fared when the Partisans arrived in

Podgorac. Is it true, as a Roman poet thought, that the good man is his own protection? "He does not need Moorish javelins and poisoned arrows." I doubt if that applies in the post-von Berks world, where one is judged not by one's temperament but by one's presumed politics.

(1947)

A Trial

The trial of General Kvaternik and five other Quisling ministers of Croatia and of Siegfried Kasche, German ambassador to the Independent State, which has just concluded in Zagreb, was of the highest importance, yet, as it happened at the same time as the Zagreb fair, it excited relatively little interest.

Croatia was for a long time the most satisfactory of the Nazi puppet states. It had a ready-made Quisling government which had only to be recalled from abroad and that government had a small and noisy following at home. The Ustashi were able to organize a constant and almost convincing parade of enthusiasm for the "liberator" and yet they could never become formidable enough to interfere with his plans. Kasche, as German ambassador, had the delicate task of exploiting the Croatian people through their government for German ends. There is evidence that he did it rather well, and in the dock he gave an appearance of resourcefulness and conviction, which was not shown by the other defendants. The trial was conducted on lines that seemed to touch the destiny of the prisoners at a tangent only because it was the manifest purpose of the judges not to prove the guilt of the defendants, which was obvious, but to show that they had the collaboration of the Peasant Party and its leader, Dr. Machek˙. The Peasant Party is the most

---

˙Vladimir Maček (1879 –1964) was a Croatian politician active within the Kingdom of Yugoslavia and into the Second World War. He led the Croatian Peasant Party

serious rival to communism in Croatia, and its leaders, like the leaders of so many other parties in Europe, appear to have behaved in a feeble, subservient way towards the Nazis, before and after the German invasion. So complete was the preoccupation of the court with Dr. Machek, that often the Croatian defendants seem to have persuaded themselves that if they, too, made eager little sallies at Dr. Machek, their own vile crimes might be forgotten. They seldom rejected any of the invitations to vilify Dr. Machek that came to them from the bench. Not so Siegfried Kasche – this horrible man grew in stature as the trial proceeded. No doubt he knew that he would not save his life by being obliging. He refused to be distracted from his purpose. His defence was that all he had done was in loyalty to the German people and its leaders. The internal affairs of the Croat people, except in so far as they affected Germany, had been no concern of his. He had not had any intrigues with any of the Croat politicians mentioned. He had sufficient control to keep the sneer out of his voice.

The three judges and Blazhevich, the public prosecutor, did not bully or rant, they were always courteous to the prisoners. The president, Ivan Poldrugatch, was a strikingly handsome man with a bronze face and snow-white hair. One of his colleagues was chubby and alert, the other was sleek, relaxed, watchful. Blazhevich had dark untidy hair and a loose unprofessional build. He sprawled across the desk to ask his questions, as if his curiosity could no longer be repressed. Whenever Machek was mentioned they all became tense as fox-terriers, their eyes brightened, they sniffed the air. But they were on the wrong scent. Machek's offences were of a very ordinary kind; Kasche, dead or alive, was important. Fascism is not extinct in a country in which a callous and cynical bully is allowed to appear so aloof and distinguished. He was like an unamused spectator at a squalid family brawl. He had a nearly bald head, bushy eyebrows and an important, ambassadorial

---

following the assassination of Stjepan Radić in 1928, and called on his supporters in 1941 to cooperate with the new Quisling regime of Ante Pavelić. (Editors)

presence. He thrust out his replies with great lucidity and emphasis, rising out of his chair slightly and then relaxing again with clasped hands. "Das habe ich nicht getan!" "Das ist nicht der fall!" "Das ist eine gemeine Lüge!" He seemed to be a man who would lie for political but not for personal reasons. Many of his sharp denials and belligerent retorts had a ring of sincerity.

The prosecution devoted too much time to proving that Kasche took large bribes for remitting death sentences. Very likely he did, but venality is a touchingly human frailty in one who had planned the deportation of half a million Slovenes and Serbs*, who had sponsored the introduction of the anti-Semite laws and had been the interpreter to the Croats of the Nazi policy of hatred and extermination. His power and his wickedness derived from his fanaticism, not from his greed for money, which was incidental. It was only by a ruthless exposure of fanaticism that Kasche could be made to appear small. The communist court was not prepared for that.

I kept thinking what a priceless psychological document the report of the trial would be for posterity, for though they had collaborated closely each had succumbed to a different temptation. Navratil for example, the air-minister, was the nicely-tailored military journalist, who had been fascinated by the technical achievements of the Nazis. He was a success snob and with his wet face, wet hair and soft ingratiating tones seemed the only one of the seven to have completely capsized. Kulenovich, an old and foxy Moslem, and Alaibegovich, his compatriot, a puffy, sad-eyed dandy, had been flattered into thinking they could protect Moslem interests better by taking part than by holding back. Koshak was a self-satisfied business man, who as a student at Frankfurt had learnt to disguise his shallow egotism with Nazi theory. Perchevich and Kvaternik were elderly men, whose sympathies

---

* This refers to the proposed resettlement of Slovenes expelled from Nazi Germany (which had incorporated part of Slovenia) on lands cleansed of Serbs in the Independent State of Croatia. (Editors)

were with the vanished Austro-Hungarian military caste. They liked
uniforms and parades and compliments and for a few years they tried
to call back to life the Zagreb of the Habsburgs. Almost all of them
raised the cry that they were simple straightforward experts, who just
did their job and let other people get on with theirs. The massacres?
The brutality? Oh yes, they had heard something about that but that
had nothing to do with their department. After this plea had been made
several times it became clear that there are few accomplices of evil so
formidable as the expert, who minds his own business.

Sometimes the speakers were not easy to follow but I reminded
myself that they would be reported in the papers. In this I was over-
optimistic. The reporting was pitiful in its inaccuracy. The answers of
the defendants were interlarded with the fatuous comments of the
reporters. I do not impute malice but laziness and perhaps the desire
to give pleasure to authority by anticipating its verdict. Kasche, in his
defence, exposed his arrogant but not unsubtle soul with clarity, yet
the reporters paraphrased and blurred his well-turned phrases as if they
were frightened of them. They explain that they were uttered with
"typical Nazi cynicism," or with "characteristic insolence," or "conscious of his own guilt." Sometimes these interpolations are worse
than silly. When Blazhevich asked Kasche if he knew his nickname,
the "Trinkgeld Diplomate," and said that even Stepinac had in his trial
referred to this weakness, Kasche, it is reported "fidgeted uneasily in
his chair and was silent." He did nothing of the kind. In resonant tones
he demanded the evidence of Stepinac's advocate. On another occasion
Kasche asserted that in all his dealings with the Croat government his
principal object had been the successful prosecution of the war against
England, and he made the curious statement that at the beginning of
the war the British Consulate in Zagreb had been filled with explosives.
This remark and the references to England were neither translated by
the interpreter nor reported in the Press.

When Blazhevitch asked Kasche what had happened to the property
of the Slovenes whom the Germans deported, Kasche replied without
a moment's hesitation, "The Slovenes were treated in the same way as

the Germans, who since then have been moved from Slovenia," but you will not find this reply in the daily papers. Once, Kasche was caught off his guard. He had been insisting on how the Germans had respected the independence of the Croatian state and Blazhevich asked him "How long would the independence have lasted if the Ustashi had shot twelve Nazis in Jelachich Square? What would you have done?" "I should have lodged a protest," said Kasche with snuffy dignity and the court roared with laughter. Yet for some reason this, the only question by which the ambassador was discomforted, was not recorded.

Obviously in Yugoslavia, a new philosophy of justice quite different from ours is shaping. Each trial seems more closely related to immediate needs than to ultimate principles. It is possible that when the need for stability becomes less urgent this tendency will be reversed. In the meantime, it must be admitted, the guilt of the accused has usually been so obvious that justice has not suffered conspicuously by the preoccupations of the judges.

Yet there is no hint that the patient diagnosis of a criminal defect might have a bearing on its cure and that treason is a trouble with which a Southern Slav government in the future, as in the past, is likely to be afflicted. There is no recognition of the fact that by the Nazis a vicious circle of hate and extermination had been established from which each nation will have to find its own way of release or perish. Yet such considerations would not have been half as irrelevant as those which actually occupied the minds of the judges. The judges were no longer interested by the seven prisoners, who had been caught. They were after Machek, who was free. If there was a young Kasche in the audience I think he would have taken heart and said to himself: "The next time we may succeed, for the Croats do not hate us half as much as they hate each other."

All seven prisoners were condemned to death. It was a just sentence and the trial, in so far as it concerned them, was fair enough.

(Unpublished typescript, 1947)

Yugoslavia:
The Cultural Background

Some years ago a Yugoslav professor came to lecture on his country in Ireland. The Central European intellectual has a passion for information and, even before he reached our shores, he was an expert on the Language Question, the Annuities and the Northern Education Act. He returned home with so many anecdotes and opinions that he decided to give a lecture on Ireland in the Dalmatian port where he was employed. It was well-attended and rather feverishly applauded. As he left the hall, he was accosted by two members of the secret police and marched away to the police-station, where he was sharply cross-examined. That was an old dodge, they told him. Clearly he was a Croat Separatist and his audience understood that "Ulster" meant "Croatia." Was he advocating partition for Yugoslavia or wasn't he? He was not released till he had produced a copy of the *Irish Independent* with a report of his Dublin lecture. It was found, on translation, to contain no heresies. He proved that he did not like partition either in Ireland or in Yugoslavia.

The Yugoslav intellectual has, in fact, a keener sense of the common interest of small nations than has his Irish counterpart. He is used to foreign analogies and the story of the Anglo-Irish struggle has often been studied as a textbook of rebellion, much as Arthur Griffith studied the manoeuvres of Hungarians against the Habsburgs. Even in peacetime a drastic censorship accustoms him to the oblique approach. The most celebrated comic paper in Yugoslavia was called *Brijani Yezh*, "The

Shaven Hedgehog"; in this ingenious journal words never bore their obvious meaning and innocent expressions like "Éire" might be charged with subversive innuendo.

Unfortunately there is no trade union of the oppressed. The brave little Hungary which inspired Sinn Féin by its nimble resistance to the Austrian oppressor used its new freedom to oppress the Croats even more than before. This was not surprising. In the centre of Zagreb, the Croatian capital, stands the statue of the Croatian general who fought against the Hungarian patriots for his Austrian overlord. To the Croats the resurrection of Hungary and the Magyar aristocracy had a different message to that which it held for the leaders of Sinn Féin.

Griffith was right, all the same, in seeing that all small nations are menaced by similar forces. The great powers have been able to obscure this fact by the manipulation of local rivalries. Centuries of Austrian diplomacy lie behind the failure of the "Succession States" to achieve solidarity in themselves or friendliness with each other. Yet except through collaboration there is no future for the small national state.

During the war a mayoress of Dublin asserted that Czechoslovakia was an English invention. There is more than ignorance behind this remarkable statement. A genteel snobbism has often kept oppressed nations apart and attracted them to the oppressors of others. Many Czechs and Serbs still think of the Irish as an obscure cross-breed of the liberal and cultured Englishman. The Irish have, in the same way, always rated the Austrian above his uncouth Slavonic subjects and for centuries the Irish Wild Geese assisted the Habsburgs in oppressing them. The mayoress was true to type.

Still, we cannot deny that in each of the new states the same pattern recurs. In Yugoslavia a simple and indigenous society appears to have defeated a sophisticated one that was privileged and anti-national. Yet both societies are equally moribund and more akin to each other than to the mechanized and impersonal civilization which is likely to succeed them. The cultural conflict has more significance than any other, but to follow its development in Yugoslavia a little knowledge of the political background is necessary.

In 1918 the small kingdom of Serbia became a great state by the accession of six historic Slav regions – Croatia, Slovenia, Montenegro, Bosnia, Herzegovina and Dalmatia, as well as territory in Macedonia and in the northern plains. Of these provinces Austria, Hungary and Italy had formerly been dominant in the north, Turkey in the south, including Serbia itself. Montenegro alone has resisted every oppressor and most external influences. The common bond between all these peoples is the Serbo-Croatian language with its Slovene and Macedonian dialects. It is a very frail bond but without it Yugoslavia would certainly fall apart. That much must be conceded to the language enthusiast.

The kingdom of Serbia is chiefly responsible for the liberation of all these peoples. For generations all their energies have been directed to this end and, after two Balkan wars and the first German war, it was finally achieved in our century. Unlike the Slovenes and the Croats, the Serbs had little time or opportunity for culture and education, nor are they noted for diplomacy. Courage and cunning were more valuable weapons against the Turk.

The history of Yugoslavia since 1918 has been a struggle between the Serbian "racial" conception of nationalism and the mellower, more cosmopolitan nationalism of the north-west. One might say that the latter is based on regional sentiment and, as such, is uncongenial to the more unsophisticated Slav, who still has nomadism in his blood. In moments of tension the Quisling with his myth of cultural superiority appears in the north, the chauvinist among the Serbs; and a familiar pattern repeats itself.

In 1929 King Alexander attempted to create a new Yugoslav patriotism by an attack on regional sentiment, replacing with modern departments the old historic territories. He drew upon himself the hatred of the Croats. In 1934 he was murdered at the instigation of Pavelitch, a Zagreb lawyer. The complicity of the Italian and Hungarian governments was suspected.

On the collapse of Yugoslavia in 1941 Pavelitch was appointed "Poglavnik" (Duce) of the puppet state of Croatia which was given an

Italian king, the Duke of Aosta. Many prominent Croats were collaborationists, for example Stepinac, the Primate of Croatia, and Sharitch,
the Archbishop of Bosnia (who published a poem to the murderer
Pavelitch, hailing him as "the sun of Croatia"), and many industrialists
and former landowners. The evidence for this comes from anti-Communist sources. We must think of Zagreb and Belgrade as much farther
apart in sentiment than Dublin and Belfast. Only a very little manoeuvring of religious and cultural antipathies by a great power is necessary
to set hatred ablaze.

I heard the news of the surrender of Yugoslavia from the Ger-
man-controlled station of Belgrade on a Yugoslav boat moored on the
Liffey. The crew sat round listening. They were friendly with each other
and seemed united in their grief. At the end they divided up into two
groups, Croats and Serbs. One walked off to the German legation and
the other to the UK office to learn their destinies. So easy is it to divide
a people whom only a common language unites.

Will it be possible to consolidate the diverse elements of Yugoslavia
into one people without spectacular abdications at both ends of the
scale of civilization? As we go north from Montenegro to Slovenia, we
pass from primitive and traditional communities to a sensitive and
highly civilized society where racial loyalties are qualified by more
sophisticated pieties. All the northern districts of Yugoslavia are still
irradiated by the sun of Vienna, which has not yet set. Zagreb is a
charming and civilized city with theatre, opera, ballet and art gallery.
In addition it has one of the best folk museums in southern Europe. It
was to cosmopolitan Trieste, in Slovene territory, that James Joyce
withdrew to write his epic of Dublin. From Trieste to Macedonia and
Montenegro an immense gulf of cultural experience is spanned by the
frail bridge of a common language. The formula for spiritual unity has
not yet been discovered, for the cultural elements, which must be
reconciled, are seldom analysed.

Starting from the south, Montenegro is the Gaeltacht of Yugoslavia,
where the last traces of a southern Slav culture survive. We find communities so self-contained that Western civilization encroaching on

every side has not yet decomposed them. Yet the mountains which protected them so long from the Turk are no longer a barrier to subtler agents of destruction. The patriarchal society of Montenegro is doomed as surely as is the Gaeltacht, and yet something perhaps can be salvaged. Before the war two codes of justice, Montenegrin, which was personal, and Yugoslav, which was abstract, ran concurrently. The last "izmirenje" or reconciliation ceremony took place at the monastery of Grbalj in 1935. (I described it in my book *Escape from the Anthill* – see "The Last Izmirenje" – and perhaps it revealed some of the spiritual torment of Yugoslavia.)* Those who can recall a society which took forgiveness rather than punishment as the true atonement for crime will not adjust themselves easily to ordinary codes of law. Why should they?

The murderer, Stevo Orlovitch, had served his term in prison for the murder of Stjepo Bauk, when he returned to Grbalj. Montenegrin law took no account of his sentence or imprisonment, his enemies had refused to bear witness against him. It was the duty of a member of the Bauk clan to kill him in vengeance for their kinsman's death. Only by soliciting a "reconciliation" could Orlovitch escape. It happened on Easter Day. Outside the chapel one hundred Orlovitchs lined up opposite one hundred Bauks, all in their gorgeous Montenegrin dress. They sang the Easter hymn. The priest read out the solemn words of reconciliation by which Orlovitch was forgiven and his first child adopted into the family of the Bauks. When it was ended, Mirko Bauk, the brother of the murdered man, stepped to one end of the two confronting lines. At the other end the murderer slipped quickly from behind the priest. He was a thin trembling figure in a cheap blue suit from Tivar, the wholesale clothier, and Bata shoes. A fountain pen was clipped to his breast pocket; he had learnt civilization and a useful trade in prison. He fingered the pen nervously to give himself confidence. Suddenly he ducked down his head and ran blindly between the ranks. "Forgive me!" he cried, when he reached Mirko Bauk. Mirko raised him

---

* H.B., 1990.

from his knees and embraced him and the hundred Bauks stepped forward and embraced the hundred Orlovitches. To those who had experienced this tremendous moment, any ceremony in the lawcourts would seem frigid and meaningless. I may appear to attribute great significance to what is only an interesting piece of folklore, but I believe that the democracy and even the Communism of the southern Slavs is still coloured by a sense of personal responsibility for each other which we have long forgotten. They adopt unwillingly and inexpertly the impersonal code of ethics which the administration of a large national state demands.

At the invitation of one of the Bauks, I sat down at the long table outside the chapel door on which the Orlovitchs had prepared a meal for them. A Bauk, magnificent in crimson and gold, seated himself beside me. Tuning himself into the English tongue with a poem beginning "My 'ome is the ocean, my earth is the ship," he then said to me, "Excuse the primitiveness of this! It is custom!" He told me that he had been, like many others in Grbalj, at the copper mines in Butte, Montana. Higher up the Dalmatian coast I had come on valleys associated for several generations with San Jose in California and with Lima in Peru. The returned exiles recover their old solidarity with their people quickly enough, but the presence of an Anglo-Saxon or an Iberian is disturbing to them, they become self-conscious and boastful. My companion had heard about the "Liberty Irish State" and a mayor who had starved for forty days.

Conditions were very bad in Montenegro, he said. The Serbs had cheated them. "Montenegrin men," he said, "should do like Irishmen, raise hell, holler!" He was blaming on Belgrade the sterile rocky soil of Montenegro which had shaped the character of his race and guaranteed their independence. Butte, Montana, had made him dissatisfied with his home but given him no idea of a society better than that which he had begun to despise.

"What will the murderer do now?" I asked a judge from Kotor, one of the two who had sentenced Orlovitch in the lawcourts; "He won't stay here anyway," the judge replied. "He learnt to type in prison and he is looking for a clerk's job in Belgrade. His relations are trying to get him to Montana but it's hard because of the quota."

"Why did he bother about the izmirenje then?"

"Just because of the rest of the family. The Bauks would persecute them. You know," he added, putting on an up-to-date expression, "it's a unique ceremony. The Press Bureau in Belgrade should have sent a chap to film it." Looking at the murderer crouched with the priest behind the buttress of the chapel, I thought that even without being filmed he had had as much publicity as he could bear. Yet could one tell what the effect would have been on this quivering little pariah of a few jolly words and a fat cheque from an experienced cameraman? What repulsive bastard will commerce beget upon ancient custom?

I drove back to Kotor with the judge in a lemon-coloured sports car. Half a mile from the town a stretch of blackened waste lay between the road and the lovely bay with its fringe of violet mountains and lacy acacias. "That," said the judge "is where they lit a bonfire to welcome Edward VIII and Mrs Simpson. It set alight to a plantation by mistake."

Dalmatia, which stretches along the Adriatic from Montenegro to Slovenia, is another of Yugoslavia's problems, and the judge's remark is a good introduction to it. Except as a tourist resort, there seems to be no future for these lovely barren shores, but tourism raises difficulties. Here is the shop window that Yugoslavia presents to the enquiring West and it is unfortunate that, though all the salesmen except 2 per cent are Croats, the goods displayed are, despite the labels, unmistakably Italian. The great palaces that fringe the shores of Kotor and Gruz were built when Venice controlled the carrying of trade of the East. Her wealth filled the churches with gold vessels and fabulous vestments. The lion of St Mark prances over town gates and on castle doorways. But Yugoslavia is fortunate to possess in Mestrovitch a great European sculptor. The fine plaque of King Peter of Serbia over the town gate of Dubrovnik, the Racic Mausoleum at Cavtat, the striking statue of Bishop Gregory, too aggressively placed in the ruins of Diocletian's Palace, are evidence that Italy has no monopoly of culture along the Adriatic coast.

The Yugoslav patriot is morbidly sensitive and in Dalmatia his feelings are constantly bruised. He has no status with the tourist of the
luxury cruise. To the average American all the territory from the Carpathians to Corfu is inhabited by "Hunkies" and little has been done
to glamorize them. No one has edited them for the shilling seats, as Mr
Bert Feldmann edited the Irish with "Tipperary" and "When Irish Eyes
Are Smiling." The Yugoslav must blow his own trumpet and he does it
without skill. When some years ago an American company proposed
to film Dalmatia, the Belgrade government eagerly collaborated, even
putting the navy at their disposal. A final polish by a publicity expert
had to be given to the film in America. He knew his job. The uncouth
Croatian names and terms were exchanged for melodious Italian ones,
familiar to the film-goer's ear: Antonio instead of Zvonko, Spalato for
Split. It was inevitable but sad.

At the head of the Adriatic lies Trieste, which will be a focus of
discord for some years. Roughly speaking it is about as Yugoslav as
Belfast is Irish, and no Italian, Austrian or Slovene can discuss its future
calmly. Once a powerful race interferes with a weaker one, it is hard
for it to withdraw when a milder mood prevails. Too many hostages
must remain behind. Trieste was built on the site of a Slovene fishing
village by a Rhineland Baron Bruck as a port for the Austro-Hungarian
empire. It became the harbour for the greater part of Central Europe
as well as for the Slovenian hinterland. Austria-Hungary, a polyglot
imperial state, made no attempt to impose a German culture upon it.
Italy was weak and divided before the Risorgimento, and the Habsburgs,
to keep an equilibrium in their empire, used to favour minority cultures. In Trieste, as in Dalmatia, there were very few Italians, but,
indulged by Austria, it rapidly became a city of Italians and Italianized
Slovenes in the middle of a Slovene countryside. On the building of
the port of Trieste, Austria-Hungary sunk over a hundred million
pounds. The railway which she made opened up the whole of Slovenia
and increased its prosperity enormously. Blasted through the Julian
Alps, it can be rivalled as an engineering feat only by the vital mountain
railway that the Austrians built from the Sava valley to the coast. An

immense amount of Austrian wealth, enterprise and talent has been sunk into Yugoslavia. After the defeat of Austria in 1918 Italy was awarded Istria and Trieste, and half a million Croats and Slovenes passed under her control. Italy, unlike Austria-Hungary, was a fiercely nationalist state. She determined that Istria and Trieste should be unmistakably Italian. All Slovene schools were closed, newspapers and books banned, and the public use of the language prohibited. Slovene-speaking clergy and doctors were expelled. An Italian doctor, who was told that his patients could not explain their symptoms to him, replied, "Nor can the cow explain her symptoms to the vet." When the Abyssinian War broke out the Fascist government conscripted the Slovenes among the first. A clear Italian majority was ultimately secured. In the dispute now raging the voice of Austria will not be raised but the Italian and Yugoslav arguments are of a type so familiar to us in Ireland that they need not be repeated.

There is no solution of this problem so long as cultural nationalism is identified with political and economic nationalism. Marshal Tito is probably an internationalist who, in claiming Trieste for Yugoslavia, finds it opportune to use a nationalist argument, but an internationalism which tries to reconcile divergent peoples by ignoring the sources of their culture can bring no permanent pacification. Nor are the histories of Fiume and Danzig so encouraging that another Free City at Trieste could be risked. Trieste will probably be granted to Yugoslavia, and in this, at the worst, there will be a certain retributive justice.

Trieste is a danger point because it lies upon a frontier, but in fact there is hardly a town in northern Yugoslavia about whose nature a similar dispute might not be raised. Yugoslavs, like Irish, are not by temperament originators of towns, railways, factories. It was as employees and colleagues of Austrians and Venetians that they gathered into the cities. Where they have lived relatively undisturbed by the foreigner, as in Montenegro, the pattern of their lives is based upon the rural community. The Turk, who unlike the Austrian was purely predatory, without the power to assimilate, has sometimes left this primitive pattern intact. The "Zadruga" of the Serbian countryside is a family cooperative society, which is dying only because all village communities are everywhere dying beneath the impact of urban civilization. The forward-looking Serbian peasant, no longer able to emigrate, looks to the city for advancement. Torn from his own social traditions, he jibs at new ones. He is so little hampered by the sense of civic responsibility that his economic progress is often as rapid as his moral decline. It is not unusual to find a peasant, who can neither read nor write, the proprietor of a block of up-to-date flats in Belgrade. How does he manage it? Possibly there are not yet enough hereditary go-getters to block the path of the enthusiastic amateur. Immense power has fallen into the hands of wealthy and ignorant peasants and to this, in part, is due the naïve egoism and corruption of the Belgrade politician, which has often alienated Croats and Slovenes to the pitch of sedition.

"Innocent" is sometimes a better word than "ignorant" to apply to the ruling classes of Balkan lands. Ignorance implies vulgarity, but the flats built by illiterate peasants are often full of the same taste and refinement that their own homes display. For centuries they have made their own clothes and their own furniture, the larger farmers have made their own pottery. Their natural taste for colour and form does not desert them as quickly as their morals. At present only the established middle classes have access to the mass-produced commonplaces of Germany and America. No doubt this restraint about domestic architecture is a transient phenomenon and would speedily be corrected by the opening of Yugoslavia to the West, but it is so striking that it deserves comment.

In such a society the word "Communism," so freely used and abused, needs careful interpretation. It is not in the first place greatly assisted by Pan-Slav sentiment which so long favoured Church and State. Both King Alexander and Prince Paul, the one by education the other by marriage, were closely associated with Czarist Russia. On the collapse of White resistance, a hoard of generals and ex-landowners and former administrators with large treasury chests descended on Belgrade. It was natural that they should be asked to assist in the government of the young and inexperienced state, natural also that they should raise a hue and cry about Communism. Unfortunately they thought they were dealing with Mouzhiks speaking a Slav patois, who could be made to understand Russian if spoken to in peremptory tones. Every Serb, on the other hand, knows that he belongs to a race of heroes which fought for centuries against the Turk and ultimately won, and in our century fought against German, Austrian, Hungarian and Bulgar, and also won. Russian superciliousness was resented. Except among Montenegrins ("We and the Russians are 170 millions!"), Serbian royalty and a handful of Croatian illuminati, Pan-Slav sentiment has had little influence. Romantic nationalism, patriarchal traditions and peasant proprietorship may retard the spread of Communism. Yet obviously there is a very strong possibility that the Balkan states, Slav and non-Slav, will pass under Russian influence and that Communist Quislings will replace Fascist ones.

Clearly the Churches can do much to bring to the Balkans a unity based on brotherly love rather than on economics but so far their contribution has been meagre and disrupting. The Catholic Church is accused of having played the Fascist and Italian game in Slovenia and Croatia and, by its clamour for privileges and concordats, of jeopardizing that brotherhood of southern Slavs which is the keystone of Yugoslav unity. The Orthodox Church still retains its prestige because it rallied the Serb against the Turk, but it is an easy-going community, more notable for its feast-days than for its doctrine or its discipline. At the time of the concordat the faithful rallied round it with fervour, but without the halo of persecution it cannot long retain its hold over the flock. Except for an understandable assault on the Moslem at the time of the liberation from the Turk, the southern Slav believes in religious toleration: "Brat je mio, koje vere bio" – "He is my brother whatever his faith."

There remains the old aristocracy. Though they are negligible in numbers and power, I believe that much depends on them if Yugoslavia is ever to become a cultured European state. Their loyalty has, like that of their Anglo-Irish counterpart, often been qualified, yet where it has been given it has been of inestimable value. They derive mostly from

the old Austro-Hungarian provinces of Yugoslavia and are of hybrid
Croatian and Austrian blood, for the Turk prevented the development
of an aristocracy in the south. Such princely families as survived in
Serbia owed their authority like the royal dynasties of Karageorge and
Obrenovitch to military prowess. They united the virtues of the patriarch and the courage of the bandit. The Croatian nobility stands at the
opposite pole; they are sometimes called over-civilized and useless,
but some blame must rest with the inexperienced state which failed
to use them. Many of them are highly educated and cosmopolitan,
thinking in three languages, often witty, intelligent, liberal. Of Slav
descent and Viennese culture, they should be the natural interpreters
between Yugoslavia and Western Europe. Though they have long ago
lost property and estates, from fastidiousness and snobbery, they have,
many of them, held aloof from the Nazis and the Quislings. It is among
the professional middle classes of Croatia, solicitors, doctors, auction-
eers, that the doctrine of race superiority and disdain for the Serb has
flourished most, small men who have to feed their self-esteem on
contempt for others. There are scores of their brothers in the smarter
Dublin suburbs. Foreign cultural bodies such as the British Council
and its opposite number, the Deutsches Haus, made converts among
this class, but at the expense of Yugoslavia. Only an educated minority,
whose patriotism is reinforced by sensibility or pride, has the power
to assimilate foreign culture without being overwhelmed or corrupted
by it.

Like every hybrid aristocracy the Croatian nobility has had its rebel
minority which has inspired the subject peoples with the dream of
liberty and rallied them to its attainment. In the Austrian provinces
the Yugoslav ideal was first fostered by the great Bishop Strossmayer,
an aristocrat of Austrian descent. He was an amazing personality, as
fervent as Thomas Davis, as practical as Horace Plunkett, as lavish and
eccentric as the Earl Bishop of Derry. He revived the national spirit of
the Croats and shaped their demands for independence.

I shall describe one of these hybrid families, typical except in one
particular. They are doubly alien in descent. Like the Nugents and

Kavanaghs of Slovenia, they are of Irish ancestry and name. This, how-ever, is only of historical significance. German is their mother-tongue and they have the dark mobile features of the Croat. Their ancestor, an Irish Catholic, forfeited his estates under Cromwell and took service with the Habsburgs in the regiment of Irish Dragoons, quartered at Prague. He rose to be a general and was granted estates in Croatia by the emperor, for it was the habit of the Habsburgs to award their foreign subjects with land in the Slav marches where they could be trusted to keep order without partiality. He must have married into Schloss Pis-chatz, the vast castle where his descendants lived, because it is far older than the seventeenth century. It is surrounded by acres of dark pine forest which the von Buttlar Moscons still own, though, by the inge-nuity of the tax collector they derive nothing from it but firewood. Outside the castle gates is a village or rather one long broad street of farmhouses. Rudi, the elder Count, showed me the spot where, a cen-tury ago, the gallows stood on which his great-grandfather strung up insubordinate villagers. "They bore us no ill will," he said. "In 1918 after the liberation, when they burnt Perovitch's house, they did not molest us at all." The von Moscons dislike Perovitch. He is very up-to-date. He worked in America before he inherited his family home, and acquired there a lot of go-ahead ideas, none of them, strange to say, either dem-ocratic or original. A specimen remark would be, "What these chaps want is a Hitler to wake them up." He is certainly a Nazi. With a small adjustment of vocabulary and opportunity, he is to be found among the Philistine ruling classes of every country.

The old Count von Moscon was a Minister of Franz Josef and they lived all the year in Vienna, except for a month of summer holiday at Schloss Krnica. Therefore they never bothered about the plumbing. Servants carried water all over the castle. On the collapse of the central powers they found themselves all at once Yugoslav citizens with Krnica their only property, and no water and no servants. Dick, the elder son, who was in the Austrian navy, transferred to the Yugoslav navy; Rudi, who was gay and expensive, recoiled from so dowdy a destiny. After a search through the family archives, he wrote to the representatives of

the Moscons in Ireland and asked them to get him a commission in the
Free State Army. In Ireland only one branch of the family had emerged
from the forfeitures of Cromwell and it had long ago made its peace
with authority. The Irish army seemed to them as comical as the Yugoslav army. They sent Rudi £2 c/o Thomas Cook, Stefansplatz, and
put his letter into the curio table. In despair Rudi took a job in the First
Croatian Savings Bank in Zagreb.

It was their sister, the Countess Wanda, who had the brains of the
family. After dealing with the family finances so that Krnica could pay
its way, she took a job in an American shipping office. Simultaneously
the Queen made her a lady-in-waiting, for decorative and honorary jobs
were still at the disposal of the old nobility. She was worried about her
brothers, though. Dick was unhappy in the navy. He had rather elaborate manners and his new shipmates thought he was putting on airs.
She got him a job dubbing gangster films in Belgrade and he left the
navy. He liked the work but did not do it very well. Though he spoke
Serbo-Croatian fluently, he could not write it well. He had been brought
up to consider it a language in which one gave orders to servants. His
sister had to assist him. Meanwhile Rudi found the bank insupportable
and he left [for] Vienna. There was a theory that he intended to marry
a rich Viennese commoner. Anyway he became an Austrian citizen
and asked for his share of the family property. Wanda had for years
been working unsuccessfully to have Krnica taken over as a national
monument. Now the furniture, which was the only thing realizable,
would have to be sold and the proceeds divided. This was a difficult as
well as a sad task. In the days of Maria Theresa a celebrated Italian
cabinet-maker had travelled round Croatia and Slovenia, staying a few
years in each castle, building magnificent furniture from the local
timber. In the salon at Krnica there were priceless wardrobes and
chests, so vast that without dismemberment they could not be brought
down the narrow winding stairs unless a breach were made in the salon
walls. The breach was made. Rudi, abandoning Yugoslavia for good,
refused to pay his share for the repair. "Let them use the castle for road
material, if they choose, the ignorant boors! I, thank God, am an

Austrian." He became a Nazi and put his knowledge of Yugoslavia at the service of its enemies. He was a very ordinary person. The challenge presented to him by the young state was crude and unimaginative, and so was his response. Their failure to be reconciled was disastrous to them both.

Dick was not ordinary. He did not sell his furniture but had it brought by lorry to Belgrade. It was to him a symbol that he was a Croatian gentleman and not a mere Austrian colonist. The problem of adjusting his furniture to a tiny labour-saving flat had a spiritual counterpart. The framework of the new Yugoslav society is crude, without the dignity of the peasant or the culture of the nobleman. Dick was good and loyal; he had that rare perceptiveness and candour which sometimes develops behind a shelter of security and privilege. He was constantly misquoted and distrusted. He did not fit in. A small group of pushing Croat businessmen cultivated him and imperceptibly he too drifted into the ranks of Yugoslavia's enemies. They were Croat separatists and the brand of Slavophile Fascism which they preached was not at all crude. Ljutic, their philosopher, was a mystic and Dostoievsky was his prophet. The contacts with Italy and with the White Russians seemed to be on a spiritual plane, the political pledges were ingeniously disguised. If it had not been for Wanda's good sense Dick would have committed himself irrevocably. His fine gifts have been wasted by his country but not used against it.

This unimportant family history is a parable applicable to any new national state with an unassimilated minority. Minorities, which from some scruple of pride or cultural superiority refuse to assimilate, often accept with resignation the choice of two destinies, exile or extinction; a handful attempts to survive by becoming Quislings. The upper classes of Yugoslavia and the other Succession States are not merging, they are disappearing. This would not matter if they left behind them the rich and fertile civilization which they acquired through generations of privilege as mediators between Slav and Teuton. Rightly this hybrid culture belongs to Yugoslavia and should be claimed by it. Otherwise it will be appropriated by Vienna. With every fresh access of educated

émigrés from the new states, the cultural magnetism of Vienna, so long
irresistible in Eastern Europe, will be reinforced. This magnetism has
possibly even been increased by political decay. Attracting unappreci-
ated talent from all the border countries, Vienna has, like London, been
able to disturb the consolidation of new civilizations politically beyond
her control. Only by the free crystallization of all cultural elements,
old and new, can these new civilizations become strong enough to hold
their own.

I have shown how the old south Slav way of life, as exemplified by
the "izmirenje," is inevitably doomed. The survivors of it are not sufficiently sophisticated to resist the encroachments of middle-class
Western civilization, nor, except in the educated classes, is there any
real cultural toughness and integrity to form the basis of a distinctive
Yugoslav civilization. Even though the new intelligentsia may appear
to take their politics from Moscow, it is predictable that, as in the past,
they will take their culture from Vienna. Typical examples of this
inevitable Austro-Yugoslav culture are the Zagreb Communist playwright Krleza, and Mestrovitch, the Dalmatian peasant boy who made
contact with Rodin and the sculptors of the West in the Viennese art
schools. The remnant of the ruling classes, if they can be won over, are
far better qualified by hereditary fastidiousness to select and transmit
these external influences than is the more easily deluded middle-class
majority.

For there is no such thing as a pure national culture. In the monasteries of Pec and Decani and Gracanica there is evidence of a lofty
Serbian art, inspired by Byzantium, yet the promise of a greater future
was destroyed by the Turk as catastrophically as were even greater
Irish hopes by the Norman. A few frescoes and ballads and some rapidly
dying social traditions are all that the Serb chauvinist has to build on,
and he is building badly after the cheapest standards of the West, scorn-
ing the assistance of those who understand the West. A common language survives, it is true, and a language unites men, so long as you can
close the frontiers, mental and physical, but it cannot give the spiritual
unity from which great cultures develop. If you looked before the war

in the popular bookshops or in the cinemas in Zagreb or Belgrade, you would see that men follow the same fashions, dubbed and adapted, as in Dublin or Cardiff. Despite all the talk of national culture, Edgar Wallace and Garbo and their Viennese counterparts have a more potent educational influence on the average Serb and Irishman than Decani or Cormac's Chapel.

I have scarcely mentioned Mihailovitch* and Tito, and the unbelievable cruelties and heroisms which in Yugoslavia have for four years usurped the place of normal development. At the moment of writing the political foreground is blurred, but I have tried to give some account of the constant forces, social and cultural, with which any Yugoslav government, of whatever complexion, will have ultimately to reckon.

(1947)

---

* Draža Mihailović (1893-1946) was a Yugoslav Serb general who led the royalist/ nationalist Serbian resistance after the invasion of the Kingdom of Yugoslavia by the Axis Powers in 1941. His bands of guerrillas (known as "Chetniks") were the first resistance movement to be formed, followed shortly by Tito's Partisans. Initially, the two movements cooperated, but by late 1941 they began fighting each other in the attempt to gain control of post-war Yugoslavia. Many Chetnik groups collaborated or established a *modus operandi* with the Axis powers (Germany, Italy, Hungary) which had occupied different parts of Yugoslavia. After the war, Mihailović was captured by the communists; convicted of high treason and war crimes; and executed by firing squad in Belgrade.

Father Chok and Compuslory Conversion

Father Ilja Chok is a frank intelligent man of middle age, with a small black beard. He is the principal priest of the Orthodox community of Zagreb, and moved up here some years ago from the wild district of the Lika, where his parish lay. In the Lika the parishes are sometimes Orthodox, sometimes Catholic, and Father Chok found himself between two large Catholic communities whose priests were Father Morber and Father Mimica. Fortunately for him Father Mimica, the nearer of his two neighbours, was friendly and kind, while Father Morber, who was not, was busy with the affairs of another Orthodox parish, Shtikada. One day, after the government had announced its programme for the conversion of the Orthodox in Croatia, Father Morber arrived by car in Shtikada and ordered the villagers to assemble at the marsh where the ceremony of conversion would take place. He explained that in this way they would escape being killed. The Orthodox came trustfully, as they were told, but a few who did not come were brought by force. However, the rumour went round that they were going to be killed in any case and some of them escaped. The others had not long to wait for very soon a band of Ustashi arrived from another village of Gudur and started to shoot them. Some weeks later the Italians took over that portion of Lika from the Ustashi and dug up 350 bodies. They said that the ammunition had evidently run short for some had been buried alive, others hacked and pounded to death with scythes and hammers.

The Italians withdrew once more and the Ustashi returned. Father Chok's parishioners became greatly agitated and they asked Father

Mimica's advice. "I could convert you," he said, "but it would not help you either in this world or the next." Instructions to convert had come for him, but the situation was more than he could bear. He asked to be transferred to Zagreb and he helped Father Chok to escape too. Most of the Orthodox parishioners fled to the woods.

"Anyway the Italians were revolted?" I asked Father Chok. He shook his head vigorously. "They pretended to be but that did not stop the Ustashi!" And he told how the commander of the 73rd Division had said to the local Ustashi, "Go on with what you are doing but not so that I can see."

Father Chok, smoking a great many cigarettes, went on with his reminiscences of the Lika in a quiet philosophical way. There had been good Catholic priests who had helped the Orthodox to get passports and escape; there had been bad priests. I could see that, like everyone who has lived in a small community, he was more interested in personalities than in generalizations.

The next year the situation became slightly better, for Pavelitch, finding that the extermination and conversion policy was not successful, agreed to recognize an Orthodox Church of Croatia with a Croatian Patriarch. All the Orthodox bishops in Croatia had been murdered and so he felt himself free to choose an *émigré* Russian from the Ukraine called Germogen, who had been living in disgrace in the monastery of Hopovo since 1922. An Orthodox bishop could not leave his See without disgracing himself. Father Chok had the passion for minutiae and the faultless memory of country people, and he told me the history of Father Germogen with many fascinating details, only some of which I recall. In 1919 the Albanians, who had become independent, wanted to have their own Patriarch, but the Patriarch of Belgrade said that this could not be decided without a conference of all the Patriarchs. But the Albanians were impatient and they asked the refugee Father Germogen to come and consecrate an Albanian bishop as Patriarch. They sent an aeroplane for him and a present of 20,000 dinars. This was irresistible; Father Germogen came and then obediently went to do penance in the monastery of Hopovo. There he stayed until Pavelitch called him to be

Patriarch of Croatia, a post which he held till he was hanged. "Germogen was a real tough," said Father Chok, "The only time I saw him he had a row of military medals on his chest." The story of the village of Shtikada was paralleled hundreds of times in Croatia. The heads of the Orthodox Church in Yugoslavia are of the opinion that the campaign of forcible conversion had the assent of many of the heads of the Catholic Church. Whether or not that is so, the majority of the Croatian priesthood seems to have accepted with resignation the expansion and enrichment of their Church. Judicial statements were made that conversions had to be willing to be effective, but at no time did they face squarely the fact that their Church, its ritual and its dogma, were used as instruments of crime. There were small sophistries by which they were able to quiet their consciences. Many priests persuaded themselves that they were saving the lives of the Orthodox by converting them, some may have believed they were saving their souls. Unlike other Churches, they had in the Vatican an extraterritorial head which could have made known to the world how their faith was being degraded by Pavelitch. The weapon of excommunication was tried against Marshal Tito's government. Was it tried against Pavelitch's? Pavelitch posed as a champion of Christianity under whom Croatia returned to its ancient role of "*Antemurale Christianitatis*," a bastion against the pagan East. If the Church had made known to the world how that role was being interpreted, Pavelitch would have lost all his influence over the devout. But instead of exposing it, the clergy of Croatia tried to belittle and ignore what was happening and to attribute the blame for everything to the Communists. Very little, either then or since, has been heard of this extraordinary chapter in the history of Christianity.

Meanwhile, overnight, Catholic parishes were doubled and trebled in size, churches were reconsecrated for Catholic use, abandoned monasteries were filled and adapted to a new ritual. To deal with the extraordinary situation a special government department was established to cope with the problems arising out of the conversions. The department's correspondence has been preserved and mimeographed so that it is possible for us to enter into its many perplexities and misgivings.

Chief among them, perhaps, was the shortage of Catholic clergy to minister to the new converts, of whom over a million were anticipated, "if things continue at the present rate." Owing to the strongly nationalist character of the new Croatia, it was thought unwise to introduce Slovenes, and it was therefore proposed that some agreement be made between the parish priests and the Franciscans by which the latter would, on suitable terms, take charge of the new parishes till permanent incumbents could be found for them. The department also had the power to pay the expenses of the friars who were sent round the country for missionary work. Converts were expected to give them their keep and also to pay a preliminary fee of twenty dinars a head, but a central board paid their salaries and travelling expenses, also postage and the printing of leaflets. Prayer-books and rosaries, of which many thousands were issued, naturally fell to the charge of the converts.

A new trouble arose; Pavelitch had decreed that only the Orthodox Church in Croatia was to be dissolved and conversions could be made to the other three Churches, Evangelical, Moslem and Greek Catholic or Uniate. The Evangelicals were few and weak and the Moslems, for whom Pavelitch had a special tenderness, were too tactful to assert themselves but Mgr. Shimrak, the head of the Uniates, did not hang back; whenever a large adjacent Orthodox parish was dissolved a Uniate priest was sent post-haste to celebrate Mass in the deserted church before a rival confession could intervene. But these were only passing differences; on the whole a spirit of co-operation between Uniate and Roman Catholics prevailed. Small difficulties were quickly surmounted. Where in some cases the ikonostasis was a fixture and could not be moved, a temporary altar was put up instead; but it was found that in many cases the Orthodox churches had been burnt or looted and the equipment and vestments were absent or could not be adapted. In that case the schoolhouse had to be used and all the necessaries, such as holy vessels and holy water, had to be brought from the nearest Catholic parish.

The newspapers give full details of these conversions, usually under some such headline as "Return to the faith of their fathers after 250 years" and we learn of the comprehensive way in which several villages were converted at one time. For example, in *Nova Hrvatska* of 9 April 1942, we read how the then Mgr Stepinac received a telegram of "devoted greetings to the head of the Church" from 2300 new converts from six different villages, assembled in the village of Drenovac. At a village near Karlovac three clergy performed the ceremony assisted by a company of 400 Ustashi, and Father Niksich, the preacher, told the new parishioners that Catholics would receive them with open arms and would accompany them every step. "Alert for Fatherland!" roared the 400. Mass was then celebrated. The band played the Ustashi hymn and the converts raised their hands in the Ustashi salute. Father Niksich afterwards had "a long heart-warming talk" with the converts, who went back home bearing the Ustashi flag.

This ritual appears to have been followed at all the conversions. Something of the substance of the "heart-warming talk" can be guessed from a leaflet headed "Friendly Advice" published by the diocesan press in Djakovo. It shows that these conversions were not just barbarous raids between rival villages. The invitation to conversion came decorously from the towns in pious words. Abridged, the leaflet reads:

> Our Lord Jesus Christ declared that there should be one flock and one shepherd. That is to say there must be one Church and one Head of the Church who is the representative of Christ on earth and the Chief Priest in the Church of Christ. Members of the Orthodox Church, we must introduce that unity into Croatia! The Bishop of Djakovo (Dr Aksamovitch) has already received thousands of citizens into the Catholic Church. As Catholics you will be able to stay in your homes and carry on your husbandry uninterrupted. In the Catholic Church you will be able to save your immortal souls according to the sacred words of Our Lord Jesus Christ.

Many will say that these missives had at worst the embarrassed connivance of the bishops, but though the concentration camps were full
with men who opposed Pavelitch's New Order, there is no record of a
bishop going there for violent opposition to the Poglavnik's intervention in ecclesiastical affairs.

As for the Uniates, Mgr. Shimrak, the chief administrator, declared
that, with the conversions, historic days had come for their confession.
"Every great work has its critics but that must not make us down-
hearted, for it is a question of a holy union, of the salvation of souls and
the eternal glory of the Lord Jesus." Mgr Shimrak died in prison and
hundreds of priests, many of them perhaps innocent, have suffered
because of the fury let loose in Yugoslavia by the compulsory conversions. Only the enemies of private judgement and Christian conduct
have profited by the hypocrisy and intolerance shown by the Christian
Churches under the Pavelitch régime. Only in one way could Christianity have made headway against Communism and that is by a frank
admission of hideous faults. Yet such an admission seems unlikely. The
Churches have made he world ring with the crimes committed by the
Communists, but the great offences committed in the name of Christianity they have passed over in silence.

I have never understood the meaning of "Return to the Faith of
their Fathers after 250 years." What happened to the Serbian Orthodox
in 1692?

(1947)

Yugoslav Papers:
The Church and Its Opponents

It was surprising to find in Communist Yugoslavia how elementary and almost perfunctory was the criticism of the Christian Churches. It seemed to be based almost exclusively on Charles Darwin and certain clerical misdemeanours of recent date. I suggested to a friend who was a translator that it might be a good plan if the works of some freethinkers, like Bertrand Russell or Arthur Weigall, who are Christians and humanists as well as distinguished scholars, were translated. He told me, however, that there would be no demand for such work. The policy of both the Church and its opponents in Yugoslavia was "all or nothing," and no attempt to salvage Christian conduct from the mythology in which, in the view of many, it had become entangled, would be countenanced. The baby, in fact, must be drowned in its bath-water or thrown out with it.

It is a very tragic situation which might, I think, be relieved by extreme candour and truthfulness on behalf of the Churches. They would have to avow more explicitly than hitherto that Christian virtues existed and could exist outside their ranks, and that, in fact, the representatives of the Churches had, in Yugoslavia, done a disservice to the Christian way of life by claiming to be its unique exponents. Their weakness and subservience had compromised fatally those in their flock, or outside it, who were neither weak nor subservient.

In Ireland interest has focused itself disproportionately on Archbishop Stepinac, whose trial was only a small episode in a struggle for

Christian values which lasted for four or five years and in which the Churches were as deeply divided as any other branch of society. At the very start the Protestant Church, which was very small, accepted the Nazis with enthusiasm, as did the Evangelical Church in Austria. The ecstatic welcome given to Hitler by the Viennese Evangelical clergy is recorded in the Dean of Chichester's *Struggle for Religious Freedom in Germany* (1938). But some effort has been made to prove that the Catholic Church in Yugoslavia was the backbone of the resistance to totalitarianism. Such an extraordinary notion could scarcely have gone unchallenged if it had not been feared that any admission of guilt would help the Communists. To do this would seem to be a greater crime than falsehood.

A large volume was published in Zagreb in 1946, called *Dokumenti O Protunarodnom Radu (Documents about the anti-national activities and crimes of a part of the Catholic Clergy)*. Some of the innumerable documents contained in it were used in the controversy. By most Churchmen they were held to be spurious. The Communist Yugoslav government was accused of faking the evidence. When I was in Zagreb I looked up ten or twelve of the most significant passages in the back number of papers published during the Occupation. They are stored in the University Library and many other libraries easily accessible. I found them all, without exception, accurately recorded. Moreover, I found that the Yugoslav government had not used a tenth of the material at its disposal. The Catholic Church in Yugoslavia for the most part received the invaders not with resignation but with transports of joy, and many of its prominent priests and friars had been preparing the way for them for many years.

Archbishop Stepinac, by his many brave sermons in defence of Jew and Orthodox, did something to redeem the welcome which he gave to Pavelitch on his arrival and the appeal which he broadcast to his clergy for submission (I saw his appeal, which has been called a fake, both in the diocesan paper of Zagreb and in two other papers.) But unquestionably his conciliatory attitude influenced others who were not capable of his restraint. So it happened that the man who organized the murder of King Alexander and was later responsible for the attempted extermination of the Serbs as well as the Jews in Croatia, was received with rapture in convents and monasteries and ecclesiastical seminaries, as well as being idolized in the Catholic press. Here is an account in a Church paper (*Nedjelja*, 17 May 1942) of a visit of 140 Zagreb theological students to the Poglavnik (or "Leader"):

> And then He entered. Himself, He opened the door of His room and stood before us. A kingly face, He raised His arm and greeted us with His wonderful deep voice, commanding and fatherly.
>
> "Za Dom!" (For Fatherland!) "Spremni!" (Alert!) [This corresponds to the Nazi greeting "Heil Hitler!"; "Poglavnik" corresponds to the Italian "Duce" and the Nazi "Führer."]
>
> A roar from 140 youthful throats, and then there stepped before Him the president of the Council of Young Clerics, Stephen Krisovitch, and addressed Him.
>
> While he spoke our eyes rested on the heir of the great Croat heroes of the past, on Ante Pavelitch! We try to watch the meaning in every feature of His face, every flicker of His eyes. And He – our sovereign – stands before us, wonderful in His simplicity. His was the holy calm of the grotto.
>
> The president finished his speech and handed to the Poglavnik our gift, five Roman missals in the Croatian tongue, and the Poglavnik enfolding us in His glance exclaimed: "Brothers!" We held our breath from excitement and a strange exhalation seemed to flow towards us from the Poglavnik. His words sketched out a new page, the loveliest and most precious of all in the history of the Seminary Youth of Croatia.

They then sang to him the Ustashi hymn and there was a further exchange of heartfelt cordiality and they went away.

As you see, capital letters are used throughout in the pronouns referring to Pavelitch. There is a photograph of Pavelitch in the midst of the 140 students. They look mild and submissive young men and I do not think they would have ventured on this demonstration if it had been displeasing to their ecclesiastical superiors or likely to prejudice their careers in the Church.

The following month there was a solemn gathering in honour of Pavelitch at the archiepiscopal church of Sarajevo, at which a choir sang Ustashi hymns and Archbishop Sharitch's "Ode to the Poglavnik" was recited; also, a young cleric recited a declamation on the Poglavnik's heroic deeds in the "Barbarous East." At that time the mass slaughter of the Serbs in Bosnia was in progress with the Poglavnik's approval, so the young man's reference to the Barbarous East was highly topical.

The pages of those papers published during the Occupation are full of such astonishing stories. Many of them are illustrated because the Poglavnik, who claimed to be religious, obtained great advertisement for himself by his association with ecclesiastics and there was usually a photographer nearby. And so he is seen as a sturdy, strutting figure surrounded by gentle nuns or eager theological students inhaling his loving kindness with eager smiles.

I have quoted hitherto the more serious papers of Yugoslavia. There are also innumerable smaller papers, like *The Messenger of the Heart of Jesus*, *The Guardian Angel*, *St Joseph's Herald*, etc., etc., which reached a less literate public. One and all they have photographs of the Poglavnik in strange proximity to angels, doves, lambs, little girls, and poems and prayers of sickly piety extolling his virtues.

It would be wrong to deride the simplicity of these people, whose fault lay in believing what they were told, if it had not had terrible consequences. We read in *St Anthony's Messenger*, June 1941, the calm announcement that "There are too many Jews in Zagreb with their aims of world domination and their perfidy and destructiveness. The Poglavnik has decided that the Jewish question must be radically solved." A few weeks later an announcement of an anti-Jewish exhibition and an article that might have been inspired by Streicher appeared. Almost the whole of the Jewish populations of Zagreb were, in fact, in those days plundered and taken to the camps of Jasenovac and executed. I believe that in spite of the Christian papers, the population regarded their fate with horror and revulsion. In the diocesan magazine of Bosnia and Slavonia for June 1941 parish clerks are notified of an important new decision: "Today it is the solemn duty of every citizen to show proof of his Aryan parentage."

It has been said that these papers were forced to print these articles under threat of suppression. But a healthy Christianity could only have been invigorated by the suppression of *St Anthony's Messenger* or, when it became a travesty of Christian principles, would have prevented its circulation. Nor do I think that "political" pressure is a sufficient excuse. Those who read *Katolicki List* will find that the editorship of the paper did not change at the time of invasion. Its new policy was merely an inflamed and exaggerated development of tendencies which had been evident before.

It is true that Archbishop Stepinac many times spoke against racial discrimination. Yet he must have been aware that such laws would follow quickly on the establishment of that government to which he had given his sanction and support. He seems to have had a curious detachment from the laws of cause and effect and to have believed that any crime committed against Russia could be overlooked. He seems to have been scarcely aware of the crimes committed on a wide scale in the name of the Church and the connivance and condonation of which many of its leaders were guilty. It is not possible that the Church leaders were ignorant of the wild and murderous excesses of hundreds and perhaps thousands of fanatical priests and monks in Yugoslavia. Yet in their statement of 8 March 1945 there is one solitary reference to these misdeeds: "When in exceptional cases a mad priest has assailed his neighbours' rights, we have not hesitated to lay a church punishment on him, and even to take away his priestly orders"!

In September the bishops also declared: "There were isolated cases of priests blinded by national and party passion who committed offences against the law and had to be put on trial before a secular court." In the same circular they tell how all the friars of Shiroki Brieg were executed without trial by the Partisans but they weakened their case against this brutal act by saying what is not true, that almost all the friars were known for their "opposition to fascist ideology." In the diocesan papers of Bosnia there are reports of ecstatic celebrations at Shiroki Brieg on the Poglavnik's birthday and other Ustashi festivals similar to that I have described. Many of the most prominent of the Ustashi leaders had been educated at Shiroki Brieg.

If the Church leaders had shown some penitence and cared about the wrongs they had done to unoffending people they might expect a more candid examination of the wrongs done to them and others in the name of Communism.

(1947)

Report on Yugoslavia

I spent a part of last summer in Yugoslavia, which I knew well before
the war, because I was a teacher in Zagreb and held a travelling scholarship from the School of Slavonic Studies. The Yugoslavs are, like my
own nation the Irish, among the least pacifist people in Europe and at
the best of times it would not be easy to persuade them that liberty
could be won or maintained except by fighting. They have good historical arguments for this view. Serbia, for example, became free after
repeated insurrections against the Turks, and the other Slav provinces
– Croatia, Slovenia, Bosnia and Herzegovina, and Montenegro – were
only added to the Yugoslav state as a result of the Great War. You might
argue that Austria-Hungary, through the growth of liberal ideas, and
Turkey through indolence, were in any case relaxing their grip on their
subjects. You might say that the Yugoslavs could have gained their
freedom by obstructiveness that stopped short of killing, by the development of cultural institutions, by passive resistance and political
manoeuvres. You might argue quite plausibly on those lines, but I am
afraid you would argue in vain. On the whole, history, as it is ordinarily
interpreted, is against the pacifist in the Balkans. He must depend on
faith, on the belief that by following his conscience he will ultimately
be justified, even though the facts of everyday life contradict him.
Only by great personal courage and high intelligence would a pacifist
in Ireland or Yugoslavia win any respect. If he depended on the ordinary
arguments of expediency, it would simply be supposed that he was a

coward or a traitor, who was anxious to shirk his responsibility to his nation.

I was not surprised to find in Yugoslavia that the small group of people who had been associated with the WRI˙ and other international movements of the kind had more or less dissolved. They had not actually been suppressed but had been voted away as superfluous by extremists within the groups themselves. These had urged their incorporation ("to prevent overlapping" is the usual excuse for this kind of cannibalism) in the officially sponsored societies, the various anti-Fascist leagues, cultural, economic, male and female. I did not find that they had been persecuted so much as rendered powerless. I talked to several men and women who before the war had been active, internationally minded people, who visited conferences all over Europe and America, who were used to lecturing and writing. I think I seemed to them, as would anybody else from our islands, a figure from the past, stirring very sad memories that had scarcely any bearing on the life they were leading. The business of living from one day to the next was absorbing all their energies. They had often lost their jobs or their incomes and had no surplus leisure for thinking of abstract problems or international movements. All their efforts were bent on securing some sort of future for their children or elderly relatives. "We are tired of living," one of them told me very sadly.

Most of the people were liberals by temperament, left-wing rather than right, so that their extinction by the Communists is a cruel tragedy. But none of those to whom I talked had gone back on their principles or come to believe in reactionary politics; they still valued individual liberty, the freedom to think and act in the light of reason. Simply they had been robbed of all power to advance their views. I think that an external pacifist organization can make very few

---

˙ War Resisters International, a pacifist and anti-militarist organization founded in 1921 and based in England. (Editors)

demands on these people. Even by communicating with us they come under the suspicion of giving information to foreigners.

You have, I am sure, heard of the trial of Jehovah's Witnesses which took place recently in Zagreb. The principal defendants were sentenced to death, the others to long terms of imprisonment. Owing, it is thought, to petitions from abroad, those sentences were in some cases revised, but there is no doubt the Witnesses had exasperated the Yugoslav government both by their pacifism and by their contact with fellow-believers in other counties. To quote the official report:

> They engaged in oral and written propaganda against the People's Republic and harmed the military power and defensive capacity of the country by persuading citizens to shirk conscription. They collected false information on the political and general situation, which they sent abroad, thus presenting a false picture of the state of affairs in Yugoslavia.

The Public Prosecutor declared that these reports of persecutions were sent abroad at the time when Stepinac was discussing "Intervention." In this way the Jehovah's Witnesses were linked with the Roman Catholic Church as collaborators in an attempt to defame and overthrow the Yugoslav government. Anyone who is aware of the relations of the Catholic Church and Jehovah's Witnesses will be amused as well as bewildered by this suggestion.

The Jehovah's Witnesses defended themselves with great courage and made no attempt to disguise their views. In the words of the official report of the trial:

> They called themselves faithful servants of Christ, to whom earthly life was of no concern. They said that they would not take up arms in case their country was threatened. At the time of the most intensive work for the rehabilitation of their country, they preached utter passivity. Their pacifism benefits international reactionaries whose agents they are.

The Yugoslav Witnesses were principally simple people, shoemakers, sanitary inspectors, mechanics, and they had a simple and fervent creed based on a literal acceptance of the Bible. There is no doubt that it was their simple faith with its rigid rules and curious dogma about the future that has enabled them to keep alive Christian pacifism in Eastern Europe. They are, I believe, almost alone in this field. Not many of us share or could ever share the views of the Witnesses, and we have to ask ourselves how, without their convictions, we can imitate their courage. Like them, we reject all the sophistries by which war is justified by leaders in political and religious life. I think we can do something by the fearless and incessant exposure of these sophistries. Stripped of them, Christianity might recover some of the vigour and universality which it has lost.

When I was in Zagreb I spent several days in the public library looking up the old files of the newspapers that were issued in the occupation period, particularly the Church papers. I wanted to see what resistance, if any, was made by organized Christianity to the ruthless militarism of Pavelitch, the Croat national leader, and his German and Italian patrons; I am afraid the results were disheartening. I did not expect to find outspoken criticism or condemnation in the Church papers because, if it had been published, the papers would certainly have been suppressed. But I was wholly unprepared for the gush of hysterical adulation which was poured forth by almost all of the leading clergy upon Pavelitch, who was probably the vilest of all war criminals. He was their saviour against Bolshevism, their champion against the Eastern barbarian and heretic, the Serb; he was the restorer of their nation and the Christian faith, a veritable hero of olden time.

As I believe that the Christian idiom is still the best in which peace and goodwill can be preached, I found this profoundly disturbing. I doubt now whether it is even wise for us to use the language of Christianity to the Yugoslav till all the vile things which were said and done in the name of Christ have been acknowledged and atoned for. I think the bitter hatred which is felt for the Churches in Yugoslavia is inflamed by all the lies and dissimulation about these things, by the refusal to admit that the Christian Church during the war connived at unspeakable crimes and departed very far from the teaching of Christ.

The principal Church in Croatia is of course the Catholic Church, but I don't think the Christian failure there is attributable to any specifically Catholic disease. There was also a small Protestant community whose published utterances make as horrifying reading today as anything in the Catholic papers. Their disgrace is smaller only because there were fewer of them. The mistake they all made was that they believed that the survival of Christianity depended on the survival of their Churches, and they were prepared to sacrifice truth and charity to an almost unlimited degree if they felt they could forward the interests of their particular confession. Instead of resisting absolutely the rise of nationalist hysteria and hatred, they thought they could guide it into sectarian channels. They believed and said that Hitler and Mussolini and Pavelitch were instruments in the hands of God for the establishment of his Kingdom. Unsatisfactory instruments, perhaps, they might admit among themselves, but God has power to turn Evil into Good. In fact as one reads through these extraordinary papers it becomes clear there was nothing they could not justify by the adroit use of ecclesiastical language. You will not misunderstand me if I say that after reading those papers for several days, certain phrases seemed to be defiled forever by the use to which they had been put. If we are to make a Christian approach to Yugoslavia, we shall have to eschew ecclesiastical phraseology.

You may think I am exaggerating, so I will explain what I mean. You will know about Pavelitch probably. I have heard him described as a guerrilla leader, and the whole Croatian struggle has been made to appear a wild Balkan affray which does not concern civilized people. It was not so at all. Pavelitch was a professional man of respectable standing in Zagreb, the writer of a couple of books, the editor of newspapers in Austria and Berlin; he considered himself the champion of Western as against Eastern values and his object was to withdraw Croatia from the Yugoslav state and from what the Nazis called

"Balkanismus." His heroes and patrons were Hitler and Mussolini, and the cruelty which he practised was copied from Western models, the concentration camps, gas chambers, the Aryan laws, the racialism and wholesale evictions, and much of it came under direct Nazi guidance. Yet he surpassed his teachers. It was a horrible blend of sophistication and savagery. You can imagine what was said of him by the Yugoslavs and you can discount some of it, but even his Fascist allies thought his cruelty in bad taste. Count Ciano, who was not a particularly fastidious person, describes him and his following, in his diary, as "a gang of cut-throats." Another Italian diplomat, Curazio Malaparte, in his book *Kaputt*, describes how he visited him in his official capacity and how he found in his study what he took to be a basket of shelled oysters beside him. Pavelitch explained that they were forty pounds of human eyes sent to him by his soldiers who were crusading among the Serbs. There are many similar stories, some of them probably exaggerated, but taken all in all we have a picture of a man and a regime for which no apology can be made. Unfortunately they had their apologists, fervent ones, and where you would least expect to find them, in the Christian Churches. This will not be forgotten within our lifetime in Yugoslavia. When Pavelitch first entered Zagreb in 1941, the Church bells rang and *Te Deums* were proclaimed by the Primate. When he left in 1945, driven out by the Partisans, it was under the floor in the Franciscan monastery in Zagreb that the State Treasure was hid, in the hope of a victorious return. It included boxes of jewellery and gold watches and gold teeth, stripped off the victims of the concentration camps.

He had managed to gain Church support by saying that Croatia was the *"Antemurale Christianitatis,"* once more the bastion of Christianity against the heathen, and whenever he visited a monastery or a convent he was received with enthusiasm and extraordinary reverence. The compliments and speeches which were exchanged on those occasions have been collected and published by the Yugoslav government, but they can be verified, as I did myself in many cases, in the back files of the newspapers in which they were always reported. For Pavelitch was very proud that in his work [he] should always be blessed in this way.

The most remarkable of all these ovations was the 22-verse ode of the Archbishop of Bosnia, Mgr. Sharitch, which was published in several papers in his own diocese and in that of Mgr Stepinac, at Zagreb.

He described how he met and embraced the great Pavelitch in the Cathedral of St Peter's at Rome, and he compared him to Leonidas, the man who never gave way:

> Each of thy days contains a sacrifice and is full of honest work.
> As the sun thou art pure and radiant...
> And the freedom is dear to thee as thine own mother.
> For her thou didst stand forth like a giant
> Against all brigands [*i.e.* the Serbs]
> And against the Jews, who had all the money,
> Who wanted to sell our souls,
> Who built a prison round our name,
> The miserable traitors.
> Thou art the first standard bearer of our country
> And thou keepest our lives free
> From that hellish Paradise, Marxism,
> From Bolshevism.

And he told how, like King David, he went forth into a strange world, where enemies lay in wait for his soul, yet God protected him.

> God has sent thee strength in foreign parts
> God has crowned thy faith with laurel
> Which will never wither, Hero of Fortune!...
> Doctor Ante Pavelitch, the dear name!
> Croatia has in thee a treasure from heaven.
> May the King of Heaven accompany thee,
> Our Golden leader!

Pavelitch's terrible campaign of compulsory conversion of the Orthodox Christians resulted in some of the worst religious massacres in European history. The Churches have denied that the Croatian hierarchy had any responsibility for all this, but unfortunately the complicity of many leading Churchmen is put beyond a doubt by their own printed utterances in their diocesan magazines and religious journals. As you have just heard, Mgr. Sharitch applauded Pavelitch's appalling measures against the Jews. As far as I know he got no official reprimand for his behaviour from his superiors. He is in exile and is referred to in the religious press as a victim of Yugoslav and Communist slander and intolerance.

You cannot go very far in Yugoslavia today without coming across traces of these fearful days. I had an introduction from Grace Beaton to a sympathizer with the WRI, a very intelligent barrister. He told me that his three brothers had been murdered in Bosnia, in the course of the conversion campaign. His sister had accepted conversion.

The Church still enjoys immense prestige in Yugoslavia, because it is regarded as the defender of Croatian nationalism and of the bourgeoisie, and it is in fact one of the few channels through which dissatisfaction with the present regime can be expressed with relative impunity. Croatia, though she entered the Yugoslav state joyfully and of her own free will in 1919, did not receive fair treatment from the Serbs and for twenty years the Croats have been discontented. Many now support the Churches for reasons which have nothing to do with Christianity. There is therefore very little likelihood that the Communist Party will risk a direct attack on the Catholic Church. It will try to assimilate by degrees, as it has already tried with some success with the Orthodox Church. In Bulgaria, for example, the head of the Orthodox Church makes frequent complimentary references to the Soviet armies. For some curious reason the Churches in all countries have been much more ready to applaud Soviet soldiers than Soviet civilians. Full use will be made by the Soviets of this strange ecclesiastical partiality.

How will be Churches react to Soviet advances? I think that they will be, on the whole, conciliatory. We can discount the cries of indignation against Communism that are raised in the Churches of western Europe. There is as yet no need for them to be accommodating. More significant is the attitude of Mgr. Rittig, the rector of St Mark's, Zagreb, and next to Mgr. Stepinac the most prominent prelate in the diocese. He holds a portfolio in the Communist government of Croatia and he gave me a signed statement about the relations of the Communist Party and the Catholic Church. This declaration is very sympathetic to the efforts of the Communists to reach an ecclesiastical settlement. Mgr. Rittig has not been disowned or discredited by the Vatican, and therefore I must assume that his policy of trying to work in with the Communists and obtain from them what concessions he can has the approval of Rome. So, whether the Church defeats Communism or is assimilated by it, it has a strong hope of survival as an institution. The Church has been called by Marxists "the opiate of the people." The hardships and discontent of many subjects of the Soviets are very great and it may well appear to their rulers that an opiate against the sufferings of this world, if it is administered by a state Church, might forestall an outbreak of rebellion. Therefore the Church is not likely to jeopardize its hope of recognition by espousing views which, like those of the pacifists, are equally unpopular with Communists and anti-Communists.

Because of this, the prospects of disseminating pacifist opinions in Yugoslavia by direct methods are poor. You can only act through individuals or through groups. The individual pacifists, as I have shown, are hopelessly crushed and the smallest gesture on their part towards international pacifism would be regarded as sabotaging the war-potential and entertaining relations with foreign reactionaries. On the other hand, the only independent institutions are the Churches and they are likely to irritate the Communists by aiding pacifism. On this subject, I had an interesting talk with her Herr Franz Zücher, the secretary of Jehovah's Witnesses at Berne, the location of the international centre to which the reports about the persecution of Christians are said to have been sent. He informed me that the trial of the Witnesses had been the result of a pact between the Catholic Church and the Communists and, if you read the Jehovah's Witnesses Year Books, you will find the same extraordinary allegations made about their misfortunes in Soviet Russia and Poland.

Is one to believe these things? I don't know. All we know is that great institutions fighting for their lives, fight quite blindly and they are able to ignore all those truths and scruples which an individual finds obvious and inescapable. In Ireland, though we have almost no Communists, there is a vigorous campaign against Communism. Possibly the object of this campaign is to invigorate the Church, by proclaiming a common platform on which Protestant and Catholic and all the divided branches of the Church may stand together.

Anyway, at the time of the trial of the Jehovah's Witnesses and their death sentences, full publicity was given to the trial in our press as an instance of Soviet brutality. Very shortly afterwards the Witnesses began campaigning in Southern Ireland and the tables were promptly turned. It was put about that so far from being the victims of Communism, the Witnesses were Communists or crypto-Communists themselves. A few weeks ago *The Irish Times* quoted on its front page from an address by the Catholic Bishop of Cork, denouncing the Witnesses on these grounds and suggesting that the police should take notice of them. *The Irish Times* is the paper of the Protestant minority, and so I wrote to explain the situation, quoting from the Public Prosecutor's speech in the Zagreb trial about the reactionary associations of the Witnesses and the grave damage they were doing to the Communist cause, damage so serious that only death alone could atone for it. *The Irish Times* refused to print this, nor have the Protestant Churches of Ireland done anything to protect this small Protestant sect against obviously sectarian slander. The friendship of Protestant and Catholic in southern Ireland is highly precarious and it may have appeared that it would be unwise to endanger it by telling the truth about an unimportant body like the Witnesses. This tacit collusion between old enemies in Ireland at the expense of the Witnesses makes it appear possible to me that the same thing happened in Yugoslavia, and that

Herr Zücher may not have been far wrong in thinking that Catholics and Communists were at one in regard to this brutal trial.

If there were no direct ways of doing propaganda for resistance to war in Yugoslavia, are there indirect ways? Serbs and Croats approach the problem of peace very differently. The Serbs, like the Russians and the Bulgars, tend to be extremists. When they become pacifists they often renounce not only war but all the other vanities of the world; they withdraw into some closed religious community with which it is hard for outsiders to make contact. It is interesting, all the same, that these groups with their extreme and fixed opinions often get recognition from the government, whereas an individual of more moderate opinions is persecuted. I believe that the small Tolstoyan community near Plovdiv in Bulgaria is still in existence and is tolerated by the Communist government. Yet, on the whole, it is among the Croats rather than among the Serbs that the international pacifist outlook, as we know it in the West, is most likely to be understood.

This sounds a paradox, because the Croats were known as great fighters and formed like the Irish Wild Geese a specially devoted corps famous for their loyalty to the emperor of Austria-Hungary. In spite of that, I would say that militarism is wholly alien to the Croat character, which is supple and imaginative. If anything, they are too docile, acquiescing from indolence or curiosity in ways of life which their intellect rejects. How was it possible that this clever subtle people tolerated Pavelitch and the Nazis so patiently? Perhaps for a time all the small pomps and ceremonies of the Independent State of Croatia appealed to them, but very soon they saw how ridiculous it was. They are cynics by temperament; certainly they no longer believe in war since it has brought them nothing but unhappiness. I think that many of them vaguely hope though that the Americans and the atom bomb will bring them some sort of painless liberation from their enemies and that they will not be obliged to fight themselves. This opium-dream of miraculous release from Communism will prevent them forming any plans for escaping service in the Communist armies or thinking out pacifist ideas. Yet there have been in the past many distinguished Croats who have been pacifist as well as nationalist. They believed in peaceful evolution and feared the contradictions and absurdities into which the military policy of their leaders might lead them.

The career of Archbishop Stepinac is a wonderful illustration of the twists and turns which an ambitious, rather conventionally minded Croat has had to make in recent years if he was to keep pace with history. His life seems to have been spent in fighting and praying for contradictory causes, and is surely the *reductio ad adsursum* of militarism and its first cousin militant ecclesiasticism. He is a Croat but was born an Austro-Hungarian subject. In the Great War he was conscripted into the Hungarian army and fought against the Italians, the allies of the Serbs. He fought loyally and well and was twice awarded the Medal of Valour. He was taken prisoner with other Croats, he changed sides, joined the Yugoslav Legion and fought for the Serbs against the Austro-Hungarians. Again he fought loyally and well and was awarded the coveted Karageorge Star. Some years later, he became a priest and very soon, with the king's favour, the Archbishop of Zagreb. On the eve of the collapse of the Yugoslav kingdom he remained loyal to the king, issuing an appeal to the Croats to stand by the young King Peter. A few days later Yugoslavia collapsed and he ordered a *Te Deum* in all the churches to celebrate the establishment by Pavelitch of the Independent State of Croatia. He was loyal to Pavelitch, praying for his victory against the Serbs and the remnant of the Yugoslav army, and was awarded by him the Grand Cross of the Order of King Zvonimir "for exposing both at home and abroad the rebels from the territory of the Independent State of Croatia," that is to say, the Yugoslavs. Pavelitch fell and the Partisans came in and established the Federal Republic. Then, his biographer Count O'Brien tells us, he became a loyal subject of the Communist government. O'Brien angrily declares that the suggestion that he remained a loyal subject of the previous government was purest calumny and in his book he prints a photograph of the archbishop watching a military parade beside the military commander of Zagreb, the Soviet military attaché and the Communist premier of

Croatia. In spite of all this, it is curious to find in this book the following anecdote to illustrate the archbishop's humanity and courage. At the height of the religious massacres, he is said to have burst into Pavelitch's room and cried out, "It is God's command! Thou shalt not kill!," and without another word, says Count O'Brien, he left the Quisling's palace. Almost all these facts are drawn from the official biography of Mgr. Stepinac which was published in Ireland, and which Cardinal Spellman laid in a bronze box on the foundation-stone of the new Stepinac Institute in America. Therefore we are expected to admire these swiftly adjustable loyalties and not observe any inconsistencies. Mgr. Stepinac was certainly a brave man, but his guiding principle was loyalty to the established authority and its armies. These changed four times during his life and he, too, was obliged to change. I do not know what he meant when he said "Thou shalt not kill!" I think he really meant: "Thou shall not kill too much!," or, "Thou shall not kill except when thou art in uniform and thy victim is, too," or something of the kind. I do not think that qualified advice like this is ever very impressive and I am sure that Pavelitch must have wondered what the archbishop meant.

It is easy to see how Christianity became unpopular in Yugoslavia. I see only two ways in which it can recover its prestige, a bad, safe way and a good, dangerous one. The bad, safe way is by the development of a new Established Church, enjoying certain privileges, in exchange for the unqualified support of the State in its wars and political adventures. That is to say, there will be army chaplains attached to Communist regiments, there will be prayers and thanksgivings for victory in return for the right to hold certain views about the next world and the preparation for it, and about sex relations. This development, particularly in a country like Croatia where the Church is strong, seems to me very probable. In the Orthodox Christian regions of the Balkans, it has already taken shape.

The good, dangerous way is so unlikely to be adopted that perhaps you will think me naïve even to mention it. It is that the Churches should become pacifist again as they were in the first centuries of

Christianity, and that they should no longer demand from the Communists the privileges which come to those who bless armies and pray for victory.

Could this mean that they would meet with the fate of Jehovah's Witnesses? There is always that danger, but it has not deterred the Witnesses. Why should it deter the older Christian communities?

I have heard it argued that it would have eased the lot of pacifists in Yugoslavia and given them status if Christian pacifists in our countries, at the time of the Stepinac trial or earlier, had pressed, not for the archbishop's acquittal, as did many Churches, but for his withdrawal from Yugoslavia by the pope. The Yugoslav government had promised not to prosecute if this withdrawal took place. It would have meant the archbishop's freedom and some relaxation of tension. The Vatican, for reasons of prestige, refused to withdraw him. I think that this prestige has been maintained at too great a cost, and that a great part of the cost is being borne by those who are not Catholics and have nothing to gain and everything to lose by the advertisement which has been given to the archbishop's views through this unnecessary martyrdom. Undoubtedly it has deepened the hatred and misunderstanding between East and West. In my country I have heard the trial described by people who took their opinions from the newspapers as a legitimate *casus belli*. Anyone who gave this question any serious attention was looked on as a Communist. Yet surely, without in any way disputing the archbishop's courage or sincerity, we here today must regret that he should be regarded as a leading representative of Christian views or a champion of Christendom. He stands surely for the principle of a state-controlled Church, with its army of chaplains and its readiness to support the state, whatever that state may be in all its military adventures, with prayers and *ovatio* and offerings of money and labour. In fact, he stands for all those things to which we here are most strongly opposed.

Those who resist this idea of a state Church with its army of chaplains will today no doubt be regarded as little better than Communists, but now that the Communists have succeeded in assimilating some of the Churches, opinion will begin to change. If the unspeakable Pavelitch was able to obtain the prayers of the Churches and chaplains for his regiments of brigands, need we suppose that Communist generals will fail to conciliate the Churches when they wish? I am sure they will not fail.

I am afraid I have told you very little that is encouraging about pacifism in Yugoslavia, yet I believe that there is no nation in the world that longs so ardently for peace. It is still a Christian country but I think that its Churches will provoke wars rather than avert them till they become pacifist. That would be a big revolution but whenever it happened, whether in the East or the West, it would quickly spread. I believe that there is no people with a greater understanding of Christian pacifism than the Slav people, if their enemies and their leaders allowed them to adopt it.

(1947)

Memorandum on the Struggle
Between Communism and Christianity

I had hoped that I should be able to give you a first-hand report from eastern Europe, but unfortunately my visas did not arrive in time for the Council Meeting. Had I gone, I think I should be able to illustrate more effectively the proposals which I made at the Shrewsbury Conference [see "Report on Yugoslavia"]; but I do not think I would have had to modify them much. They are based on facts which are known to many of you and which I have carefully verified.

Third World War as a Crusade

You may remember that I maintained that much of the impulsion towards a third world war comes from the belief that it would be a crusade of Christian civilization against Communism. I asked if we should not somehow try to counteract that force and I made a short memorandum stating the case for an appeal or a declaration. Some of you thought something of the kind would be practicable, others not. But whatever your decision it seemed to me urgent that we should collect and examine the facts of this Communist-Christian conflict and interpret them in the light of pacifist principles. Such a compilation would be valuable on its own account or as a reinforcement of appeal or declaration.

The Pressure from the Roman Catholic Church

The Communist struggle with the Churches has intensified in the past
year and there have been corresponding reactions in the West. I think
I referred to my own country, whose spokesmen, including our Minister for External Affairs, have repeatedly explained that a third world
war would be for Ireland a Holy War. I think too I mentioned that it
was in the excitement of the Stepinac trial that Cardinal Spellman
gave his blessing to conscription in the USA. Since then, the Mindszenty trial has given the Cardinal a further excuse for expressing similar
views. To quote an article in *The Economist*, 19 February 1949, from its
US editorial staff:

> Roman Catholic groups now seem to be doing their best to
> incite the country to a war with Russia. The burning words
> of Cardinal Spellman on the Mindszenty trial aroused the
> apprehension of many Americans, who had hoped that the
> Cold War was being kept from growing warmer. Americans,
> who do not belong to organized minorities, are discussing
> with a new and far from academic interest the legitimate
> uses of minority pressure.

I do not think the writer exaggerates the force or the danger of this
pressure. Though it comes from a relatively small group, that group is
highly organized and has close contacts with other countries. The
Roman Church in America and elsewhere played a considerable part
from a distance in influencing the Italian elections of 1948, and the
writer of the article infers that "the sense of powers and exaltation
engendered by that recent success undoubtedly plays a part in this new
crusade."

Pressure Derives from an Uncompromising Philosophy

We are rightly shy of introducing any element of religious controversy into the pacifist movement. We like to think that the gospel of peace is one which men of every Church and no Church can equally well promote. Many of us have friends in the Roman Church: we find them personally tolerant, wise and good. They do not interfere with us or we with them. That certainly is my experience in the Irish Republic, where we who are not Roman Catholics are in a minority of 2 or 3 per cent and are always kindly treated by our neighbours. But I am not thinking of personal pressure – there is very little – but of the soft, irresistible pressure of an uncompromising philosophy. According to that philosophy, all other Christians are renegades from the one True Church which will in due time reclaim them. And all those who are not Christians must be made so at all costs. I say "at all costs," for many popes (Pius IX, for example, in his Syllabus of 1864) have asserted that it is heresy to maintain that the Church has no right to employ force. Let me quote from the current number of the *Dublin Review*, the leading intellectual quarterly for Catholics in England: "Russia has become a vast field for missionary activity and will no doubt prove to be a fertile field as soon as the Iron Curtain is lifted." How does the writer expect the Iron Curtain to be lifted? How are the Orthodox Church and the Communist Party to be liquidated and his dreams fulfilled? There is no direct mention of war, but it is very clear that war is in the mind of all those who are looking for the conversion of Russia to the Catholic faith. And, if war is in their minds, the words of peace upon their lips cannot carry conviction.

Fellow Travellers of the Catholic Church

The influence of the Catholic Church extends far beyond its own members, and in a confused way millions who are not Catholic or members of any Church have come to accept the Catholic view of a sharp antithesis of Christian and anti-Christian divided from each other by a geographical frontier. Forgive me if I am platitudinous and tell you what you already know, but the Catholic propaganda is so plausible and persuasive that unless we remind ourselves constantly of obvious facts we are liable to be influenced by it.

Four Objections

Firstly, west of the Iron Curtain there is now only a very small minority of practising or believing Christians. Secondly, these Christians are so deeply divided that the only bond between them is often their common allegiance to what I must call "the fundamental Christian ethic," the belief in forgiveness, charity, universal brotherhood. Thirdly, it is not yet certain that this fundamental Christian ethic has been repudiated in Communist countries. Fourthly, the battle which is raging round the Churches in eastern Europe is not concerned with the Christian ethic, but with politico-ecclesiastical matters, the relations of Church and State, religious education and other matters which since the Reformation have always been subjects of controversy. I am not belittling the importance of this struggle or its possible bearings on human liberty. I am merely emphasizing its special character.

Beleiving Christians a Minority in the West

To prove my first point, let me give you some figures to show that the conception of a Christian West is now little more than a metaphor. A well-known Catholic writer, Montgomery Belgion, declares that in France, nine out of eighteen million urban workers are completely indifferent to religion. In the whole country only one in ten now communicates. In Czechoslovakia, while it was still under Western influence, a careful poll was made through the Charles University in Prague, acting on a suggestion from the BBC in March 1946. It was found that only 32.8 per cent believed that Christ was the incarnation of God, only 38.4 per cent believed in an afterlife. Similar figures could be given for many other countries in northern Europe, where Communism has hardly any foothold.

We hear only very little about this huge unbelieving majority. They are unorganized and hence inarticulate. There are only a few militant free-thinkers and they are seldom allowed to write in the press or speak on the wireless. The passive free-thinkers, either from good breeding or inertia, do not obtrude their opinions. There is from their side no serious challenge to the Catholic slogans about a Christian West and an anti-Christian East, even though they know them to be monstrously untrue.

Of Christian Unity the Christian Ethic Only Survives. It Survives Also in the East

My second point was that if you are to find common ground among the Christian sects of the West, you must dig very deep, so deep that you come to those fundamental principles of human brotherhood which are now shared by all civilized people. There is nothing exclusive about them, and we cannot say that the agnostic or the Communist is outside the range of their application.

For example, on the extreme wing of Protestantism are the Jehovah's Witnesses, who are now so active all over Europe. They believe that the Kingdom of God must be established by resistance to nearly all ordinances of the State. The Catholic Church, on the other hand, believes deeply in the State, provided that it is subject to Catholic influence. These opposed views bring them into bitter conflict with each other and with the Communists. The tactics of the Witnesses are fairly well known to us. The Witnesses are uncompromising and fanatical and face death for beliefs which are based on a very curious interpretation of the Bible. But I think that to the vast body of Christians and non-Christians in the West, the Roman Catholic standpoint is also

wholly alien and their methods of fighting Communism are as repugnant to many of us as Communism itself. They seem to have no dislike
for ignorance, credulity, destitution, provided they can exploit them
for their Church. If you think this judgement a harsh one, refer again
to that distinguished writer in the *Dublin Review*, Mr Tomberg, whom
I have already quoted. He is full of hope for Russia, because the peasants
have been seeing fiery crosses in the sky on the sites of desecrated
churches, and because there had been a panic in a cinema in eastern
Ukraine, when instead of the expected film, the Mother of God had
appeared on the screen weeping bitterly. Did Mr Tomberg himself
believe in this apparition or is he merely rejoicing that former Communists believed in it? To the non-Catholic, both attitudes would be
equally distasteful and extraordinary.

In the same journal a learned Jesuit, Father Martindale, surveys
another episode in the Catholic struggle with Communism, the apparition of the Virgin in 1917 to three small children at Fatima in Portugal
on the eve of the Bolshevik Revolution. The Virgin, it is said, gave the
eldest child, Lucia, a message about the conversion of Russia. On the
anniversary of the vision, there was another apparition before huge
crowds, and accompanied, according to the evidence of many clerics,
by "a Great Fall of the Sun" and a miraculous shower of white roses of
which a photograph has been published in Dublin. On 31 October 1942
Pope Pius XII, speaking in Portuguese and obviously influenced by the
apparition, complied in part with the message given to Lucia and later
he referred to it more explicitly. The apparitions had a tremendous
influence on Portuguese politics, and Father Martindale has described
them as the "spiritual coefficient" of Dr Salazar's government. Cardinal
Mindszenty also spoke in one of his sermons of the apparitions at Fatima, and on another occasion described how he himself had seen the
tears of joy flowing down the cheeks of a wooden statue of the Virgin,
when it was restored to the niche from which it had been looted.

The miracle of Fatima has now had great publicity all over the world,
and particular emphasis has been laid on the revelations about Russia,

which Lucia wrote down from memory some twenty years afterwards at the request of her bishop. Two different versions were circulated of Our Lady's announcement to little Lucia. In one, the word, "Russia" was used; in a later one, issued during the war, "the world" was substituted. Father Martindale explains how this difficulty "can be at once eliminated." "It is now known," he writes, "that this change was deliberately agreed on lest 'neutral' Portugal should seem to be taking sides against Russia. Since 'Russia' is now replaced throughout, there is no point in dwelling on this." Father Martindale does not say by whom this deliberate agreement was made. By Our Lady, by Lucia, by the Portuguese hierarchy, by the government, by the War Office? The questions on which Father Martindale is disinclined to "dwell" are very numerous. As many as 500,000 people go on every anniversary of the apparition to the site of it in Portugal, on which the largest church in the land has been built. The cult has spread to many lands accompanied by lecturers and images of the Virgin. It is impossible to dissociate it from the anti-Communist campaign.

Surely we must admit that most Western Christians find no point of contact with the philosophies that employ the cult of Fatima against the Communists or, like the Witnesses, preach the imminence of the Armageddon against them. The façade of Christian unity can only be kept up by the most specious window-dressing. We can relegate the Witnesses to the background as hysterical and unimportant, but we cannot make terms with or ignore the Catholic use of supernatural phenomena. Our Catholic friends will tell us that I have exaggerated the significance of these cults. They will say that belief is optional but, if you invite them publicly to denounce a cult such as that of Fatima, you will find that they excuse themselves. They will explain perhaps that the cult of Fatima is meant for simple people whose minds are impressed more easily by fantasy than by reason. This argument is wholly repugnant to the Protestant mind. There can be no united Christian front against Communism where such weapons are used.

The Christian Ethic Not Repudiated
in Communist Countries

My third point was that it is not clear that Communists, who have
crushed some Churches and reduced others to submission, have rejected the Christian ethic. I don't intend to start a discussion as to
whether Marxism and Christianity are compatible, because I doubt
whether the present Communist society is much more Marxist than
ours is Christian. In practice, Russians and their neighbours are heirs
like us of Western civilization, which owes so much to the Christian
ethic, and I do not think that influence is easily shed. In the West, the
Christian belief in universal brotherhood and charity survived the
Reformation, the Inquisition and the penal forced-labour camps,
though it may wear an unfamiliar name. For that reason, too, the antithesis of Communism versus Christianity seems to me false and
dangerous.

Communist Struggle with the Churches Is Principally
Politico-Ecclesiastical

Fourthly, I claimed that the imprisoned or persecuted Church leaders
are often presented to us as champions of those spiritual liberties and
humanist values in which in the West we all of us, believers and unbelievers alike, place our trust. Yet a little examination would show
that what they stood for was in most cases quite different. It concerned
the rights and privileges of the Churches, the control of education and
property, and the maintenance of certain traditions, such as the supremacy of the pope, which have been controversial subjects long
before the Nazi and the Communist.

In illustration of this last point, in Czechoslovakia, Archbishop
Beran, a very brave man who opposed the Nazis, has seemed to many
of us to be fighting the cause of us all against the Communists. But in
fact, his struggle is primarily ecclesiastical and is the recrudescence of

an old dispute about the supremacy of the Vatican which flared up after the liberation of 1918 when a million Czech Catholics left their Church and joined a new Czech National Church. Their reason was that the Catholic Church had been used by the Habsburgs as an instrument for the suppression of Czech nationalism and that the Vatican had always been closely associated with the Austro-Hungarian imperial house. No doubt the Communists are explaining in their own interests an ancient grievance but they are not the originators of it. Archbishop Beran is fighting an old battle against a new and formidable enemy. He is not likely to add to his difficulties by fighting for other liberties than those prescribed by the Catholic Church. Those who look to him or his Church for an uncompromising defence of democracy will find themselves disappointed. For instance, some time after the Communist coup took place, Mgr. Beran, at the Communist leader Gottwald's request, celebrated a *Te Deum* at Prague Cathedral. He evidently thought he might make better terms for his Church if he appeared to give the blessing of God on the methods by which Gottwald assumed power. Today a favourable concordat might convert him from being an opponent of the regime into being its supporter. In the three celebrated trails in Yugoslavia, Hungary and Bulgaria, it is impossible to see, as we have been asked to see by our press, a straight fight between Communist and Christian values. The protagonists in each case undoubtedly believed that the interest of their Churches could be forwarded by wars, *coups d'état* and physical force. They were champions of that militant and political ecclesiasticism which it is our duty here to censure.

The Humiliation of the Churches
Through Militant Ecclesiasticism

It should be our task to make a study of the relationship of the Churches and the totalitarian regimes from our standpoint. I not think it has been done before. We could show the perversions the Churches have had to suffer because of this same militant and political ecclesiasticism.

Church leaders have been again and again reduced to the most shameless opportunism and compromise. They have had to take political somersaults while maintaining that the Church of God is *semper eadem*, always the same.

In the paper at Shrewsbury I related how Archbishop Stepinac, owing to political changes in Central Europe, had received medals for valour and devoted service to the State from three different hostile powers to which his country had alternately been subject – Austria-Hungary, Yugoslavia, and Independent Croatia – and how he had also tried to work with the government of Tito, attending his military parades and being photographed at them. I suggested that this was the *reductio ad absurdum* of militant ecclesiasticism, but these *volte-faces* are so frequent as to excite no comment.

Very few, for example, have censured the gyrations of Cardinal Schuster of Milan and possibly that is because each side in turn had hopes of profiting by his opportunism. Most English people were gratified when at the fateful Italian elections, the cardinal passed sentence of excommunication on all those who voted Communist. They did not question any of the methods by which the election results were achieved, the threats of eternal damnation, the nodding statues, the miracles and all the rest. The severest criticism I have seen of him comes not from the left wing but from the right. In a Milanese paper I read some time ago a letter from the mother of two Fascist sons who had been killed without trial on the day when the Italians had risen against Fascism. It was a copy of a letter to the pope, in which she lamented that the cardinal had rung all the church bells on this day of civil slaughter and on its anniversary had put it under the blessing of the Blessed Virgin. She recalled that the cardinal had been one of the most ardent supporters of Fascism. Was he now by these dedications and ringing of bells trying to efface the memory of his former political sympathies? Surely this Fascist mother was right? Anyone who questions the support which the cardinal gave to Mussolini and the Fascists has only to turn to Professor Binchy's *Church and State in Fascist Italy*, in which you will find a record of some of the cardinal's passionate sermons.

Protestant as well as Catholic Church leaders made these compromises and somersaults. Their struggles also were ecclesiastical and, as a rule, had little bearing on the fight for universal charity, peace and freedom. Let us take the case of the famous Pastor Niemöller. I do not wish to disparage his courage or sincerity but merely to show that he only opposed the Nazi philosophy where it impinged on the independence of his Church. At his trial in February 1938, in his defence he reminded the court that he had voted for National Socialism in 1924 and preached a sermon in favour of the movement in 1933. That is to say he was one of the earliest of the Nazis and long after *Mein Kampf* had been published he must have believed that its philosophy could be reconciled with Christianity.

In Austria it was not only Cardinal Innitzer who greeted the invading Nazis with "Heil Hitler!"; the heads of the Evangelical Churches gave them an even more ecstatic welcome. In their manifesto of April 1938, two months after Niemöller's trial, they referred to Hitler as "a tool in the hands of the Almighty" and promised him everlasting loyalty. Similarly in Yugoslavia, the head of the Evangelical Church, Bishop Popp, supported the Quisling Pavelitch and received form him "an Order with Star for sincere collaboration as head of the Evangelical Church."

Militant Ecclesiasticism on the Left

I shall have given a wrong impression if I have suggested that Christian opportunism shows itself principally by collaboration with right-wing totalitarianism. This is not so. The intimate association of the Communist governments and the Orthodox Church is well known to all. I shall not dwell on it here, because it is constantly condemned in our press, whereas ecclesiastical opportunism on the right is far more tenderly handled. Yet from the example of Russia and her neighbours, it should now be obvious to all that a Church which supports right-wing militarism will ultimately, after a successful revolution, transfer its support to the militarism of the left. A Christian community can only keep its integrity by being absolutists for peace and universal charity and by refusing all such privileges from the state as might deflect it from these ideals.

Rebel Clergy in the West Today

There were, of course, many clergy in the West who against their own interests refused and are still refusing support to the right-wing governments which came to power by *coups d'état*, in Spain, for example, and in Greece. We are not permitted to hear much about them and so while we can applaud their courage we cannot yet judge their motives. Yet as we are being incited against the Soviets by stories of the trial and degradations of clergy in central Europe and Bulgaria, we should remind ourselves that in the West also, with less publicity, proceedings are taken against clergy who were in the wrong political camp. For example, in Greece at least two bishops were deposed without trial because they continued their support of the Greek resistance movement. Trials were not necessary, because the patriarch, who had been more elastic in his loyalties, simply deposed them. If in a similar way Mgrs Mindszenty and Stepinac had been deposed by their ecclesiastical superiors, their trial also would not have taken place.

The Greek paper (*Eleftheri Ellada*) in which one of these bishops, Dr Joachim of Kozani, stated their case, has now been suppressed, and I think his statement is the last public utterance from the group of Greek bishops and clergy who participated in the resistance movement against the invader and whose activities once had the applause of the Anglican Church and the Allied governments. The bishop in his article complains that English bishops, who had made protests about the Communist persecution of the clergy, had been silent "when he and his colleagues had been deposed, without any of the Church rules and laws guaranteeing human rights being observed... because they played their part in the leadership of the Greek people's struggle for the Allied cause."

I am not asking you to regard these deposed bishops as martyrs. I merely want to show how political discrimination is always being used when some deposed Church leaders are hailed all over the world as martyrs, others quietly consigned to oblivion. And apart from Greece, how few of us are aware that in Spain, a cardinal suffered exile, and bishops and countless priests, Spanish and Basque, were penalized, sometimes by death, for their opposition to Franco. We hear nothing of them. There are no protest meetings, nor public prayers nor appeals to the UNO.

Lack of Candour about the Bulgarian and Other Trials

And about the trials of Stepinac, Mindszenty and the Bulgarian pastors, our papers give us for the most part emotional judgements but no facts. Here and there a brave voice is raised – the Bishop of Sheffield, for example, in England, and Dr Jones of the Protestant Council of New York in the USA – warning us that everything is not as easy and simple as it is made to appear. There are few blacks and whites but much grey.

The trial of the Bulgarian pastors must be of special interest to us because one of the accused pastors, Ivanov, was connected with the pacifist movement. Are the charges against them totally untrue? Or did he despair of pacifism and come to think that only American and British military intervention could save his country and his creed from being submerged by Communism?

In these Bulgarian trials the names of some twenty English and American officials were given great prominence and the real facts of the situation must have been known to very many in England and America. If the Bulgarian charges are wholly false, why has not a detailed refutation been made, the twenty people concerned relating truthfully what conversations, if any, they had with the pastors? Not one has made any such statement. The British papers have simply declared that the confessions were forced ones and the whole trial a device for suppressing the Protestant Church in Bulgaria.

Anyone who has read the Bulgarian report of the trial must feel that this is a strange oversimplification. We cannot fully accept the Bulgarian statement any more than the British. The confessions are full of small misstatements, which may derive from physical fear or the pastors' desire to ingratiate themselves or simply from ignorance. And yet it is not possible to escape the conclusion that the Protestant Churches in Bulgaria, so closely allied as they were to Britain and America, were being used as a cover for military investigation by the British and American Intelligence Service. Many people who are not pacifists could defend this. Few, I believe, could with honesty deny it. Yet it has been almost unanimously denied.

I believe that Ivanov lost faith in pacifism and that his reasons were his fear of Communism, his admiration of Britain and America and his friendship with some of their representatives. All this was fairly natural in the Bulgarian Protestant clergy who had mostly been educated at American colleges.

It seems to me that pacifists will not be proof against these powerful influences if they are afraid to investigate candidly the circumstances in which fellow-pacifists succumb to them.

Mindszenty and Stepinac

As for the others, it is not pleasant to attack those who are undergoing punishment for crimes which are so usual that they appear almost to have historical justification. Yet Mindszenty* and Stepinac are

---

* József Mindszenty (1892 – 1975) was the Archbishop of Esztergom and leader the Catholic Church in Hungary from 1945 to 1973. He opposed the communist regime and was imprisoned from 1949 to 1956. During the Hungarian Revolution of 1956, after being freed, he was granted political asylum by the US embassy in Budapest, where he lived confined for the next 15 years. He was finally allowed to leave Hungary in 1971 and died in exile in Vienna. (Editors)

ecclesiastical politicians whose political manoeuvres failed; they are in no sense martyrs for those Christian values, charity, forgiveness, brotherhood, in which we all of us believe, whatever our attitude to revealed religion. Unquestionably, they contemplated without horror a third world war, which might relieve them of their embarrassments and restore the Catholic Church to its former privilege. I think that the Christian ethic comes into justifiable disrepute in Communist countries when these men are represented as its martyrs.

War Resisters and the Christian-Communist Struggle

You will say perhaps again that all this only indirectly concerns the War Resisters. I disagree. In most people's view, the Churches remain the chief organizations in the world committed to the belief in the supremacy of moral over physical force. When the Churches betray that faith so signally as they have done, all those who believe with them in the pre-eminence of moral force, suffer from the discredit that falls on the Churches. The pacifist bodies, whose strength lies in their absolute belief in moral force, must defend that belief wherever it is held. That is why I think we should make it our concern to show how militant and political ecclesiasticism have led the Churches into hopeless inconsistencies and cruelties and perhaps ultimate ruin. We should collect all the facts we can and publish them, and if in certain circumstances we can intervene, however feebly, to reduce the tension between Communist and Christian, we should try to do so. Though our numbers are very small, we have one great source of strength which might well give us the leadership of all those who do not see conflict as inevitable. Our belief that war can be avoided is not an opinion but a dogma, and those who know are always stronger than those who merely think.

Archbishop Stepinac, a Test-Case

I mentioned at Shrewsbury, as a test-case for possible intervention, the imprisonment of Mgr. Stepinac in Yugoslavia. Here, on the face of it, one would say was an absolutely insoluble situation. The inflexible policy of the Communist Party is pitted against the inflexible will of the Vatican. Both sides seem to be reconciled to the continued tension, though it is fraught with danger to the whole world, most of which is neither Communist nor Catholic. To Catholics, Stepinac in prison is a far more glamorous and important figure than ever he was when free. I do not think they would wish him released, unless he was triumphantly vindicated. On the other hand, the Yugoslav government is no longer interested in protesting about the justice of the trial. They would like Stepinac simply forgotten, and for this they reckon confidently on the irresponsibility of the modern press, which will drop a man and a cause as soon as they cease to have news value.

The Yugoslavs are wrong. Myths and martyrs have more authority over us the less we know of them. The Stepinac legend is not dwindling, it is growing. I don't think the tension can be relaxed till the question is brought out again into the light of day. Can this be done?

The Alleged Inflexibility of the Communists

I think if you look closer the inflexibility of the Vatican and the Communist Party is not as impressive as from a distance. It is well known that Stepinac, like Mindszenty, would not have been tried had he agreed, with the Vatican's assent, to leave his diocese. That is to say the Communist governments of Yugoslavia and Hungary were prepared to stay proceedings against men who later they condemned on the charge of high treason. That suggests a certain flexibility of policy in the Communists.

The Alleged Inflexibility of the Vatican

Now let us look at the background of Vatican inflexibility. In *The Tablet* of 22 January 1949, Bishop Santin of Trieste is quoted as saying of Mgr. Stepinac:

> There is no indication that he is ill-treated. I am convinced that the Yugoslav government would be happy to release him if the Holy See would consent to transfer him to another country, but the Holy See cannot betray the Yugoslav people and is immovable on this point.

Brave words, if they came from a champion of liberty and democracy and a true friend of the Yugoslavs, but strange ones if you refer back to Bishop Santin's own record. As Bishop of Fiume, under the Fascists, he was a determined supporter of Mussolini's policy of Italianizing the 15,000 Yugoslavs of Fiume. He refused them a single sermon in their native tongue. He threatened the Slav priests with suspension if they refused to give religious instruction in Italian to the Yugoslav children in the schools. He abrogated some ancient privileges which the Slav Catholics had enjoyed for centuries. The result of his tyranny was that in Abbazia more than sixty households joined the Protestant Adventists and in one village, Vodice, the Carabinieri had to be sent to prevent the villagers from seceding in indignation from the Catholic Church. You will find these particulars and many more about Bishop Santin not in a Communist book, but in a book published in 1936 under a right-wing government of Yugoslavia (*Life and Death Struggle of a National Minority* by Dr Lavo Cermelj, pp.125-9).

All this has now been forgotten, forgiven or more likely never known by the British and American occupying authorities. Bishop Santin is now esteemed as a champion of democracy and Yugoslav Christians against the totalitarian menace from the East. I have seen his views on the present Yugoslav-Italian tension quoted at great length and very respectfully in a British conservative newspaper. It is natural that, to quote Mgr. Santin, "The Holy See is immovable" about the Stepinac case. If any guilt was admitted in Mgr. Stepinac, Bishop Santin is still doggedly impenitent. And he derives some of his assurance, I think, from the naïve British and American occupying authorities in Trieste, who are so ready to forgive all sins that are not committed against Anglo-American interests.

I think, therefore, that the Vatican refusal to compromise on the Stepinac issue is not as inflexible as it may appear. It is based partly on misinformation among Roman Catholics, partly on the moral support given to them by the non-Catholic public in the West.

I think it is from ignorance rather than from cynicism that *The Tablet*, the leading Catholic weekly, quotes Mgr Santin in support of Mgr Stepinac and allows him to pose as a champion of Yugoslav Christians when really he was one of their most bitter opponents.

It is harder to account for the British and American support of the Vatican over these issues. I think what the British and the Americans revere in Mgrs. Stepinac and Mindszenty is not their pity but their nuisance value as foci of resistance to the Communists. If the majority of them asked themselves, "Do we stand for the same things as Stepinac and Mindszenty stand for?" they would give the same vigorous, outraged "No!" which their ancestors gave so often and so tempestuously in the past. I think they would take a different attitude to these trials if they looked more candidly into their hearts and I doubt whether the inflexible Vatican policy could for long stand the strain of British and American disapproval.

It does not often happen that the best way to secure a man's release from prison is to show that he is not innocent of the charges brought against him. Yet in the case of many of the imprisoned Church leaders this paradoxical situation seems to have arisen. They are kept in prison principally because the West has chosen to regard them as fearless champions of truth and freedom. If it could be shown that this reputation was not earned and probably not even desired and that they were simply fighting for an ecclesiastical standpoint that has been repudiated by a majority of Western peoples – and the proof of this is very easily forthcoming – they would no longer be considered dangerous people and their release would only be a matter of time.

A Policy for WRI

That would be a particular policy for WRI and as such necessarily subordinate to a general policy. In general we ought to collect and collate information to show how, in county after country, Christian leaders, by their subservience to the military policy of the state, have been led into hypocrisy, self-contradiction, base compromises and active complicity in crime. There is so much material in proof of this that our problem would principally be one of selection and arrangement. Next we should show that the antithesis of a Christian West and an anti-Christian East is a dangerous and out-of-date simplification of the facts. We could show how the Christian ethic is respected by millions of men all over the world who are not members of any Church or believers in any revealed religion. Though these people, for the most part, see a gulf between Christian and Communist ethic, the line of cleavage is not where most Church leaders would have us put it. It runs along no geographical frontier. That is to say to the vast majority the ideals of Stepinac and Mindszenty are every bit as antipathetic and totalitarian as the ideals of Karl Marx. It is because of the politicians that millions of men of good will have been confused into thinking that there is an identity of interest between those who are fighting for individual freedom and those who are fighting for clerical control of the schools, the supremacy of the pope, or the narrow sectarian views of the Protestant missionaries and revivalists in the Balkans.

The Camp-Followers of the Churches

I must not be thought to be condemning those who believe sincerely in these causes, I am referring to their unbelieving camp-followers. Millions of men today are lining up behind slogans in which they do not believe because they think a struggle is imminent and they must close ranks and suppress their private scepticism. Some think this broadminded, but it is the facile broadmindedness of those who inherited and did not have to struggle for their freedom of thought. They are defending the Churches not because of a new reverence for the Christian ethic but simply from fear of Communism which makes them look for allies wherever they can be found. And they are bringing the Christian ethic into disrepute by their cynical championship of it.

Militant and Political Christianity
a Powerful Enemy of Peace

We cannot disregard the Church issue, because peace and charity among men have never been preached so compellingly as in the words attributed to Jesus Christ. These words still have immense influence even over those men who have rejected the ecclesiastical interpretation of them. They are powerful in Russia still and in every Communist country. They cannot possibly be made into an occasion of conflict between East and West. On the contrary they should be an instrument of healing. Yet many Church leaders are trying to twist these Christian phrases so that they appear to justify a war against the Soviet Union. Political Christianity is almost always also militarist Christianity and when statesmen and ecclesiastics come to terms it always happens that, in return for certain privileges, the Church gives its blessing to the military forces of the state. Therefore, I think that members of this Council will agree with me in seeing an enemy in political and militarist Christianity. A soldier who is taught that he has the blessing of heaven on his work of destruction is surely more formidable than a soldier who lacks that conviction. You may disagree with me as to how best we may combat this ecclesiastical teaching, but I think you will share my view that it is a very evil one.

The Problem is Not One for the Pacifist Groups of the Churches Only

I do not agree that this is a matter for the pacifist bodies within the Churches and not for us. They are too small and weak, and we are all of us concerned. We have never adequately estimated the strength which the armed forces draw from the Churches. And I am not now thinking only of the West but also of eastern Europe. It was in time of war that the Orthodox Church received its greatest privileges from the Communist state in Russia. The privileges were not given simply from love of Christianity. The supernatural sanction which the Churches call down upon the armies are obviously considered to have military value. So too do their solemn and beautiful ceremonies in time of war.

Strike at the Root Not at the Branches

Therefore when pacifists rage against armies and generals, they are striking at the branches when they ought to be attacking the root. They are wasting their efforts. If the Churches withheld their support of war, there would be no chaplains, no *Te Deums*, no absolution for killing, no blessings of armaments, no anthems, remembrance days, cenotaphs. All these things are done on *both* sides, let us reflect, of the Iron Curtain. And I think that without them, state armies would in time wither away.

I don't mean that man would cease to be a fighting animal, but states would no longer be able to profit by his pugnacity and exploit it with such ease. Soldiers are usually honourable men. They like to have a good conscience and to be reassured that what they are doing is right.

Because of discipline, there is much more church-going among the armed forces than among their civilian brothers. And for many it is still from the Churches that directly or indirectly they draw reassurance and a supernatural sanction for their profession. But it should be impossible for Christians to give such sanction.

For all these reasons, I think that if we could expose the pitiful and ignoble results of militant ecclesiasticism, we should be striking at the roots of modern war.

(1949)

The Compuslory Conversion
Campaign of 1941: I-III

I

An Unpublished Letter from Archbishop Stepinac to Pavelitch

When I was in Zagreb this September, I secured through the Ministry of Justice some documents relating to the Stepinac trial. Most of them were already familiar to me, but the letter, which I have translated below (though not the resolution that accompanied it) was new to me. Though it is of great importance, neither the enemies nor the champions of Mgr. Stepinac have made use of it. The letter is not helpful either for the Communist prosecution or the Catholic defence. It reveals a confused human situation, where angels and devils are not easily identified.

The gigantic massacre of 1941, which was linked with Pavelitch's conversion campaign, has often been declared, particularly in Ireland, to be a fabrication of Chetniks or Communists or the Orthodox Church. Mgr. Stepinac's letter, once and for all, establishes its actuality. In a more peaceful age it would have been a great historical landmark, for the dead outnumbered the total of the victims of the massacre of the Albigenses, the Waldenses, and of St. Bartholomew's Eve. Figures can only be approximate still, but those given by the leaders of the Orthodox Church have been so often repeated that they must be treated with some respect. They are 500,000 killed, 250,000 forcible converts*. These figures have been used by Bishop Iriney of Dalmatia, by the Metropolitan Arsenius of Montenegro, and during the war by the Serbian Orthodox *Herald*, which was published in London.

The Archbishop's letter reveals the regret and revulsion which the violent methods used by Pavelitch's missionaries inspired in the Catholic hierarchy. The resolution, which was passed by the Bishops in Conclave in November, 1941, was an attempt to bring the conversion campaign under the control of the Church, and to check the rule of violence. The attempt was belated, since the fury had spent itself by July, 1941, three months earlier.

If we exclude Archbishop Sharitch, the author of the celebrated odes to Pavelitch and the fervent advocate of all his designs, the letters of Mgr. Stepinac and the four Bishops, whom he quotes, are moderate and humane. Why was the hierarchy so utterly impotent to check this inroad of fanatical barbarians into the purely ecclesiastical domain of conversion? I think the answer can be seen by a close examination of the letters. Pity for the heretic had always to be qualified, and was sometimes neutralised by zeal for the extension of the Catholic Church. Never once did they say, "Let there be an end to conversions! There can be no talk of free will and voluntary change of faith in a land invaded by two armies and ravaged by civil war!" Their concern is all for the right ordering of things, the appointment of suitable missionaries, and

---

* After much research unavailable in the postwar aftermath, the best contemporary scholarly estimate (according to the United States Holocaust Memorial Museum) is that between 320,000 and 340,000 ethnic Serbs, and at least 25,000 Roma, were killed by the Ustaše. Ivo Goldstein (*Holokaust u Zagrebu/Holcocuast in Zagreb*, 2001) gives a highly researched figure of 30,000 Croatian and Bosnian Jews also either killed directly by the Ustaše, or deported to Nazi death camps. Together, these figures make the tripartite Ustaše genocide easily one of the ten largest of the twentieth century. Philip J. Cohen (*Serbia's Secret War: Propaganda and the Deceit of History*, 1996) estimates that 250,000 Serbs were forcibly "converted" in a six-month period in 1941. (Editors)

a recognition of the legitimate claim of the Greek Catholic Church, equally with the Roman Catholics, to make converts from the Orthodox. A great opportunity had come to them. They must use it wisely, and not barbarously, for the saving of souls, but use it they must.

It is particularly to be noted that the second of the Council of Three appointed to regulate the conversions, by the Bishops' resolution, was Mgr. Shimrak, who had expressed himself forcibly in favour of the conversion campaign in his diocesan magazine of Krizhevtsi. (See my article in the *Gazette* of 11th March, 1947.)

It is not, therefore, possible to accept Count O'Brien's claim in his biography of Mgr. Stepinac (page 17) that by this resolution the Archbishop "made his (Pavelitch's) evil plan impossible." The resolution was too late, too generalized, too evasive. From the Bishop of Banja Luka's letter, it is plain that it was principally the intervention of Communists and Chetniks that brought the campaign to an end. Indeed, an anti-Communist writer, Stephen Clissold, says that it was the conversion campaign which first drove the Orthodox into the arms of the Partisans. And thus the Communist control of Yugoslavia was assured by means of the Catholic conversion campaign. (The same view was advanced by Bishop Valerian, Vicar to the Patriarch in *Martyrdom of the Serbs*, Chicago, 1943, page 249: "without doubt the Communist control of Yugoslavia was greatly assisted by the Catholic conversion campaign.")

What are we to make of O'Brien's anecdote that in June, 1941, Mgr. Stepinac "went to Pavelitch's office and said, "It is God's command! Thou shalt not kill!," and without another word of explanation he turned and left the Quisling's Palace"? Can we reconcile this story with the differential tone of the letter to Pavelitch, five months later, in which, it will be seen, the Leader is exonerated from all blame for the bloody deeds and complimented on his public condemnation of violence? Surely the story belongs to hagiography rather than history?

Public interest has been focused exclusively on the unhappy flood-lit figure of Mgr. Stepinac. Very few are interested in the tremendous massacre carried out by the flock whose shepherd he was. One day its cause and its effects will have to be traced. The story is obscure and tangled, but not hopelessly so.

In a memorandum published recently in London, the exiled Ortho-dox Bishop Iriney of Dalmatia tried to expose some of the "sheer, de-liberate lies" which had been hurled at his Church by Communist and Catholic alike. He introduces his section on Pavelitch's Croatia with these words: "I am, unfortunately, the only Bishop of the Serbian Church, from the whole territory of the Axis-Ustashi creation, called the 'Independent State of Croatia,' who has witnessed events in 1941 and survived. I owe it to God and to His Church and to history to bear witness to the truth. I do it here by simply summarising the main facts, for many large volumes will have to be written about the terrible fate of the Serbs and their Church in the 'Independent State of Croatia.'"

Owing to the difficult circumstances of Yugoslavia today, there are many obstacles in the search for the truth. Inevitably much evidence is being destroyed, much lost through death or failing memory. It is essential that what scraps of information we possess should be care-fully recorded.

II

Letter from Mgr. Stepinac to Pavelitch, the "Leader" of Independent Croatia, 20th November, 1941

LEADER!

The enclosed decisions of the Croatian Episcopate have been shaped under the influence of an intense love and care for the Croatian people, for the Independent State of Croatia, and for the Catholic Faith, which is the Faith of the vast mass of the Croatian people.

Here we speak only of the mistakes which have prevented the conversion of the Orthodox from proceeding with that widespread success which it would otherwise have had.

For these mistakes we do not blame the Government of the N.D.H.; we do not wish to present them as systematic, but as acts of irresponsible persons who were not conscious of their great responsibility and its consequences.

We know that these acts were the reaction to the State policy of the last twenty years in particular and to the crimes of the Chetniks and the Communists, who committed so many bloody deeds on our peaceful Croatian people.

We thank Almighty God that through your intervention better circumstances are prevailing, and, therefore, the Croatian Catholic Episcopate brings the following facts to your notice, not for the sake of recrimination, but so that in the future all actions of irresponsible elements may be completely checked; so that we may discover why, up to this, the work of conversion has not been successful, and what course should be taken so that the enterprise may continue in a normal, well-considered way without fruitless experiments.

May I be permitted, Leader, in this place to quote the opinion of the most outstanding members of the Croatian Catholic Episcopate which they wrote to me on the occasion of this Bishops' Conference.

Here is a letter from that old "Croatian warrior" from Banja Luka, His Excellency Bishop Mgr. Fra Jozo Garitch, dated the 4th November, 1941: "On the subject which most urgently needs our decision I do not know what I can say. I am not at all optimistic. Many, not only individuals but whole villages, will, in my opinion, fall away when the occasion arises. Already in some places the Chetniks and the Communists are taking revenge on those who passed over to the

Catholic Faith. They are burning their houses, taking away their cattle and other livestock, and so on. Moreover, the Moslems have begun to slaughter, in the most atrocious way, the wretched Orthodox population. When they are called to account they urge in their defence that they acted on orders. Many Orthodox have perished in the districts of Bihac and Cazin, who had already been converted to our Holy Faith; they were forced by violence to pass over to Islam. Then they were killed. The only consolation in these misfortunes is that the clergy who had the care of souls acted nobly in caring for these miserable people. They have paid no attention to threats. Banja Luka has earned an ill-repute. But Banja Luka is a gentle mother, if we think of the cruelties which have been committed in other places. The movement for conversion is abating in those places where the Chetniks and Communists are in command; and these are making attacks on the whole territory of my diocese, except the Livan district."

The Bishop of Mostar, His Excellency Mgr. Fra Mojsije Mishitch, writes on the 18th of August this year, No. 968/41: "The circumstances under which we live are from every point of view unsatisfactory. One must see and admit that it is difficult for the higher State authorities, but it is also difficult for the Holy Church in relation to its Divine task and its work for immortal souls. Quite a large proportion of the Greek Orthodox in the Mostar Diocese is disposed to accept the Catholic Faith. The principal State authorities in Zagreb have several times issued orders which had to be obeyed about conversions to another faith. But in fact these instructions are not such as could be conducive to the general well-being of the Holy Church or even of the State. By the mercy of God there was never such a good occasion as now for us to help Croatia to save the countless souls, people of good will, well-disposed peasants, who live side by side with Catholics; they know the Catholics and the Catholics know them.

Conversion would be appropriate and easy. Unfortunately the authorities by their narrow views are involuntarily hindering the Croatian and Catholic cause. The leaders are not to blame; there is interference from all sides. Instead of reflection and good sense there is callow, unqualified inexperience; there is fire and violence. It is no wonder that there have been very unfavourable consequences for the Croatian and Catholic cause... In many parishes of Mostar diocese, for example, Duvno Polje, Stolac, Klepce, Gorance, Gradac, etc., very honest peasants of the Orthodox Faith who live side by side with Catholics, have registered in the Catholic Church; they go to Holy Mass, they learn the Catholic Faith, they baptise their children... But then outsiders take things in hand. While the newly-converted are at Holy Mass they seize them, old and young, men and women, and hunt them like slaves... they nearly hound them to death in masses. All this does no good to the Holy Catholic or to the Croatian cause. Every single person will condemn this irresponsible activity, but in present circumstances we are letting slip excellent opportunities and advantages which we could use for the good of Croatia and the Holy Catholic cause. From a minority we might become a majority in Bosnia and Herzegovina. Let us not expect kindness from others' hands, let us do kindness ourselves. I look upon this as our sacred and exalted cause. I make this declaration to the reverend Presidium in the interests of Croatia and Catholicism, as I hope we shall do everything possible to prevent fatal consequences and remove all obstacles in the path of our good cause. In such a way we may bring about happier days for Croatia and Catholicism."

The same Bishop writes on 7th November this year (1253/41): "At one time there was a likelihood that a great number of schismatics would be united to the Catholic Church. In the meantime men appointed as Ustashi

functionaries have abused their positions, profited by the
abnormal instincts of the masses and worked upon their
weak human frailties. Terrible things have resulted. There is
no remedy against it... People were captured like wild beasts.
They were killed and murdered and thrown living into
ravines. Women and mothers with children, grown-up
daughters, boys and girls, have been flung into pits. The
Vice-Governor in Mostar, Mr. Bajic, a Moslem, publicly declared (as a State employee he ought to have held his tongue)
that in Ljubina alone 700 schismatics have been thrown into
one pit. From Mostar and Chapljina the railway carried six
waggons full of mothers, girls and children under eight to
the station of Surmanci, where they were taken out of the
waggons, brought into the hills and thrown alive, mothers
and children, into deep ravines. They were knocked on the
head and killed. In the parish of Klepca seven hundred schismatics from the neighbouring villages were killed. Shall I
continue? I might go too far. In the town of Mostar itself
hundreds of the Orthodox have been bound, carried outside
the town and then killed like beasts. Then there have been
deportations to Serbia, cries and lamentations and sorrow,
frenzied appeals; a deputation has even gone to Mussolini in
Rome. What have they said and petitioned? You can guess
for yourself. The consequence was a new Italian occupation
of Herzegovina. The Italians returned, took over the whole
authority, military and civil. Schismatic churches immediately came to life again, the Orthodox priests who had previously been in hiding appeared freely. The Italians were
well-disposed and friendly to the Serbs. The Catholic Church
is not inclined to violence. It condemns it, and on this occasion condemned it. But the Italians went to extremes in a
startling way. The new occupying authorities began immediately to act indulgently towards the Serbs and harshly towards the Catholics. There were imprisonments and even

executions. Needless to say, the Ustashi commanders and the cut-throats took to their heels on all sides, and left the poor people to pay for their crimes. Naturally all this has had a disastrous effect on the prospects for the conversion of the schismatics to Catholicism in Herzegovina. The wholesale butchery by the Ustashi commanders, the savagery of individuals, the incompetence of the higher authorities, have done grave harm not only to the Faith but to the nation. If God had given to those in authority the understanding and the sense to deal effectively with conversion, so that it could have been carried through more ably, more smoothly and by degrees, if that had been so, the number of Catholics might have been increased by at least five or six hundred thousand. Such a number is required in Bosnia and Herzegovina if there is to be an increase from 700,000 to 1,300,000."

The Archbishop of Upper Bosnia, His Excellency Mgr. Dr. Ivan Saric, writes on the 15th Novemeber, 1941 (No. 4107/41):

"The civil Government has taken the standpoint that as many as possible of the Greek Orthodox should be converted. But unfortunately it has in many cases acted very incorrectly. We have received complaints from many quarters that the civil authorities where Moslems are in control are rejecting the petitions of Orthodox who wish to be received into the Catholic Faith. In other places high taxes are imposed for changes of religion which the poorer classes cannot pay. It was so in Sarajevo, where the Town Council demanded a tax of 500 kuna, and we were obliged to approach the Government in Zagreb and beg it to suppress this regulation. Needless to say, such behaviour of local authorities is a great obstacle to conversion."

Further, His Excellency the Archbishop speaks about the propaganda of the Evangelical Confession. Its representatives have said that it is unnecessary for the Orthodox to become converted to the Catholic faith, and that their priests will return to them, but that if they are to be converted at all, it will be better for them to become Protestants, and so on.

His Excellency Pavao Butorac, the Bishop of Kotor and the Apostolic Administrator of the Diocese of Dubrovnik, writes on the 4th November, 1941 (No. 10/41):

"I well understand the importance of the subject to be discussed. From the recent instructions of the Ministry of Internal Affairs it can be seen that in the highest circles a better understanding of the conversion to the Catholic Faith begins to prevail. Any pressure could be fatal for the repute of the Catholic Church. We must reckon with every eventuality and even the possibility that the Serbs, out of defiance, may decide to be converted in masses to Islam. On that account it is my opinion that we must choose our missionaries among the Serbs with special care, and on no account entrust the problem to monks or priests who have no tact at all and who would be much better suited to carry a revolver in their hands than a cross."

LEADER!

From this report from the Croatian Bishops and also from the oral depositions of individual Ordinaries at the conferences, it is clear that many great mistakes have been made in the conversions.

The source of these mistakes lies in the fact that the work of conversion was not entrusted to that forum to which alone it should have been entrusted, according to the Law of God and the Canons of the Church – i.e., the Croatian Catholic Episcopate, who alone are authorised in this spiritual task to give the seal of the apostolate, and of holiness and of love. In this holy work they should act for the welfare and advantage of the Holy Catholic Church and the Croatian people united and liberated in the N.D.H. The work of conversion has been carried out by people who often acted as if there were no Church authorities. It is natural that they should have made mistake after mistake.

Above all, they did not have it before their eyes that the rites of the Church are not a dead thing or a formality which can be easily set on one side. There are customs which are not from yesterday but from the first centuries of Christianity. They have lived in the souls of men for more than sixteen hundred years. They give the tone to piety and to the whole spiritual life, they guide our feelings. They have become a part of the souls of the simple people, often more even than the truth of the Faith. The Holy Congregation of the Eastern Church, in its Declaration of 17th July, 1941, on this account, urges that Roman Catholic priests in Croatia should be instructed by their reverend superiors that in the case of conversions of schismatics, their natural return to the Eastern rite should not be impeded.

In addition, it must be affirmed that the psychological aspect of this problem is very important. Above all, we must be aware of the nature of the man whom we approach with the Catholic truth. We must know his past, his traditions, his feelings, then we must know the Orthodox Church in its structure in the past through the centuries and at the present time. It is not sufficient merely to know the differences of faith and to interpret them on the occasion of conversion, but it is necessary to know what echoes such distinctions may have in the dissident soul. We must know Orthodoxy not only in its dogmatic but also in its social and political field and in the field of culture. Everywhere one finds its terrible errors, as, for example, in Communism, which only in Orthodoxy could find such nourishment and support. The schism derived from resistance to authority; resistance gave birth to passions and, above all, to hatred; hatred has torn the

soul and the mind to shreds. In all fields of human activity
it has led to negation and revolution, to nihilism and extermination. That has been most evident not only in Russian
Bolshevism, but also long before in the religious struggle in
Russia between old tradition and new movements.

We must not deceive ourselves: Orthodoxy through the
centuries has moulded men here too, and they cannot overnight be changed in their ideas, they cannot overnight become something different in a mechanical way. In conversions
mere machinery may cause fatal consequences. That was
revealed in the conversions in Poland. Everything that had
been mechanically contrived, without fundamental education of the spirit, collapsed at the first favourable opportunity
like a house of cards. That was evident long before in Spain,
which is a really terrifying example of mechanical conversions because the converts turned against Catholicism and
the Spanish people and almost threatened the existence of
them both. That, too, was evident in the Latin Empire in
Constantinople. Mechanical methods brought hate with
them. For a little time it lay concealed and then burst out in
the flames of passion at the appropriate hour. Mechanical
methods have always built houses which were founded on
sand and not on rock, and when the winds and the storm
came there was nothing left of that house but great ruins.

Another fundamental mistake in conversions is that the
local authorities and the Ustashi functionaries on their own
account, in spite of the circular of the Government of the
Independent State of Croatia on 30th July, 1941, often forbade
any conversion of the Orthodox to Catholicism of the Greek
rite. Worse still, such conversions were often forbidden in
those districts in which Greek Catholics have been settled
for centuries in union with the Catholic Church. They were
only recently turned aside from unity and Croatia through

forcible Serbian propaganda, and united to anti-Croatian policy. It seems that these conversions were forbidden out of persistent political fears which, in any case, have no foundation, because the Greek Catholic clergy through three centuries in the most difficult circumstances and struggles have testified in their work to its Croatian character. On the other side, the work of this clergy has been crowned with success, as can be seen best among the Greek Catholic intellectuals and in the broad peasant masses of the people in Zhumberak and elsewhere.

Could not this Greek Catholic clergy of the Diocese of Krizhevtsi* do the same today there as in other districts with the same results, seeing that it has behind it the experience and traditions of centuries? In the Diocese of Krizhevtsi, instead of granting freedom to carry through conversions in the sense of the above-mentioned circular of the 30th July, Greek Catholic priests, such as Aleksandar Vlasov at Dishnik in Gareshnitsa district, was threatened because he carried out conversions in the territory of this parish, observing in every respect the circular, Article I. He was expelled across the frontier as an unwelcome guest, though he was a citizen of the Croatian State. In other places, as in Veliki Zdentsi in the same district, conversions of the Greek Orthodox to the Catholic Faith of the Greek rite were simply annulled, although they have been accomplished not only according to ecclesiastical but also according to civil regulations, which were in force at the time; in addition, they had the special permission of the Ministry of Justice and Religion. In other

---

* Križevci, near Zagreb, is the see of the eparchy of the Byzantine Church of Croatia, Serbia and Montenegro: that is, the Uniate or Eastern Rite Catholic Church in these territories. (Editors)

places again the local authorities, such as Dr. Jurina in Sokolovats at Koprivnitsa, issued a leaflet for the elders against the
"Uniate" Church. He threatened indirectly anyone who dared
to pass to the Catholic Faith of the Greek rite, saying that he
will not be guaranteed his civil rights. In other places again,
as, for instance, in Krizhevtsi during the Service of God in
the Cathedral Church, those who had been converted according to civil and ecclesiastical laws were dragged out of the
church under the eyes of the faithful and sent to concentration camps.

Further, communications from the State Office for Reconstruction have been sent to Greek Catholic priests. In
them without any intimation to the local Ordinary they have
been threatened with penalties, and Greek Catholics are
treated just as if they were Orthodox. In further cases, as it
was done by the secretary of the village Council of Gareshnitsa, it is maintained that only those are allowed into the
Greek Catholic Church who distinguished themselves in the
struggle against the Croatian people, though the exact contrary is the case. Only those who have been converted signed
the letter sent to the Leader in which they expressed their
sincere loyalty to Independent Croatia and to the Leader;
they confessed that they are happy to have been united to
the Croatian people, to which they have always been attached, but from which they were recently parted by violent
propaganda.

Apart from that, the Chetniks and the Communists in
the district of Prnjavor drove away all the Greek Catholic
priests except one from their parishes and plundered all their
houses; they took one of them as a hostage. So, on one side,
the Chetniks were converted to the Greek Catholic Faith, on
the other they became its bloody adversaries. It is to be noted
that the same Dr. A. Jurina, Town Clerk of Sokolovats, made

a further announcement in regard to the Uniate Faith, as he calls it. Such a name does not exist in Independent Croatia; it was used only by Yugoslavs and Serbs when they wished to curse the Catholics of the Greek Catholic rite and to divide them thereby from Croatia and Catholicism. So that you can judge for yourself about this action of Dr. Jurina, we enclose an authorised copy of these regulations and attached to it his order to the village elders against "the Uniate Faith and Church."

LEADER!

No one can deny that terrible crimes and cruelties have taken place since you yourself, Leader, have publicly condemned the violence of the various so-called Ustashi. What is more, you have had them executed on account of the crimes they have committed. Your determination that Law and Order should prevail in the land should deserve every recognition.

Up to this the Croatian people [has] behaved in accord with its thousand-year-old culture and Christian civilisation. Therefore, we expected that in practice, now that it has attained its freedom, it will show itself nobler and more humane than those who governed till lately.

The Church must from the standpoint of the Gospel condemn all crimes and outrages of irresponsible elements and immature youths, and it must demand complete respect for the human personality without regard to age, sex, faith, nation or race, because all people are the children of God and Christ "qui vult omnes homines salvos fieiri," died for them all.

We believe, Leader, that you share this opinion with us, and that you will do what is in your power to restrain the violence of individuals, so that only the responsible authorities may rule and govern the land. In the contrary case all work for the conversion of the schismatics is illusory. Receive, Leader, the assurance of my sincere respect.

A.S., Archbishop, P.M.
Zagreb, 20th November, 1941

III

The following is the resolution passed by the Bishops' Conference in November, 1941, which accompanied Mgr. Stepinac's letter to Pavelitch:

Resolution of Conversion
17th November, 1941

LEADER!

The Croatian Catholic Bishops gathered together in their annual plenary conference on 17th and 18th November of this year, have made the following decisions about the conversion of the Orthodox to the Catholic Faith:

(1) They consider it a dogmatic principle that the solution of all questions touching the conversion of the Orthodox to the Catholic Faith falls *exclusively* within the competence of the Catholic ecclesiastical hierarchy, which alone is authorised by the Law of God and by the Canons of the Church to supervise religious conversions and to impose rules, so that no action is taken contrary to the authority of the Church.

(2) On that account no one outside the Catholic ecclesiastical hierarchy has the right to appoint "missionaries" to attempt the conversion of the Orthodox to the Catholic Faith. Every such "missionary" must obtain appointment and authority for his spiritual work from his local Ordinary. In

addition, it is against dogma and canon law that "missionaries" should, without consent of the local Ordinary Bishop, obtain missionary authority from the local or regional offices, from the Ustashi functionaries, from the Department for Religious Affairs of the State Board for Reconstruction, or from any other secular sources.

(3) Every such "missionary" must in his spiritual task be responsible only to the local ordinary either directly, or indirectly through the local parish priest.

(4) The Catholic Church can recognise as valid only those conversions which have been carried out or shall be carried out according to these *dogmatic principles.*

(5) The secular authorities cannot "annul" those conversions, which have been registered by the Church not only according to the Laws of the Church but also according to the Laws of the State.

(6) The Croatian Catholic Bishops on this account have chosen from among themselves a committee of three, as follows: The President of the Episcopal Conference; the Bishop of Senj, Mgr. Dr. Viktor Buritch; and the Apostolic Administrator of the Bishopric of Krizhevtsi, Dr. Janko Shimrak. This committee shall apply itself to the solution of all these questions which come within the province of the conversion of the Orthodox to the Catholic Faith. It will work in collaboration with the Minister of Justice and Religion in whatever affects the civil regulations about conversions.

(7) As a Working Executive Committee regarding the conversion of the Orthodox to the Catholic Faith the Croatian Catholic Bishops have chosen: Dr. Franjo Herman, Professor of the Theological Faculty of Zagreb; Dr. Augustin Juretitch, consultant of the Bishops' Conference; Dr. Janko Kalaj, Lecturer in Divinity in the middle schools and reader in the Glagolithic in the Theological Faculty; Nikola Boritch, Director of the Chancellery of the Zagreb Archbishopric; and Dr.

Krunoslav Draganovitch, Professor in the Theological Faculty. This Committee will solve all questions relating to the conversion of the Orthodox to the Catholic Church under the control of the Episcopal Committee for Conversion.

(8) Only those can be received into the Catholic Church, who go completely of their own will without any constraint, from innermost conviction of the truth of the Catholic Faith, and who have fulfilled the Laws of the Church in their entirety.

(9) As regards the rites of conversion the Croatian Catholic Episcopate adopts in its entirety the regulation of the Sacred Congregation of the Eastern Church of the 17th July, 1941, Prot. N. 216/36, which was sent to the President of the Bishops' Conference, and which runs as follows: "The Sacred Congregation of the Eastern Church draws Your Excellency's attention to the fact that Roman Catholic priests in Croatia shall be enjoined by their reverend Bishops that, in the event of the conversion of schismatics, they do not oppose their natural return to the Eastern rite, when dealing with those who were previously members of the Catholic Church of the Eastern rite, but under the threats and pressure of the Orthodox departed from the Catholic Faith. If Your Excellency explains this requirement to his honourable brethren in Croatia he will once more earn merit by his valuable contribution towards right development where so many hopes exist for the conversion of the schismatic. I gladly profit by the occasion to renew the expression of my respect and I sign myself, Your Excellency's devoted brother, Cardinal Eugen Tisserant, manu propria, secretary; Ant. Arata, Archbishop of Sard, manu propria, assessor."

The Croatian Catholic Episcopate received precisely the same instructions from the Holy Apostolic See on the 18th October, 1941, which runs: "Wherever there already exists an organised parish of the Greek Catholic rite, such schismatics as wish to return to the Faith may be directed to such parishes; but supposing that the schismatics will not or cannot maintain their Eastern rite, they must be permitted to adopt the Latin rite."

These two regulations have been adopted by the Croatian Catholic Episcopate; moreover, they are, in general lines, in accord with the rulings of the circular of the Government of Independent Croatia, 30th July, 1941, No. 46468/1941, in clause 1, on condition:

(a) That under Greek Catholic parishes we are to take into account not only the administrative centre of the parish, but also its territory, as this has been defined by the Canons of the Church and State in times past – that is to say, not only the parent parish but also its affiliated branches;

(b) That conversions to the Catholic Church of the Greek Catholic rite, where conducted in conformity with the Church Law, cannot be annulled. That would be in conflict with Canon Law; in such cases, too, all the civil laws will have been observed.

(c) That all who are not in accord with this standpoint should bring their problems to the Committee of the Episcopate for conversions, which will solve them.

(d) In this connection, the local authorities are forbidden to interfere. In the spiritual work of the Church no secular organisation at all must intervene, because that could only injure the good work.

(10) The Committee of the Catholic Episcopate for conversions will organise courses for those priests who are accomplishing conversions from the Orthodox to the Catholic Church. In these courses they will receive theoretical and practical guidance for their work.

This text of the resolution of the Croatian Catholic Episcopate is sent to all Roman and Greek Catholic Parochial Councils with the instruction that it be strictly observed in

the question of the conversion of the Greek Orthodox to the
Catholic Church.

DR. ALOISIUS STEPINAC,
President of the Bishops' Conference

From typed draft, omitted in printed resolution:

(11) A psychological basis for conversion must be created
among the Greek Orthodox inhabitants. With this in view,
they must not only be guaranteed but also granted all civic
rights and, particularly, the right of personal freedom and
the right of ownership. All illegal activities against the personal freedom and the property of the Greek Orthodox must
be most strictly forbidden; penalties must be imposed on the
Orthodox, as upon other citizens, only after due legal proceedings. It is of the first importance that every destructive
attack by an individual upon Orthodox churches and chapels
must be most strictly punished, so, too, with the expropria-
tion of Orthodox property.

The following notes, in the handwriting of Dr. Budak, were found
among his papers after the liberation:

Dr. Mile Budak, Minister of Religion and Education:
Notes for Talk with the Archbishop

Conversion of Serbs:

(1) The problem of Serbs cannot be solved by imprisonment and killing and persecution.
(2) We wish to solve this problem for now and always by
the method of conversion.

(3) I consider that the Catholic Church cannot be opposed to a definite, well-thought-out and methodical plan for the conversion of the Serbs.

(4) The Government authorities are prepared to lend all their moral and material means to support the organisation and accomplishment of conversion.

(5) We consider that in a scheme for conversion the following should be taken into consideration:

(a) A central committee should be formed. It would be composed of priests and would always be active, examining every possible course, making decisions in concrete instances, giving advice and promoting the accomplishment of conversion. The council would not be appointed by the public, but would come under the exclusive control of the Archbishop of Zagreb, but if similar sub-councils should be formed in other dioceses, then such sub-councils should come under the control of the Bishop in the dioceses concerned.

(b) Opening of monasteries in our bigger centres of Orthodox population; they should receive the greatest moral and material support from the state.

(c) The best and most active Croat priests should be appointed to those places in which conversion has been successfully started.

(d) There should be a special, well-considered plan to try to influence into conversion those people who have been married to Orthodox Christians.

(e) Accurate statistics should be drawn up about conversions and the State authorities should be informed immediately.

(f) A special monthly, weekly, or something similar, for the newly-converted, should be issued.

(g) Every possible facility, which the Catholic Church permits, should be given for entering the Catholic Church;

perhaps special facilities from the Vatican should be obtained.

(h) The Minister of Religion and Education should be informed about the course of conversion, its difficulties, etc., so that in this way it could be arranged for conversions to be carried out in the most satisfactory and complete way.

(1950-1951)

A Visit to Lepoglava

The prison of Lepoglava, which I visited with four Quakers, lies to the south of Varazhdin, some 100 kilometres north of Zagreb. We drove through small wooded hills and beside maize fields, where golden pumpkins crawled in the stubble between the stooks. In the vineyards the grapes had been stripped but the farmers had not yet started to harvest the buckwheat or the hemp and sunflowers. It is a hedgeless country where cows and pigs wonder about attended by some old woman or a child. I noticed that there were many roadside shrines and it was hard to believe that we were in a Communist country.

The prison itself, sitting in a valley to the right of the road, is a large rectangular space enclosed by a wall with corner turrets. In the centre is a battered church. As we drove up, we saw a group of blue-uniformed soldiers at the entrance and a young, rather bewildered officer asked to see our passports and then changed his mind and said he didn't require them. We went into a hall decorated with the usual frescoes of the Partisan War and the "industrialized collectivized Future" and then up a temporary-looking staircase to the governor's office. He was young and squat, in a new brown suit and brown cloth cap, with gold black teeth. Harold Evans explained why we had come. The governor then invited us to call in on him after we had seen Mgr. Stepinac: he promised to answer any of our questions. He led us out the way we had come, outside the prison walls and through another gate, to a small courtyard at the end of which was an ornamental red-brick building. At the top of a flight of steps we found a short passage, and opening the second door on the right, we found ourselves face to face with Mgr. Stepinac.

Those who have not visited a prison before would have been disconcerted at the smallness and bareness of the cell and the helplessness of the prisoner in face of intruders. But my Quaker friends told me that as cells went, it was a good one – the semi-circular window, which was high up, was large enough, there was a washstand with an enamel basin, a shelf with about thirty books, a hanging cupboard for clothes and a low iron bed. Through a door on the left we could see a small chapel and we were told that there were two priests, free men living in the prison, to assist at Mass. The archbishop had been working at his typewriter but now, as he stood upright against the wall, I was struck by the slightness of his figure and his sad, strained expression. His colour was good and his black hair unmarked by grey.

Harold Evans spoke to him at first in English – he told him what great interest the trial had excited in America and said that when he returned he would be eagerly questioned about this visit. "What can I tell them about you?" he asked. When this was translated, the archbishop asked in French if any of us spoke that language. We said we did and the archbishop, continuing in French, answered that in the circumstances in which he found himself it was better for him to say nothing – "Rien," he repeated emphatically.

I went over to him then and said that I was an Irishman, and that his case had roused great interest and sympathy in Ireland too. He seemed pleased at my saying this and when I explained that I was a Protestant, he interrupted me pleasantly to say that that made no difference. I had not gone to the prison out of idle curiosity and, as soon as I got a chance, I was determined to ask certain questions of the archbishop. I said I had read a letter he had written to Pavelitch, the Quisling leader of Croatia, protesting against the barbarity with which the conversion campaign had been conducted and that I had never doubted his dislike of cruelty. But why, when he wised to regulate this campaign, had he chosen as one of his two collaborators Mgr. Shimrak, Apostolic administrator of the Greek Catholic (Uniate) Church? Mgr.

Shimrak's enthusiasm for the disgraceful conversion campaign had been well known and publicly expressed. I had myself looked up his published address in his diocesan magazine of *Krizhevtsi*. I added how awkward I felt as a free man asking these questions and admitted I had no right to press for an answer. The archbishop gave the stock reply he had so often given at his trial (which incidentally has become the stock answer among the flippant of Zagreb to any awkward question): "*Notre conscience est tranquille.*"

William Edgerton, I am glad to say, persisted. The question is of supreme importance for all thinking Christians. Edgerton asked whether the compulsory conversions could not have been stopped if the Croatian bishops had together solemnly and formally denounced the campaign. Mgr. Stepinac possibly did not understand the question: he said with some heat that he had never urged forcible conversion of a single soul and that the Catholic Church had never done so, and he repeated, "*Notre conscience est tranquille.*" Asked if he thought there was anything Christians could do to avoid another war, the archbishop replied, "At the present time there is no recourse but prayer," and to the question of whether spiritual ends could ever be reached by war, he answered, "Spiritual error can only be conquered by spiritual methods" – "*La guerre est un moyen très mal... mais ici je ne sais rien du monde, rien, je n'entends rien.*" His French was rather bad, and it occurred to me that he avoided German because at the time of his imprisonment it had given offence in Yugoslavia, though now, after four years, it is again freely spoken.

We asked him if he had everything he needed and he said, "*Je suis content. Si c'était nécessaire, je resterais ici heureusement, non sieze ans, mais cent sieze ans. Je sais pourquoi je souffre!*" He told us he was translating from the French into Croatian some *Lives of the Saints* which had been published in Paris. He said books were permitted, and I got the impression he might like to be sent them. Then we thanked him, he replied politely and we left. Our visit may not have given him pleasure but I don't think that it annoyed him.

My Quaker friends catechized the governor closely in his upstairs room, asking him questions about the treatment of his prisoners, about Prisoners' Aid Societies, educational facilities, etcetera. The impression we got was of a regime of average enlightenment, applied perhaps with some roughness. Then William Edgerton remembered to ask about the Jehovah's Witnesses, eighteen of whom had been condemned to death, commuted to life sentences and various terms of imprisonment in 1947. As their trial, a much publicized one, had been in Zagreb, it would be natural to suppose they might be in Lepoglava, but the governor had heard of neither them nor their trial. Their case had been so little understood – they had been accused of reactionary activities of behalf of foreign imperialists – that it would not have surprised us if they were, in fact, in Lepoglava, with the exact reason for their detention unknown. We determined to enquire about them further in Zagreb. A sect whose members were attacked in Ireland as agents of Communism were apparently punished in Yugoslavia as agents of foreign capitalism, a comic situation if it were not desperately tragic for these poor fanatics. In fact, till Armageddon, they were wholly committed to pacifism.

The governor told us that prisoners were allowed to receive parcels and letters twice a month, and Mgr. Stepinac had been offered special food but had refused to accept preferential treatment. When I got back to Zagreb I learnt from the British Consul that the prison governor was a more sympathetic character than could be judged in our short encounter. A Yugoslav, well-known to the staff of the Consulate, had been imprisoned there for a time in a cell adjoining Mgr. Stepinac's. He had been visited by members of the British Consulate and, on his release, had discussed his experiences freely. He said that the governor had always listened carefully to complaints and petitions and, where possible, agreed to amelioration.

Mgr. Stepinac in prison is a figure who commands respect. What he did, he did in the belief that it was right. Christians who think otherwise – and there are many millions of them – would mostly agree that while he remains in prison, the focus of violent emotions, there is little hope of a dispassionate enquiry into the tragic story of 1941. He must be an embarrassing prisoner, but his cause has been mishandled by ill-informed champions. I was told by M. Wimpulsek, the President of the Court which condemned him, that it is unlikely he will be released so long as the Yugoslav government fears that clemency will be interpreted as capitulation to pressure from the West.

The whole Stepinac question is very much more complicated than the ordinary man is aware but it is not necessary to go to Yugoslavia to learn this. A glance at *The Martyrdom of the Serbs*, published in Chicago by the Serbian Orthodox Church, will show that this is not a simple issue of Communist versus Christian. Had Mikhailovitch, the Serbian monarchist, and not Tito, been the victor in the war against the Germans, the trial of Mgr Stepinac could scarcely have been avoided. Tito offered to suspend the trial if the archbishop was withdrawn to Rome, but the offer was rejected. It is just possible that what was refused to a Communist government might, if requested, have been conceded to an Orthodox one.

(1951)

The Invader Wore Slippers

During the war, we in Ireland heard much of the jackboot and how we should be trampled beneath it, if Britain's protection failed us. We thought we could meet this challenge as well as any other small nation, and looking into the future, our imagination, fed on the daily press, showed us a technicolour picture of barbarity and heroism.

It never occurred to us that for ninety per cent of the population the moral problems of an occupation would be small and squalid. Acting under pressure we should often have to choose between two courses of action, both inglorious. And, if there was moral integrity about our choice, it certainly would not get into the headlines.

We did not ask ourselves: "Supposing the invader wears not jackboots but carpet slippers or patent leather pumps, how will I behave, and the respectable Xs, the patriotic Ys and the pious Zs?" How could we? The newspapers only told us about the jackboots.

The newspapers have by this time worked the subject of resistance to the Nazis to death. They have passed on to livelier issues, so it is possible to anatomize this now dessicated topic in a quite callous way. We can forget about the heroic or villainous minority or those other irreconcilables who adhered to some uncompromising political or religious creed. We can look only at the ordinary people, the Xs, the Ys and the Zs, about whom there is a mass of documentation. By a little careful analogy and substitution we can see ourselves, and a picture of our home under occupation emerges with moderate clarity. It is more like an X-ray photo than a war film. It is quite unglamorous and perhaps it is only by the trained mind that the darker shadows can be interpreted.

In totalitarian war human nature is reduced to its simplest terms and a skilled invader can predict with fair accuracy the behaviour of the respectable Xs, the patriotic Ys, the pious Zs. Of course there are innumerable divagations but in an avalanche it is the valleys and the riverbeds that count, the hundred thousand cart tracks can be disregarded.

I know that we Irish were not more complex than anyone else and that our percentages of Xs, Ys, and Zs were about average and known to every likely invader. And I dismissed as inapplicable to us the propaganda stories of the jackboot with which the allies tried to shake our neutrality. We did not, I thought, like most of the Slav regions, belong to the area of German colonization in which extermination and spiritual enslavement would be practised. And it seemed to me that the respectable Xs who told us the reverse were speaking either without reflection or with concealed motives. It was surprising when the inevitable volte-face came after the war. The people who had been threatening us with the jackboot in places where no sensible invader would dream of using it, began to applaud his restraint. Indulgent things were said of generals, even jackbooted ones like von Manstein, "who simply did their duty," and Rommel's biography was widely read in those pleasant Dublin suburbs where the Xs live.

It seems to me that we civilian Irish, finding indulgence where we had been led to expect violence, might easily have been tricked into easy-going collaboration. Yet small peoples should become specialists in the art of non-cooperation with tyranny. It is the only role we can play when the great powers clash, and we are hopelessly untrained in it.

Careful observation of precedent and analogy is the first need. This can be done best in small circumscribed regions, whose characters are fairly homogenous. I found three such occupied zones within my reach, where the tactics of the invader with the Xs, Ys and Zs severally were displayed as on a small diagram which could be indefinitely enlarged.

There were the Channel Islands where the respectable Xs were in the majority, Brittany, where the influence of the romantically patriotic Ys was strong, Croatia, where the Ys were reinforced by the fervently pious Zs.

The policy of the invader in all these places, and the response it met, is best studied in the newspapers of the occupation. Reminiscences of course are helpful but they are usually written by men who are exceptional either for their independence of mind or their complacency. They are edited to flatter the vanity of their compatriots, seldom to chasten it. But the newspapers show the invader at his highly skilled task of manipulating the Xs and Ys and Zs. Reading between the lines you can judge of his success.

I think it was only in Zagreb that I found easy access to the files, though even there I was met with some suspicion and surprise. The reason was that in Zagreb a revolution had taken place which had, temporarily at least, undermined the natural desire of every nation to conceal its weaknesses from itself, or in the smooth phraseology of self-deception, to "let bygones be bygones." Somebody before me had been over the files in the university library with faint pencil marks and an incriminating collection of the acta and dicta of the Xs, Ys and Zs had been published.

This had certainly not been done in Rennes, the capital of Brittany. In Jersey there is an excellent museum of the occupation but it deals with the behaviour of the Germans and not with that of the Jersey people themselves. And in the newspaper room of the British Museum I searched in vain for the Jersey newspapers which were published all through the war, and had to be content with the incomplete Guernsey file, the personal gift of a Guernsey man. This indifference of the British archivist to the history of the Channel Islands under occupation struck me as curious and significant. Has the national mind, like its individual prototype, some Freudian censor, which automatically suppresses what is shameful or embarrassing?

The public does not want a truthful account of occupation. It prefers to switch over from extremes of reprobation to extremes of

condonation. You will see what I mean if you read the most authoritative book on the occupation of Jersey by R.C. Maugham. The publisher
appears to be about four years behind the author. On the dust-cover
the title, "Jersey under the Jackboot," is illustrated by a big cruel boot
crashing down on a helpless little green island and the blurb talks of
the "courage and fortitude of the islanders" and "the misery, ignominy
and privations that marked the trail of the Nazi hordes across the face
of Europe." But the author makes it plain that the islanders were subjected to a more subtle instrument of pressure than the jackboot. They
were very liberally treated indeed. The small island parliaments and
courts continued to function, provided al their measures were submitted to German sanction. It was by an ordinance of the Guernsey Royal
Court that all talk against the Germans was made punishable; thus
when the manager of the Rich's stores was cheeky to a German cus-
tomer, it was before the Guernsey Court that he appeared. He got off
by explaining that it was all a mistake, that the German officers had
all been charming and his son-in-law was taking German lessons. Divine service with prayers for the Royal family and the Empire were
permitted. So were cinemas and newspapers.

In an organized society our dependence on the newspapers is abject.
The readers of the *Guernsey Evening Post* were shocked and repelled no
doubt to see articles by Goebbels and Lord Haw-Haw, but not to the
pitch of stopping their subscriptions. How else could they advertise
their cocker spaniels and their lawn mowers or learn about the cricket
results? Ultimately Haw-Haw became an accepted feature like the
testimonials for digestive pills, and an edge of horror and revulsion
was blunted. Here is the printed summary of events for an October day
in the first year of the occupation.

"Dog-biscuits made locally. Table-tennis League of Six Teams
formed. German orders relating to measures against Jews published.
Silver Wedding anniversary of Mr and Mrs W.J. Bird." The news of the
deportation and torture of local shopkeepers is made more palatable
by being sandwiched between sport and domestic pets and society
gossip. "Lady Ozanne had passed a fairly good night." "Mr Stephen

Candon is as comfortable as can be expected." There was Roller Skating at St George's Hall and "Laugh it Off" was still retained at The Regal and "the bride looked charming in a white georgette frock." Lubricated by familiar trivialities, the mind glided over what was barbarous and terrible.

The *Herrenvolk* philosophy judiciously applied, as it was in the Channel Islands, can be swallowed easily enough if you have not too sensitive a digestion and belong to a ruling race yourself. Flowerbeds were trampled, housemaids whistled to, garden tools unceremoniously borrowed, but formal apologies, printed receipts were often forthcoming if applied for. "I must record," wrote Mr Maugham, of the German soldiers in his garage, "they did their best to give us as little trouble as possible, were perfectly polite and grateful for any slight help which they received from us," and the Procurator of Guernsey officially declared: "The Germans behaved as good soldiers, sans peur et sans reproche."

Such behaviour is plainly more formidable than the jackboot, we are hypnotized by the correctness of the invader into accepting invasion itself as correct. The solidarity of our resistance is undermined by carefully graded civilities, our social and racial hierarchies are respected. For example in Jersey there were Irish tomato pickers and Russian prisoners at whose expense German prestige was adroitly raised in British eyes. When wireless sets were confiscated the Irish, with disdainful correctness, were paid for theirs as they were neutrals. This punctiliousness was more repaying than jackboots since it drove a wedge of jealousy between English and Irish. When later on a feud broke out between the "correct" occupation troops and some "incorrect" naval ratings who daubed the shop fronts of St Helier with swastikas, the authorities blamed this breach of etiquette upon the Irish, and there were some gentlemanly headshakings between the German and English officials over these vulgar antics of an inferior breed.

I don't think the Germans on the island had a difficult task in making the Russians in Jersey detested. Some of the Russians, who were employed in the fortification of the island, were convicts liberated from prison in the German advance into Russia. They were worked hard, fed little and flogged. A whip that was used on them can be seen in the Jersey Museum. They were inadequately guarded. Almost mad with hunger, they broke loose and pillaged the neat holdings of the Jersey farmers, taking hens, pigs, cabbages, clothes from the line. These raids began through the carelessness of the guards, continued through their connivance and finally had their active encouragement. The guards indicated the eligible premises and exacted a huge percentage of the plunder. When the Jersey people asked for protection they were met with a humorous shrug from the officials. "Well, they are your allies. Must *we* protect you from them?"

It is hard for the Xs to keep a balanced judgement in such circumstances. Other problems too arise. Should they acknowledge the salute of the aimiable Rittmeister, who had known their cousins at Weybridge? Should they turn the other cheek when a degenerate Mongol ally robs the hen-roost? These problems are more disintegrating to the resistance of the Xs than bombs or jackboots, and a competent invader will make them inescapable.

In a Zagreb newspaper of 1942, *Deutsche Zeitung in Kroatien*, I read that Ireland, with Croatia and Slovakia, was to be one of the three model "allied" states in German Europe. In other papers too there was much of flattering intent about the common loyalty of Croats and Irish to Faith and Fatherland, our similar histories, romantic temperaments and literary gifts. Irish plays continued to be played in Zagreb, when English were tabu.

All the same I think that Brittany under the Nazis offers more profitable analogies for us in Ireland than does Croatia. In Brittany the German attempt to exploit the patriotism of the Ys and the piety of the Zs, which in Croatia had been triumphantly successful, was only half-hearted. The Nazis had no doubt of the need to disintegrate Yugoslavia, they were undecided about France. Perhaps, after defeat, France might be won over more easily if her unity was not impaired, perhaps a separatist and Celtic Brittany might slip out of German influence and look westward to Celtic Wales. Also in Brittany the Catholic Church did not support the separatist movement, as it did in Croatia. There was no wide-scale convergence of patriotism and piety. By conciliating the patriotic Ys, the Germans might risk offending the pious Zs.

For all these reasons Nazi policy in Brittany was very inconsistent. The Germans sheltered the Breton rebel leaders, Mordrel and Debauvais, as they had once sheltered Roger Casement and they too were invited to recruit a rebel army to fight for independence among the prisoners of war. The Breton prisoners responded in the same halfhearted way as the Irish had once done. The Germans, however, continued to support the Breton movement till France had been brought to her knees. Then they made terms with Vichy, withdrew all aid from the Breton separatists and allowed them to operate only against the Maquis. They led the Bretons the sort of dance that cannot be done in jackboots.

I think the Nazi policy in regard to Ireland would have been equally agile and ambiguous. The Celtic nationalist would, as in Brittany, have been regarded as a valuable tool for undermining a non-German hegemony, but of decidedly less value for the reconstruction of a German one. The nationalist would have been manoeuvred, not kicked, out of his privileged position.

Judging by the Breton analogy, I think the first impact of the changed policy might have been borne by the handful of single-minded German Celtophiles, who would have been entrusted with the early stages of the programme. A successfully double-faced policy requires at the start the complicity of many single-minded idealists, native and foreign.

I think when the success of the invasion had been assured, it would have emerged that the respectable Xs, the Anglo-Irish *Herrenvolk* of Ulster and the Dublin suburbs, would prove the more satisfactory accomplices in establishing the German hegemony. The Jersey treatment would have been applied to them, insofar as they were civilians. There would have been a dazzling display of "correctness." It is probable that at Greystones and Newtownards, as at St Helier and at Peterport, divine service with prayers for the King and the British Empire would

continue to be permitted in the Protestant churches. Certainly the
inevitable bias of German correctness would have been towards the
Anglo-Saxon, towards bridge and fox hunting, and away from the Irish,
from ceilidhes and hurley matches and language festivals. A master
race will be at times indulgent to these regional enthusiasms but will
not participate in them. Ultimately this bias would have led to a complete reversal of policy, more in keeping with the *Herrenvolk* philosophy. Lord Haw-Haw, an Irishman himself, seems to have been in closer
sympathy with the Mosleyites than with the Irish republicans. The
British Naziphiles were romantic, traditional, imperialist. Irish separatism would have been incompatible with their Kiplingesque ideal of
a merry, beer-drinking "old" England, allied with Germany, grasping
once more in her strong right hand the reins of empire and dealing out
firm justice to the lesser breeds. I do not see how the Irish could have
raised themselves permanently into the *Herrenvolk* class from which
Czechs and Poles had been excluded. Of course the Croats had arrived
there. But they must have felt their position precarious, because two
well-known Croatian scholars, Father Shegitch and Professor Butch,
developed the theory that the Croats were really Goths who had slipped
into a Slav language by some accident. Pavelitch, the "Leader" of Croatia, who had a private passion for philology, favoured the theory and
brought out a Croat lexicon in which all words of Serbian origin were
eliminated, a work of great ingenuity because the Serbian and Croatian
languages are all but identical. We Irish would inevitably have felt
uneasy. There had been in Ireland eminent German Celtic scholars
who had not managed to conceal their contempt for the modern representatives of those Celtic peoples whose early history enthralled
them. Nazi philosophy was permeated with race snobbery and we are
outwardly a rustic and unpretentious people. When a Nazi leader,
Ribbentrop, visited Ireland, it was with a Unionist leader, Lord Lon-
donderry, at Newtownards that he stayed. In the Nazi hierarchy of
races the Irish would not I think have ranked high.

It is likely that ultimately more attention would have been paid to
out piety than to our patriotism. Its pattern is universal and familiar

and so more easily faked, whereas patriotism has so many regional variations that no ready-made formula could be devised to fit them all. Many of the pious Zs would have responded to skilful handling. The other day I read in an Irish newspaper the sermon of a well-known preacher. "The world," he said, "may one day come to be grateful to Hitler." He was thinking, of course, of Communism and it was the constant preoccupation of the Nazis that the minds of the pious should always be inflamed with the fear of it. In that way charity and humanity, where they were only superficial, could be skinned away like paint under a blow-lamp. But in the technique of perverting piety it was in the Independent State of Croatia that the Nazis first showed their consummate skill. Pavelitch's Croatia deserves the closest study.

When an incendiary sets a match to respectability, it smoulders malodorously, but piety, like patriotism, goes off like a rocket. The jackboot was worn by the Croats themselves and used so vigorously against the schismatic Serbs that the Germans and the Italians, who had established the little state, were amazed. Pavelitch, the regicide ruler of Croatia, was himself the epitome, the personification, of the extraordinary alliance of religion and crime, which for four years made Croatia the model for all satellite states in German Europe. He was extremely devout, attending Mass every morning with his family in a private chapel built onto his house. He received expressions of devoted loyalty from the leaders of the Churches, including the Orthodox, whose murdered metropolitan had been replaced by a subservient nominee. He gave them medals and enriched their parishes with the plundered property of the schismatics, and he applied the simple creed of One Faith, One Fatherland, with a literalness that makes the heart stand still. It was an equation which had to be solved in blood. Nearly two million Orthodox were offered the alternatives of death or conversion to the faith of the majority. The protests of the Xs, Ys and Zs were scarcely audible.

Yet, as I read the newspaper files in Zagreb, I felt that it was not the human disaster but the damage done to honoured words and thoughts that was most irreparable. The letter and the spirit had been wrested violently apart and a whole vocabulary of Christian goodness had blown inside out like an umbrella in a thunderstorm.

It is easy to illustrate this from the newspapers of a single week in spring 1941. In one Zagreb paper, for example, the king's speech on the bombing of Belgrade was published with appropriate comments of April 10.

"On the morning of Palm Sunday," he said, "while children slept their innocent sleep and the church bells were ringing for prayer to God, the German aeroplanes without warning let fall a rain of bombs on this historic town…" and the king went on to describe the terror of the women and children, who were machine-gunned as they fled from their homes, by low-flying planes.

The following day the Germans in Panzer divisions arrived in Zagreb. Flags were out in the streets to welcome them and the same paper wrote in solemn phrases: "God's providence in concord with the resolve of our allies has brought it about that today on the eve of the resurrection of the Son of God our Independent Croatian State is also resurrected… all that is right and true in Christianity stands on the side of the Germans"!

When Pavelitch fell, the Zs had to take a third somersault. Words had by then lost all relation to fact and thereafter there was something schizophrenic about the exaggerations of the Croatian Zs and their sympathizers. Rather than admit their horrible inadequacy, they plunged about in contrary directions, sometimes whitewashing Pavelitch, sometimes making him blacker than life.

Many were able to turn head over heels in a quiet, gentlemanly way. For example the Bishop of Djakovo, Dr Akshamovitch, who received the Delegation from the National Peace Council, of which I was a member, in a very friendly way, was a kind old man of whom we already knew a little. Under Pavelitch circulars flowed from his diocesan printing press headed "Friendly Advice," reminding the Serbs that Jesus had said there was to be one flock and one shepherd and that, as Catholics, they could stay in their homes, improve their properties and educate their children.

When Tito came to power the bishop is said to have invited the Central Committee of the Croatian Communist Party to lunch. He certainly attended a Peace Meeting in Belgrade. His photograph was printed in the press, as was his speech, in which warm praise was given to Tito. Should one charge him with opportunism? At this range one cannot judge him, but what is clear is that both governments valued his support and profited by it.

In future wars, if there are any, the formulae of corruption will be a little different but the principle will be the same. It may be said that the respectable Xs will only be wooed by the invader if he comes from a capitalist country, but that, if he is Communist, no dangerous flirtations need be feared. I am not so sure. Acquisitive, tenacious, timidly orthodox people are not confined to any class or creed. It is a matter of temperament rather than of social standing or of politics. They have the force of inertia, which all invaders will wish to have on their side. As for piety and patriotism, whether they are deep or superficial, they are ineradicable from the human race. In the long run the modern state, east or west, will try to assimilate the Xs, Ys and Zs, not to exterminate them.

Horace once wrote that the honest man, innocent of crime, could protect himself without Moorish javelins, without his bow or his quiver full of poisoned arrows. But is ordinary innocence enough nowadays or must he cultivate the unseeing eye? Must he not "mind his own business" like the professional man, or "simply do his duty and carry out orders" like the soldier, or like the tradesman "just get on with the job?" (The Channel Island papers are full of cheery synonyms for connivance!) Are we really obliged to admire the armour-plated innocence and respectability of General Rommel, that "preux chevalier" of the subscription libraries? He concentrated so fiercely on his professional duties that ten years after Hitler came to power he was still able to be ignorant of, and shocked by, the Jewish extermination policy, by gas-chambers and the destruction of Warsaw. I don't think these questions can be answered unless we isolate them and study them in a small more or less homogeneous area. It is clear that small peoples are used as guinea pigs by the great powers. Experiments are tried out on them which are later applied on a wider scale. Their suffering and their reaction to suffering are studied but only for selfish, imperialistic ends. Should not the results of these experiments be recorded now while the memory is still fresh and accuracy and candour are available? For though such knowledge will not of itself bring us the will or the courage to resist tyranny, it will prevent us from dispersing our strength in fighting against shadows. By learning from which direction the most insidious attacks are likely to come, we may acquire the skill to forestall them.

(1950)

Ireland and Croatia

Few events in Europe excited such widespread interest in Ireland as the trial of Archbishop Stepinac and the struggle between the Catholic Church in Yugoslavia and the Yugoslav government. It was as though after six years of discreet silence, we had at last found a subject about which we could safely vent our repressed indignation. Croatia is a remote, little-known part of Europe, and this made it very strange that our press, our parliament, our county council, which had been silent when one country after another had been overrun by Germany, should suddenly pass resolutions of protest in the strongest and boldest language. Some would say that we dared so much because we were not likely to be punished for our candour. I think it would be more true to say that fundamentally we are idealists and suspected that ideals had played a subordinate part in the war from which we had abstained. On the other hand the victims of the Yugoslav government appeared to be both Croatian patriots and Christians... and patriotism and piety particularly when they have gone hand in hand have always earned applause in Ireland. It seemed in fact a clear case where Truth and Error were squarely confronted.

I was brought up an Irish Protestant and I think it is implicit, if not explicit, in our belief that the Truth, which is a phrase we seldom use, is built up of many lesser truths, or perhaps it is always in the process of rebuilding, for as we grow wiser we grow more fastidious. We demand a higher standard of accuracy, a keener courage in applying it. No single man has at any time the right or the power to say what is true and what is not. We shrink from pontificating and taking sides, and at its worst, this tendency degenerates into complacency and indifference. Of course, there are many brands of Protestantism that are militant and dogmatic, and I am, perhaps, being unfairly selective in admiring the ones that are neither. I believe there is most future today for Protestantism where it is least dogmatic – when, that is to say, it is most concerned with the patient discovery of the truth rather than the violent propagation of The Truth.

I don't think I have exaggerated the commotion caused in Ireland by the Stepinac trials, though I have found a strong tendency among Irish editors of the liberal stamp to dismiss it with a shrug of the shoulders. Don't argue with those people, they say, you'll get nowhere at all. Write where you'll be understood, write in England, and write in some serious monthly where people use their reason and not their primitive instincts. This seems to rest on the assumption that we write for those who agree with us only, and that the best way to confute error is to talk about it with those who have not erred, because they have never had the temptation. Controversy in Ireland is usually barren, because when we are hard pressed, and conscious that the Irish Majority is against us, we raise our voices in the hope of hearing a reassuring echo from across the Irish sea. That echo, when it comes, is full of ill-omen; it turns disagreement into discord and any hope of an understanding is destroyed. I write as an Irishman, an Irish provincial, and it is the impact on our country of the events in Croatia that interests me, or, if one must widen the range, the impact on us of some external interpretations of those events.

I will be told, I know, that I have greatly exaggerated this impact, and have attached importance to demonstrations, resolutions, sermons, ceremonies and tracts which they don't in fact possess. Irish people have only the vaguest interest in Croatia. Certainly, in casual conversation, you will meet none of that crusading spirit, the exalted passions, with which their representatives credit them on public occasions. They are aware that no human problem is simple, and that we live on the edge of a complex and disordered world, where our homemade remedies will make small impression. All the same, the crusaders hold the floor in Ireland, I have never once seen them publicly criticized except in a Communist weekly which is not handled by newsagents. The disagreement of those who are too cowardly or too discreet to express their views has no validity and, therefore, I am justified in taking the demonstrations at their face value.

They have been of a more or less ritual nature. The phrases that are used might be called empty, because they betray no evidence of mind. Yet we know that we can be hypnotized by the repetition of meaningless words and under their influence can perform acts from which reason recoils. It is in the vacant mind that the foolish idea can establish itself unchallenged. And the crusaders have shown a special genius for exploiting the vacuum.

I have made a cuttings-book in the past three years of the references to Yugoslavia and it is humiliating for me to find that the stupidest comments, the silliest manoeuvres, come from Ireland. It is true that it was M. de Bedoyère, editor of *The Catholic Herald*, who sponsored the scheme that picture postcards of Archbishop Stepinac should be circulated among those too illiterate to read the newspapers for themselves. It was Archbishop Spellman who gave an address on Mgr Stepinac to 1731 American schoolgirls, drawn up in the form of a rosary on a polo ground. Yet it was in Ireland that the life of Mgr Stepinac was printed, a little book which contains more misstatements to the square inch than any which I have previously encountered. It is symbolic of the decay of our civilization that this book should have been put into a bronze box and built in the corner stone of the four-million-dollar Stepinac Institute in America.

I would think it unkind and unchivalrous to belittle the courage and endurance of anyone who suffers for an ideal, if it was not well known that Mgr Stepinac's martyrdom had been deliberately courted and that his opponents offered him his freedom if he left the country, and only imprisoned him with reluctance and embarrassment. In the last seven years some two million Yugoslavs met silent and painful ends; some of them died heroically for ideals for which we have little sympathy. Many of Mgr Stepinac's fiercest antagonists had themselves endured long terms of imprisonment. In a world of widespread and underserved suffering, there is something callous in this engineering of sympathy, which should be natural and spontaneous, towards a sectarian end.

Some of these manoeuvres seem to be almost obscene in their cynicism. What is one to think of Father Schwartz, who got front-page prominence in our Irish newspapers by inducing 4000 natives of the Pacific island of Guam to express their horror at Mgr Stepinac's trial? I had not heard of Guam so I looked it up in Willard Price's book on Pacific islands. This is what I read:

> It was not until 1668 that the Jesuit missionaries came to the island and erected the Sweet Name of Mary Church in Aganya. The missionaries were accompanied by soldiers. Conversions were made at the point of the sword. Drums beat in the hills and the natives rose in bloody riots. The Spaniards fortified the Sweet Name of Mary, turned their capital city into an armed camp and made war on the stubborn unbelievers. Slaughter of innocents followed on a Hitlerian scale. Those who could, escaped from the island. The native population, about 55,000 when the Spaniards came, dwindled to 100 in only eighteen years.

In Croatia, in 1941 and 1942, conversions on a far wider scale than at Guam were carried out and the slaughter far exceeded 55,000. Was Father Schwartz ignorant of this? Was he so insensitive as to have been blind to the parallel? Could he not have spared those poor half-breeds that silly pantomime?

As for Mgr Stepinac, I believe he underwent martyrdom in order that the truth should be misrepresented. There had been a great massacre of the Orthodox Christians by the Catholics which he had been unable to prevent. I have not described this myself because for me it is all hearsay, though it is hearsay that I firmly believe. I am eighty-eight and have lived all my life among Roman Catholics, and though we have differences of opinion about many subjects – divorce, privacy, celibacy, abortion and much else – neither I nor any of my friends or relations have ever suffered in any way because of our heresies. Yet I believe that what Gierowski told me and wrote in his journal' is true. His faith, that of the Orthodox Christian beyond the frontiers of Russia, is under strong pressure from Communism on the east and Roman Catholicism in the west. In the West, we are aware of the gentle pressure that in time of peace a dominant religion exercises upon its neighbours, and how it can intensify in time of war.

The First World War began because Austria-Hungary wished to impose its Germanic culture on the Southern Slavs. The Archduke, who came with his Slav wife on a conciliatory visit to Sarajevo, the capital of Bosnia, which had recently been annexed, was assassinated. The war that followed led to the disintegration of the German and Austro-Hungarian empires; the Russian Empire, though on the victorious side, dissolved in 1917 after the Bolshevik Revolution. New states came into being: a new Poland built from fragments of the German, Austrian and Russian empires, a new Czechoslovakia, a new Yugoslavia. The huge rump of the old Russian Empire, stretching from the Ukraine to the Pacific Ocean, was under Communist control, though often the old tribal and religious loyalties survived dormant under the new allegiance. The new nations had been built by the architects of the League of Nations, who had endeavoured with great care to draw their frontiers to correspond as far as possible with the race and religion of their inhabitants. This was difficult because the old empires had, like the Roman empires before them, tried to impose a uniformity of

---

' *Svobodnoye Slovo* (*Free Word*); see "A Three-Day Nation: Alexei Gierowski and Carpatho-Russia." (H.B)

culture and religion on all the nationalities they subdued and hoped
to assimilate.

I will conclude with the persecution of the Orthodox in Yugoslavia.
All historians know that those who live through a time of terror and
suffering seldom minimize what they have endured or seen others
enduring. We get different accounts of the same event. And those who
inflicted the suffering will give a diametrically opposite account of
what happened. Are bishops, monks, cardinals and clergy in general
more truthful than other men? I do not know but I believe that when
they distort the truth, it is by silence or evasion, not by lying. Here is
what Dr Iriney Georgevitch, the Orthodox Bishop of Dalmatia,[*] wrote
from exile in New York in 1948 of the sufferings his people endured
from their Roman Catholic neighbours:

> Being the only Orthodox bishop alive and living in a free
> country who has escaped the fate of his slaughtered brethren
> in Roman Catholic Croatia, I deem it my duty to acquaint
> American public opinion with the truth about how hundreds
> of thousands of Orthodox Christians were tortured and slain
> in Yugoslavia because of their Orthodox faith by Roman
> Catholics who were instigated and led by Roman Catholic
> clergymen with the knowledge and the approval of the high-
> est Roman Catholic hierarchy.
>
> I have come to the United States from Italy in April 1945.
> I have kept quiet up to this day. I was sick and exhausted
> physically and morally by what I have gone through after
> having been arrested and deported to Italy, where I have been
> kept in jail for three and a half years under intolerable

---

[*] Bishop Georgevitch's pre-exile residence was in Shibenik in Dalmatia. The city was
occupied during the Second World War by the Italians, who arrested Georgevitch
and deported him to Italy for being the founder and president of the "Society of
Friends of Great Britain and America" in Yugoslavia. (H.B.)

conditions. It took me more than a year after my arrival in America to recover to a certain degree.

Then, in 1946, Aloysius Stepinac, the Roman Catholic archbishop of Zagreb, was arrested and brought to trial. With him chiefly lay the fault for the mediaeval persecutions of the Orthodox in Yugoslavia during the war. I remained silent because I was not sure that he would get a fair trial. On the other hand, it was repulsive to me to help in any way the Communist regime in Yugoslavia for which I have no sympathies whatsoever. The verdict was surprisingly mild, and I don't grudge it to Stepinac. It was his good luck that that he was not tried at Nuremberg where German generals were sentenced to death for crimes of which many of them know much less than Stepinac knew of the unspeakable atrocities which his bishops, his priests, and his monks committed against the Orthodox in Yugoslavia.

Even after the trial I was still reluctant to speak. Last year, when I was interviewed by some American journalists about Church affairs in Yugoslavia, I declined to talk about the Stepinac case. But on mature consideration of the matter, I have come to the conclusion that it was my duty to speak out. First of all, because the truth should be known. I owe it to the dead who cannot speak for themselves anymore. Among them are thousands of the faithful of my own diocese of Dalmatia, even priests whom I have ordained and who were tortured and murdered together with their families in a most gruesome manner.

I owe it to four Orthodox bishops, among them two metropolitans, who were put to death.

I owe it to my Serbian people, hundreds of thousands of whom have been slain, and I owe it to the millions of Orthodox in the Balkans and elsewhere in Eastern Europe who are threatened by the same fate in the near future if ever the Roman Catholic hierarchy should think that another opportunity has presented itself to exterminate non-Roman-Catholic Christians in order to expand the frontiers of the Vatican's realm farther east.

By now it is a historical fact that the Roman Catholic hierarchy had decided since the 1920s that Yugoslavia should be destroyed and that, for that purpose, the Roman Catholic hierarchy conspired with the Fascist Italian government, in spite of the fact that the Roman Catholics enjoyed full freedom and equality in Yugoslavia and that the Yugoslav government tried to appease Rome by all means. Father Koroshets, chairman of the Roman Catholic Clerical Party, was a member of almost every Yugoslav Cabinet, even Premier of Yugoslavia.

It is further a historical fact that the Roman Catholic hierarchy was in contact with Anthony Pavelitch, the head of the gang which, in October 1934, murdered King Alexander of Yugoslavia. The archbishop of Sarajevo, Ivan Sharitch, went from Yugoslavia to Rome and met there, in the Vatican, Pavelitch after the latter had been sentenced to death in absentia for the murder of King Alexander, by a French and a Yugoslav court.

On the very same day the Germans occupied Zagreb (on the 10th of April 1941), the independence of Croatia was proclaimed, a Roman Catholic state in which two million Orthodox were included and outlawed. This new Roman Catholic Croatia, headed by Pavelitch, the convicted murderer of the Yugoslav king, was immediately recognized by Stepinac who, in a pastoral letter, appealed to his flock to support Pavelitch.

With Archbishop Stepinac's connivance, a campaign of extermination and forcible conversion of the Orthodox was inaugurated in Croatia. The result was the massacre of several hundred thousands of Orthodox Serbians. The exact number of the slain has not been established. According to Orthodox sources about 800,000 have been murdered. Some Roman Catholics assert their number was only 350,000˙.

The Roman Catholic bishop of Djakovo, Akshamovitch, had leaflets distributed in his diocese in which he gave "the inhabitants of the Greek-Eastern faith the friendly advice" to turn Roman Catholic in order to be allowed to remain in their homes. In the province of Bosnia leaflets were distributed advising the Orthodox Serbians to become Roman Catholics in order to save their lives and their property.

It is also a historical fact that many Orthodox churches were defiled, destroyed, and burned by the Roman Catholics under the leadership of Franciscan monks who occupied all the Orthodox monasteries in Roman Catholic Croatia.

It is historical fact that the pope and the Roman Catholic hierarchy in Yugoslavia have done nothing about the crimes committed against the Orthodox, and there is a well-founded suspicion that some of the chief-criminals, like Pavelitch and Archbishop Sharitch, who cannot be found, are hiding in the Vatican.

It is a historical fact that the destruction of Yugoslavia and the ensuing crimes have been prepared in Yugoslavia during many years prior to the war by the Roman Catholic hierarchy through the Catholic Action and its affiliates. "The Great Brotherhood of Crusaders," "the Great Sisterhood of Crusaders," the "Saint Mary Congregation," and others.

These facts clearly show that the spirit of the Holy Inquisition is still alive in Rome and that Rome does not shy from mass murder nor from the destruction of states to further its worldly aims of domination.

I think it is to the interest of all non-Roman-Catholic Christians and of the Roman Catholics themselves, who in

---

˙ See footnote on page 178. (Editors)

their overwhelming majority are God-fearing and honest people and in no way responsible for their hierarchy in Rome, to uncover those pernicious activities which threaten the freedom, the peace, and the very lives of all peoples and of all nations.

In my opinion, the above facts should be verified by an impartial American committee in order to prevent a recurrence of events similar to those described above in case of a new war, which the Vatican plans to exploit for the establishment of a "Central European" Catholic Federation, the frontiers of which would go far beyond Central Europe and comprise millions of Greek Orthodox who thus would be at the mercy of Rome. Many of the perpetrators of the atrocious crimes in Yugoslavia, among them the Fascist chieftain Pavelitch and Archbishop Sharitch, are still at large and they are ready to serve the Catholic Action as they did in Yugoslavia.

(1948, 1988)

The Sub-Prefect Should Have
Held His Tongue

In countries where the old beliefs are dying it is the custom for educated people to handle them with nostalgic reverence. It is thought crude and undignified for a sophisticated man to take sides in a religious squabble, and it often happens that, the less he believes in himself, the more indulgent he is to the time-honoured beliefs of others. I have been reproached several times by sincere and civilized unbelievers for my efforts to find out the details of the vast campaign in Croatia in 1941 to convert two and a half million Orthodox to Catholicism. "Why not let bygones be bygones?" they say. "If we rake these things up we'll merely start trouble at home and play into the hands of the Communists. And anyway, they are always killing each other in the Balkans." I once heard an ambassador in Belgrade argue like that, and indeed I have never heard a British or American official abroad argue in any other way. When in 1946 I went to Zagreb and looked up the files of the war-time newspapers of Croatia in which the whole story was to be read, it was obvious that no foreign inquirer had handled them before, and the library clerks regarded me with wonder and suspicion.

Yet it seemed to me that for a man as for a community too high a price can be paid for tranquillity. If you suppress a fact because it is awkward, you will next be asked to contradict it. And so it happened to me when I got back to Ireland, and gave a talk about Yugoslavia, the country and its people, on Radio Éireann. I did not mention the

Communist war on the Church, or Archbishop Stepinac, who had just been sentenced to imprisonment for collaboration with Pavelitch, the Quisling ruler of Croatia, and for conniving at the forced conversion campaign. I could not refer to the Communist persecution of religion without mentioning the more terrible Catholic persecution which had preceded it, so I thought silence was best. But silence did not help me. In the following week our leading Roman Catholic weekly, *The Standard*, published a long editorial diatribe against myself and against Radio Éireann. I had not, it declared, said a word about the sufferings of the Church and its ministers under Tito and, by sponsoring me, Radio Éireann had connived at a vile piece of subversive propaganda. The officials of Radio Éireann, knowing I was no Communist, supported me, and finally *The Standard*, under pressure from my solicitor, agreed to print a long reply from me. I received the proof-sheets, corrected and returned them, but the reply never appeared. Months later, a muddled, amiable explanation reached me, and my friends said "let bygones be bygones." I did. That is the way things happen in Ireland.*

But it became increasingly difficult to be silent. The foreign editor of *The Standard*, Count O'Brien of Thomond, published a little book called *Archbishop Stepinac, The Man and his Case*. It had an introduction by the Archbishop of Dublin, and commendation on the dust-cover from a couple of cardinals, Canadian and English, and half a dozen bishops and archbishops. Cardinal Spellman laid a copy of the book on the foundation stone of the new Stepinac Institute in New York, USA, and told 1700 schoolgirls, drawn up on a polo-ground in the form of a rosary, what they were to think about Croatian ecclesiastical history. Yet it seemed to me that there was a major error of fact or of interpretation, or a significant omission, on almost every page of this book. Meanwhile all the county councils and corporations in Ireland met and passed resolutions. Extracts from Count O'Brien's book were hurled

---

* See Appendix (page 540). (Editors)

about, and fiery telegrams despatched to parliaments and ambassadors. But the climax of my discomfort was reached when our Minister for Agriculture, Mr Dillon, addressing some law students, advised them to model themselves on Mindszenty, Stepinac and Pavelitch, who had "so gallantly defended freedom of thought and freedom of conscience." Those who knew Yugoslavia were aghast, for Pavelitch, one of the major war criminals, was the Yugoslav counterpart of Himmler, and it was under his rule that the gas chamber and the concentration camp were introduced into Yugoslavia and the forced conversion campaign initiated. Clearly Mr Dillon was speaking in ignorance, not in bigotry, but ignorance rampaging with such assurance and harnessed to religious enthusiasm is like a runaway horse and cart. It must be stopped before serious mischief results.

I felt that the honour of the small Protestant community in Southern Ireland would be compromised if those of us who had investigated the facts remained silent about what we had discovered. In many Roman Catholic pulpits the sufferings of the Catholics under Tito were being compared to the long martyrdom of Catholic Ireland under Protestant rule. "Yesterday and today Herod abides." If we agree that history should be falsified in Croatia in the interests of Catholic piety, how could we protest when our own history was similarly distorted?

In letters to the newspapers I replied to Mr Dillon and many others who had expressed similar opinions. A well known Irish Jesuit, Father Devane, assuming a Slav name, Mihajlo Dvornik, to lend force to his accuracy, solemnly declared that there had been no forced religious conversions in Croatia, but I could find no one ready to argue the details. Mostly they quoted at me passages from Count O'Brien, or, on *a priori* grounds, accused me of vile slander. "The Catholic Church had always

---

* In my own county town, Kilkenny, a muddled but enthusiastic alderman insisted that Tito was in Dublin in the capacity of Yugoslav ambassador, and proposed at the Corporation meeting that he should be told "Get out, Tito!"(H.B.)

insisted that conversion must be from the heart. *Ad amplexandam fidem Catholicam nemo invitus cogatur.*" I was alleging the impossible.

Soon afterwards it was announced that Tito was to visit London, and in Ireland, as in England, various anti-Yugoslav demonstrations were arranged. My friend, Owen Sheehy-Skeffington, a lecturer in Trinity College and now a member of the Irish Senate, invited me to a meeting of the Foreign Affairs Association, at which the editor of *The Standard* was to read a paper on "Yugoslavia – the Pattern of Persecution." The Association had been modelled on Chatham House as an international fact-finding society and Arnold Toynbee himself had come over to give his blessing to the first meeting. In the *Survey of International Affairs* of 1955 he was later to express himself as strongly as I had about the persecution of the Orthodox. This is an undenominational society with a tradition of free speech. The lecturer had never been to Yugoslavia, and I believe that all the others on the platform were in the same position, though one of them said that on a cruise down the Dalmatian coast he had met members of a Yugoslav football team. I decided that at the end of his paper I would try to make those points which he had failed, despite his promise, to publish for me. I would try to show how variegated was the pattern of persecution in Yugoslavia, and how misleading our crude simplifications would be. What followed has been told by Paul Blanshard, whom I met for the first time that evening, in his book *The Irish and Catholic Power*. It is enough to say here that the Chairman's attempt to close the meeting at the end of the paper was ruled out, on a vote, as unconstitutional. I got up, holding in my hand *The Martyrdom of the Serbs*, a book published by the exiled Serbian Orthodox Church in Chicago, in case anything I said required authoritative corroboration. It had been given me by archpriest Nicolitch, the head of the Serbian Orthodox Church in England. But I had spoken only a few sentences when a stately figure rose from among the audience and walked out. It was the Papal Nuncio, of whose presence I had been unaware. The Chairman instantly closed the meeting, and there was an appalled silence, followed by a rush of reporters in my direction. They had understood nothing in the confusion. There was, consequently, some lively reporting, and two leading dailies quoted me as saying that the Orthodox Church, not the Communists, had initiated the persecution of the Catholics in Yugoslavia. In gigantic letters in the *Sunday Express* (Irish edition) I read: "Pope's Envoy Walks Out. Government to Discuss Insult to Nuncio."

Blanshard has described the measures taken against Skeffington in Dublin and myself in Kilkenny. The persecution was of a familiar pattern, and I try to see in it not a personal hard-luck story, but material for a study in the modern indifference to evidence, but I think both of us knew that had we been less fortunate in our backgrounds we would have been ruined. Skeffington, the son of a father executed by the British in 1916 – or, to be more accurate, murdered at the orders of a hysterical British officer – is at his happiest when he is fighting, and shortly afterwards he had fought his way into the Irish Senate. For myself, I am grateful for the few inherited acres which have helped me to survive the disapproval of my neighbours. All the local government bodies of the city and county held special meetings to condemn "the Insult." There were speeches from mayors, ex-mayors, aldermen, creamery managers. The County Council expelled me from one of its sub-committees, and I was obliged to resign from another committee. Although my friends put up a fight, I was forced to give up the honorary secretaryship of an archaeological society which I had myself founded and guided through seven difficult years (see Appendix). My opponents hoped that my liquidation would be decorous and quickly forgotten, but my friends and myself were little inclined to oblige them, and for a time our small society enjoyed in the metropolitan press a blaze of publicity which its archaeological activities had never won for it.

I decided that before I resigned I would tell our two or three hundred members something about the forced conversion campaign in Yugoslavia. Much of the evidence, including the utterances of the Orthodox Church and its bishops, and Archbishop Sharitch's "Ode to Pavelitch," with its sonorous denunciations of Serbs and Jews, I put aside, because I was certain that it would not be believed. Finally, I decided to publish the long letter written by Stepinac to Pavelitch on the subject of the

forced conversions˙. I had translated it from a typescript in Zagreb in
1946, and it seems to me a document of vast importance which deserves
a prominent place in the annals of religious history. Its reception was
disappointing. Many were confused by the outlandish names and inextricably complicated series of events, and I was taken aback when
one friendly disposed reader congratulated me on "my interesting
article on Czechoslovakia."

There is in Ireland a historic loathing of proselytism. The well-meaning Protestants who plied the starving peasants of the west with soup
and Bibles after the famine of 1846 have never been forgiven. Religious
apprehensions as strong as these survive in Yugoslavia, and I had hoped
that some of my neighbours would be capable of the necessary mental
adjustment and would see the parallel. Surely it would be obvious to
them from the Stepinac letter that the Croatian bishops, while denouncing the use of force, were delighted with the opportunities for
mass conversion which the chaos and defeat of Yugoslavia afforded
them. There was, for example, Dr Mishitch, the Bishop of Mostar and
the kindliest of mortals, whom even the Communists have praised for
his clemency. He too had made quite plain the hopes which he had
entertained at the beginning of Pavelitch's régime:

> By the mercy of God (he wrote) there was never such a good
> occasion as now for us to help Croatia to save the countless
> souls, people of good will, well-disposed peasants, who live
> side by side with Catholics... Conversion would be appropriate
> and easy. Unfortunately the authorities in their narrow views
> are involuntarily hindering the Croatian and Catholic cause.
> In many parishes of (my) diocese... very honest peasants of
> the Orthodox faith have registered in the Catholic Church...
> But then outsiders take things in hand. While the newly-con-
> verted are at Mass they seize them, old and young, men and

˙ See "The Compulsory Conversion Campaign: I-III" on page 177. (Editors)

women, and hunt them like slaves. From Mostar and Chapljina the railway carried six waggons full of mothers, girls
and children under eight to the station of Surmanci, where
they were taken out of the waggons, brought into the hills
and thrown alive, mothers and children, into deep ravines.
In the parish of Klepca seven hundred schismatics from the
neighbouring villages were slaughtered. The Sub-Prefect of
Mostar, Mr Bajitch, a Moslem, publicly declared (as a state
employé he should have held his tongue) that in Ljubina alone
700 schismatics have been thrown into one pit.

Elsewhere in his letter the Bishop wrote:

> At one time there was a likelihood that a great number of
> schismatics would be united to the Catholic Church. If God
> had given to those in authority the understanding and the
> good sense to deal effectively with conversion, so that it could
> have been carried through more ably, more smoothly and by
> degrees, the number of Catholics might have been increased
> by at least five or six hundred thousand. Such a number is
> required in Bosnia and Herzegovina, if there is to be an in-
> crease from 700,000 to 1,300,000.

The other three bishops, whose letters Stepinac quoted, all took the
normal human view that it is inadvisable in the name of religion to
thrown waggon-loads of schismatics over cliffs; they were critical of
the conversion campaign, but they did not find the occasion for it unseasonable. Had there been no cruelty, and if possible a little soup, they
would have welcomed it. But compared with Mgr. Mishitch's letters
theirs are cold, calculating and self-righteous. Archbishop Sharitch
opined that the town council of Sarajevo was imposing too high a tax
on the Bosnian Orthodox for their change of religion. The Bishop of
Kotor, Dr Butorac, declared that the missionaries to the Serbs must be

wisely selected. "We must not entrust the problem," he wrote, "to monks or priests who have no tact at all and who would be much better suited to carry a revolver in their hands than a cross." And he expressed the fear that if the Serbs were driven too hard they might, out of defiance, pass over in a body to Islam.

I must confess that I find Mgr. Stepinac's comments on these letters and the situation that provoked them curiously narrow and thin-lipped. He scolds the miserable, hunted Orthodox for their terrible errors, deriving, he declares, from "hatred and schism," and he blames them for the Russian Revolution, just as he blames the crimes of Pavelitch and his gang on the Chetniks – that is, the followers of Mihailovitch – the Communists, and the Royal Yugoslav Government. He considers that the best way to convert the Orthodox might often be found through the medium of the Greek Catholic Church, which recognizes the authority of the Pope while preserving its Orthodox ritual. He ends his letter, as he began it, by exonerating Pavelitch from all blame in the crimes that had been committed.

Yet Count O'Brien tells us in his little book that at this time, in defence of the Orthodox, the Archbishop had swept into Pavelitch's office. ""It is God's command!" he said, "Thou shalt not kill!" and without another word he left the Quisling's palace."

Stepinac's long and respectful letter to Pavelitch at this date proves the anecdote to be a hagiographical fabrication. Yet it was quoted at me several times in the press of Kilkenny and Dublin. The letter was obviously the longest and most important that Stepinac had ever written, and it struck me as odd that though I had published it twice in Ireland – for my critics in Kilkenny and also in *The Church of Ireland Gazette* – nobody in the British Isles, at a time when so much was written and said about the imprisoned Archbishop, ever commented on it, quoted from it, or wrote to me to enquire how I had secured it. Three years later, however, Richard Pattee published in America a lengthy book in defence of Stepinac, and among his documents the letter belatedly appears. Yet I believe that my translation is the more accurate of the two. Mr Pattee has thought it best to omit a sentence or two here and there. He leaves out, for instance, Mgr. Mishitch's calculations of the number of conversions required in Bosnia and Herzegovina. Again, wherever the word "conversion" appears in the text Mr Pattee reads it as a "legitimate conversion," thus adding an epithet which I could not trace in the original. Stepinac's admiring description of the Bishop of Banja Luka as "that old Croatian warrior" likewise disappears, presumably because Mr Pattee does not wish his readers to infer that the bishops were Croatian separatists trying to ingratiate themselves with Pavelitch.

About the same time Mr Michael Derrick published in *The Tablet* a paragraph or two from Mishitch's letter, but he attributed it to Stepinac, and he omitted the extraordinary parenthesis about the Sub-Prefect who told of the barbarities inflicted upon the Orthodox, and the bishop's comment that "as a state employee he should have held his tongue." In the succeeding issue of *The Sword*, Mr Derrick published my translation of Stepinac's *The Regulations for Conversion* without acknowledgement! Anybody who read these regulations with an open mind, and particularly an Irish Catholic with his inherited horror of "souperism," would have to admit that they bore every trace, except soup, of *illegitimate* conversion. For instance, Clause 11, an appeal that the Orthodox be granted full civic rights, has been much applauded, but it begins, "A psychological basis for conversion must be created among the Greek Orthodox inhabitants." If still in doubt as to the bearing of these regulations one would have only to read the manifesto of Dr Shimrak, editor of the leading Catholic daily, and chosen by Stepinac as one of his two colleagues in the supervision of conversion:

> Every priest must have before his eyes that historic days have come for our mission. Now we must put into practice that which we have spoken of in theory for centuries. In the matter of conversion we have done very little up to this, simply because we were irresolute and dreaded the small reproaches and censure of men. Every great task has its opponents, but we must not be downcast on that account, because it is a

question of a holy union, the salvation of souls and the eternal glory of the Lord Christ. Our work is legal in the light of the ruling of the Holy See... also in the light of the ruling of the Holy Congregation of Cardinals for the Eastern Church... and finally in the light of the circular sent by the Government of Independent Croatia, July 30, 1941, whose intention it is that the Orthodox should be converted to the Catholic faith (*Diocesan Magazine of Krizhevtsi*, No. 2 [1942], pp.10-11).

Count O'Brien, an Austrian of Irish descent, had been until he came to Ireland after the war the editor of an important Viennese paper, and he claims in his book to have known Shimrak intimately for twenty years. He also writes that all the Croat bishops had opposed Pavelitch's "evil plan" for the forced conversion of the Orthodox. This seemed in such strong conflict with Shimrak's declaration that long before the "Insult" I had visited Count O'Brien to ask for an explanation. An explanation was forthcoming. The Count replied at once that Shimrak had not been a bishop at the time, but only an administrator. It appeared from his reply that it was actually after he had proved himself in sympathy with Pavelitch's plan that Shimrak was appointed to the bishopric and to Stepinac's committee for regulating conversion. I then asked how it came about that, if all the bishops were hostile to Pavelitch and his plans, Archbishop Sharitch of Bosnia, one of the greatest of them, had been able to print his *Ode to Pavelitch* in the ecclesiastical papers of his own archdiocese and that of Zagreb. I had made a translation of his ode in twenty-six verses, describing his meeting with Pavelitch at St Peter's in Rome, and I now ventured to remind Count O'Brien of a few lines:

Embracing thee was precious to the poet
as embracing our beloved Homeland.
For God himself was at thy side, thou good and strong one,
so that thou mightest perform thy deeds for the Homeland...
And against the Jews, who had all the money,

who wanted to sell our souls,
who built a prison round our souls,
who built a prison round our name,
the miserable traitors...
Dr Ante Pavelić! the dear name!
Croatia has therein a treasure from Heaven.
May the King of Heaven accompany thee, our Golden Leader!

Count O'Brien had an explanation for that, too. He said: "The Archbishop was an abnormal man, very emotional. He was always embracing people. Whenever we met, he used to kiss me on both cheeks. He can't be taken seriously."

These replies made me feel very helpless, since they could not have been made if venal indifference had not reigned around us. When I went home I was feeling as emotional as the Archbishop, and I remember that I wrote a poem myself on the Massacre of the Orthodox, though I must admit that it was the massacre of the truth that really outraged me.

Milton, if you were living at this hour,
they'd make you trim your sonnet to appease
the triple tyrant and the Piedmontese.
"Why for some peasants vex a friendly power?
We'd like to print it, but Sir Tottenham Bauer
and half the Board would blame us. Colleen Cheese
would stop its full-page ad. They're strong RCs.
It's old stuff now, and truth, deferred, goes sour.
So cut those lines about "the stocks and stones"
and "slaughtered saints," or keep for private ears
that fell crusade, for even in undertones,
it breeds disunion and the Kremlin hears.
Say nothing rash or rude, for it is right
that all the godly (west of Kiel), unite!"

I thought my poem almost as good as the Archbishop's, but I had some difficulty in getting it published. In the end it appeared in a pacifist weekly, but very inconspicuously and in very small print. The Archbishop had been luckier. His had appeared in *Katolicki Tjednik (The Catholic Weekly)* on Christmas Day, with a signed portrait of Pavelitch and a decorative border of Christmas tree candles and little silver bells.

I suppose that the small community in which I live has about the same significance for the world as the community of Mr Bajitch, who as a state employé "should have held his tongue" about the massacres, so I need not apologize for returning to it. My friends and neighbours were memorably kind and supporting; for they knew that I had not intended to insult anybody. But others were puzzled. I was not, like Mr Bajitch, a state employé, and some found it difficult to make their disapproval materially felt. This problem would not have baffled them for long had it not been for the courtesy and good sense of the local Catholic clergy. I was most vulnerable through the Kilkenny Archaeological Society. This had been a famous Victorian institution, with the Prince Consort as patron and the Marquess of Ormond as President, but it had shifted to Dublin as an All-Ireland Society, and when I revived it in Kilkenny in 1944 it had been dead there for half a century. In a couple of years the new Society became a real bridge between Protestant and Catholic, Anglo-Irishman and Celt. The friendliness which it created was perhaps our main achievement, but we did other things, too. Mr O.G.S. Crawford made for us a photographic survey of old Kilkenny such as no other Irish provincial town possesses; Dr Bersu, the Director of the Institute of Frankfurt, made his principal Irish excavation on a hill fort outside Kilkenny and reported it in our journal; we had a centenary celebration of the old society in Kilkenny Castle; and the National Museum co-operated in a very successful Kilkenny Exhibition. But I think I was proudest of having organized a week's visit from the principle archaeological society in Northern Ireland; for cultural fraternizations between North and South are as rare as they are valuable. I feared that all this work would be wasted, so I decided to appeal to a certain Stephen Brown, a Jesuit, who had attended meetings of our Society. He had escorted the Nuncio to the fateful meeting, and afterwards in the *Irish Independent* had defended the Croatian hierarchy against the charges of illegitimate proselytism, with copious quotations from Count O'Brien but, as it seemed to me, with a total ignorance of Yugoslav conditions. Father Brown received me warmly. He said he was satisfied that I had not intended to insult the Nuncio, that he strongly disapproved [of] the introduction of the incident into the affairs of an archaeological society, and that in any case the Nuncio had visited the meeting by mistake under the impression that he was bound for a meeting of a Catholic society with a similar name. Father Brown said that he would send me a letter making these three points, and that I might publish it in any paper I chose. The letter never arrived. It seemed, however, that a compromise had been reached in the matter, for a few days later a paragraph appeared in *The Standard* under the heading "Mr Butler rebuked." After commending all the denunciations by public bodies, the passage ended:

> It is well that such repudiation should be known. But we doubt if any good purpose would have been served by the proposed step by which Mr Butler would have been deprived of office in, say, the Kilkenny Archaeological Society, of which he is presumably an efficient functionary, and into which he can scarcely introduce sectarian issues. If he has any regard for public opinion he must know by now that his action met with not alone local but national disapproval. That is sufficient.

It was difficult for me to return as a presumably efficient functionary to a Society which I had myself founded, so I never after attended a meeting, but my friends, both Catholic and Protestant, still support the Society and I am glad today that it continues.

I hope I have not appeared to diagnose in my Catholic countrymen a unique susceptibility to a disease with which we are all of us more or less infected. Speed of communications has increased, and we are expected to have strong feelings about an infinite series of remote events. But our powers of understanding and sympathy have not correspondingly increased. In an atmosphere of artificially heated emotionalism truth simply dissolves into expediency. This shifting current of expediency may be illustrated by a chronicle of the changing attitudes to Pavelitch in the past ten years. In Croatia, upheld by the victorious Germans, he had for four years been regarded as a great Christian gentleman and patriot. All the Catholic bishops and the Evangelical bishops were among his panegyrists and had received decorations from him. Then the Nazis collapsed, and Pavelitch was regarded by the outer world as one of the basest war criminals, while in Croatia all the dignitaries hastened to disavow the compliments they had paid him. A former Italian fascist, Malaparte, in his book, *Kaputt*, has described how, as correspondent of *Corriere Della Sera*, he visited Pavelitch in his office in 1942 and saw behind him what appeared to be a basket of shelled oysters. "Are these Dalmatian oysters?" Malaparte asked. "No," Pavelitch replied, "that's forty pounds of human eyes, a present from my loyal Ustashe in Bosnia" – eyes, that is to say, of the Serbian Orthodox. I am ready to believe that this story is an invention, like Stepinac's visit to "the Quisling's Palace," and that stories like this were repeated by the ex-Fascists, who thought that if they made the whole world black their own shade of dirty grey would be less conspicuous. But in 1948 no one told Malaparte that he was a liar. Indeed, writing about *Kaputt* in *The Irish Times*, Mr Kees van Hoek, the biographer of the Pope, said that Malaparte was "the most accurate observer and reliable witness."

That was the universal Western view of Pavelitch seven or eight years ago – a monster of iniquity, an ogre out of a fairy-tale. But since then Pavelitch has become more respectable, and if he was wanted again in a campaign against Communism in the Balkans it is possible that he and his friends would be used. He now lives in South America and two or three papers and journals are published in his interest. Five years ago he issued postage stamps commemorating the tenth anniversary of Independent Croatia, and he has cashed in very effectively on the Stepinac legend, since one of his Ustasha clubs in the Argentine is called after the famous Cardinal. Archbishop Sharitch, the devoted admirer of both Pavelitch and Stepinac, lives in Madrid, but still publishes his odes (rather modified), as well as ecstatic reminiscences of Stepinac, in *Hrvatska Revija*, a Croatian separatist quarterly of Buenos Aires. I once visited Mgr. Stepinac in prison and found him a gentle and serious man, who obviously acted as he thought was right. Surely it must be one of the hardest blows that fate has dealt him that both Pavelitch and Sharitch speak well of him?

In one way or another the memory of a terrible crime against humanity is being confused and effaced, so that many people believe that it never happened at all or that it has been monstrously exaggerated. I have seen Pavelitch compared in Irish papers with Roger Casement and Patrick Pearse as a simple-hearted patriot who merely did his best for his country in difficult circumstances. In October 1952 he was interviewed for an Italian picture paper, *Epoca* of Milan. He was photographed basking in the South American sun with his wife and family, stroking a pet dog. He told how he had escaped from Croatia through the Allied lines, how he had paused for weeks at a time in Naples, the Vatican City, and Castel Gandolfo. He was to be considered a romantic fellow, the carefree immunity which he enjoyed no more than his due.

How has all this happened? Three centuries ago Milton gave undying notoriety to the massacre and forced conversion of the Waldenses, and Cromwell sent out emissaries to collect information about the sufferings of this tiny Alpine community. We are mostly now immune from the religious fanaticism which once intensified racial antipathies and to which Cromwell himself was no stranger; why has it become unwise to censure or even to take notice of an explosion of those ancient passions fifty times more devastating than that which Milton observed? There were scarcely ten thousand Waldenses to be persecuted in Piedmont, while the decrees of Pavelitch were launched against more than two million Orthodox, and 240,000 were forcibly converted.

Looking for a reason, I can only conclude that science has enormously extended the sphere of our responsibilities, while our consciences have remained the same size. Parochially minded people neglect their parishes to pronounce ignorantly about the universe, while the universalists are so conscious of the worldwide struggles of opposing philosophies that the rights and wrongs of any regional conflict dwindle to insignificance against a cosmic panorama. They feel that truth is in some way relative to orientation, and falsehood no more than a wrong adjustment, so that they can never say unequivocally "that is a lie!" Like the needle of a compass at the North Pole, their moral judgement spins round and round, overwhelming them with information, and telling them nothing at all.

(1956)

Appendix

A Statement to the Committee and Members
of the Kilkenny Archaeological Society
by the Honorary Secretary, Hubert Butler

November 10th, 1952

A Committee Meeting is being summoned on Wednesday next, at 8.30 p.m., in the Technical Schools, Kilkenny, to discuss the effects upon the Society of the incident at the International Affairs Association. I think it would leave you freer to discuss the matter if I did not come to the meeting myself but sent to each of you a statement which you could study before you reached the meeting.

I expect that some of you will think I ought to resign without more ado and others, who bear me no ill will and realize that I spoke without any intention to give pain to anyone, will think I ought to give up the secretaryship in order to tide things over and prevent the Society from dissolving.

I need not emphasize how desperately sorry I would be if the Society did break up along sectarian or other lines, and how ready I shall be to co-operate in any effort to keep it going. We are, I think, unique in having survived so long without a trace of bitterness or dissension. So I have to think hard what is the right thing to do.

In the first place, I do not believe that my resignation now would save the Society as an interdenominational one to which people of every shade of opinion could belong. Secondly, pressure has been exercised to make me resign. That makes resignation impossible for me for it would imply that I admitted that what I did or said was wrong, and that I cannot admit.

As I have been secretary for seven years, of which the recent year, in which we organized the exhibition in the Tholsel and the visit of the Belfast Field Club, has been the most successful, I should have to consider the request to resign as a mark of disapproval. I could not take it in any other way.

Before you make a decision I would like you to look back over the many pleasant summer afternoons we have spent together in the past seven years, and how often we might have split upon just such issues as this and yet we survived. Do you remember, for instance, the outing to Carrickshock, when Father Clohosey spoke to us on the Tithe War at the memorial to the three men who had been killed in an attack on the tithe collector, Edmund Butler, who, with twelve policemen, lost his life? Most of the Protestants went home from the bottom of the hill, but I went to the top, because I knew that Father Clohosey could be relied on to give an impartial account of this bitter controversial event. And that is just what he did do. And, if you remember, it was I who offered him the thanks of the Society when the evening ended at Ballybodan. Yet that was an issue which, had I been a bigoted person, might have affected me strongly. My great grandfather, Richard Butler, the Rector of Burnchurch, near Bennettsbridge, had been mobbed and molested so frequently by the agitators that in the end he had to leave his home for several years. Yet in fact, he thought, as I think, that the tithe agitators had right on their side. He did not, and no more could I, make a sectarian issue of it.

I mention myself because I have been attacked, but each one of us has acted in the same way. Our little Society, under our chairman, John O'Leary, has been doing Christian work healing the sores of history and reconciling conflicting opinions. I am quite certain that His Excellency, the Nuncio, could not possibly wish it to come to grief.

It would not have been surprising if we had split on some local issue of Kilkenny history, the Confederation, Cromwell, the Penal Laws, but it is to me almost unbelievable that we should be in danger of disintegrating because of two different interpretations of tragedies that happened eleven years ago in the plains of Slavonia and the wild hills of Bosnia and Herzegovina.

As I would like you to understand something of the issues at stake, I will quote you the letter I wrote to the Nuncio, but I gather at present he does not want it to appear in the press.

> Maidenhall
> Bennettsbridge,
> Co. Kilkenny.
> Nov. 2, 1952
>
> Your Excellency,
>
> I would like to express my regret at any embarrassment or pain I may have caused you by my remarks after Mr O'Curry's talk. I felt, as I have felt for six years, that vital facts were being suppressed and that, though their discussion might at first be very bitter, worse would follow if they were ignored.
>
> I think the enclosed letter from Mgr Stepinac, which I translated and published Dec. 29, 1950 in *The Church of Ireland Gazette*, discloses a complex situation in Yugoslavia, which could not possibly be ignored in any discussion on "Yugoslavia, the Pattern of Persecution." You are not, I think, likely to have seen this letter, because it was never published in Yugoslavia or mentioned at the Archbishop's trial by his

accusers. The Communists were at that time holding him responsible for the barbarities of the conversion campaign and this letter shows too clearly that he was not responsible for them.

Nonetheless, it also shows (the quotation from Mgr Mishitch in particular) that force was being used to affect opinion, or, to put it differently, the violence of the times was being exploited for the purpose of proselytism. Since these were the methods used then and later by the Communists for their proselytism too, an unfair and unbalanced view of persecution in Yugoslavia would have been obtained if Mr O'Curry's paper had not been discussed in the light of these facts.

The International Affairs Association with its membership drawn from all creeds seemed the only forum in which these delicate issues could be soberly discussed. I went as the guest of a foundation member, who assured me that unfettered discussion had always been the order of the day.

I had gone, I admit, with the intention of disputing Mr O'Curry's interpretations, which I already knew, but, believe me, the last thing I wished to do was to insult you, your Church or Mr O'Curry.

My family is Irish, I was born here and have lived here most of my life. My experience and the experience of most Irish Protestants is that the kindliness, toleration and good will of Irish Catholics towards their Protestant fellow countrymen is such that it is hard for us even to conceive what bitterness and violence can exist in other lands.

In conclusion I would like to assure your Excellency of my sincere esteem and good will.

Yours sincerely,
Hubert Butler

As for the charge that I spoke uncharitably of Mgr Stepinac, I hope that one of the Kilkenny papers will print the account which I published over a year ago in *The Chuch of Ireland Gazette*, 20 April 1951, of a visit paid to Mgr Stepinac with four Quakers. It will show that I never thought him "a dupe" (a misreporting) and that my feelings towards him have always been respectful.

I will here quote one extract: "Mgr Stepinac in prison is a figure who commands respect. What he did, he did in the belief that it was right. Christians, who think otherwise—and there are millions of them—would mostly agree that while he remains in prison, the focus of violent emotions, there is little hope of a dispassionate enquiry into the tragic story of 1941."

I attach also a translation of the letter from Mgr Stepinac to Pavelitch, which I have sent to the Nuncio. It is long and difficult, but I took great pains to translate it accurately from the Serbo-Croatian, and I am rather surprised that here, where Mgr Stepinac is so greatly venerated, it excited so little interest on publication nearly two years ago. No Irish paper asked permission to republish it, yet I believe it is the most important letter the Archbishop ever wrote. The facts to which he refers are all corroborated in the publications of the Serbian Orthodox Church.

Those who read the letter will admire Mgr Stepinac for his courage and humanity, though some may share the views of the Serbian Orthodox Church, expressed very strongly in their wartime publications, that he could have helped them best by witholding his recognition from the Government which decreed their compulsory conversion. But I do not think we are likely to divide on this point along the obvious lines. It is a question upon which each person will have his own individual opinion.

The Archbishop's letter will show that Count O'Brien, who is quoted against me in the Dublin and Kilkenny papers, is a wholly unreliable historian. Of the gigantic compulsory conversion campaign he writes on page 16 of his book on Mgr Stepinac, published by *The Standard*, "It was through Mgr Stepinac's firm stand that Pavelitch's endeavours to impose the Catholic faith by force ended in complete failure." Mgr Stepinac, who is modest as well as brave, shows in the attached letter how wildly untrue this statement is. The compulsory conversion campaign in Croatia, 1941, was one of the most terrible in the history of Europe.

I am glad to say that these problems do not touch us here, where for several generations we have shown tolerance and not tried to force our faith upon each other. Yet, at the meeting in Dublin, having expert knowledge relating to a subject which was being very seriously investigated, I felt it my duty to speak as I did. I could not have done otherwise.

(1952)

The Artukovitch File

I

Reflections on a Croatian Crusade

Some years after I had written "The Sub-Prefect Should Have Held His Tongue," I was in New York and read how the Yugoslav Government was urging that Artukovitch, Pavelitch's Minister of the Interior, who was living in California, should be extradited. I went to the Yugoslav Consulate to enquire about this and was handed a fat yellow booklet called *Artukovitch, The Himmler of Yugoslavia* by three New Yorkers called Gaffney, Starchevitch and McHugh.

Artukovitch first won notoriety in October 1934. He had gone to England at the time of King Alexander's murder at Marseilles. After his visit to Paris, the king had intended to see his son, Crown Prince Peter, at Sandroyd School, so, in case the Marseilles attempt failed, Artukovitch had been deputed to arrange for the king's assassination in England. It did not fail so Artukovitch waited in Czechoslovakia and Hungary till the Nazi invasion of Yugoslavia. He then returned with them and held various ministerial posts under Pavelitch from 1944 to 1945 in the Independent State of Croatia. Very few people have heard of him, yet if his story were told with remorseless candour, we would have a picture not only of Croatia forty years ago, but of all Christendom in our century. Everything that the New Yorkers relate was already known to me, except for one startling paragraph, an extract from a

memoir by Artukovitch himself. After describing how he escaped to
Austria and Switzerland in 1945, he goes on:

> I stayed in Switzerland until July 1947. Then with the knowl-
> edge of the Swiss Ministry of Justice I obtained personal
> documents for myself and my family, which enabled us to
> travel to Ireland. Using the name of Anitch, we stayed there
> until 15th July, 1948. When our Swiss documents expired, the
> Irish issued new papers and under Irish papers we obtained
> a visa for entry into the USA.

So evidently we in Ireland had sheltered this notable man for a
whole year. He was not, like Eichmann, a humble executive, but himself a maker of history, dedicated to the extermination not of Jews
alone, but also of his fellow-Christians, the Serbian Orthodox. He was
a member of the government which in the spring of 1941 introduced
laws which expelled them from Zagreb, confiscated their property and
imposed the death penalty on those who sheltered them. Some twenty
concentration camps were established in which they were exterminated. Why do we know so little about his sojourn in among us? Did
he stay in a villa at Foxrock or in lodgings at Bundoran or in some se-
cluded midland cloister? And who looked after him? The Red Cross?
And did we cherish him because he presented himself to us as a Christian refugee from godless Communism? That seems to me rather likely.

Nowadays we usually estimate cruelty by statistics and Gaffney
and Co. use the figures normally recorded for Croatia by Jewish and
Orthodox writers, that is to say, 30,000 Jews and 750,000 Orthodox
massacred, 240,000 Orthodox forcibly converted to Catholicism[*]. Even
if these figures are exaggerated, it was the most bloodthirsty religio-racial crusade in history, far surpassing anything achieved by Cromwell
and the Spanish Inquisitors. I am sorry that Gaffney and Co. give so

---

[*] See footnote on page 178. (Editors)

many photographs of headless babies, of disembowelled shopkeepers, of burning beards soaked in kerosene, for Artukovitch was, like Himmler, a "desk-murderer," who deplored the disorderly and sadistic way in which his instructions were carried out. He was respectable, and it is the correlation of respectability and crime that nowadays has to be so carefully investigated.

The three writers tell Artukovitch's story with much emotion, because, as is plain, they want him to be extradited and hanged. But in itself the story is of the highest importance, for no earlier crusade has been so richly documented. If the abundant material were coolly and carefully studied, how much could we learn about human weakness and hypocrisy! We could observe how adroitly religion can be used in the service of crime. When Pavelitch and Artukovitch and their armies retreated, they were sure that, on the defeat of Germany, England and America would turn upon Russia and they could return to Zagreb. Therefore nothing was destroyed, the state documents were stored in the Archiepiscopal Palace, the gold (dentures, wrist-watches and all) was hidden below the deaf and dumb confessional in the Franciscan monastery and cemented over by the friars themselves. The newspapers of the time, secular and ecclesiastical, are still to be seen in the Municipal Library, but this huge pile of documents, the Rosetta Stone of Christian corruption, has not yet been effectively deciphered.

These terrible Church papers, 1941 to 1945, should destroy forever our faith in those diplomatic prelates, often good and kindly men, who believe that at all costs the ecclesiastical fabric, its schools and rules, its ancient privileges and powers, should be preserved. The clerical editors published the Aryan laws, the accounts of the forced conversions, without protest, the endless photographs of Pavelitch's visits to seminaries and convents and the ecstatic speeches of welcome with which he was greeted. Turn, for example, to *Katolicki Tjednik (The Catholic Weekly)*, Christmas 1941, and read the twenty-six-verse "Ode to Pavelitch," in which Archbishop Sharitch praises him for his measures against Serbs and Jews. Examine the Protestant papers and you will find the same story. Is it not clear that in times like those the Church doors should be shut, the Church newspapers closed down, and Christians, who believe that we should love our neighbours as ourselves, should go underground and try to build up a new faith in the catacombs?

Why did our professional historians not deal with all this long ago? They seem to wait till history is dead before they dare to touch it. But does a good surgeon only operate on corpses? They have wholly misinterpreted their functions, for it is their duty to expose the liar before his contagion has spread. While Artukovitch was on his way to Ireland, a Dublin publication told us authoritatively that the massacre of the Serbian Orthodox had never happened. In Count O'Brien's book* on Mgr Stepinac, to which I have already referred, we read:

> They [the Orthodox] were offered by Pavelitch the choice between conversion to the Catholic faith or death... But the Catholic Church as a whole, all her bishops and the overwhelming majority of her priests, led by the Archbishop of Zagreb, made this evil plan impossible.

Some of the correspondence between Artukovitch and Stepinac has been published in England by Richard Pattee** and, collating with Gaffney, we see how Stepinac, a brave and merciful though very simple man, was hopelessly compromised by his official connection with the state. It was only his own flock whom he could help, and even them very little. For example, he appealed to Artukovitch on behalf of one of his priests, Father Rihar, who had defied Pavelitch. His failure was absolute, for this is how Artukovitch replied:

> Zagreb. 17th November, 1942. In connection with your esteemed request of 2nd November, 1942... notice is hereby

---

* A.H. O'Brien, *Archbishop Stepinac, The Man and His Case* (London: 1947). (H.B.)
** Richard Pattee, *The Case of Cardinal Aloysius Stepinac* (London/Milwaukee: 1953). (H.B.)

given that Francis Rihar by the decree of this office of 20th April, 1942, No. 26417/1942, was sentenced to forced detention in the concentration camp at Jasenovac for a period of three years... because as pastor at Gornja Stubica he did not celebrate a solemn high mass on the anniversary of the founding of the Independent State of Croatia... nor did he consent to sing the psalm *Te Deum Laudamus*, saying that it was nowhere prescribed in ecclesiastical usage...

Stepinac appealed again, but Rihar had been already three months at Jasenovac and, therefore, according to the rules of this camp, he was killed.

How, anyway, could Stepinac defend Father Rihar with any authority, since he himself had done what Rihar refused to do? Gaffney and Co., on page 42, reproduced seven photographs of the celebration of Pavelitch's birthday on 15 June 1942, and a letter from the Archbishop exhorting his clergy to hold a *Te Deum* after High Mass the following Sunday, 17 June, because of "Our Glorious Leader."

Since Pattee omitted this very relevant letter, it is strange that he printed Stepinac's correspondence with Artukovitch about the Jews, for this makes it clear that in acknowledging the authority of Pavelitch, the Archbishop, for diplomatic reasons, felt obliged to accept the terminology of the anti-semites and their human classifications. For example, on 30 May 1941 he urged Artukovitch "to separate the Catholic non-Aryans from non-Christian non-Aryans in relation to their social position and in the manner of treating them."

Much has been written about Communist distortions of history, but only recently has our own inability, as Christians, to report facts honestly been closely investigated. Now, after twenty years, the dam has burst and the truth, a turbid stream, is inundating our self-complacency and irrigating our self-knowledge. Catholic scholars are leading the way. For example, Professor Gordon Zahn has shown how selective is the documentation on which the biographies of Christian heroes of the resistance are based. Their sermons and speeches were pruned of all the compliments they paid to Hitler and his New Order and no row of dots in the text marks the excision of these now-embarrassing ecstasies.

In the long run, remorseless truth-telling is the best basis for ecumenical harmony. Hitler once explained to Hermann Rauschning how he intended to use the Churches as his propagandists. "Why should we quarrel? They will swallow anything provided they can keep their material advantages." Yet Hitler never succeeded in corrupting the Churches as effectively as did Pavelitch and Artukovitch, who professed to be Christians. We shall not be able to estimate the extent of their success and how it might have been resisted, while a single fact is diplomatically "forgotten." It is well known that those who suppress history have to re-live it.

* * *

How did Artukovitch (alias Anitch) get to Ireland? I wrote to Yugoslavia, to America, France, Germany and questioned Yugoslavs in Dublin and London. The Yugoslavs, both Communist and anti-Communist, had no information. A friend in London, who had been to Trinity College, Dublin, remembered someone saying: "I'd like you to meet a very interesting chap called Anitch," but the meeting had never happened. In the end Branko Miljus, a former minister of the pre-war government in Belgrade, who now lives in Paris, got some news for me from a friend in Switzerland. If I seem to give too many names and details, it is so that his story can be checked and completed.

The first stage of the journey is fairly well known. Pavelitch and Artukovitch had escaped to Austria when the Croatian state collapsed. They seem to have been arrested by the British in Salzburg and, after "a mysterious intervention," released and there was an interval of hiding in monasteries at Sankt Gilgen and Bad Ischl. The Yugoslavs were in hot pursuit, so Pavelitch fled to Rome, disguised as a Spanish priest called Gomez. Artukovitch stayed on till November 1946, when he met the learned Dr Draganovitch, Professor of Theology at Zagreb, who was touring the internment camps with a Vatican passport. He had secured the release of many hundreds of Croat priests who had fled with Pavelitch. Now he obtained for Artukovitch papers under the name Alowz Anitch and put some money for him in a Swiss bank. Two other priests, Fathers Manditch and Juretitch, also came to his aid. The former, the treasurer to the Franciscan order, controlled a printing press at the Italian camp of Fermo and assisted the Ustashe (Croatian nationalist) refugees with funds and propaganda. Juretitch had been sent on a mission to Fribourg by Archbishop Stepinac, so he and Manditch, both former students of Fribourg University, were able to secure a welcome there for Artukovitch. Archbishop Sharitch, Pavelitch's poet-champion, had got there ahead of him. Both Draganovitch and Juretitch had been appointed by Mgr Stepinac to the Commission of Five for the Conversion of the Orthodox in November 1941. These three were important people to have as sponsors. The ecclesiastics of Fribourg must have been impressed. They recommended Artukovitch to the police who got him a *permis de séjour*. There were other difficulties, which, according to report, Artukovitch smoothed out by the gift of a Persian carpet to an influential official.

But meanwhile the Federal Police had learnt that Anitch was the war criminal Artukovitch. They told him he had two weeks in which to leave Switzerland. Once more the Franciscans came to his aid. The prior of the Maison Marianum at Fribourg recommended him to the Irish Consulate at Berne. And so it happened that in July 1947 Artukovitch landed with his family on the Isle of Saints, sponsored by the disciples of that saint, who had prayed:

> Lord, make me an instrument of Thy peace!
> Where there is hatred let me sow love,
> Where there is sadness, joy!

I do not know where Artukovitch spent his Irish year, but one day, as a matter of history, and perhaps of religion, we shall have to know. If Artukovitch had to be carried half-way round the earth on the wings

of Christian charity, simply because he favoured the Church, then
Christianity is dying. And if now, for ecumenical or other reasons, we
are supposed to ask no questions about him, then it is already dead.

On 15 July 1948 Artukovitch with an Irish identity card left Ireland
for the USA where he settled as a book-keeper, near his wealthy brother
in California, still under the name of Anitch. It was over two years
before his true identity was discovered. The Serbian Orthodox were
slow to move. Oppressed by the Communists at home, dispersed as
refugees abroad, they still managed to publish the facts in books and
papers in London, Chicago, Paris. In 1950 Branko Miljus, and two other
prominent monarchist politicians in exile, sent a memorandum to the
Fifth Assembly of the United Nations urging it to implement its resolution of December 1946, which had branded genocide as a crime
against international law. They asked that its member states should
take into custody, till a Commission be appointed to try them, some
120 Croat nationals, who had taken refuge among them. On the long
list appended, the names of Artukovitch, Archbishop Sharitch, Fathers
Draganovitch and Juretitch and many Franciscans were mentioned,
and some of the scarcely credible Franciscan story was related. It is
stated that a Franciscan had been commandant of Jasenovac, the worst
and biggest of the concentration camps for Serbs and Jews (he had
personally taken part in murdering the prisoners and Draganovitch,
with the rank of Lieut. Colonel, had been the chaplain). The memorandum relates how the focal centre for the forced conversions and the
massacres had been the Franciscan Monastery of Shiroki Brijeg in
Herzegovina (Artukovitch had been educated there) and how in 1942
a young man who was a law student at the college and a member of the
Catholic organization, The Crusaders, had won a prize in a competition
for the slaughter of the Orthodox by cutting the throats of 1360 Serbs
with a special knife. The prize had been a gold watch, a silver service,
a roast sucking pig and some wine.

How can this be true? One recalls that great hero of Auschwitz, the
Polish Franciscan Father Kolbe. But it was true and rumours of it had
reached Rome. Rushinovitch, Pavelitch's representative at the Vatican,

had reported to his Foreign Minister in Zagreb the remarks of Cardinal Tisserant, with whom he had an audience on 5 March 1942:

> I know for sure that even the Franciscans of Bosnia-Herze-govina behaved atrociously. Father Shimitch, with a revolver in his hand, led an armed gang and destroyed Orthodox Churches. No civilized and cultured man, let alone a priest, can behave like that.

Tisserant had probably got some of his information from the Italian general of the Sassari division at Knin, who had reported that Shimitch had come to him as local representative of the Croatian Government and had told him that he had orders to kill all the Serbs. The general had had instructions not to interfere in local politics, so he could only protest. The killing, under Franciscan leadership, had begun. The following year the Superior of the Franciscan Monastery in Knin was decorated by Pavelitch for his military activities with the order of King Zvonimir III.

The Croat bishops themselves were aware of what was happening. The Bishop of Kotor, Dr Butorac, while agreeing that the moment was propitious for mass conversion, wrote to Mgr Stepinac (4 November 1941) that the wrong type of missionaries were being sent – "priests in whose hands revolvers might better be placed than a crucifix."

In parenthesis, I should say, how fascinating are Rushinovitch's accounts of his audiences in Rome with Pius XII, with Cardinals Tardini, Maglione, Sigismondi and Spellman. Only Tisserant, and to a lesser extent Mgr Montini, the present Pope, appear to have fully grasped what was happening in Croatia. In Cardinal Ruffini the Ustashe had a firm supporter.

The memorandum made little impression on the United Nations, since it had no member state behind it. It had accused Tito's Government, which *was* a member state, of sheltering many Croat criminals and using them to break down the anti-Communist resistance of the

Serbs. However, in 1952 Tito appealed to the USA for the extradition
of Artukovitch. The California Courts to whom the case was referred
argued that the extradition treaty of 1901 between the USA and Serbia
had never been renewed and that therefore Artukovitch could not be
handed over to Yugoslavia. Six years later the Supreme Court rejected
this view (by 7 to 1) and decreed that the case must be tried again in
California. In the meantime Artukovitch had become a member of the
Knights of Columbus and a much-respected figure who gave lectures
to institutes and interviews on TV. When he was arrested again 50,000
Knights sent petitions on his behalf to Congress, and the West Penn-
sylvania Lodges of the Croatian Catholic Union forwarded a resolution
that "his only crime is his ceaseless fight against Communism" and
that he was a champion of the rights and freedoms of all the peoples
of the world.

That was the way his counsel, O'Connors and Reynolds, presented
him, too, and Father Manditch, who had helped him in Switzerland,
was once more by his side, in charge of another printing press and now
Superior of the Franciscan Monastery in Drexel Boulevard, Chicago.
His papers *Nasha Nada* and *Danica* (*Our Hope* and *Morning Star*) not only
supported him but in their issues of 7 May 1958 urged their readers to
send subscriptions for the Ustashe refugee fund to Artukovitch at his
address in Surfside, California.

Another very useful ally was Cardinal Stepinac's secretary, Father
Lackovitch, who had sought asylum at Youngstown, Ohio. In Europe
Stepinac had been almost beatified for his implacable hostility to
Pavelitch and Artukovitch, but now *The Mirror News* of Los Angeles
(24 January 1958) reported Lackovitch as saying that he had seen Artukovitch almost daily and that he had been "the leading Catholic
layman of Croatia and the lay spokesman of Cardinal Stepinac and had
consulted him on the moral aspect of every action he took." The murderers of the Old World had become the martyrs of the New.

The American public was so ill-informed that it was possible to get
away with almost anything. Pattee prints a statement that 200,000
of the converts from Orthodoxy were returning "with a right

intention" to a Church, which "for political reasons" they had been forced to abandon. In fact, of course, the Serbian Orthodox had been in schism for some three centuries before the Protestant Reformation. Cardinal Tisserant, who had a rare tolerance of disagreeable truths, denounced Rushinovitch vigorously when he tried out this argument on him:

> I am well acquainted with the history of Christianity and to my knowledge Catholics of Roman rite never became Ortho-dox… The Germans helped you kill all the priests and you got rid of 350,000 Serbs, before you set up the Croatian Orthodox Church. What right have you to accuse others and keep on telling us that you are guardians of culture and the faith? In the war with the Turks the Serbs did just as much for Cathol-icism as you did and perhaps more. But it was the Croats, all the same, who got the title of *Antemurale Christianitatis*.

When I was in California, I went to see Father Mrvicin of the Serbian Orthodox Cathedral at West Garvey, near Los Angeles, and asked him why the Orthodox and the Jews of California had tolerated so many lies. He told me that at the time of the extradition trial he had circu-larized close on a thousand Serbs, who must have known well about Artukovitch, urging them to give evidence, but very few had replied. Life in the USA was hard for them as refugees, they did not want to affront a powerful community, McCarthyism was not yet dead and they were shy of associating themselves with an appeal that came from a Communist country. A naturalized American, who took the matter up, died violently and mysteriously.

As for the Jews, though 30,000 with their 47 rabbis had been mur-dered in Croatia, Croatia was far away, and many who had escaped to USA had owed their safety to holding their tongues. Even so, the Jewish War Veterans of California, *The Valley Jewish News* and some Gentile papers like *The Daily Signal* of California came out against Artukovitch.

But most Americans felt for the unknown refugee and his five children the easy charity of indifference. Finally the Yugoslav Government did some profitable deals with the USA and became indifferent, too. It is now interested only in proving that Artukovitch was a helpless stooge of the Nazis and that therefore the Bonn Government should pay compensation to Yugoslavia for the damage that he and the Ustashe had done.

The other day I came across a *History of Croatia*, published by the New York Philosophical Library. The author, Mr Preveden, acknowledges various "inspiring messages of commendation and encouragement." One of them comes from "Dr Andrija Artukovitch of Los Angeles." He is quite a public figure. He may have changed his address but his telephone number used to be Plymouth 5-1147.

Now many people want him hanged but there would not be much point in it. He was an insignificant man, who got his chance because there had been a great breakdown in the machinery of Christianity and he was able to pose as its protector. Why did this breakdown occur? Can it be repaired and, if so, how? So long as we are obliged to pretend that the breakdown did not happen, we shall never find out.

(1970)

Postscript 1971. There has since been an easing of tension between Communism and Christianity, most notably in Yugoslavia, where diplomatic relations with the Vatican have been resumed and there has been friendship between Catholic and Orthodox. For example, in a Christmas message, Bishop Pichler begged forgiveness of the Orthodox Church and their Serbian brothers for all the wrongs done to them and funds have been raised by Catholics to restore the destroyed Orthodox churches.

Some of the leading Orthodox are not wholly happy about all this. Is it spontaneous or Government inspired? Is it possible that Tito fears the deep-rooted and passionate nationalism of the Orthodox more than Catholic universalism, which can be manipulated by external arrangements? Under the amnesty to political offenders, many Ustashe have returned home, notably Father Draganovitch, one of the five "regulators" of the Forced Conversions, who escorted Pavelitch and Artukovitch to safety. He is in a monastery near Sarajevo editing the Schematismus, a sort of ecclesiastical year-book, whose publication has been suspended since 1939. Some of his returned colleagues are more active politically.

There is, of course, everything to be said for peace and conciliation, but the brotherly love that is brought about by diplomatic manoeuvres is often a little suspect.

II

In Search of a Professor of History

I could not get it out of my head that eighteen years before, Artukovitch had stayed for a year in Ireland. How had he come here? Who had sheltered him and where? In the spring of 1966 I was in Dublin for a week and I decided to find out. I was convinced that only some highly organized international body could have brought a wanted man so secretly and efficiently across Europe and, since the Franciscans had been so closely associated with the Ustashe in Croatia and had many international links I was confident that it was they who had brought him. I have never heard anything but good of Irish Franciscans but they were an institutionalized body and as such able and anxious to protect their members who get into trouble abroad.

There were a dozen Franciscan Houses in Ireland and I wrote to the Provincial in Merchant's Quay, Dublin, and also to four or five other houses, which, because of their remoteness, I thought were likely. Most of them answered with polite negative replies. The Provincial told me there had been a Croat Franciscan at their Galway house for some time but his name, Brother Ivanditch, was on the list of their Order and they had no doubt of his identity.

It was not till Branko Miljus sent me his copy of *The Mirror News* of Los Angeles that I made any progress. Artukovitch had been interviewed by the reporter, Henry Frank, who for the photograph had arranged him at a piano, grouping his wife and five handsome children round him. The Rev. Robert Ross of the Blessed Sacrament Church was there too as a friend and advocate. He told Frank how, as Minister of the Interior, Artukovitch had helped the Jews and been a formidable foe to the Communists.

"Artukovitch listened gravely and said with quiet dignity, 'I put my faith in God'."

Frank spoke of Artukovitch's "strong, seamed face" and his "modest well lived-in living room." He told how his daughter, Zorica, had won an essay competition in Orange County High School and his nine-year-old son, Radoslav, had been born in Ireland.

Here was a clue. The children had been exploited sentimentally to mask the truth, so they could be used to rediscover it. I went to the Customs House and after prolonged search I found Radoslav Anitch's birth certificate (A. 164, No. 75). He was born on 1 June 1948 at the Prague House Nursing Home, 28 Terenure Road East; he was the son of Alois Anitch, Professor of History, of 6 Zion Road, Rathgar.

On the strength of this discovery, I sent a letter to all the Dublin dailies, explaining that I was writing an account of the Independent State of Croatia (1941-45) and that I wished information about the former Minister of the Interior, Andrija Artukovitch, (alias Alois Anitch) who had lived at 6 Zion Road, Rathgar, in 1947. Only *The Irish Times* printed my letter, turning him into a lady called Audrey.

In the meantime I visited the two houses, which were close to each other. No. 6 Zion Road is a two-storied house of red brick with an ivy-tangled sycamore and an overgrown privet hedge, but it had changed hands so often that it told me nothing about Artukovitch's Irish sponsors.

No. 28 Terenure Road, a tall building of red and white brick with much ornamental ironwork, has ceased for some years to be a nursing home. Nobody knew where the former owner had gone and it was not till I paid two visits to the Guards Barracks at Terenure that one of them recalled where she now lived. It was not far off at 7 Greenmount Road and I went there immediately. The matron was a charming and intelligent woman and after eighteen years she remembered the Anitches perfectly. She had found them a pleasant and pathetic couple. He had spoken little English, Mrs Anitch had spoken fluently and, because of that, she had asked that he should have lunch with her in the Nursing Home. "He is my baby," Mrs Anitch had said, "he wouldn't know how to get lunch without me." They had two little girls who were at the Sacred Heart Convent, in Drumcondra Road, and now they wanted a boy. "If it's a girl," said Mrs Anitch, "don't call him till the evening." But when on the morning of 1 June Radoslav had been born, she was so delighted that he said her husband must be called at once. Anitch came and in his joy he had embraced the matron, much to her embarrassment. The Anitches had behaved nicely paying all their debts with money from America. After they had gone some months Mrs Anitch had written a grateful letter, which the matron showed me.

Only one person besides her husband had visited Mrs Anitch in the Nursing Home. He was a Franciscan who had been in Croatia, but the matron was not clear whether or not he was a foreigner. The Anitches had told her that the Communists had been particularly vindictive against the Franciscans.

My anticipations that the Franciscans had helped Artukovitch in Ireland had now been confirmed so I went to see the Provincial at Merchants' Quay. This time he agreed with me that the friar at the Nursing Home must have been the Croat at the Galway House. His name, he said, was Ivanditch. He was a supporter of Pavelitch and had often gone from Galway to Dublin.

Yet a Croat friar could not have made all these arrangements without powerful Irish assistance. Where had it come from?

The process by which a great persecutor is turned into a martyr is surely an interesting one that needs the closest investigation. I had only four days left in Dublin, so I could not follow up all the clues, but I made some progress.

First I went to the Sacred Heart Convent, 40 Drumcondra Road, a big red building on the left hand side of the street. I was shown into a little waiting-room and was received by a charming and friendly nun. I told her I was trying to trace the family of two little girls called Zorica and Vishnya Anitch, who had been at the convent in 1947 when they were four and five years old. She went away to look them up in her register and I sat for a very long time contemplating the plate of wax fruit and the little figurine of St. Anthony. Then the nun returned and told me that the two little girls (but they were called Katherina and Aurea Anitch) had been admitted on 9 August 1947. Their parents had lived at 7 Tower Avenue, Rathgar and had taken the children to the USA on 15 July 1948. She did not recall them herself but suggested that I ring up an older nun, Sister Agnes, who would certainly remember them. She was at St Vincent's Convent, North William Street. I rang Sister Agnes, who remembered them all vividly. The little girls were sweet and she had found the two parents "a lovely pair" and Dr Anitch was "a marvellous musician." She did not remember that anybody came to visit the children except their parents, but a Franciscan monk, a nephew of Dr Anitch's, who had escaped with them from Croatia, was with them and had helped them to find lodgings.

Next I visited 7 Tower Avenue and was directed to a previous tenant, who worked in an ironmongery in D'Olier Street. He said he did remember having a lodger with a name like Anitch. He added, "He was black, you know." I tried other houses in Tower Avenue. Everybody was helpful and interested but I got no further clues.

After this I returned to Mrs O'Donoghue in Greenmount Road and found she had been keenly interested in what I had told her and herself had been trying to find out who had been the landlord in 6 Zion Road when the Anitches had lived there. She said I should get in touch with

Patrick Lawlor, 32 Hazelbrook Road, who had sold the house to some woman in 1947.

I wrote to him and the next day he rang me up. He said it was so long ago that he could not remember the woman's name, but the auctioneer might know. After that I made some dozen visits and twenty telephone calls. They would be boring to relate but I found them exhilarating, as each clue led to anther clue. I telephoned the doctor who had delivered Radoslav and examined the parish registers in Terenure and Rathgar for christenings. I went to the Valuation Office and telephoned the Voters Register, the Irish Red Cross, the Aliens Office and the International Office of Refugees. I enquired at the city hall about Corporation Rates. In the end I got onto the solicitor who had acted both for Mr Lawlor and for the woman to whom he had sold 6 Zion Road. His clerk made an unsuccessful search for her name and then suggested, "Why not call on Thom's Directory?"

I went there the next day and the secretary took down from a shelf the directories for 1947 and 1948 and found Patrick Lawlor's name in both. "But that's impossible," I protested. "He sold the house to a woman in 1947." "Yes, but there might have been a delay in publishing after we collected the information." She took down the directory for 1949. "The woman's name was Kathleen Murphy," she said. I was off like a shot to a telephone-box.

There were three Miss K. Murphys in the directory and five Mrs Kathleen Murphys and several K. Murphys, who might be either male or female. It was lengthy business for some were out and I was asked to ring later and some were testy at being catechised by a stranger. The fifth answered very suspiciously. "Who are you? Why do you want to know? Yes, I was at 6 Zion Road, but if you want to know more you must come down. I remember the Anitches and, if you're friends of theirs I'd be glad to see you. Do you know them?" I said I did not but that a friend of mine in Paris, M. Miljus, would like to get in touch with them.

So we drove down to 6 Barnhill Road, Dalkey, a fine broad street with handsome villas. My wife waited outside in the car writing letters, while Mrs Murphy, a friendly middle-aged woman talked to me in her drawing-room. A friend of hers was just leaving when I came in, an Ulsterwoman with a nice downright manner, whose husband had been a bank manager in Kilkenny. She remembered us straight off when I said my name. "Yes, I know who you are. I read your letters and articles in *The Irish Times*. I remember you got into a row with the Nuncio, Dr O'Hara, and it was on the head of you he got the boot!" She and Peggy talked together while I was with Mrs Murphy, who I could see had a powerful affection for this foreign family who had lodged with her. In particular she admired "Dr Anish," whom she connected with "Czech-oslavia." This confusion is not very surprising. Artukovitch would not have mentioned Yugoslavia, which did not exist for him, and not much was known in Ireland of Croatia, though one of those who were kind to him in Dublin said he came from Craishe. In general he was be-friended as a foreign refugee from Communism and hitherto I have found no trace of sinister international intrigue among those who gave him hospitality.

Mrs Murphy reproached herself repeatedly for not having kept in touch with the "Anishes" in California. Several times they had written charming letters. What a delightful family they were! "They made a wonderful impression all round," she said. "I'd like to show you some snaps I have of them." Mrs Murphy took down a photograph album with a large bundle of snaps in the middle. She rummaged through them all the time we were talking but never found what she was look-ing for. I explained to her that some time after Dr Anitch had got to California he had been the subject of bitter controversy and I showed her the picture of the family in *The Mirror News*. "Ah, how old he has got to look, poor man! And that big girl must be Katerina and that one Aurea. And goodness me that young chap must be Radoslav! How time flies!" When I told her what his enemies were saying she shook her head indignantly. "People will say anything! I don't think he thought of politics at all. All he cared about was his family. He was a wonderful father and husband! He was a very good man you know. He was rather like President Kennedy. He wanted justice for everybody. And he loved the Church. They were daily communicants." Then I asked her how she had met him in the first place and she said she thought it had been at some party. Maybe some priest had introduced them. She became a little vague on the whole in this pregnant conversation. I was being the sly one, she the candid one. I asked did she meet a Franciscan with him and she said, "Oh, yes, there was one came to lunch a couple of times. But the Anishes lived very quietly. They hardly saw anyone. You see he was a very retiring scholarly man. He once or twice gave a lecture at UCD, but otherwise they just thought of the children." I subsequently made enquiries about those lectures at UCD but with no success.

Then I told her what remorseless enemies he had and explained something of the collapse of Yugoslavia. I showed her *Artukovitch, the Himmler of Yugoslavia*, turning the pages rapidly so as to reach some not too emotive pictures of him in the days of his glory. There he was giving the Nazi salute to a German general and there again greeting Hitler's envoy at the head of his Security Police, and there with his wife at a cocktail party in the Hungarian embassy. I skipped some horror pages, headed with heavy irony ANDRIJA ARTUKOVITCH'S HEROIC DEEDS and including a picture of a soldier scissoring off the head of a seated peasant with some shears. Except for their attribution, such photographs are probably genuine. As I have said, Artukovitch was probably a desk murderer only. Mrs Murphy must have caught a glimpse of the scissored head for she stiffened and started to fumble again in her album for her friendly snapshots.

"Everybody in Dublin seems to have liked him," I said, "but why did he come here with a false name?"

"Probably he was forced to. Lots of people are. He couldn't have been a Nazi, though he may have been forced to take that side. I'm a good judge of character. I've travelled in sixteen countries and know a good man when I see one."

"But he signed all those laws against the Jews" (I thought it would be too complicated to talk about the Orthodox she might not know who they were).

"Well, look what the Jews are doing to other people!" (I suppose she was thinking of the Arabs.)

Then we said good bye. As I left she repeated; "They just lived for their children. They thought the world of them."

The next place I had to visit was the Franciscan House in Galway from which Dr Anitch's nephew, Brother Ivanditch, paid visits to Dublin to see him.

When we reached Galway I went round to the Franciscan House, which is a few streets away from Eyre Square. Beside the big church I saw a small private door through which some traveling clerics with suit-cases were being hospitably ushered. I waited till they had all been welcomed before I went in and, after a few moments, the Father Superior appeared. Though he was preoccupied with his visitors he received me kindly. Seeing my attaché case he thought I was a commercial traveller, but when I explained I had come as a historian interested to find out about a Croat friar called Ivanditch, who was in Galway in 1947, he said, "I'm afraid I don't know the good man. I'm only here three years, but, if you come tomorrow, when we've a bit more time, I'll get Brother Bede onto you. He was here in 1947."

The following day I went round to the Franciscan House at 11.30 and Brother Bede received me. Yes. He remembered Brother Ivanditch well and had looked him up in the "Schematismus" of the Order. He was from the province of Bosnia, near Sarajevo. He was a very striking looking chap and must have been over six foot. He was born in 1913. "He wasn't here but at our hostel, St Anthony's College along the Moycullen Road, so I didn't see much of him. But they say he spent all his time at the wireless listening to the news in German, French, Italian, Spanish; he was a very intelligent fellow, learnt English quickly. But he was broody, reserved and melancholy. All soul, you might say."

Brother Bede had spent the war years in Rome. In the Franciscan headquarters the Croats had been more prominent than any other Slav group. Apart from Father Manditch, the treasurer of the Order, there was Father Jelachitch, a great canon-lawyer, and Brother Balitch, an eminent palaeographer who had written about Duns Scotus. "You've no idea what confusion there was in Rome at that time. As for us, we put all the Slavs in one basket, a terribly passionate lot. We couldn't unscramble them."

"Who sent him here? Oh, I suppose it was the General of our Order in Rome. I think it was Schaaf at that time, but I could look that one up. It was a question of obedience, you know."

I told him that the Ustashe ambassador to Rome, Rushinovitch, had been given audiences by many cardinals and had sent his impressions of them back to Zagreb. It was obvious that not only the Irish but all the clerics at Rome had been highly confused by what was happening in Croatia. Only Cardinal Tisserant, I said, had a clear idea. On the other hand Cardinal Ruffini was a vigorous supporter and protector of the Ustashe!

"Ruffini!" Brother Bede laughed. "Yes, indeed. He was a Sicilian, a great nationalist! They are as excitable as the Slavs. We took everything they said with a pinch of salt."

As for Ivanditch, he had stayed for about a year in Galway and then gone to Canada. But there was a rumour that he was in Valencia, Spain, now. He was still alive or he wouldn't be in the Schematismus.

Brother Bede did not think I would get much more information from St Anthony's College as they were always changing their staff there, but there was a Brother David who might remember him. "Worth trying anyway. Cross the salmon-weir bridge along the Moycullen Road till you come to a long grey building on the left."

They were widening the road and the surface was terrible so it must have been very close to the Brothers' dinner-time when I got to St Anthony's. The most pleasant thing about the building was the fine stone wall, a new one, that surrounded it. Most of the Galway walls are still excellently built and of stone, as unlike as possible to the new walls of the midlands, which, maybe because of the rich stoneless soil, are built of concrete, which submits itself readily to many vulgar and modish fancies.

I waited in a very clean and polished parlour under a picture of Jesus mediating on the Mount of Olives, till Brother David came along. He and his colleague, Brother Edmond, remembered Ivanditch well, and Brother David showed me a photograph of himself and Brother Ivanditch and a Galway lady, Mrs O'Halloran. They were a handsome group. Ivanditch, whose religious name was Brother Louis (Croatian Lujo), was dark, clean-shaven, spectacled. A pleasant serious person he looked in his long-brown habit with its white cord.

"But he was very hysterical," Brother David said. "He'd been sentenced to death by the Communists and he spent all his time listening to the ups and downs of Communism on the wireless. He was with us about a year, sent here by the General at Rome, waiting for instructions where to go. He was a professor of Dogmatic Theology. According to what he said, he was second-in-command to the Provincial at Zagreb. He had been given the seal of the Province of Croatia – he had it with him here – when the Provincial was imprisoned."

I asked him if Artukovitch (Anitch) had ever been to visit him. "No, he had no visitors at all though once or twice he went to Dublin."

"He brooded the whole time. He said the only hope for us was to have a third world war immediately. He thought us a very weak lot. There was a milk strike in Galway at the time and he could not understand why we did not settle it straight away by shooting the milkmen. And we should invade the six counties and settle that matter too *immediately.*"

"What amazed us about him," Brother Edmond said, "was the way he ate jam for breakfast... sometimes nearly a whole pot, and without any bread, just with a spoon. And though he got to know English very well, he used some very funny expressions. When we used to ask him if he would like another helping of anything, he would say, "Thank you, no, I am fed up!" But he made a great friend in the town who could tell you more about him than I can, Joe O'Halloran of the Corrib

Printing Works. He was working in O'Gorman's book shop in those days and he and Brother Louis used to see a lot of each other. Joe is the son of Mrs O'Halloran you saw in the snap shot."

It was difficult to believe that the Galway Brothers belonged to the same order as the Ustashe Franciscans. What was nearest to Brother Edmond's heart was a scheme for building houses for the homeless by voluntary groups. He had been considering this idea, while he was with the Order in Louvain.

Joe O'Halloran was in a white coat working at the Corrib Printers when I called. He asked for a few moments to change and then he joined me at the Imperial Hotel and we had vodka and orange together. He had only been eighteen when Brother Ivanditch was in Galway, and he had been hugely impressed by this glamorous and passionate foreigner who had fled from his country under sentence of death, who had seen his Provincial sentenced to five years' penal servitude and his Primate, a world famous cardinal, condemned to sixteen years imprisonment by a Communist government. They had spent every Sunday together and Joe's parents had been equally captivated by this engaging person, who bore with him the seals of the Franciscan Order in Croatia and the responsibility to make its sorrows known to the world. It was his dream to establish a Croatian Seminary in Dublin. Ireland must know what Croatia had suffered and was still suffering in the name of Christ. She must know that the fate that had befallen Croatia awaited all Europe. They must be prepared.

Brother Lujo counted on Joe O'Halloran's support in this sacred cause. But after a year the orders came from Rome for him to cross the Atlantic. He sailed from Liverpool to Montreal and Joe O'Halloran saw him off in Dublin. But though he had left Joe in charge of a sort of crusade, he had not replied at all regularly to his letters and slowly they had lost touch with each other. Joe learnt, though, that Brother Lujo had been appointed chaplain to the Croat workers at Windsor, which is on the Canadian side of the Detroit river. They worked in the Ford factory at Dearborn and Brother Lujo built for them the Chapel of St

Joseph. Later on he had heard that he had been secularized and had left
he Franciscan Order and it now occurred to Joe O'Halloran that this
might have been because the French-Canadian Franciscans did not
like Ivanditch's Croatian politics, which a few years later resulted in
the murder of the Yugoslav consul in Stockholm and a curious entente
with the Communists.

I asked about Artukovitch-Anitch and also about Count O'Brien,
but Joe knew nothing of them. The only layman in Galway that Ivanditch saw was Mr O'Flynn, the County Manager, who invited him to
tea, because his niece had once taught in Zagreb. Ivanditch had however
told Joe that he had an uncle in Dublin who had been a Minister in the
government of Croatia. Joe O'Halloran stressed that Ivanditch had
totally failed to inflame the Franciscans in Galway and was very much
disappointed in the Irish. He had been in Galway when the Republic
was proclaimed in Eyre Square, and he was amazed that the Government had tolerated an opposition for so long. Why had not they just
shot them?

In the past eighteen years Joe had changed. Ivanditch, were he to
return, would no longer have the intoxicating effect which he had had
on him as a very young man. In those days he had been puzzled that
his elders should be so apathetic. For example, Father Felim O'Brien, a
well-known Franciscan, had been lecturing in Galway and had treated
very coolly Ivanditch's passionate appeals for a crusade. O'Brien was
known all over Ireland for his dislike of "liberalism." Two or three years
later, in 1950, he engaged Owen Sheehy-Skeffington in a long controversy in *The Irish Times* later published as a pamphlet, on *The Liberal
Ethic*. I had contributed to this controversy so I have kept some records
of it. O'Brien had maintained that in Ireland we owe our freedom of
expression more to the clerics than to the liberal doctrine of tolerance,
and that in Europe the Catholic clergy are the chief champions of
liberty.

We got back late from Galway and it was a day before I was able to look up Ivanditch in my books. I found only one reference to him. He was referred to on page 20 in the report of the Stepinac Trial, *Sudenje Lisaku, Stepincu, Salicu I Druzini*[*], in connection with the trial of the Provincial of the Franciscan Order, Father Modesto Martinchitch. The Provincial is said to have given Brother Lujo (Ivanditch), an Ustashe, a large sum of money to enable him to escape abroad. Brother Lujo was not one of the five friars who helped the Provincial bury the thirty-four trunks of Ustasha treasure under the confessional in the Franciscan Church in May 1945, and I find no record of any activities that in Communist eyes were criminal. I think that when he claimed to have been sentenced to death by the Communists, Ivanditch was trying to make himself more glamorous. He seems to have escaped early on with an ample travel allowance and the seals of the province. Whether or not Artukovitch was really his uncle, it may have been his task to escort him abroad in safety.

Since Brother Bede had mentioned Dr Balitch, the eminent palaeographer, at the Vatican, I looked him up in the vast book *Magnum Crimen* by Professor Victor Novak of Belgrade, not expecting to find anyone so scholarly and remote in this record of horror. But there he was on page 900. "Brother Doctor Karlo Balitch, Professor at the Franciscan University at Rome." His offence seems to have been slight but significant. When Marshal Kvaternik, the Commander of the Ustashe Forces, had arrived in Rome and visited the Institute of St Jerome in February 1942, Professor Balitch had been there to receive him, together with several other distinguished Croatian clerics and the whole staff of the Institute. Dr Balitch seems to have listened appreciatively while Dr Madjerec, the Rector, praised Kvaternik and the leader Pavelitch for their illustrious deeds in the cause of Christ.

The St Jerome Society was a very old and established Croat

---

[*] Translation: "The Trial of Lisak, Stepinac, Salić and Others." (Editors)

Institution with headquarters at Rome. Every year, even when Novak published his book in 1948, there were celebrations in honour of Pavelitch's birthday, attended by Croat Jesuits, Dominicans, Capuchins, Benedictines. When Marshal Kvaternik addressed the Institute prais-ing its work for the Ustashe there was loud and prolonged applause. This was in Rome, yet we have been told repeatedly that it was only under the strongest pressure that in Croatia itself the hierarchy lent their support to Pavelitch.

After the St Jerome Society had been suppressed in Croatia by Tito, Mgr Stepinac declared in his speech of defence: "The St Jerome Society has ceased to exist. Its suppression is a grave offence against the whole people." But surely it was rightly suppressed.

In an authoritarian community, when there is hypocrisy and con-nivance at the centre, the ripples from them spread outwards to the remote circumference: "In vain do they worship me, teaching as their doctrines the precepts of men."

In 1985 there is news of Dr Draganovitch, who helped Artukovitch to escape. I have been reading Tom Bower's story of Barbie, "the Butcher of Lyons" who eluded French justice after the war in 1951 by the "Rat line," an escape-route which the Americans set up for people who were valuable to the CIA. They were equipped with fake passports and iden-tity cards, but a contact was needed in Genoa, the port of embarkation, to supply the Rats with immigration papers for South America. Dra-ganovitch, who had helped so many Ustashe escape to the Argentine, was obviously the man for the job. His fees for the Rat Line, according to Tom Bower, were $1000 for adults, half-price for children and $1400 for VIP treatment.

Surprisingly, though his services to the escaping Ustashe were well-known and though he had been on the infamous Committee of Five for the conversion of the Orthodox, he was permitted legally to return to Yugoslavia.

Is it possible that just as Barbie had useful information to give the

Americans about the Communists, so Draganovitch had useful information to give the Communists about the Americans?

Artukovitch himself is still in California and, as I have related, sometime in the sixties the Yugoslav Government tired of asking for his extradition. Among other reasons, maybe, they thought that a sensational state trial in Zagreb might revive animosities between Serb and Croat.

However, in July 1981, the Board of Immigration Appeals in the USA, in view of a 1979 ruling of Congress, ordered that Artukovitch be deported. This was followed by further legal proceedings, appeals, counter-appeals, hearings and re-hearings.

In spring 1984 a civil suit against Artukovitch was filed in Los Angeles by relatives of twelve Yugoslav Jews murdered "in the death camps." An *Irish Times* report (2 April 1984) said, "US officials familiar with the case always expressed puzzlement at how Artukovitch obtained sanctuary in Ireland and then received a visa to visit the US where his brother, a contractor, lived." How much of the puzzle have I solved?

The US Justice Department acted on a legal reform excluding "Nazi collaborators" from seeking refuge and on 14 November 1984 "three carloads of federal marshals, guns drawn," burst into Artukovitch's house at Seal Beach and took him into custody (*The Sunday Times*, 12 January 1985). He is now eighty-five and, according to his Dublin-born son Radoslav, he has Parkinson's Disease, a congestive heart condition, and is also blind and suffering from delusional paranoia. It is uncertain whether he will be competent to take part in an extradition hearing and its sequel, deportation to Yugoslavia and a show-trial at Zagreb.

(1985)

Artukovitch: A Postscript

Much of what follows was published in Le Droit de Vivre, May, *1966 (a Jewish paper of Paris) and in* Glas Kanadskih Srba, August 4, *1966 (The Voice of Canadian Serbs). (H.B.)*

Sometime after publishing my *Twentieth Century* article I discovered that in Ireland we were championing Stepinac at the very time when we were sheltering a man who was supposed to be one of his principle adversaries. Andrija Artukovitch, who lived in Ireland from July 1947 to July 1949, was Minister of the Interior to Pavelitch and had introduced and signed the laws which expelled the Jews and Serbs from Zagreb, confiscated their property and imposed the death penalty on those who sheltered them.

On July 15 he had left Ireland for California and it was not for a couple of years that his identity was discovered (he had lived in Ireland as Dr Alois Anitch, a Professor of History), and his extradition as a war criminal demanded. At this time Father Lackovitch, Mgr. Stepinac's secretary, who was living as an honoured refugee in Youngtown, Ohio, had come to his defence and, according to the *Mirror News* of Los Angeles, had said that Artukovitch had been "the leading Catholic layman of the Croats, who had consulted Stepinac on the moral aspect of every action he took." Much similar testimony came from other leading Catholics and after many hearings his extradition was refused.

His sojourn in Ireland never was discussed, so I decided to investigate it. No one knew anything. I visited the leading Serbian Orthodox

clergy in Los Angeles and at Libertyville, near Chicago, and in New
York Alexander Gierowski, who was legal adviser to the Holy Synod in
Belgrade. I went to Paris and saw Branko Miljus, a minister in the pre-
war government of Yugoslavia, who had composed the petition which
had been sent to the United Nations by the monarchist government
in exile, demanding the extradition and trial of Artukovitch and others
(1950).

In the end I discovered the following facts, greatly condensed from
a long and complicated story. Artukovitch's escape from Yugoslavia
had been engineered by the Franciscans. Passing from monastery to
monastery, he had arrived at the Marianum in Fribourg in Switzerland,
where Archbishop Sharitch was already in hiding. Then his identity
was discovered, but he had powerful friends such as Manditch, the
treasurer of the Franciscan order at Rome and its General (who was I
believe at that time Dr Schaf) and Dr Draganovitch, a Zagreb Professor
of Theology, who was touring the internment camps with a Vatican
passport. The Prior at the Maison Marianum gave him an introduction
to the Irish consul at Berne, and when the order for his expulsion from
Switzerland came, he passed on inconspicuously to Ireland. He was
escorted by Brother Lujo Ivanditch, the Acting Provincial of the Franciscan Order in Croatia, who bore with him to Galway the seal of the
province. The Provincial had been imprisoned for his Ustashi activities.
He had 34 cases of their treasure under the floor of the Franciscan
church, when Pavelitch had fled. It had included the loot, gold-teeth,
watches, jewellery, collected from the massacred Jews and Serbs.

Where had Artukovitch stayed in Ireland? It took me a long time
to find out. He had lived both at 7, Tower Avenue, Rathgar, and at 6
Zion Road. These houses had changed hands many times since, 17 years
before, Dr Anich and his wife had lived there. It was a fortnight before
I succeeded in talking to one of his landladies and to the matron of the
Nursing Home where his son, Radoslav, had been born. I talked too to
the nuns at the Sacred Heart Convent in Drumcondra Road, where his
two little girls had been housed. Everywhere the Aniches had created
an excellent impression, his music, his jokes, his love of children and

above all his piety. He was "a daily communicant" and his landlady for the purity of his idealism and of his family life could only compare him to President Kennedy. He had given a lecture, she said, at University College.

After this I went to St Anthony's College at Moycullen near Galway, where Ivanditch had been sheltered, because I wanted to find out to what extent Artukovitch's Irish visit had been sponsored by Irish ecclesiastics. I believe that possibly one or two highly placed prelates knew that we were giving asylum to one, whom millions regarded as a major war-criminal. I do not think the Franciscans of Galway knew this. I was struck by the candour, gentleness and wisdom of those to whom I talked. Ivanditch had impressed them with his crusading zeal, but he had been a mystery and an embarrassment. They were relieved, I think, when the General of their Order sent him to minister to the Ford Factory workers (Croatian Catholics), at Dearborn near Detroit. While there he built the Church of St Joseph and published a book called *Praznovjere* or "Superstition."

I have talked about Artukovitch and Ivanditch to many people but only Jews and Serbs are interested. Most people think we did right to show mercy to a fugitive from justice however disreputable he may be. They are deceiving themselves and their charity is based not on the warmth of their hearts but its coldness. They were simply indifferent. The press, which had excited their sympathy about the Kennedy assassination and the Moor murders (what ecclesiastic would have helped those criminals escape?), had played down the Croatian massacres.

Artukovitch had profited by murdering in the name of religion, for nowadays even unbelievers respect it as a sort of social cement, which it is imprudent to damage. Even communists now think in that way, on occasion.

There were two other factors. The tremendous scale of the Croatian religious persecutions made them look more like war than like ordinary brutality. Hence they were to be judged by different standards.

Secondly the Yugoslav government publication, *Artukovitch, The Himmler of Yugoslavia*, is a stupid propagandist work, which was readily scrapped, when some satisfactory commercial agreements were made with the USA. In it Artukovitch was made responsible directly for barbarities for which he bore only a politician's responsibility.

Very few are interested in the complex morphology of modern cruelty. Yet one should scrutinise very carefully every link in the long chain of complicity, which binds some small sophisticated connivance at the top to the primitive savagery at the farther end.

At the upper sophisticated end we must always be prepared to find accomplished and outwardly respectable people.

(1966)

Cardinal Seper and the Ulster of Yugoslavia

I

I was very pleased when I was sent by the School of Slavonic Studies to Zagreb nearly forty years ago. It looked to me at the time as though my own country, which had broken away from an empire and insisted on the resurrection of its native culture, might become the leader of all the small countries of Europe whose history had been so similar. The institution for which I was working, the Anglo-American Yugoslav Friendship Society, [which] had been founded by Dr Georgevitch, the Orthodox Bishop of Dalmatia, was highly ecumenical, for most of my pupils were Catholics or Jews. It was not very interesting, the Catholics mostly wanted to learn English to become waiters and waitresses in the tourist hotels, the Jews, conscious of what awaited them, were training for emigration to the UK or USA. Ireland had been left out of the society's title, so I tried to remedy that by an exchange of visitors between the little countries.

But my immediate superior, Dr Milan Curcin, was a fascinating man. He was the editor of a paper *Nova Evropa* and with his friend Prof. Seton Watson and Dr Georgievitch he might be considered one of the founders of the Yugoslav state. They were very close to each other and Georgievitch, whom I rarely met, was the godfather of Seton Watson's son Hugh, now head of the School of Slavonic Studies and a noted expert on Central European affairs.

The state had been founded by the three Slav peoples, Serbs, Croats and Slovenes, of whom the first two spoke an almost identical language. All of them had been wretched and rebellious under the Austro-Hungarian supremacy and though the Serbs had played the main part in its destruction each people had contributed something and the union had been joyously accepted. The friction, which soon appeared between Serbs and Croats, was almost exclusively religious for the Serbs were Orthodox, the Croats were Catholics. And this friction had reached a climax the day before we arrived. The little town was draped in black and even the railway engine had put on a black bow round its funnel; expensive pot-plants were being moved into the first class waiting room, for the following day the body of King Alexander was halting in Zagreb on its last journey to Belgrade from Marseilles where the king had been murdered through the agency of Anton Pavelitch, the leader of the Ustashe, who wished to destroy the Yugoslav state and set up an independent Croatia. The whole of the next day great processions of mourners streamed to the railway stationers. I still have a black bordered copy of Novosti with the list of the principal mourners, among the first [was] the name of the Catholic Archbishop Bauer [with] his suffragan, Mgr. Stepinac. For Stepinac, a Croat, had joined the Serbs against the Austro-Hungarians, [and] been decorated by King Alexander to whom it was said he may have owed his rapid promotion in the church.

Dr Curcin had some years before been to Ulster, because the Yugoslavs knew much more of Ireland than we knew of them. These knowledgeable ones called Croatia the Ulster of Yugoslavia and wrote about our problems in Nova Evropa. At first I did not see the parallel, for the Croats, who wished to break away from the Yugoslav ideal were Catholics, the Ulstermen, who loathed the all-Ireland ideal were very much Protestant. Curcin, an Orthodox himself, saw the point of view of the Ulster Protestants and the Croat Catholics. You could swap round the religions, the cleavage remained the same. You had a sophisticated rather bourgeois minority in the north, frightened of being absorbed by a majority in the south, whom they regarded as primitive, and full of peasant superstitions, without industry or education.

I wish I had attended to Curcin more closely for as the years passed the problems of Ireland seemed more and more like those of Yugoslavia. And I found that the Irish at home had no sympathy at all for these little peoples whose rebellions they had half inspired and whom they might have influenced and led. How many times I heard Irishmen regret that the Austro-Hungarian empire had ever been dissolved. "Czecho-slovakia and Yugoslavia are just a rag-bag of a kingdom invented by the British." What wilful self-deception! These little peoples had all kept their language and their cultures, for generations after the Irish had lost theirs to the British. The only small succession state power for which they had any tenderness was Poland. I saw the reason. Poland alone among the new peoples had an assured Catholic majority. It was in a position indeed to suppress its Orthodox minorities, which it most urgently [?] did. These issues were judged by religion, only the Irish did not concede to other small peoples the right they claimed for them-selves, the freedom to preserve their own culture, language, traditions.

I had left Yugoslavia when the shameful pact with Hitler was made and the government was overthrown by enraged patriots, headed by the Orthodox Patriarch Gavrilo. He is one of the great Yugoslav heroes, who is never mentioned. The Croat troops in the Yugoslav armies all passed over to the Nazis, and this brief Serb-led rebellion was rapidly quelled. Gavrilo, insulted and dishonoured, spent the last days of the war in Dachau. Pavelitch the regicide, sponsored by Germans, Hun-garians, and Italians to whom large portions of Yugoslavia, even Cro-atian Dalmatia were ceded, returned with his Ustashe, as head of the Independent State of Croatia. He wrote to the Pope saying that he in-tended to establish "Christ's Kingdom on earth." The Pope gave him an audience and many complimentary [missing word]. There were nearly two million Orthodox Serbs in the new realm. But what really happened is well described in a booklet published by *The Standard* in 1947, with an introduction by the Archbishop of Dublin. The author, Count O'Brien, writes on page 14: "They were offered the choice of conversion to the Catholic faith or death."

After this statement of fact the rest of the book is fairy tale. Arch-bishop Stepinac, it is alleged, and all his bishops, opposed this evil plan so that it came to nothing. All those who asserted that the massacre[s] and the forced conversions had in fact taken place were said to be victims of communist propaganda. How could such lies have been told, in a country so sensitive as ours to religious oppression? How could our scholars, Catholic and Protestant, have been so ignorant or pusillanimous, as not to look at the evidence which the Orthodox Church in exile had published several years before the communists came to power? Published in America or England, these books and journals are written in English. There is *The Martyrdom of the Serbs* published in Chicago in 1943 by the Orthodox Church in America with an introduction by Dr Manning, the Episcopalian Bishop of New York; there are issues of *The Serbian Orthodox Church Herald* published in London during the war through funds raised by King Peter himself. The facts are related in full. All but one of the Orthodox bishops of Croatia had been massacred or like Dr Dosithej, Orthodox Metropolitan of Zagreb, beaten up in the streets so that he became insane and died in a German hospital.

Count O'Brien does not even mention the dead Metropolitan but (page 16) commends Stepinac for establishing an "autonomous Croat Orthodox Church" in Zagreb. He does not mention that the head of this Church was not a Croat but an émigré Russian and that at all the services prayers for Pavelitch had to be offered.

In fact so far from resisting the advent of Pavelic it was welcomed with *Te Deums* in all the Catholic Churches. The bishops may well have been kindly men but they had released something they could not control. Their appeals for clemency for this one and that one scarcely changed the general picture. This picture is depicted for us in the most precise detail in a large Croatian volume (I abridge its long name to *Dokumenti*), which gives photostates and dated extracts from all the church papers of the Pavelic period. They seemed to me so incredible that when I was invited to accompany a delegation of the National Peace Council to Yugoslavia in 1954 stopped off to check them in the library at Zagreb. All those I checked were correct and by a strange accident one of those I confirmed was an ecstatic account by a certain

Father Kolb of a visit by Dr Seper and the seminary of which he was rector to the Leader. I have already quoted much of this in *Grille*, Autumn 1968. There is a photograph of Seper standing beside Pavelich with the 140 seminarists grouped around them in the form of the letter U for Ustashe.

Here is a passage I did not quote:

> Our Leader himself opened the door of his room and stood before, grave and dignified, a kingly face. We try to catch the meaning in every feature of his face, every flicker of his eyes. He our sovereign stands before us wonderful in his simplicity. His was the holy calm of the grotto...
>
> A strange exhalation of loving kindness seemed to flow to us from our Leader. His words sketched out a new page, the loveliest and most precious of all in the history of the religious youth of Croatia.

Pavelitch in his reply had told them that without his young priests he could never have come to power and every page of *Dokumenti* seems to confirm this.

What can a wise and kindly cleric, and Dr Seper may well have been all this, have done in the face of such an uprush of holy and patriotic sentiment? Had he resisted maybe he would have been repudiated by his flock and imprisoned by Pavelich and maybe executed as was Rihar, because he refused to celebrate High Mass with *Te Deum* on the anniversary of the foundation of the Independent State of Croatia (see *New Blackfriars*, February 1971).

It is hard for one man to stand alone, and maybe in time of war men must be judged collectively for their crimes and their complicity and not individually. By and large these men had all assented, some had even inspired the crusade against the "heretic and the schismatic." In his diary Stepinac condemns Protestantism, but because the Yugoslav Evangelicals were mainly of German descent, no crusade against them was possible. On the other hand Stepinac in his diary (Falconi, page

273) had mentioned with satisfaction Pavelic's determination to uproot the sect of Old Catholics, "a mere society for divorce" and the Serbian Orthodox Church as "not a church but a political organisation." Falconi comments that Stepinac must have known that such a programme would unleash a religious war. He knew and did not care.

The war ended, the communists came to power and the inevitable Orthodox revenge was stayed by the suppression of both churches. Monarchist leaders like Branko Miljus say that the Vatican was grateful for this at first and permitted and encouraged its clerics to take posts in the communist government.

(19??)

II

Lately the Croatian Ustashe came into the news again. In April 1971 to commemorate the thirtieth anniversary of the Ustasha state of Croatia, headed by the regicide Pavelic in April 1941, they murdered the Yugo-slav ambassador to Sweden. A year later they hijacked a Swedish air-liner and forced the Swedish government to release the seven Croats who had been found guilty of the murder.

Pavelic had been cherished for years by the Axis powers and released upon Croatia when the Yugoslav army had capitulated to the Nazis, after the defection of all the Croat troops to the enemy. The Independ-ent State of Croatia lasted till 1945, when Tito and the Partisans arrived in Zagreb. Pavelic fled to the Argentine where he formed a shadow Ustashe cabinet which probably still exists.

Now Croatia might make headlines again for a much favoured can-didate for the Papacy is a Croat, Cardinal Seper, head of the Congrega-tion of the Doctrine of the Faith. Men will ask what part he played when he was rector of the Diocesan Seminary in Zagreb. A great many nice people will ask "why rake all this up now?" It will be hard to answer and yet in Ireland of 1974 an answer is essential for it concerns the status of religious minorities.

Pavelic had assured the Pope that he intended to establish Christ's Kingdom in Croatia and on May 17 1941 Pius XII had given him an audience. But the Leader found an obstacle to his plans in the two million Serbian Orthodox with whom the Croats had to share the new Croatia. In a book published by *The Standard* in 1947 its foreign editor, Count O'Brien, explains how he proposed to overcome it.

"They (the Orthodox) were offered the choice between conversion to the Catholic Faith and death."

Unfortunately O'Brien then goes on to say that "this evil plan was brought to nothing by the entire Catholic hierarchy and most of her priests" and he suggests that anyone who argues differently must be a communist.

But the facts were quite different and now easy enough to ascertain. It is true that most of the books written by the Serbian Orthodox leaders and their supporters are now hard to obtain or else like Novak's very detailed *Magnum Crimen* written in Srbo-Croatian (Novak is a very enlightened Croatian Catholic). But recently Bernard Wall translated Carlo Falconi's *Il Silenzio di Pio XII* and the latter half of the book deals with Croatia under Pavelitch. From all these books it is clear that the "evil plan" was carried out on a gigantic scale. Falconi estimates the Orthodox victims at 700,000 but in this figure he includes, I think, the 240,000* forced converts. They reveal how all the Orthodox bishops in Croatia were murdered except Georgievitch, the Bishop of Dalmatia, who was imprisoned by the Italians and the Metropolitan Dosithej who was beaten up by Ustashe women in Zagreb and later died insane. It is also clear that the Catholic hierarchy greeted Pavelitch with *Te Deums* in all their churches, and with poems in all the church papers and that none of the bishops had anything against the

---

* The figure appears in the text as 24,000, but this is almost certainly a misprint.

conversion campaign, though they were often shocked by the barbarity with which it was carried out.

None of these writers, not even Avro Manhattan, the London humanist, who wrote a booklet on the subject for Ian Paisley, mentions Mgr. Seper. Yet a certain Father Grgic, writing in *The Tablet*, March 2, 1968, says that he spent those terrible years helping the Orthodox and the Jews and meditating on ecumenism. Father Grgic is, however, the Croat equivalent of O'Brien and one has to dig deep into *Dokumenti* by Horvat and Stambuk in order to refute him before one finds that Seper behaved like all the others. *Dokumenti* is a huge volume containing relevant photostats and extracts from all the Church papers of Zagreb under the Ustashe. On page 304, 305 and 323 you will find account of the visit the Diocesan Seminar paid to the Leader in the April of his arrival and in the April of the following year another commemorative April visit was paid. There is a photograph of Seper, the rector standing beside the Leader in the middle of his 140 seminarists, who are grouped around him in the form of the letter U for Ustashe. We are told of the missals and illuminated addresses that were presented to Pavelic, the rapturous speeches of the seminarists, the grateful enthusiasm of the Leader not only for the visit but for all that the young priests of Croatia had done in the past to make his return possible. "You have been my right hand," he said.

But why go on? I have translated some of these speeches in *Grille* and it is the ordinariness of these episodes rather than their horror, which is dulled by time and distance, that appals me. It is now routine for all our churches, Protestant, Catholic, Orthodox, (with the exception of a few dotty fundamentalists), to abase themselves before any government, however barbarous, that guarantees their institutions. It is routine for the churches to lie about it afterwards, to pretend that the crimes and abasements never happened or were due to communists, or "understandable" or "much exaggerated."

The churches of the Reformation have as many heads as the hydra, the Church of Rome has one, yet all react to pressures in the same way. To show that the hydra-headed Protestant Churches are as prone to these abasements as the One Universal Church of the Catholics, I attach for the editor to print if he chooses, the declaration of some ten leaders of the Evangelical Church of Germany proclaiming their support of Hitler and his anti-semitic crusade, indeed promoting it.

How does the Christian in the age of mass communications preserve his integrity? By having no institutions or very flexible ones like the wandering Bible Christians? I think not; our continuity, stability, traditions are valuable to us. We could not face the solitude that would meet us if we abandoned them.

I was astounded when Harold Wilson lately threatened the Ulstermen with a new St Bartholomew's Eve, if they did not mend their ways. Why did he dig up that sad old affair of the 5000 Huguenots, who were murdered 400 years ago, when in his own life time a massacre 100 times as terrible had occurred?

The reason is that St Bartholomew's Eve is now like a mummified or pickled cadaver, something for the museum or the laboratory, while the Croatian massacre is like a battered week-old corpse, which fond relations have buried and which would cause much unpleasantness to exhume for a post-mortem.

Yet it is deeply relevant to us, since we may be on the eve of bloodshed though we do not know who will be the aggressor, who the victim. When I was in Croatia forty years ago, (The School of Slavonic Studies had sent me to teach in the Anglo American Yugoslav Society; its founder-president was that Dr Georgievitch, Bishop of Dalmatia, from whose statement about the massacres I quoted in *Grille*), I constantly heard how Croatia was the Ulster of Yugoslavia. Though all my pupils were Catholics, my immediate superior, whom I revered, was Milan Curcin, an Orthodox Serb. He was the editor of *Nova Evropa*, a quarterly which was supported by the English Slav enthusiasts of the day, men like Seton-Watson and Wickham Steed and all the Yugoslavs who worked for peace and harmony between the races and creeds. In their writings the Ulster analogy constantly cropped up and Curcin had even been to Belfast and visited the Orange and the nationalist leaders. He had attended Pen Club meetings in Edinburgh and Dubrovnik. (When later I tried to get him invited to a Pen Conference in Dublin, the answer was "No!" He came from a communist country.)

The Ulster of Yugoslavia was a busy prosperous community, who feared domination by the Serbian Orthodox, whom they regarded as backward and superstitious. There were of course sharp difficulties about the analogy. The Yugoslav "Ulstermen" were Catholics and shared both race and language with the Southerners, whom they scorned and feared.

To me the Croats always seemed a mild, kindly and cultivated people. With its opera house and theatres and kafanas, Zagreb had the friendly charm of a tiny Vienna. Why should we be surprised that they suddenly became savages? Did it not happen in Vienna too?

Why all the same? For thirty years we have turned our backs on such questions and discussed instead the Pill, the communist menace and Princess Anne's wedding.

To elect Cardinal Seper to the Papacy, however familiar the dilemma in which fate once placed him, would be to close a door which should be kept wide open. At present those who mention the massacred are merely considered tedious bores and possibly bigoted. But if Cardinal Seper is elected to the Papacy, assuredly *Dokumenti* will be translated and a fire will be lit that no man can extinguish.

(Unpublished typescript, 1973)

From the Butler Album

Oxford years, 1919-22

After Oxford, probably 1920s or 1930s

1947, possibly from a visa or passport

With wife Peggy, baby daughter Julia, and friends,
17 April 1936, Belgrade

With wife Peggy, probably 1970s or 1980s

1980s

With the poet and Nobel Laureate Seamus Heaney, 1980s

Butler's oeuvre, before *Balkan Essays*

PART TWO

The Cultural Pattern

"Hubert Butler was what in Central Europe they call a *feuilleton* writer. The word has misleading echoes of leafy lightness and even weight-lessness. But for a century and a half it has meant a special kind of intellectual journalism, witty and often angry, elegant but piercing, and revealing great learning lightly borne, interested in the 'epiphanies' which make currents of social and political change visible through the lens of some small accident or absurdity."

Neal Ascherson
"Foreword"
In the Land of Nod
(The Lilliput Press, 1996)

"[Butler's] acuteness about Ireland, about Europe, about Ireland in Europe will ensure his continuing influence, but that perception, and those preoccupations, are based on philosophic foundations and literary genius which put him in a far greater tradition than simply that of political commentator or historian. In an age when the intellectual market is dominated by vast, distended, catch-all histories dealing with 'millennia' or 'civilizations,' churning out words which say nothing at all, Hubert Butler stayed in his fields along the Nore, and in essays which often covered fewer than ten pages said more about world history than the most inflated blockbuster or television series. The view from the front porch of Maidenhall is emblematically Irish, but it stretches far beyond the water-meadows, the river, the distant ruined

Norman castle and much older Celtic church: west to American Utopias, east to Sarajevo and Riga Strand, sweeping through lost memory, failed aspirations and great hopes..."

Roy Foster
"The Salamander and the Slap: Hubert Butler and His Century"
The Irish Story: Telling Tales and Making It Up in Ireland
(Allen Lane, 2001)

James Bourchier:
An Irishman in Bulgaria

I wonder what is thought of my compatriot James Bourchier in Bulgaria today? Is there still a street called Bourchier Street: or have you become critical of the man who was once held in such high esteem in Bulgaria that when he was buried near Rilo Monastery in December 1920, a day of national mourning was declared in Sofia? An issue of postage stamps was made to commemorate him. Perhaps that is now of interest only to the stamp-collectors, or is Bourchier himself still remembered with affection?

Now, in every country, reputations change rapidly and we judge the great men of the past according to different standards. James Bourchier was a man of his time and the Bulgaria of a generation ago, with all its special problems, has passed away. I ask you, though, to think of him now not simply as a political partisan, a man whose strong champion-ship of Bulgarian claims certainly changed history. Think of him in-stead as a warm-hearted and intelligent foreigner, an Irishman who rose above the prejudices of his nation, his class and his profession, and who tired always to speak the truth about Bulgaria even when it made him enemies.

It is not generally known that James Bourchier was an Irishman. The greater part of his life was spent in English service so his Irish origin escaped notice. Yet he was very much an Irishman belonging to the Protestant minority. Unfortunately for us who remain at home, the Protestant Irishman is often bound to England by close ties of self-interest and imperial service as well as of religion. His working days he gives to others. Ireland is a place for childhood and holidays and old age. That was what it was to James Bourchier.

The Bourchiers were a Huguenot family from Bruff, Co. Limerick, who had taken refuge in Ireland almost three centuries ago when Protestants were being persecuted in France. James's mother, Sarah Aher, came from my neighbourhood and her home, La Rive, became his home whenever he came back from Bulgaria. So when I was a boy I remember seeing him in the village of Castlecomer where his home was. It is a small mining village, the only mining village in Ireland, with one long street shaded with lime trees, and his house was comparatively new for the original house had been burnt down in the rebellion of 1798 when the Irish had tried to throw off English rule. Bourchier, as an Irishman born in 1850, must have heard from his boyhood of rebellion and civil war. He must have been familiar with the rival claims of nationalism and imperialism. The Irish problem is not unique, and those who have grown up with it will not be easily baffled by the problems of other small peoples who have powerful neighbours. Bourchier put all his gifts of imagination and understanding at the service of Bulgaria; he played no part in Irish politics. I say this with regret because I think in his own country he could have exercised a great and good influence where it was badly needed.

When I saw him he was already an elderly man, bowed and so deaf that it was almost impossible to communicate with him. It was in 1919 and at that time, as a century before, our neighbourhood was in the grip of civil war. Houses were once more being burnt down and Ireland was only in sight of that political independence which Bulgaria had reached a generation before.

It was a queer chance that brought Bourchier from Ireland to Bulgaria in 1888. When he had left Trinity College, Dublin, and King's College, Cambridge, to which he had won a scholarship, he first became a teacher at Eton. He was a bad teacher: for even then he was very deaf and he could not keep discipline. One evening, when he was taking class, the boys turned all the lights off and had a firework display. After ten years there his deafness grew worse and the school had reluctantly to dismiss him. He was greatly liked but he was obviously unfitted for his profession.

What was he to do? He chose journalism and soon he found himself as correspondent of *The Times* in the Balkans. He travelled in Greece, Romania, Crete and Serbia – but it was Bulgaria to which he finally gave his heart and in which he established his headquarters.

The work of a correspondent of a great paper is not easy. How can you tell the truth consistently and keep your job? Inevitably, the policy of the paper may be in conflict with the private views of the correspondent, and Bourchier was often charged with being unwisely pro-Bulgarian. But he never compromised. He wrote back angrily when he was chided, and a couple of times he was saved from dismissal only by the fact that he was known to be the most accomplished journalist in the Balkans. In any case he was no blind partisan. If he thought the foreign policy of the Bulgarian government at fault he said so, though this made him unpopular. King Ferdinand, for example, never forgave him for being too candid in his criticism of the King's ministers and their policy.

Bourchier's deafness was such an appalling handicap that only a man of supreme talent could have overcome it. Often urgent telephoning was necessary and he had to get his servant or a hotel porter to do it for him. All his private negotiations had to be conducted at the top of his voice. When he was on an important mission in Greece he chose the slopes of Mount Pelion for his private talks with Venizelos. Riding there every day, they were able to bawl at each other from horseback. It was in this way that Bourchier acted as intermediary between Greece and Bulgaria in forming the alliance that preceded the First Balkan War.

Bulgaria was, when Bourchier arrived, only just emerging into partial freedom and independence. Eastern Roumelia[*] was still held

---

[*] Roumelia (also known, in English, as Turkey in Europe) was the Ottoman word for the empire's Balkan provinces. (Editors)

for the Turks by a Christian governor. Macedonia was wholly Turkish. Every year Bourchier used to spend a few weeks exploring Macedonia, arranging secret interviews with the men who were conspiring to overthrow the Turk. Bourchier was passionately pro-Bulgarian but he was an even more passionate advocate of the truth. Let me explain how he fell out with King Ferdinand.

The Moslems were constantly attacking the Bulgars in Macedonia and inevitably the Bulgars would retaliate with reprisals on the Moslems in the territory they controlled. On one occasion the village of Dospat was burnt to the ground, and many Moslems, as Bourchier wrote in *The Times*, were massacred. The Bulgarian government published an indignant denial but Bourchier stuck to his guns. *The Times* insisted that the report must be verified or withdrawn. Bourchier received threats of assassination.

Finally, the Bulgarian government permitted Bourchier to go to the spot and investigate himself. He went and found the village a charred and looted ruin, as he anticipated, but he also found the number of massacred greatly exaggerated. As usually happens, neither side was satisfied with his revised account of the massacre. But though Bourchier made enemies, yet even they ultimately began to respect his integrity and his desire for the truth at all costs. He cared nothing for popularity with the powerful and often he would intervene when he found, for example, that some village was being encroached upon by the authorities. It was seen that he was not out for profit and that he did not change his loyalties easily.

To the staff of *The Times* Bulgaria was a remote and unimportant country. The problems of Macedonia were insignificant compared to those of India. "Is it wise," the editor once wrote to Bourchier, "to risk annoying the Moslems, subjects of the British empire, by supporting the Bulgarians against the Moslem rulers in Bosnia?" Bourchier argued out this point with heat. He hated all this high diplomacy; *The Times* was not, he maintained, a branch of the British Foreign Office and should not reflect its policy. As for the need to placate the Indian Moslems, had they been in the least gratified by the British protests against the annexation of Bosnia by Austria-Hungary? Had they been annoyed when the British had supported the Greeks in their expulsion of the Moslems from Crete? *"Magna est veritas et praevalebit."*

Bourchier was, as you will have deduced, rather a lonely figure – or perhaps I should say not "lonely" but spiritually isolated. He never lacked warm and loyal friends, either in England or Ireland or Bulgaria. But he was always at war with the cynical imperialism of the great powers to which small peoples like the Bulgars were continually sacrificed. He was repelled by the commercial competitiveness of great newspapers like *The Times*, which valued early news more than true news. His life was soured for years by "an infamous telegram," as he called it, which *The Times* sent him; in it he was blamed because another paper had forestalled *The Times* in announcing the proclamation of the total independence of Bulgaria by the King in 1908. As a matter of fact, by an odd chance, the news had first been released in Paris and Bourchier was not even technically to blame. But Bourchier was deeply wounded that the telegram dismissing him was sent for all to read and that another English journalist was sent to replace him. However, Bourchier was, it proved, the only man for the job and soon he was at it again. But a year later he noted in his diary: "Today is the anniversary of the infamous telegram." Bourchier was too sensitive and scrupulous to make an entirely dependable journalist and there were frequent breezes of this kind. But he was irreplaceable and he knew it. He stayed on.

As mentioned, Bourchier played a very influential part, acknowledged by all the Greek and Bulgarian leaders of the time, in cementing the Graeco-Bulgarian alliance of 1911-12. It was a fine achievement, for Bulgars and Greeks had been enemies for close on eight centuries and there were still bitter memories of the attempt by the Phanariot Greeks to suppress Bulgarian culture. Bourchier's tact and persuasiveness turned the scale in favour of the alliance.

It was not only the prominent Bulgarians who were grateful to Bourchier. A group of Macedonians sent him as a prized gift a horse called "Yaver" and a letter which ran as follows: "The Bulgarians will never forget your defence of their national ideals and your fight for their realization in past and present, when the whole world has turned against the suffering Bulgar nation." Bourchier cherished this horse all his life and used to ride it every day from the Boris Gardens along the Constantinople Road.

Bourchier was distressed when the Greeks refused to withdraw from Adrianople which had been awarded by treaty to Bulgaria, but he was equally taken by surprise at the Bulgarian attack on their former allies which led to the disastrous Treaty of Bucharest, when Bulgaria lost almost all that she had gained. Had he known, he would have tried to avert this quarrel by those methods of conciliation at which he was such an adept. He believed strongly in the friendship, perhaps the federation, of the Balkan peoples, but at that time the enemies of Bulgaria regarded Bourchier as the leader of a conspiracy to keep them apart.

A Greek newspaper, *Atlantis,* in February 1914 wrote how Bourchier had been given a vast estate from a confiscated monastery and how he used to spend hours in the Bulgarian Foreign Office concocting and circulating faked atrocity stories about the conduct of the Greek troops in Macedonia. Of course there was not a word of truth in all this.

One amusing episode occurred illustrating the great influence of Bourchier, and the efforts made by the Greeks to counteract it. A well-known London actor called Arthur Bourchier was approached by some prominent Greeks and invited to go to the Balkans at their expense. From there he was to send articles to a rival English newspaper. He was to sign them "Bourchier," but he need not, they kindly explained, write them. That would be done for him. It was hoped that the British public would be so confused by seeing the famous name affixed to Greek propaganda that they would think that the great man had either gone out of his mind or else changed it. The tempting offer of a free holiday was declined.

When the war of 1914 broke out Bourchier tried to make the Allies promise to Bulgaria the provinces that were hers by right of population. He was bitterly disappointed with his failure. When Bulgaria sided with

Germany, as a British subject Bourchier had to leave. But he left with the goodwill of the Bulgarian people. In gratitude for Bourchier's service the government released Ivan, his old servant and friend, from conscription in the army, so that he could look after Bourchier's affairs for him, and in particular his horse Yaver, given him by the Macedonians.

From Bucharest Bourchier wrote: "Though you have chosen the wrong side in the war, I do not forget your cause is just and, when peace comes, I shall defend the legitimate rights of the Bulgarian nation."

But by the time peace arrived Bourchier had become an old man and tired. In the violent passions aroused by war there was little scope for his calm, well-instructed intervention. He returned for the last time to Bulgaria and there he died, at Sofia on 30 December 1920. He was buried, as he wished, in a valley near the monastery of Rilo.

How did it come about that an Irishman could exercise so great an influence in the affairs of a foreign people? An Irishman would not be puzzled by that question, for Ireland too owes much to foreigners, who have sympathized with her cause and presented it truthfully and generously in the press and parliament of more powerful nations. And Bourchier not only served the Bulgarian cause but he loved the Bulgarian land and its people, and described them in prose. He gave an unforgettable account of Trnovo with "its houses clustered like seabirds on the ocean crag," and he studied the birds, the flowers and the antiquities of Bulgaria. His paper on the Pomaks of Rhodope still has value. He wrote well and persuasively.

The days when a single man could exert so big an influence in a country not his own are perhaps long passed. We cannot wish them to return. Bourchier would now appear a very outlandish figure to most of us. Many of his views would strike us as old-fashioned and wrong. But it is not his views for which I ask your attention and respect but his loyalty, his warm-heartedness and his devoted search for justice and truth.

(1948)

Endnote: This talk was written rapidly in London to be delivered in Sofia or, as a secondary choice, on the BBC or Radio Éireann. It was "intended to suggest bridges for friendly intercourse" and drew principally from Lady Grogan's *Life of J.D. Bourchier* published in 1924. In a note to the text the author has added:

> I've tried to give an objective account of Bourchier as a man who was by temperament tied to no particular régime. Obviously his traditions and upbringing were such that he would not have been friendly to Communism, but that is a point I have naturally not stressed. Indeed it is irrelevant. His sense of justice often overcame his traditional conservative outlook. He would, I think, have remained today a firm and valuable, though probably critical, friend of Bulgaria.

It was never broadcast. (Antony Farrell, The Lilliput Press)

Escape from the Anthill

"Introduction" to Escape From the Anthill *(1985)*

These essays are not so heterogeneous as they look. They are all skew-ered together by a single idea. Or perhaps I should call it an obsession, a mental necessity that turned into a physical one. When I was a boy of fourteen I decided I was going to live in the place where I was born and where my father, grandfather and great grandfather had lived before me. It seemed then an easy and obvious thing to do, since I was my father's eldest son and he had a house and farm in Kilkenny. There was also another reason, which influenced me, even when I knew how insubstantial it was. Though we have long been unimportant people, the Butlers, of whom my family is a junior branch, had ruled the neigh-bourhood since the fourteenth century, and there is scarcely a parish in Tipperary or Kilkenny that does not bear some trace of our some-times arrogant, sometimes kindly interference. Could I not interfere too?

It was some time before I grasped how difficult this was going to be and noticed that not only was all my education slanted away from Ireland but that the whole island was tilted eastwards. It was very hard to stand upright unsupported on this precipitous slope, for as many people were pushing me from the west as were pulling me to the east. And ambition was tugging me vigorously the whole time towards the land of opportunity. And in fact, in a strongly centripetal world, staying at home is scarcely even respectable; certainly no one thinks it pub-lic-spirited. The man who does it can surely have no feeling for "broad horizons" and mighty enterprises, for the unity of mankind and the exploration of the universe? Even in a manual worker it can be a discreditable thing to do, for our economists often moralize now about the need to make labour more "mobile" so that it can be drafted to those spots where it is most needed. It is perverse and selfish to resist.

And if living in one's own neighbourhood is difficult, to write about it is harder still. Who, anyway, are our neighbours? Our real neighbours, both of the spirit and the flesh, both those we know and those we don't, seldom live near us nowadays. We keep contact with them by telephone and plane and car, or else we have one-sided commerce with them through books and television screens. In spite of that, though the familiar hills and rivers seldom now enclose a stable or self-sufficient community, I think they are only waiting to recover their plundered significance. The canals that once diverted the rivers are all choked and after five generations the railway cuttings that ravished the hills are collapsing. Why should the great dams at Ardnacrusha and Poulaphouca, or the television mast on Mount Leinster, or the huge roads that level out villages and raths and esker ridges, prove more enduring? They are all linked with certain ways of life and thought, and ideas have never been as ephemeral as in the twentieth century.

But to look ahead like this is not very comforting to the beleaguered country-dweller. At eighty-four I am, like everybody else, very disillusioned but only averagely discontented. Fundamentally I think as I always did. The post to which I am willingly tethered still holds firm and I have grazed around it in a sufficiently wide circle. Close-cropped grass comes up again fresh and sweet, and whoever comes along next may find my patch slightly improved.

So even when these essays appear to be about Russia or Greece or Spain or Yugoslavia, they are really about Ireland. We choose some of our experiences and others are forced on us, but they have little meaning till they are related to some central focus of ideas and this focus for me has never varied. Many of the irrelevant things that have happened to me have been boring or nasty, but not all of them. For example, like many Europeans, I have exchanged a couple of dull sentences with

Chou Enlai and seen the Great Wall of China, but I have no idea how to profit by this fascinating adventure, for I think we Westerners can mostly only sense the sweetness of China, we can bring nothing home with us. We are like honey bees which can get nectar from white clover but not from red, because their sucking apparatus is too short. And I do not believe that we should be spiritually impoverished if for a century or more we were excluded from all Asia and all Africa beyond the shores of the Mediterranean.

But nowadays can we exclude ourselves from anything? Can the ant ever escape from his anthill? Even the most sedentary and homebound person is obliged to roam the world in spirit ten or twenty times a day. The newspapers and the radio and television release a million images of remote places and people. They settle like butterflies on the brain till every cell is clogged with the larvae from their unwanted eggs. How can one protect oneself from the ravages of secondhand experience? Here and there perhaps one can replace this pre-digested stuff with experiences of one's own. But to most people this seems an affectation, like the quest for free-range eggs or vegetables from "organic" farms.

While we are more or less committed to mass travel and to information that is canalized for press-conferences, the experiences that nourish us are individual, not collective. Few of us have been of use to any Indian, Negro or Chinaman, and the regard we have for them is unmixed with personal gratitude; yet many generations of vicarious involvement have caused us to think we are necessary to each other, and it will take as many more to unlearn this.

When this happens we shall recognize again that within a few square miles we should have everything which we can possibly need. Here in Kilkenny the earth is fruitful and the neighbours are intelligent, imaginative and kind; their minds are well-adapted to poetry and jokes and the propounding and solving of problems. Though it is not easy to be independent of tinned pineapples and the Dublin dailies, we could be, at a price. But even the tinkers and the retired colonial administrators are more restless and discontented than they used to be. The colonials, travelling round the earth, have lost the country-man's acquiescence in seemingly immutable things like temperature and rainfall and local prejudices. It is now easy to avoid what one cannot change, so they move about. And though our tinkers come back every summer to the same lanes and clearings, the last ones who came here had spent the winter washing dishes in the Cumberland Hotel at Marble Arch. They play the familiar tricks with a touch of urban sophistication, and it is hard to see them as neighbours whom it is one's duty to love.

All this sounds misleadingly nostalgic. In fact nothing has happened that cannot be reversed if it is accurately recorded. That is the purpose of these essays, in which I try to show that the countryside, where mean and silly things happen because energy and intelligence have been drained away, is an essential part of the world pattern which too few have studied. In "Boycott Village," for example, I complain that no one has investigated why ordinary people with nice intentions and neighbourly instincts proved to be such incompetent guardians of freedom. I do not know what the answer is but, if we relate the facts as we see them, posterity will perhaps handle them less clumsily than we have done.

I grew up before the great emigration of the Anglo-Irish in the twenties had begun, when some of the pioneers of the Irish Literary Revival were still alive and active, and through the *Irish Statesman* AE was still confidently elaborating his plans for a co-operative Ireland. These were dreams with reality and achievement behind them but they could not stand up to the Gaelic dream of Patrick Pearse, for it had been sanctified in blood. Now that dream too has faded, though the blood sacrifice still goes on, like the fire that smoulders slowly towards the forest when the picnic is over.

Now there are no dreams left to sustain us and all we have is a rag-bag of tangled notions and prejudices, of which I have exhibited a sampling in "Envoy and Mr Kavanagh." I do not doubt that a new generation, with fresh ideas and the vigour to carry them through, will solve some of our problems, and yet in times of troubled peace like ours, when the old idealisms have lost their magic, the future, I believe, lies with the solitary individual of whom Chekhov used to write. I quote from one of his letters:

> I see that our salvation will come from solitary personalities, scattered here and there over Russia, sometimes educated, sometimes peasant. Power is in their hands even though there are few of them. No man is a prophet in his own country and these solitary individuals, of which I speak, play an imperceptible role in society; they do not dominate it but their work is visible.

It was in the same way that Vershinin reassured the three sisters that knowledge and intelligence were never wasted. He said there was no town so boring and dead that three people of intellect and education could not make a faint impression; they would get swallowed up, of course, by the dark masses, but not without leaving some slight influence, and after them there would be six, then twelve, till at last they would be a majority. "In two or three hundred years life would be unspeakably, amazingly lovely."

Yet now something has happened to thrust this future loveliness even farther away. Vershinin had not forseen that as culture, under official patronage, became increasingly centripetal, Feeny, Meany and Sweeny, the three people of intellect and education, would fall under the irresistible, techno-cultural influence of the capital. Long before the three had propagated six and the six twelve, each nourishing his successors with the rich decay of his talents, the tempter would address himself seductively to them. Feeny and Meany would persuade themselves that they could serve their little town best from outside. Feeny would get a plum of a job as adviser to Channel 3 on South-Eastern Regional Culture, and Meany, no longer his ally but his rival, would draw a smaller income from his Friday afternoon talks on rural problems; Sweeney would stay behind, a new element, jealousy, penetrating his loneliness and distorting his judgement.

And what of the dark masses? They would be just as dark as before but with no trouble to themselves they would be given extension lectures and loan exhibitions, so that even Sweeney in his unpopular enthusiasms would seem superfluous and the task of swallowing him up would be greatly eased.

It is in fact a problem of men, not methods, and we can hope for little from the clever educational gadgets with which we try to irrigate the intellectual deserts. The soil that has been robbed of its natural creativity cannot be restored to health by fertilizing chemicals. Make it possible for Feeny, Meany and Sweeney, the "solitary individuals," to live in their own homes, for nature has planted them there like antibodies in a diseased constitution. Only they have power to regenerate it.

This, of course, is contrary to all current notions. Everything that is seminal or germinative in the way of ideas is thought to develop in the great centres of culture, where intellectuals congregate. It is in the press, the theatres, the clubs of the metropolis that revolutionary ideas are expressed and challenged. Things are openly said that could scarcely be thought in a provincial town. Yet there is something self-destructive about these great congestions of originality. A sense of doom hangs over them as over the exuberant freedom of the Weimar Republic.

Here is one of the reasons. In a vast society like ours, "the man of intellect and education," as Chekov saw him, is one among several thousands, a natural solitary, in fact. His function is to be the pinch of bread-soda in the dough, and not to foregather with other ex-solitaries and form a bread-soda pudding. Yet an Irishman sees this happening every year. Feeny and Meany, drawn away from their solitude, bring with them to the city their instinct to defy. They gather together with other ex-solitaries; then they are no longer solitary and what is more they find they are no longer original. Their insights and perceptions, which surprised and often vexed their fellow-citizens, are banal and irrelevant among the exuberant heterodoxies of their new community.

In place of the known neighbours whom it was their duty to challenge, there are faceless strangers who can only be met with abstractions. To get attention in such circles, the ex-solitary may have to turn in his tracks, to sacrifice the particular to the general, and to accept as valid some mass-produced consensus whose insufficiency he would quickly have detected among the familiar diversities of his native town. In this way the cities acquire fanatics at the same rate as the provinces lose their solitary individuals.

Am I exaggerating? Probably, but there is evidence from Russia and Italy and Germany that totalitarian beliefs spread from the cities to the provinces where sharp antagonisms had been held in check by a long history of neighbourly interdependence.

So I go on believing that the strength to live comes from an under-standing of ourselves and our neighbours or the diaspora that has re-placed them. If we could focus on them all the curiosity and wisdom that we disperse round the world, as we focus all the rays of the sun through a burning glass on a pile of dead leaves, there is no limit to the warmth and life we could generate. It is easier of course to collect the dead leaves than to make the sparks to kindle them. Yet I believe the life which Chekhov prophesied, "unspeakably, amazingly lovely," is not out of our reach, though it may now be a century or two farther away than he calculated.

Some of this material is unpublished (the latter portion of "The Artu-kovitch File"), some has been recast ("Beside the Nore," "Divided Loyalties"), updated ("Boycott Village") or extended from the original ("Peter's Window") – sources will be found under Acknowledgements – but for the most part these essays are unaltered, though a few of them deal with problems that appear to have been solved or episodes that have long been forgotten. We have lived through two worlds wars and, in Ireland, rebellion and civil war. Yet the basic things remain the same. When I was a boy of ten the Ulster Unionists were saying Home Rule is Rome Rule and civil war was threatened. Now I am eighty-four and the Ulster Unionists are saying Home Rule is Rome Rule and civil war does not seem immeasurably far away. It is as though we were on a scenic railway in a fun-fair. We pass through towering cardboard mountains and over raging torrents and come to rest in the same well-trodden field from which we got on board.

I have lived for long periods at home and my garden, with its vegetables and raspberry canes, its orchard and neglected flower-beds, has had to take the place of people and events. Thirty-three years ago my life of active involvement in enthusiasms which I shared with my neighbours ended abruptly. I have described how this came about in "The Sub-Prefect Should Have Held His Tongue." I shall not refer to this again as my affection for my neighbours has not changed. We were all of us victims of events beyond our control. Ireland was caught in the backwash of a tremendous religious struggle in Central and Eastern Europe, which we did not understand and for which we were unprepared. It was inevitable that there should be casualties.

Are we here in Ireland any nearer to that eighteenth-century dream "to unite the whole people of Ireland, to abolish the memory of past dissensions, and to substitute the common name of Irishman in place of the denomination of Protestant, Catholic and Dissenter"?

The idea of a religious war is so abhorrent and disgraceful that many prefer to think that it is for loyalty to the British Crown that Ulstermen will fight. They are wrong, because Ulster loyalty is to a Protestant monarch and would not survive if the monarch became a Roman Catholic. In fact it is the old insoluble conflict between authority and private judgement. Though all of us sometimes defer to authority, sometimes judge for ourselves, the moment we cease to act as individuals and think collectively, what was a matter of choice becomes a matter of principle and a clash between Catholic and Protestant is likely.

Can ecumenism help? In Ireland 160 years ago there was a vigorous ecumenical movement. The circumstances were more favourable than now but it ended in a deadlock. I have told the story in the following pages.

In "The Bishop" I write of an eighteenth-century young man,

agreeable and popular, who could not resist the fleshpots of an ascendancy he knew to be doomed.

In "The Eggman and the Fairies" the Captains and the Kings have all but gone and taken with them their sophistication and learning, their love of their home and their self-knowledge by means of which what looked irremediable might have been remedied. The Clearys in their cruel innocence and isolation could only escape from poverty and ignorance into fairyland.

Most of the other Irish pieces are self-explanatory.

When I was thirty-one and Soviet Russia was fifteen years old I taught English for a term in Leningrad. I was very happy there and would like to have stayed longer but the pull of my home and those I loved was too strong for me. I came back with as little understanding of Marxism and Communism as I went but I made many friends whom I still remember with affection. There was a multitude of small misunderstandings and difficulties but they all counted for nothing compared with the imaginative kindness with which I was welcomed. In "Peter's Window" I tell the story of that time.

Men and women are surely more important than the systems in which they imprison themselves. Yet it is not easy to disentangle ourselves and to commit ourselves unreservedly to personal relations. Organized religion cannot liberate us for it is a system too, and there is nothing more bitter than the conflict of two religious systems, as I have found both in my own country and the foreign country I know best, Yugoslavia.

Three years after I returned from Russia I went to teach in Zagreb in the Anglo-American-Yugoslav Society. It had been founded by my friend, Dr Milan Churchin, the editor of *Nova Evropa*, the leading liberal journal of Central Europe, and by Dr Georgievitch, the Orthodox Bishop of Dalmatia. I also had a small scholarship from the School of Slavonic Studies in London.

Yugoslavia had been born in 1918 after the defeat of

Austria-Hungary and the rise of the Succession States. For the southern Slavs it was the fulfilment of an ancient dream of harmony between four neighbouring and kindred peoples. I was at Oxford then and there was springtime in the air. There were Serbs, Croats and Czechs, there were Irish too, all rejoicing in their new-found freedom. We all had minority problems and I was surprised that Ireland, least scarred by war, did not identify herself with the other small new states more warmly, share experiences and take the lead for which she was qualified. The Croats knew about Ulster and some of them talked of Croatia, ruefully, as "the Ulster of Yugoslavia." This needed a readjustment of roles, but one knew what they meant. They were Catholics and to them Zagreb, the Croatian capital, was "a little Vienna." They wondered how they would fare in union with the more primitive Serbian Orthodox, who had fought for freedom while they had mostly fought for Austria-Hungary.

The day we arrived in Zagreb, 9 October 1934, news had just come that King Alexander, a Serb, had, with Barthou the French Foreign Minister, been assassinated in Marseilles by agents of the separatist Croat leader, Pavelitch. Zagreb was plunged in well-organized mourning with portraits of the king surrounded by black crape in the shop-windows and black bows on the funnels of the railway engines. Two days later the king's body arrived from Split, where it had been shipped from Marseilles on its way to Belgrade. It lay for a couple of hours, surrounded by pot-plants, in the first class waiting-room at the station, where it was visited by mile-long processions. One of those who prayed beside the royal coffin was Archbishop Bauer, the Catholic Primate, accompanied by his Auxiliary Monsignor Stepinac.

During our time in Yugoslavia the shadow of the assassination hung over the whole country. Hitler had come to power in Germany and Jewish refugees were flocking to the Dalmatian coast. In Italy and Hungary, Pavelitch and his helper, Artukovitch, were training the army of the Croat rebels, who were, in 1941, to sweep into Yugoslavia with the Nazis and proclaim the Independent State of Croatia.

And yet my recollections are of peace and beauty. There was almost no traffic in Yelachitch Trg, the central square. Fat amethyst pigeons strutted through the market stalls looking for pickings and panicking when the church bells rang. The scent of mimosa and wood-smoke, holy candles and freshly tanned leather drowned the faint whiff of petrol. On Sunday, we walked up Slijeme Mountain, where wild cyclamen and hellebore grew through the beech woods. In our room I rooted oleander cuttings in bottles between the double windows. And when my pupils were on holiday I wrote down the story of Mr Pfeffer.

Zagreb, in the thirties, was a very cultivated little town; it had an opera house and theatres, and there were still remnants of an Austrianized aristocracy in the leafy suburbs. Dalmatia was Italianate and Belgrade was still largely Turkish in character. When one went south and penetrated to Montenegro, one seemed to pass from our cruel, complicated century to an earlier one, just as cruel, where each man was responsible to his neighbours for his crimes and where organized twentieth-century barbarity had not yet emerged. Possibly in "The Last Izmerenje" I have idealized what I saw. To know what Montenegro was really like you must read Djilas's superb autobiography, *Land Without Justice* (1958).

The war came and Yugoslavia was carved up by Germany and her allies. Croatia, which had not resisted the Nazis, was rewarded with her Independent State under the rule of Pavelitch, King Alexander's convicted murderer.

Then in Zagreb an Aeschylean tragedy was enacted. The same young priest who had stood beside the coffin of his murdered king, reappeared before his countrymen as Archbishop at the right hand of his king's assassin, helpless in the face of Pavelitch's resolve to exterminate the Orthodox by expulsion, massacre or forced conversion. Unhappy but icily correct, Stepinac considered himself to be the servant of a power that is higher than the king or his murderer, and one that has rules for every occasion. His conscience was clear.

Violence came a second time to the city. Caring neither for king nor priest nor pope nor assassin, the Communists swept in, resolved to make all things new. I have written about this period in my two pieces,

"The Sub-Prefect Should Have Held His Tongue" and "The Artukovitch File," yet I would like here to recall the historical background to the events I have described. There are three great sources of power and influence in Eastern and Central Europe: Roman Catholicism, Byzantine Orthodoxy and Communism. Orthodoxy, which broke away from Rome five centuries before the Protestant Reformation, was once, with its Patriarch magnificently enthroned at Constantinople, the rival of Rome in power and splendour. Now the Orthodox Church is a shadow of its former self. With Saint Sophia a secular museum, the Patriarch lives on sufferance from the Turks in a small quarter of Istanbul. Since the Russian Revolution the other Patriarchs over whom he reigns as *primus inter pares* are weak and scattered. Communist Moscow threatens them from the East and the Catholic powers from the West. Those Russian Orthodox who survived beyond the borders of Tsarist Russia and later the Soviet State, have had to fight for their faith and culture against the politico-religious scheming of Austria-Hungary and her successors, Czechoslovakia and Poland.

A powerful instrument in this little-known struggle is the Uniat Church, devised by King Sigismund III of Poland and the Pope in the sixteenth century to attract the peasants of the eastern border-lands away from Orthodoxy. The Orthodox received into this Church retained their ritual and their married clergy but Rome, not Moscow, became the focus of their obedience.

This Uniat Church has been used many times in our century by the Western Powers for political purposes. At the beginning of the war in 1914, when the Austrians were advancing against the Russian Ukraine, a detailed memorandum about its occupation was formulated by the Uniat Archbishop, Count Szepticky of Lemberg in Austrian Galicia. Apart from the military and juridical arrangements, the Orthodox Church in the new Protectorate was to be detached from the Moscow Patriarchate and subjected to Szepticky himself, as Uniat Metropolitan. Prayers for the Tsar were to be forbidden and prayers for the Emperor substituted. The Muscovite saints were to be eliminated from the calendar. The new Prince of the Ukraine was to be Archduke Wilhelm, who had changed his name to Vasily, learnt Ukrainian and wore an embroidered Ukrainian tunic. But the Russians struck back, occupied Lemberg, arrested the Archbishop and published the Memorandum in the Petrograd papers. Soon after this the Revolution occurred.

In the Second World War the Uniat Church was active in Croatia; in 1941-2 Dr Shimrak, the Uniat Bishop, played a notable part in the campaign for the conversion of the Orthodox.

For many years the Czechs and Slovaks used the Uniats to secure and, if possible, extend their eastern frontier, where Carpatho-Russian Orthodox were settled along the Ukrainian border. They revived for themselves the old Austro-Hungarian dream of a vast Ukrainian protectorate and for this purpose rechristened Carpatho-Russia "Carpatho-Ukraine" and supported the Uniats against the Orthodox. The story of this often violent struggle has been told month by month in *Svobodnoye Slovo (Free Word)*, the organ of the many *émigré* Carpatho-Russian Orthodox in the USA.

In Europe it is now only in Greece that a free Orthodox Church survives. When in 1964 there was a friendly meeting in the Holy Land between the Pope and the titular head of the Orthodox Church (the Patriarch in Constantinople), Chrysostom, the Primate of Greece, and his bishops refused to participate and even asked for the dissolution of the Uniat Church. The world was shocked that when all Christendom is craving for unity the Primate of Greece could be so intransigent, yet it is intelligible enough. The Greeks are the countrymen of Aesop, who wrote so many fables about small animals to whom large ones made friendly overtures. It is natural for them to dread the Uniat embrace.

Should we involve ourselves with complex happenings in far countries? Sometimes we have to, but we misinterpret them at our peril.

On May Day 1949 a crowd of 150,000, said to be the largest ever seen in Dublin, assembled in O'Connell Street to protest against the imprisonment of Archbishop Stepinac of Yugoslavia and a Hungarian Cardinal, Mindszenty. There were bands, speeches, telegrams, women fainted and a young man, wrongly suspected of distributing Communist leaflets, was struck on the head and taken to hospital.

In America there were even greater demonstrations and many thought that with so righteous a cause, and Russia still weak after the Nazi invasion, the moment for a third world war had arrived.

I know nothing about Cardinal Mindszenty but I knew that the struggle in which Stepinac was involved was totally misconceived. It was a pre-Communist and inter-Christian one. As in Ireland, race and religion go together, Catholic Croat confronted Orthodox Serb and Hitler's war had triggered off a massacre of the Orthodox by the Catholics. Hugh Seton-Watson, the well-known historian of Central Europe, wrote in 1945: "The Communists saved Yugoslavia from a bloody civil war on racial lines, which would have been inevitable, if Mihailovitch (the Serbian Orthodox general) had come to power."[*] This is something which in Ireland we would be reluctant to believe. Who could wish a Communist solution to our own racial and religious problems?

We live and think under a nuclear cloud and stretch our brains, built for solving human problems, into thinking cosmically. If sooner or later they fail us, friend and enemy will be destroyed together. How soon can we return to being men, not human adjuncts to machines, and handle again man-sized problems? How soon can we escape from the anthill which we have built round ourselves?

(1985)

---

[*] Hugh Seton-Watson, *Nationalism and Communism* (London 1945), page 90. (H.B.)

Croatia, Gaj, Etc.

(Editors' Note: This essay was transcribed from a handwritten and sometimes nearly illegible manuscript. The use of [?] indicates a unclear word or passage, whilst [] indicates where an obviously missing word has been inserted.)

Croatia has often been called the Ulster of Yugoslavia, but for the thoughtful [?] Irishman to grasp the appositeness of this title a great deal of difficult but beneficial mental gymnastics are necessary. We have to put Catholic instead of Protestant, Orthodox instead of Catholic, republicanism instead of monarchy, and separatist autonomy instead of imperialism, eastern instead of western. We would not, I think, trouble to do all this elaborate rearrangement of concepts, if we felt that any of these represented a fundamental antithesis. They are all, as above [?], secondary differentiations. The primary opposition is between freedom and subordination. Croatia, a small Catholic and historic state, in spite of ties of blood wishes to be free to dissolve her alliance with a monarchy [it] does not wish to be subject to, and to be an autonomous republic; Ulster, a small Protestant parvenu state, wishes to be free to refuse association with an autonomous republic and to unite herself with a monarchy. The only common ambition is freedom—but because of ties of blood, the analogy is held to be good and acceptable to Ulstermen and Croats, [and] we see that in many minds freedom is a feeling [?] which has precedence of everything else even religion.

Yes, even religion—a bad religion which is our own—is more dear to us than a higher one, which is forced on us by violence or material considerations. Even when we criticize its mythology, we resent any infringement of our freedom to practice it. It is, still, in most cases, the spiritual history of the society which shaped us and in which we were born. It is the key to a great many of our defects and virtues. Only if we decide to shape ourselves in quite a new way, can we divorce ourselves from it and become members of a new society. It is a difficult and delicate process, if it is to be painless; so many ties of association have to be severed, but it is only when the change is made under abrupt compulsion that men consider that a tragedy has taken place. That is to say, the view that religion is an absolute good to be inculcated at all costs like the desire for freedom is no longer held. The forcible conversions that disfigured Croatian history were profoundly unnatural, a disaster that resulted as a secondary effect of the war through which men lost whatever freedom they enjoyed.

No Catholic has today tried to justify [?] the conversion [campaign], not even dishonestly, [and] instead set himself the task of proving [?] better what happened [the rest of this sentence is illegible].

Yet nothing happens without a reason, and it would be possible I think, by tracing carefully the history of the Croatian people, to discover why their religion all at once became perverted and homicidal. I shall not try to do this, for I think it is a task that only a Central European could undertake – but the main lines of such a development are easily guessed. The Croats were more favoured than any others of the Slavonic peoples. They inherited one of the most splendid and unified [?] of the provinces of the Roman empire. For Illyria and the Dalmatian coast lay over against the Italian mainland and was sprinkled with wealthy villas and flourishing towns. They had been wrecked but not destroyed by the Avars, who preceded the Croats; and the Croats, settling among the ruins, developed a civilisation that was full of promise and originality. They were enslaved by Venetians, Hungarians, Turks and finally Austro-Hungarians, but there was considerable rivalry among their oppressors, who were often forced to present servitude in its most attractive form. On the whole Croatia fared better than

Ireland, though having not one covetous neighbour but several; and they continued to keep their language and many of their customs, even when as under the Moslem Turks in Bosnia they were forced [to] a change of religion. The Hungarians were, I think, the worst of their oppressors, and were the only ones till our time to make a serious onslaught on the Croatian language. They were themselves an oppressed people, who had to fight the Austrians for their right to be themselves, and perhaps as they were a simple unsubtle people they were not certain they were truly their own masters till they were the masters of someone else. And so we find during the period of Hungarian rule the attempt gradually to replace the Croatian language by Hungarian, beginning with the civil service in the innocent nationalist way. But the Hungarians ruled only the through Austrian connivance, the Austrians always endeavoured to oppress by proxy; they managed to keep their many subject peoples in subordination by making them jealous of each other. Also they managed to attract the ruling nobles of Croatia by giving them titles and confirming their estates. The Croats were considered splendid fighters and had a reputation for devoted loyalty to the throne. There were many anecdotes and songs to illustrate this. They were credited with the ingenious loyal virtues that Irish soldiers have in the pages of [unclear name] or Kipling.

I do not know how it came about that the Croats retained their language, while the Irish lost theirs, and how the English, though they had to cross a sea to do it, imposed a uniformity which Turks and Austrians, Hungarians and Italians failed [at]. I suspect that it had something to do with prestige. The Croats were familiar with the idea that there were many ruling languages and no single one of them enjoyed overwhelming prestige. Also I think it would be true to say that like many very efficient up-to-date people the English were more practised than the Turk in the less dramatic forms of oppression. The Turk crucified, raped and burnt but he had not the patience to carry out a detailed campaign of spiritual degradation. The spirit of the Irish was broken by many generations of well-run committee meetings, admirable schools and railways, earnest proselytisers, and the expert manipulation of jobs. That too was how the Austrians worked, so that they acquired in Jugoslavia a more intimate control than the Turks ever achieved, and yet never earned the same ill-fame. To Serb and Croat there was unspeakable infamy in any form of dealing with the Turk, but with the Austrians the Croats in particular were seduced into many small complicities and prostitutions. The sharp distinction of oppressor and oppressed was blurred by small concessions and careful phrases. The Serbian attitude to Austria, when it was dictated by the Serbian country folk rather than the court, was direct and simple, the Croat attitude was tortuous and perplexed. Just as Irish history is complicated by the fervent expressions of loyalty to the English crown from many leading Irish patriots like Daniel O'Connell or in early days rebels like Mountgarret, so Croat nationalism first appeared as a qualification of loyalty to the emperor rather than a repudiation of [it]. As time went on more and more drastic qualifications were dared, but as so often happens the leadership was taken, not by the oppressed whose spirit had been broken, but by generous men, who hated injustice. They wished to extend to others the privileges they enjoyed themselves, the refuge from oppression. They started *the Ilyrian movement*. This movement was generous, romantic, easily ridiculed, but in this it was similar to every other movement by which a kindlier attitude to others, a wiser system of justice and social morality, is initiated. Good men, who have inherited no power beyond that of mind and heart, are usually driven by desperation to be leaders in religion or armed rebellion. The initiative for a peacefuller transfer of privilege from the few to the many, has always come from the privileged themselves, a tiny but friable minority with an intimate knowledge of the weaknesses of their class and the best methods of exploitation and persuasion. Ljudevit Gaj and Count Yanko Drashkovitch˙, the founders of Croatian

---

˙ Ljudevit Gaj (1809-1872), of Huguenot origin, was a Croatian linguist, journalist, writer and politician. He was one of the central figures of the pan-Slavist Illyrian Movement. (Editors)

nationalism, sacrificed security and easy popularity and conventional friendships to build up the Illyrian movement. Its name "Illyria," like "Éirin," betrays its period and its methods. It had its Tom Moores, its Emmets and Edward Fitzgeralds. Many poems were written and old legends and folklore recovered from oblivion and scholars lent themselves gladly to the task of investing with glamour the ancient and obscure history of the Croats.

Gaj was only half a Croat, for his mother was German. He had big sorrowful dark eyes and a black and drooping moustache: and he wore the jacket of the Croatian national dress richly embroidered in crimson and gold and had a handsome Byronic appearance. His mother tongue was German and as a school boy his first publications were a German translation from the Latin of a tourist guide to his native Croatian village, and some German poems of his own. Then he went to the Austrian University of Graz where it was that he became conscious not only of Croatian nationalism but also of the common ties that bound Croats to other Slav peoples, Serbs, Bulgarians, Poles, and Czechs, all of whom had their patriotic societies in the Austrian Universities. He learnt much of his nationalism in the University's libraries in Vienna and Graz and Buda Pest. He became a doctor in Leipzig but most of his time seems to have been spent between Croatia and Vienna struggling for the recognition of Croat rights. After three years of waiting in 1835 he secured the right to publish the first newspaper in the Croatian tongue in Zagreb. He was a diplomatist, [and] by concentrating on culture rather than politics, his work was tolerated at the court. At that time a dispute was going on in Croatia about the rights of the Protestant Church. Gaj by supporting (1837) the Catholic party secured their support for nationalism. The Bishop Algovitch of Zagreb and all his clergy encouraged him and he obtained the right to found a printing press. He had the idea to publish an edition of his paper in Serbia in the Cyrillic script and he even went to Russia to borrow 20,000 roubles to effect it but in this he did not succeed.

In 1843 a ruthless Hungarian governor called Haller arrived in Zagreb. The Hungarian patriotic movement, under the celebrated

Kossuth, was underweight, and Haller saw the Croats as a backward
and rebellious people, who tried with archaic ways [and] absurd reviv-
alism to resist the splendid advance of the Hungarian regime of religious tolerance and economic freedom. Haller's predecessor as Ban˙ had
been the mild and progressive Bishop Haulik, who had favoured the
Croatian Movement and had thought to liberate the Croatian church
from its dependence on Hungary. He was accused in Vienna of giving
financial aid to the Croat rebel movement and he was removed. Haller
found among the Croat upper classes a certain amount of support. The
Illyrians were suspected of being "Russophile," of wishing "Yugoslav
separatism," of agitating for the curtailing of the privileges of the aristocracy. Word went to Vienna and the Vatican that the Illyrians were
concocting heresy, that Croats were apostatizing to the Orthodox
Church, that they were disseminating the pernicious ideas of the
French Revolution and aiming at an independent Illyrian kingdom.
Even the Russians, hearing of all the Slavophile activities of the Illyrians, were alarmed and disapproving. As the Illyrians were subjects of
Austria, Russians feared an Illyrian movement in the other Slav countries of the Balkans, which would bring them under Austrian influence.
The Turks, more naturally, hated the Illyrians, because they dreaded
the spread of romantic nationalism among their Croat subjects in Bosnia and Herzegovina. The Croats who sympathized with Hungary
industriously tried to part Croats and Serbs, on the religious issue,
where they were most sensitive. They hinted to Serbs that the Illyrian
movement was an attempt convert them into Catholics, to the Croats
it was to turn them into Orthodox. The gentle and generous Croatian
nationalism grew up with savage enemies and cynical suspicious
friends always around it. Sometimes it was flattered, sometimes attacked, its nature was slowly perverted, and finally it came to power,

---

˙ Under the Habsburg Monarchy of Austria-Hungary, the Ban was the chief
government official (effectively, the royal viceroy and prime minster) in what is
now Croatia. (Editors)

a warped and terrible phenomenon, savage and remorseless as to those within its power, as Hungarian nationalism had once been. The pattern of Croatian history is complicated and traditional and deeply human: it is repeated again and again with minor variations of time and place. It has the [slight yellowy?] conventional beauty of their embroidered clothes.

Haller as soon as he arrived forbade the use of the Illyrian idea, vetoed all political meetings and imposed the strictest censorship. It had been the custom for all business in Croatia to be treated in Latin: from now on Hungarian was to be substituted. There was the wildest indignation, and on the 29th of July 1845, there was a riot on St Marks Square at an election at which 16 men were killed. It was one of those historic occasions on which ordinary people have to bear the weight of destiny, and small misunderstandings become symbolic of irreconcilable discord. A Hungarian soldier had fired into the air from a window pleasure at the results of a gerrymandered election and had hit a young student. His friends had charged at the house from which the Hungarian had fired. They were met by a round of fire from some soldiers on guard. Wild panic and slaughter. There was an immense funeral. The hideous black invitation card to the funeral ceremony of the victims can still be seen. The words of Ban Heller, "Nur nieder schiessen die Hunde!"[*] have passed into legend. A patriotic countess raised a subscription and over the grave in the Yuryev cemetery a lion crouches upon a sarcophagus. Odes were written to the "July martrys" and what had been a cultural movement became a political one. "The national movement," writes the historian Jaksha Hertzeg, "was christened in blood."

The next thing that happened was the revolution of 1848 in Vienna, the flight of Metternich and the emperor, and the premature exaltation of Kossuth. The Croats boldly pressed on with their demands; they wanted a university, and an archbishopric for their Zagreb bishop, who

---

[*] Translation: "Just shoot down the dogs!"

was independent of Hungary. And they declared that Croatia had never been a subject but a partner under the crown of St Stephen. "Where is Croatia?" was Kossuth's reply, "I cannot find it on the map."

What followed is fairly well known.

(Unpublished handwritten manuscript, late 1940s)

In Serbian Macedonia

Skoplje, the chief town of Serbian Macedonia or Vardarska Banovina*, as it is now called, is a night's journey by train from Belgrade. The Vardar runs through it, a broad and rapid river, dividing the old Turkish town from the growing modern city that has sprung up around the railway station. On the far side of the bridge lie mosques and minarets, and a Turkish bazaar, where in booth after booth bearded Moslems sit combing wool, slapping it with long-handled rakes, stuffing and embroidering eider-downs, ironing fezzes or stirring delicious vegetable stews on long crescent shaped ovens. Here too are the shops of the Albanian silversmiths, where all day they sit making filigree rings and necklaces. They are Roman Catholics, mainly, and once they enjoyed the favour of Franz Josef, who built them a church. Today like the Turks of Skoplje, they are considered undesirable intruders in a land of Serbian Orthodoxy, an unpleasant reminder of a squalid past to be kept as far as possible from the tree-shaded boulevards of the near side of the Vardar. Still further out and still lower in the social scale is the gipsy quarter.

---

* "Serbian Macedonia," captured by Serbia in the Balkan Wars (1912-1913) at the expense of Turkey and Bulgaria, refers to the territory that would eventually become, under Tito, the Yugoslav People's Republic of Macedonia, and is now independent Macedonia. "Skoplje" is the older spelling of Skopje, the capital. "Banovina" was the name given to provinces in the Kingdom of Yugoslavia after 1929, until the state's dissolution in 1941 by the Axis Powers. Banovinas were mostly named after their main river. (Editors)

All the gipsies seem to be boot-blacks and every morning they swarm in and squat along the pavement beside their little stools. Some privileged ones sit in the Hotel lounge gazing with desperate concentration at the legs of the hotel visitors, at their leather suit cases, at everything polishable and brushable, making tireless suggestions.

Beyond the gipsy encampment stretches the Roman aqueduct, a quarter of a mile long; it once fed the town of Skupi, the Roman parent of Skoplje, which shortly is to be excavated. The Romans here, to judge by the inscriptions on their tomb stones were simple souls, their Latin was none too good and their Greek was worse; no doubt they talked among themselves in some Illyrian or Thracian patois. The Albanians claim to be descended from these Romanised Illyrians, pushed back into the mountains by Slav invasions.

Of the new town at Skoplje there is nothing much to be said; it has almost realized its ambition, common to all progressive little towns, of looking like everywhere else. It has a goodish hotel, a university, and a zoo and some hideous but imposing public buildings. An occasional little shop selling Halva and Turkish Delight, almond nougat and sesame-seed candy is the only reminder here that Skoplje was once the capital of a Turkish province. The main street was built thirty years ago in honour of the Sultan of Turkey, who was to pass along it on his first state visit to Uskub, as Skoplje was known to the Turks. From Uskub he went to Kosovo, the famous battlefield, "The Field of the Blackbirds," where in 1389 Serbia lost her freedom for five hundred years. There was a legend that the Turkish Empire would fall if ever a Sultan went to Kosovo, the scene of the Turkish triumph. The Sultan went and a few years later in 1912 the Turks were driven from North Macedonia.

The monastery of Sveti Naum, where I was going, was across the mountains but it was the end of March and there had been no snow for weeks. "You'll get there all right," everybody said, so I started: but I did not get there. The bus drive, which should have taken eight hours, instead took thirty six. As we got higher into the mountains, the snow fell thicker and lay deeper. It rose in great banks on either side; through the windows we saw nothing but snow. At last with a groan and final shudder the bus died; its wheels spun round ineffectually, and it sank back against a snow bank. We got out and pushed and two men who had spades dug. Our efforts released the bus, but, instead of going on, it came crashing back on top of us. We scattered with huge leaps in all directions into the snow drift and a soldier was knocked over and almost crushed. We left the men with the spades and walked on for five or six miles, then the bus overtook us; but that afternoon we stuck five times in the snow. In the evening we decided it was dangerous to go on, and spent the night in a mountain hut. It was clean and comfortable. There was a big stove round which we dried our clothes. Some people slept on the floor but I was lucky enough to get a room which I shared with a Bulgarian Professor of Theology from Sofia. He had been giving lectures at Tirana in Albania and now he was making his way back across the mountains to Skoplje and thence to Sofia, (for no less than three bus loads had got stranded in the hut.) He had like many Orthodox clergy a great black beard and a deep awe-inspiring voice which terrified the Macedonian boy who kindled our stove, so that he sang back at him in the same tone like a dog to a piano.

"I am not a Chauvinist" said the Professor, "I am an individualist, and national problems don't worry me, but there's no question that Macedonian is much more like Bulgarian than Serbian. They have an article like us, and like us they put it after and not before the noun." "Serb nationalists are like all other nationalists" said a schoolmaster, "If they can't prove Macedonian is a dialect of Serbian they'll just suppress it."

"Bulgarians won't do that, not because they're so enlightened, but because they've too many Macedonians. Actually we all speak Slav dialects – Bulgarians, Serbs, Macedonians, Slovenes and Croats. We're one people. Some day there'll be a Greater Yugo-Slavia that will include us all."

The next morning the sun was shining when we squeezed again into our buses to continue the journey. The rest of the way was downhill yet even so we often stuck but this time it was a pleasure to stretch our cramped legs and walk on through the snow. We were very high up. The tops of the mountain were dead grey stone, so bald and vertical that no snow seemed to have caught on them; a stream ran in the valley below us, now and then tumbling over waterfalls through a trellis of icicles. The branches of the pine trees were weighed down with gleaming snow. The only passenger who was annoyed at the delay was a fat business man, who was standing for Parliament in the May 5th Elections and had to make a political speech in a remote Macedonian town. We got to Debar on the Albanian frontier in the afternoon, and there we found a new bus to replace our old one which had collapsed under the strain. Debar is a decaying little town which lost its market, when the frontier was drawn a mile or so away from it. The road from Debar to Ochrid, which runs along the Black Drin river was also Albanian till a few years ago when it passed by agreement to Yugo-Slavia. Willows, scarlet and golden, fringed the edge of it; there are frequent eel-traps and weirs. We stopped at the foot of a rocky pass to let off an austere Serbian officer who was returning from leave in Belgrade to his post on the frontier. He was met by some soldiers with mules. As the bus moved on, we saw the officer and his troop disappearing up the lonely mountain road. The wooden saddles were piled high with portmanteaux and basket trunks, while the local innkeeper trundled a tin wheelbarrow stacked with martial accoutrements. At the rear of the little procession stalked the officer himself. For the rest of the way there was nobody in the bus but a sailor who had come from the Fleet at Dubrovnik to patrol Lake Ochrid in a motor boat and harry the smugglers who trade between the Albanian and Yugo-Slav sides of the Lake. Soon we were skirting along Lake Prespa and Lake Ochrid, two of the most beautiful lakes in the Balkans but it was almost dark and I scarcely saw them. I had lost twenty eight hours because of the snow so I had to leave Sveti Naum unvisited. It is the most famous of the South Serbian monasteries, built before the days of the Tsar Dushan, the ruler of the mediaeval Serbian empire, one of whose palaces was at Skoplje. Some of the monks at Sveti Naum were Russians who had left a monastery in Finland owing to some clerical ordinance which had offended them. Half had crossed over into Soviet Russia and there had been promptly imprisoned, the rest had come to Yugo-Slavia.

The bus for Bitolj left at seven the next morning so I scarcely saw Ochrid; brown-tiled Turkish houses mounted in tiers on the sides of the hill, their windows had high green shutters outside and sometimes even the garden wall had a palisade of matting and hurdles and broken boards, so zealously must the Moslem protect his womenfolk from prying eyes. There was a sudden burst of pipes and concertinas from half way up the hill and a crowd of children rushed down singing and playing. The leader had a conical hat three feet high, red and blue and white, with paper streamers, the others had home-made masks and necklaces of dried paprika and tomatoes. They were celebrating the last day of the Orthodox fast. We gave them some pears and offered a couple to two boys in fezzes who had been watching. The smaller one accepted and was promptly slapped by his big brother; I suppose to accept pears at a Christian party smacks of heresy.

In the highlands between Ochrid and Bitolj we were again stuck in the snow and had to dig a path nearly a quarter of a mile long for the bus to pass along. Bitolj, where we at last arrived, is not far from the Greek frontier and the largest town of the district. As Monastir it was well-known in the War, to English, French and Americans who left a smattering of their languages behind them in shops and restaurants. The Bishop of Ochrid and Bitolj is Father Nikolai, one of the best-loved priests in Yugo-Slavia; he is well-known in the British Isles too which he often visits, and he is a hospitable friend to the rare English visitors to Bitolj. The house where he now lives was shelled in the War and sixty townspeople who were sheltering there were killed. Bitolj too has been injured by the nearness of the frontier but a new railway is being built to the Skoplje line which will link it up more closely with the rest of Yugo-Slavia. Roads have been improved and new streets have been built. Through all Macedonia and Southern Serbia one is aware of the great efforts of the Government. The country was devastated by the War and before then by five centuries of Turkish misrule and in spite of natural riches recovery must be slow. There have been many set-backs. The neighbourhood of Skoplje was once famous for its grapes until the whole stock was ruined by phylloxera. Only in the last couple of years have they started with Government subsidy and advice to replant the vineyards with disease-proof American vines.

The Government deserves the support of Southern Serbia and will no doubt get it in the May elections, but in spite of all they have done to raise the standard of living, there is still much poverty and distress there. For generations Macedonians, unable to make a livelihood on their farms, have emigrated to America, and now that America will no longer take them, and there is less demand than ever for the meagre produce of their farms, many families are faced with destitution. For the Yugo-Slav Government, the economic problems of Macedonia are almost as grave and as urgent as the political problems of Croatia.

(Unpublished typescript, 1930s)

The Barriers

Out of over twenty small states in Europe now, only four, including Ireland, are free and at peace. It is hard, however, to make an Irishman's flesh creep with foreign analogies. Most of the defunct states were British protégés or part-creations, and it is through British channels that news of them comes; it is therefore regarded sceptically here. The Czechs had a far longer history of national independence than the Irish, they had a still living and vigorous language and a very distinctive culture, but their fate did not trouble Ireland deeply. "It is all British propaganda," said a prominent Republican at the time of the German Occupation. Still – it is quite possible that of all the small nations which after the war devoted themselves to self-sufficiency, Ireland alone will survive.

Just as our island is physically protected by the sea, there is an ocean of indifference and xenophobia to guard our insularity and to save us from foreign entanglements. Whatever its political value, culturally this self-sufficiency has been and will be a disaster to Ireland as to the other small states. It is a strange time to maintain the theory that a distinctive culture cannot exist without cultural intercourse, but since the mainspring of our freedom was not political theory but the claim that Ireland possessed and could develop a unique culture of her own, it is seasonable to examine this claim. It need not take us long, not longer than a walk down O'Connell Street past the bookshops, the cinemas, the stationers, the theatres, the hotels. By the time we are in Parnell Square we can have no doubt that after twenty years of effort, the culture of Ireland is still overwhelmingly Anglo-Saxon, nakedly or in word-for-word translation. The machinery of the national culture is of the approved (international) model, but the wheels have never once gone round.

If we cross to Europe or even England itself a surprise awaits us; everywhere in books and plays and even in temper of mind we find traces of Irish culture, if we can use that phrase for the influence of Irish exiles. To take the best known, there is not a culture in Europe that has not been radically influenced by Shaw's distinctively Irish habit of mind. I doubt if since Voltaire and the French ascendancy in Europe any national genius has had so wide a range as ours. On a later generation James Joyce has had a more selective but scarcely less widespread influence.

What is the significance of this contrast? It surely is that individual genius is the cement by which a nation is given shape and substance. A nation cannot be created negatively by elimination or strategic retreats into the past. It must crystallize round the contemporary genius that interprets it. The interpreters will be those who can see the national life as well as live it. To acquire this detachment, they will need to have access to other forms of society, so that they can see their own lives objectively and in totality from the threshold, and unless they can obtain from their own country this approach to other civilizations, by spiritual channels or by personal contact, their allegiance either to their country or to their interpretive mission will weaken.

It is not necessary to labour the point that self-sufficiency is in fact insufficient for a national culture. It is a fact, whether or not the explanation I have given is the right one. Great cultures have always risen from the interaction of diverse societies. And where that interaction has been varied, easy and reciprocated, as between the city-states of Greece, or during the Renaissance, national genius has expressed itself most freely. Its flowering period has been briefer and less abundant where it proceeds from a long interbreeding between two peoples, often involuntary and conditioned by geography rather than by mutual attraction.

In the eighteenth century French culture was as dominant in Germany as English culture in Ireland. In both cases the ultimate result was a bitter recoil to self-sufficiency, pedantry, mythology and linguistics.

The problem of a struggling national culture is thus an international one. It can preserve itself only if the spiritual channels by which it can communicate with foreign cultures are kept free and its intercourse is equal and reciprocal. In Ireland intercourse with England only was possible and that could not be on equal terms. Anglo-Irish culture, which should comprehend all literature from Swift to Edgar Wallace in translation, could never become the focus of a nation. The same might be said of the old Austrian civilization, on which the Succession States of Eastern Europe tried to base their new national cultures*. It was too strong and powerful to be assimilated. As soon as this was apparent, they dedicated themselves, like Ireland and the new states of the Baltic, to cultural self-sufficiency. Their only contact with each other was through consuls and diplomats, tourists and bagmen, and always in the interests of politics or commerce. There was none of that easy social intercourse by means of which the cultural centres of the Middle Ages were nourished. These little states were formed to protect and foster small cultural units. They failed. Everything that was unique and spontaneous in their national life was smothered behind the barriers reared to protect it.

It is unlikely that these small units will ever be revived in a political shape. A total Anglo-Saxon victory will probably bring some federal solution; a total German victory, a still further disintegration of non-German peoples into small administrative blocs, Bretons, Marcomans, Ukrainians, etc. Whether these federal or linguistic units will possess sufficient unity and freedom to attract to themselves the genius

---

* The 12 European Succession States are generally considered to be the following: Austria, Hungary, Yugoslavia, Czechoslovakia, Poland, Estonia, Latvia, Lithuania, Finland, Soviet Union, Turkey – and the Irish Free State. (Editors)

of a national culture or whether that genius will emigrate once more, cannot be predicted. None the less a national culture, since it depends more on individuals than on governments, has a continuity that survives political changes.

It is a big leap from the Czar to Stalin; the passage from Chekhov and Gorki to Zoshchenko, Leonov and Romanov is gradual and easy. Accident, which plays such a large part in the political relations of peoples, where their genius is only lightly engaged, is far less prominent in their cultural intercourse, where the relatively permanent and fundamental is brought into contact.

It would be easier to influence the cultural than the political future of Europe. And if what I say about the necessity for intercourse is true, then it is not premature or absurd to ask where we are to look for the spiritual channels between the peoples.

In the last decade cultural intercourse has loomed very large in the political schemes of the great powers. Russia started with Voks and Intourist and the Society for Cultural Relations. Her example was followed by German Bunde and Kraft durch Freude cruises; by French Institutes and holiday courses; by British lecture tours and university exchanges. Lesser powers like Italy advertised themselves by exhibitions, cheap railway fares and presents to national museums. Was there any reciprocity or spontaneity about this? Scarcely. It was a one-way traffic. Culture was the jam by which the nasty taste of political penetration was disguised. The small states, which were most in need of foreign contacts, had to satisfy themselves with resisting political influence since they could not exert it. Intercourse with their neighbours had a purely commercial bias. It was often startlingly unpolitical. Some Yugoslav journalists who applied for facilities at the Irish Tourist Association are said to have been refused with the reminder that one English city like Liverpool was of more importance to Ireland than the whole continent of Europe.

It was in the most backward and improbable parts of Europe, where cultural isolation was most deeply felt, that lively efforts to combat it on the right lines were made. In Serbia, Croatia, Slovenia and parts of

Romania and Bulgaria, life in the provinces is not unlike our own. People are lazy, sociable, individualistic, with a passion for gossip and a deep attachment to their land. They began to solve the problem of international intercourse by welcoming foreign visitors to the small provincial clubs, originally formed for the study of foreign languages. A plan was made to link up some of these clubs in each country in a single scheme, by which they entertained in succession travellers from outside. As their organization became recognized, it began to receive official favours in the form of railway tickets, wireless engagements, visa reductions, while remaining cautiously independent about official patronage. The audiences were small and intimate and the visit was sometimes more like a party than a lecture.

Once an Irish singer came and in the small clubs of Macedonia Irish songs alternated with Serbian ballads. That was not the only contact with Ireland, for the visit was returned some months later by a school-teacher from Novi Sad, who lectured, travelled and broadcast in Ireland. It was curious how those who were attracted by the scheme, which had no money in it, were seldom mere travellers. Artists, writers, folk-lore students, professional men, they did not often lack talent or personality.

Soon the spontaneity of the plan was spoiled by the potential implications of English culture round which many of the clubs were built. Big halls were hired to hold big audiences gathered to listen to bigwigs with titles and other recommendations based on public services. The faint smell of power politics pervaded the atmosphere; reciprocity gave place to rivalry, personal exchange to diplomatic courtesies. The scheme changed beyond recognition under official patronage and international snobbery.

There is no reason why it could not be revived in its original form. The smaller peoples must take the lead once more and hold it tenaciously. Round the most ordinary British traveller there hangs an aura of wealth and Waterloo and the British navy, which either antagonizes or enthrals. The traveller from a lesser country, rich in traditions but politically weak, can meet and mix fruitfully on a reciprocal basis, as himself alone. Travellers like these in an unromantic age might take the place of the craftsmen, crusaders or minstrels, who by their wanderings kept alive the spiritual unity of Europe through the Middle Ages, and at the same time enriched the cultural diversity of its provinces.

It was in the eighth century, when she was most closely in touch with Europe, that Ireland enjoyed a native culture of her own. Irishmen had in Christianity a motive for exploring the world. They had a new message, freshness of fervour, a clear field. Ireland is not so fortunate today. Here contact with foreign culture must be organized on more artificial but not less personal lines.

Today we are cut off completely from the outer world, and between north and south, between cities and provinces, the barriers are rising. The war has forced on us a cultural self-sufficiency more complete than the most fervent separatist could have imposed by law. Now that we have seen its dangers, we can fight against them. We must create some social organism to overcome the barriers between ourselves, so that it can extend its scope outside our island when peace returns.

(1941)

The Two Languages

It is fortunate that men are as a rule well insulated from each other, that is to say they do not absorb more of each other's sorrows than they can conveniently exude in sympathy and assistance. Now and again, of course, we commit ourselves to a surfeit of fellow-feeling, and compassion that we are forced to inhibit turns to exasperation and dislike. Men protect themselves from such over-indulgence by withdrawing into groups, communities, states, for an aggregation of men exposes a smaller surface of sensibility to outer impressions than does a loose collection of individuals. It is the principle of the potato clamp.

In spite of that we go on expecting that states and governments should show the same susceptibilities as those who compose them. We expect them to be sensitive to appeals to pity and honour and, when they are unresponsive, to exhibit signs of shame. In fact it is only through the fissures in the fabric that such influences travel. A solidly built state will show only a surface reaction. Thucydides is still the best interpreter of the humours and idiosyncrasies of the small community. His chronicle of the Peloponnesian War should convince us that it was only those cities which were divided against themselves, in which there were Laconizing, Medizing and Philathenian parties, to which it was ever worth addressing appeals for help, reminders of past friendships and common causes.

Our Irish state has kept its course through the distractions of war with a composure which the warring peoples, forgetful of former phases of their own collective existence, find neither natural nor decent. Is it the indifference of the untroubled, undivided community? Hardly. I think it masks a deep suspense. Of the dozen states which were created from fragments of empires a score of years ago (Russian, German, British, Turkish, French, Dutch), ours alone is intact. The others were told that they had never existed, they had been amputated, not born. Those who sponsored their liberation could not save them from extinction. The same arguments have been heard in Ireland for centuries. Unuttered, they are no less formidable than before. We are deeply uncertain of ourselves, less frightened of what we might be made to suffer than of what we might be made to think. With one or two exceptions, those other states (Czechoslovakia, Yugoslavia, where there was a German minority) were destroyed more by schizophrenia than by violence. Therefore we welcome every sign of solidarity and are proud that the cleavages in our state have not gone so deep as to violate its integrity. Control has not passed from the body to its members. The sympathies of the citizens have been warmly dictated by those impersonal laws which regulate the intercourse of all small communities.

What proof have we that such laws exist? The small modern state is overgrown and artificial, and much further removed from the realities of human nature than were the city-states of Thucydides. All the same, as if in a discoloured mirror, it reflects something of the natural forms and phases of human association. In its struggles and factions and epic catastrophes, a recurrent, inevitable pattern is traceable. The evidence of such affinities is, however, unwelcome. Small modern states resent the imputation that their destiny is dominated by their social structure rather than by those distinctive racial qualities from which they derive their right to be free. Their claims to be unique have been recognized so that their behaviour, in time of war, has become the subject of moral judgements rather than of sociological analysis. They are credited with the same good and evil qualities which we distribute among their citizens. But surely, from the moment they were created, they were as different from the component individuals as is a crystal or a molecule from the atoms out of which, in elaborately formal arrangement, it is combined. Men do not pool their qualities in a community like flavours in a pudding. Association truly changes them, thaws the queer shapes into which the individual is cast, disperses the film of idiosyncrasy with which he protects himself. The whole is not the sum of the parts. The moral laws which develop out of the intercourse of persons have, therefore, no authority over the intercourse of communities.

Only an accident of geography preserved our state from the fate of the other eleven, and there is evidence enough that in our position they would not have acted differently. Men as individuals can be chivalrous, generous, impressionable, but a community of men can accept no obligation that threatens its existence. At the first sound of war we have seen the small modern state abjure all the enlightened sympathies of its citizens, contracting into a tight ball like a hedgehog at the bark of a dog, seeing nothing, hearing nothing, smelling nothing. At such a moment a hedgehog cannot think of other hedgehogs. It cannot permit itself a single twitch of curiosity or compassion.

How is it that, while the state is so circumspect in all its movements, many thousands of its citizens have been able to betray their sympathies in action? I think it is because we have always been realists about our state, however many delusions we have had about the Irish nation. We have grown up with it and never thought of it as transcending common experience or giving more than a vague and precarious expression to that corporate existence of which we believe ourselves capable. We have never made it the guardian of our social conscience or expected it to speak prematurely with the voice of the National Being.

In this we are unlike older countries and easily misunderstood by them. When someone says, "Slums are a disgrace to England," "The loss of Alsace-Lorraine is a wound in the side of France," even the most matter-of-fact can see for a moment a bowed monumental figure symbolizing a bad conscience, a sunk ship, an unflinching resolve. If free Ireland had been born at the same time as Belgium or even Norway, we should have some such substantial, rather domineering phantom to blush for us, grieve for us, expect us to do our duty, confuse us in fact into thinking that the solidarity we aim at it moral rather than biological. But there is none.

The Ireland for which men died, even when as Cathleen ni Houlihan she took a human shape for them, was aloof and indifferent, demanding but not preaching. She was a projection of their yearnings and frustrations, not of their designs for a social order. In the favourable air of the Victorian age, when social consciences were crystallizing, Ireland was not yet a sovereign state. So our internal affairs are very little influenced by abstract and humane ideas. Our politics are highly personal. We blame people and we praise people. Our slums are not a disgrace to Ireland but to Mr So-and-so who owns them, and he is made to feel this just in so far as pity for the poor, an elusive abstract thing, can overcome our concrete liking and respect for Mr So-and-so. That is how things work and it might be worse. The throne from which the National Being might speak is empty but at least it has never been profaned.

Because of that it is only as individuals, as free elements on the surface of our state, that we respond to the moral climate of the world. That this response is active enough few would deny. Not many small states have so deep a zone of free elements: people, that is to say, whose attachment to our state is so loose as to be precarious, who are at any moment more accessible to influences from outside than to those within. If these outer influences were to penetrate deeper, the nuclear solidarity of our state would be dissolved, as a state we should cease to exist. It does survive, because, as in all agricultural communities, there is an ultimate impermeable core of obtuseness and self-sufficiency, which is at once our shame and our salvation.

This is the explanation why many Irishmen feel profoundly and personally implicated in the moral problems of Europe and at the same time are passionate supporters of Irish neutrality. Wireless sets, newspapers, tell them of free nations like their own being destroyed, of men being bullied and tortured, of free minds being enslaved, but they feel that it is they themselves and not their nation who are being addressed. They do not wish their neighbour across the hill to be coerced into feeling this shame or into pretending to feel it. For such feelings are the price that is paid for a range of interest and sympathy wider than his. They stand on the periphery of their nation, he at the core. Their hearts are not warmer than his, merely the warmth ranges outwards and not inwards and is more widely diffused. When he goes to England for a job in the building trade and later dies in Cyrenaica, they feel that it was through the flaws, the wormholes in their state that the challenge to which he responded reached him. In such a way a Czech or a Croat peasant, released from the claims of his state by its disintegration, might easily enough be recruited for a remote crusade in Russia. By their natures such men are fitted to play a creative part only at the heart of their community; drawn outside it, they become passive elements, equally serviceable for good or evil ends. The community to which they belonged suffers by their defection, for all the warmth of their natures was needed to preserve its cohesion and integrity. It is only when its integrity is guaranteed that the community has a life of its own and, through the men of the periphery, radiates an influence greater than the sum of their individual contributions.

Modern states correspond only roughly to the natural organic community, and in them men seldom play the part for which they are fitted by nature. All the same, in any society which lays claim to organic unity, we must expect to find this impermeable core. Those who compose it are as a rule inarticulate or express themselves in reach-me-down language a size too big for their thoughts. If they could speak naturally, as the Greeks did, and censorship of thought played as small a part as at Athens, I think they would talk about the war as did the farmers and charcoal burners of Aristophanes. The peasants of Attica had suffered unspeakably, their olive trees had been cut down, their farms and vineyards destroyed by the Spartans. They were not pacifists or anti-anybody or anything, for that suggests the power to think about the war abstractly. They just wanted peace. It is clear that you could not make idealists of such people any more than you could transplant carrots. Here is Trygaeus, the vine-dresser, appealing to the goddess Peace:

We have been praying to you for thirteen years. Do now put away battles and tumults! Put a stop to our suspicions of each other and our tale-bearing! Blend us Greeks as before with the balsam of friendship and temper our minds with a milder fellow-feeling. Grant that our market be filled with all manner of good things, with garlic, early cucumbers, apples, pomegranates and little cloaks for slaves, and that we may see people bringing from the Boeotians geese, ducks, woodpigeons and sandpipers and let baskets of eels come from Lake Copais!

The Peloponnesian War dragged on for twelve years, waged by men who saw far beyond the horizon of the peasants, men of high ideals and brilliant attainments, who expected far more of life than eels and sandpipers. Thucydides put speeches into their mouths in which they balanced remote probabilities, estimated the claims of honour, loyalty, friendship, justice. In contrast to Trygaeus, they were typical men of the periphery, pursuing remote sympathies so far that often they lost touch with their base – like Alcibiades and Themistocles, betraying their countries in the interests of oligarchy or pan-Hellenism or mere ambition, whose lofty scale robbed it of vulgarity. The war ended in total ruin and the ultimate subjugation of Hellas to Macedon. Is the moral that the Trygaeuses should be the arbiters of war and peace? No, the moral is that there is an outer and an inner language talked in every state and if no one is coerced into talking a language other than this own, the life of a community will be preserved even when its material existence is threatened.

This, like all social generalizations, seems far too simple and also far too elaborate. But societies as they grow seek to fill out the patterns we suggest to them. The feudal system must have become more like a pyramid the more it was interpreted as a pyramid. Today society is dominated by a subtler, truer conception of itself as an organic system of separate parts which grow, contact, coalesce and disintegrate again according as some vital force ebbs and flows in one direction or another.

Men associate in "cells" or, in Russian, in "little eggs." We remind ourselves how we submerge our personalities in groups, reassert ourselves as individuals, claim for ourselves the qualified autonomy of the highly differentiated cell. We are struggling to use these ideas for our happiness and every time we apply them we have to act the part of creators as well as interpreters.

We must therefore apply, as well as accept, the idea that groups of men – states or nations or whatever association claims for itself a conscious solidarity – communicate with each other by means of their surface elements and that if the surface is too deeply penetrated the group's integrity is undermined. In time of war the natural social processes are reversed and the group contracts upon itself, the feelers with which it explored the world becoming bristles for repelling it, but war cannot last for ever and soon the natural processes are resumed. In the peace which follows the war the conditions will be as strange and difficult; the sudden relaxation of tension, the expansiveness and quick renewal of contacts, may be as fatal to the integrity of the small state as war itself. Racial affinities are rarely powerful enough to hold men together in the face of opportunities and enterprises which the convulsions of war make accessible. Many communities have been exterminated by violence, but more have perished by outgrowing their strength, responding too readily to the seductions of the world outside. Apart from smaller peoples, what became of the Normans, the Goths, the Gauls, all of them conquerors or favoured by their conquerors?

In so far as a nation has developed an organic life of its own, the impact of the outside world will be met and answered upon the periphery. The energies of the greater part will not be deflected from their true function, which is to maintain the strength and solidarity of the nation. It is only when that solidarity exists that the men of the periphery will represent more than themselves and become in a true sense the interpreters of the National Being.

History, which respects above everything political unity, has done less than justice to that queer unpolitical cohesion which enabled the minor peoples of Europe to resist assimilation. For generations prudence has obliged them to avoid the overt mechanical forms of association and to develop an interdependence that is warm, personal and clandestine. One day men will move away from political combinations towards more organic forms of association. When that happens there will be more understanding for those who, like the Irish and the Czechs, learnt for long years to keep their communities alive without political sanctions.

Will our nation be dispersed before it is resurrected to organic life? The pious have collected the bones, the wise can reassemble them; but that process of nature which can clothe them with flesh is not yet at our command.

(1943)

Appendix

Airton House,
Tallaght,
Co. Dublin
November 27th, 1943

Dear Hubert,

Sean sent me your TWO LANGUAGES article. It's probably too deep for me, and for any ordinary reader I'm sure it wants expanding. I'm afraid I have marked your MS in red pencil for my own convenience; I hope it will rub out, but I haven't got a rubber! I don't know if you want my opinion, but for what it is worth here it is.

The whole article stimulates my interest and imagination, but it does *not* illuminate my understanding. It's rather as the eye may be directed to an aspect of the landscape by a shadow falling on it! You doubtless know your stuff, but the uninstructed (like myself) need to be soothed with FACTS. Some of these you could give without adding much in the way of words – e.g. the names of the twelve states referred to at top of page 2*, and the names of the two exceptions later on the same page. And you ought to have a foot-note to say that "Students of Political History will not be perturbed by the apparent anomaly of such states as Switzerland, Belgium, and those of the Scandinavian and Iberian peninsulas." I am not a Student of Political History, and I should need that much reassurance. On the same page, I don't understand the passage from "Control" to "communities"; it needs expanding and linking to its context. Further on you say "What proof have we…?" and you don't anywhere fulfil the implied promise. Again, one wants examples of *modern* states being removed from the realities of *human* nature (from the nature of the primitive "state"?). At the top of page 3 you speak as though morality were wrongly attributed to the State, but on page 4 you speak of a "social conscience." At the bottom of that page you suggest that we are "realists" about our state, but at the bottom of the previous page you have suggested that small states (with no hint of exception) tend to be "romantic" about themselves. On page 3 you suggest that we have been saved by "geographical accident," but on page 2 you suggest that we have been saved because certain "cleavages" have not gone deep enough. These may be contingent facts, if so, they might be stated contiguously? Top of page 5 – there seems to be some confusion between the "individual" who is accessible to outside influences and the "state" into which they might penetrate. Further down the page you seem to assume that your chap who is not open to these outside influences is the one who is most likely to get himself killed in Cyrenaica – but *is* he? Why? On page 6, the opinions of the peasant Trygaeus seem to me identical with most informed Pacifist opinion of today – to be oddly enlightened, in fact. Page 7, what is the difference between the "life" of a community and its "material *existence*"? Page 8 – "social consciousness" (like "social conscience") implies a very advanced organism. Something of the sort, having a

---

* See note on page 343. (Editors)

"race-memory," seems to be needed by Freud and Jung, but it's pure myth, surely? Your thesis rather depends on this, but you don't demonstrate it, and if there is a "social organism" (other than those of the Hymenoptera) it has only been demonstrated as something at a very low level – certainly not as having reached consciousness? Further down the page you talk of war and peace conditions in a confusing way (to me). On page 9 you say "only when solidarity exists, etc.," implying that it does not yet exist (here?), but on page 5 you have attributed to us an "impermeable core of self-sufficiency."

My criticisms may be due to my stupidity, but they could be got over by expansion and FACTS – at least I hope so!

Love,
Geoffrey

Maiden Hall,
Bennettsbridge

December 8

Dear Geoffrey,

I was awfully pleased that you took so much trouble with my article. It is easier to be vaguely polite and non-committal when no contact is made, so I was very grateful for your extremely intelligent comments and even disposed to accept the truth of about 15 per cent of them. With your knowledge of writers you'll admit that is pretty handsome of me.

It's difficult, without a better technique than I present at present, to put an idea across and to work on it at the same time, and in the article I sent I was thinking mostly of putting it across. Though you'll be sceptical of this, I *am* able to pick my way through all those confusing synonyms, and they didn't confuse *me*. In fact as I felt fairly certain where I wanted to get, and there wasn't much space, my idea was to hustle the reader (for his own good) past all the forks and turns and *not* picnic at each cross-roads and take him into my confidence. That would have been a different kind of a journey. I was quite ready to make it, but not in that article. I think you are the wrong sort of reader for me as obviously before one submits to be hustled by someone else and agrees to suspend a certain kind of criticism (some sort of suspension accompanies all reading), one must want to arrive at the same place as the writer does, and you probably don't. I have a picture of the sort of society I would like, so have you; if either of us could describe it we should be almighty geniuses. As it is we can only poke about hopefully among analogies and parallels and be rather pleased when the same one takes our fancy. Because of this I didn't feel reproached by your suggestion that I was indicating a point on the landscape by casting a shadow on it. Better that way than none. I usually find indirect methods the best and have sympathy with the man who gave his son a good slap so that he would remember having seen a salamander.

Inevitably the terms one uses are fluid. To take an example of possible confusion which you did not mention, I have used words like "group," "community," "society," etc., with very little effort to distinguish between them. In fact I avoided too much precision as I feel it is premature to be precise about sociology. Inevitably all the terms one uses have a different aura for all of us. What, for instance, is an Irishman or a Czech? Clearly what is written in his passport (and that is what would chiefly concern many sociologists) has nothing to do with it. I myself made several Irishmen like that out of Viennese Jews.

I don't know whether you are right in wanting more "facts." Historical facts have that gritty, substantial feel about them only in the examination schools and their too-extensive purlieus. I discard them as building material because they are really too plastic to use except as ornament. For example, in a small state like Yugoslavia you could get a purely factual account of its creation from a dozen representative citizens, Croat, Bosnian, Slovene, Macedonian, etc., or from representatives of the various economic and religious cross-sections, and each would give a different but quite truthful picture. When Yugoslavia comes to be reorganized, facts will be so cogent and clamorous and innumerable that they will be used just as seasonings to the theoretic puddings made by the powers. Subjective considerations will weigh the most, shaped by the views of society current at the time. In 1918 the pundits of the moment, Seton-Watson, Pares, Miss Durham and others, felt queer atavistic attractions towards primitive forms of society, and were able to ignore the irresistibly dominant Austrian culture. I feel the same attraction and so have only sympathy for this astounding *tour de force*, but it is due to mental gymnastics and has nothing to do with the facts. Ireland, as a state, is the same sort of intellectual concoction, emanating probably in part, like Yugoslavia, from Anglo-Saxon brains. There are such things as real human societies, in *posse* if not in *esse*, but they are masked by these political figments, not revealed.

I left out Belgium, Holland, Spain, etc., quite deliberately. I ought to have explained that I was collecting only those Succession States which were formed at the same time (1918-21), and under the influence of much the same ideas. I don't think it is remembered now to what an extent they were created in the brains or the bile of Professor So-and-so. I counted a dozen because I felt that committed me less to precision than eleven, but I can, if forced, count a dozen, with many tedious qualifications, e.g. Finland was less a creation than Lithuania*.

The gist of my article was the extraordinary similarity of their reactions to similar stresses, which could not be explained *only* by their birthdays, their common origins in the professor's brain-pans and other contingent facts. I believe there must be some constant factors in all human associations, some rules of growth in the human community similar to those in our bodies. If they existed once in the primitive community, what became of them? Herbert Spencer ran the organic analogy to death for his contemporaries, but I believe it could profitably be restated for ours. If I groped, it was not for facts. In fact I

---

* See note on page 343. (Editors)

conscientiously sieved out a page or two as I feared it would make the article still more indigestible.

Your comments were really helpful and showed me why I failed to explain myself. What was nicer was that I felt the defects you found were fairly remediable.

Love, Hubert.

P.S. I ought to take one of the passages you complain of and see if I can prove that I had a meaning which can be conveyed. Peggy, too, finds my views on Trygaeus obscure so I shall take him.

Trygaeus is a normal element in most states. He likes peace but defended himself bravely against the Spartans, who interrupted the routine of his life. He isn't in the least, as you say, an "enlightened pacifist." He has no philosophy (an enlightened pacifist surely believes in pacifying, not just in being peaceful). In fact he only starts to function when and where there is discord. Otherwise he would be a quietist or something of that kind, if, as Trygaeus doesn't, he *wanted* an "ism."

Put such a Trygaeus in an average small state, say Czechoslovakia. Though he is a pious Catholic, it is most improbable that while that state is intact he would ever have had the inclination, apart from the opportunity, of going on a crusade against the Bolshevik Antichrist. A few enlightened Catholics might, and did, but not he. But later on the whole state collapsed and these influences penetrated quite easily to him. They started to take effect on him. Even if they had always filtered through to him in the form of newspaper propaganda, his faith in his immediate surroundings and the demands they made on him gave him kind of immunity to them. But now he is recruited without difficulty for this religious crusade. Thousands like him have gone off not too reluctantly to the eastern front. I expect he thinks it rather fine and perfectly in line with what he has always been taught. All the same the fact that he is accessible to such a stimulating idea proved that something had gone wrong with the state. Similarly, I said that when our Trygaeuses in Ireland respond, as they do, to the "appeal of the allied nations etc.," something is wrong with *their* state. The section of the community to which they belong would not show any strong reaction to such external stimulus if the fabric of the community was in perfect condition. It's like an orange: the weather only ripens it when it meets the outside alone, but rots it when it gets inside through a crack.

I am constantly struck by the way that many ordinary Irishmen with strong healthy roots here can say about foreign events, "Oh, how bad! Oh, how sad!" and be receptive to newspaper propaganda about the war, but yet feel emotionally quite uninvolved. This seems to me, for their type, normal, and quite *abnormal* when the propaganda really strikes home. This in my experience happens first with those Trygae-uses who, for one reason or another, already stand in a bad relation to the community.

Probably I tried to telescope this up far too much. If I was to improve the article as an article (I mean make it readable for the ordinary reader) I could only afford to expand it there, if I eliminated here.

You are probably confused by my habit of not explaining when I am referring to a "social organism" that really exists, and when it is a purely imaginary ideal of perfection. I don't see why one can't use the idea fairly loosely. After all one says that somebody has a triangular table or even face, and yet one knows there is no such thing as a triangle and never could be, since by definition it is composed of lines without breadth. In a short article one wishes to escape stating all one's axioms. Maybe one can't.

(1943)

Endnote: This essay is accompanied by the intellectual exchanges of magazine editor (Geoffrey Taylor, literary editor of Sean O'Faolain's *The Bell*) and author – the one pleading for clarification, the other giving a brilliant and sustained defence of his ideas and their expression, re-fusing to "picnic at each cross-roads." In sum, they form a fascinating commentary on the original as well as giving an insight into the thought processes of a writer-at-work as he seeks to articulate the moral and communal notion of self, or the identity of that creature called man – or Irishman, or German, etc. – in the midst of a world war in which Ireland played no formal part. (Antony Farrell, The Lilliput Press)

Fiume, Sushak and the Nugents

Lately I have been reading Elizabeth Hickey's *Green Cockatrice* (1978) which is in part a history of the Nugents of Westmeath and in part a celebration of one of their most interesting members, William Nugent, the Gaelic poet. It reminded me that nearly thirty years ago I had visited Fiume and its neighbouring town, Sushak, where the last of the Nugents, an elderly woman well remembered in the town, had recently died.

Fiume, at the head of the Adriatic where Italy and Yugoslavia meet, takes its name from the river or "flumen" which divides it from Sushak. This small stream was for twenty years the frontier between the Slav and Latin peoples, but now the Yugoslavs have joined the two towns with a broad flat bridge and under it the little Fiume or Rijeka as stream and town are now called, never very impressive, has become almost unnoticeable. The bridge is more like a big square than a bridge and is planted with rows of chestnut trees under which the citizens of Fiume and Sushak mingle and listen to the band. It is a symbolic bridge.

For d'Annunzio too the bridge, an earlier narrower bridge, had a symbolic significance. He had with his young Arditi seized the towns in 1919 from the Yugoslavs to whom they had been awarded by the peace treaty. The Arditi were the forerunners of the Fascists and their cry "Eja, Eja, Alala!" with which they marched across the bridge was adopted by them. When shortly afterwards by a new treaty, Sushak, but not Fiume, was awarded once more to the Yugoslavs, the bridge was not abandoned without a struggle in which it was destroyed. It was photographed and widely advertised as the saddest of all the casualties.

When I was there the Italians and Croats had almost forgotten the hectic days of d'Annunzio, and I bought a history of his short reign for a few shillings. The first page was covered with a dedication in his own dashing handwriting to his glorious comrade-in-arms Attilio Bijio and there were fifty photographs of ecstatic triumphs and processions and conquests of Dalmatian islands – all now forgotten*. Or are they entirely forgotten? I was told how a little before a foreigner missed his wife, Eva, in a crowd at Fiume railway station. He called after her shrilly "Eva! Eva! Allo! Allo!" It was almost his last cry because he was battered by his fellow travellers with suitcases and umbrellas. They thought he had been crying "Eja, Eja, Alala!"

A steep rocky hill rises above Sushak. On top of it are the castle, church and village of Trsat. One tower of the castle is Roman, for there where Sushak now stands was the old Roman town of Tersatica. The rest of the castle was built by the Francopans, an ancient Italian family of unknown lineage, who claimed like Dante and Thomas Aquinas to be descended from the Patrician family of Aricius, and who ruled Croatia for several generations and became more Croatian than the Croats. At the beginning of the last century it was bought by the Irish General Laval Nugent. He had left Westmeath some forty years before and taken service with the Habsburgs. When Napoleon had set up an Illyrian state in Croatia the Austrian emperor had been powerless to evict the

---

* Italian irrendentism was a political movement of the nineteenth and twentieth centuries seeking the annexation by Italy of a large part of Adriatic Dalmatia. Several of the partially Italian-speaking Dalmatian islands as well as parts of its coast (all of which had been part of Austria-Hungary) were occupied by Italy after the First World War; and, in 1919, the famous Italian nationalist and poet D'Annunzio even led a force of several thousand Italian troops which seized the large Istrian city of Fiume (now Rijeka, Croatia) and declared the short-lived, *opéra bouffe* state, "Italian Regency of Carnaro" (1919-1920), which sought unification with Italy. Later, one of Mussolini's famous rallying-calls would be "Dalmazia Nostra" (Our Dalmatia). (Editors)

French. So Nugent had taken the matter in hand himself. Mustering the Croats of Istria and Dalmatia he had pushed the French far back into Italy. By the Austrian emperor he was later made into a count and a marshal. He restored in part the old castle, built a chapel there and below it a pleasant modern house for himself.

I found a remarkable old man living in the Nugents' house, which was badly battered by bombs. He had been a Feldwebel in the Austrian army, then he had become an Italian, now he was a Yugoslav. He had known well the last of the Nugents, an old woman who had died aged ninety in 1941, blind and alone, and he had read and knew by heart all the history of the neighbourhood. The Yugoslav government had made him a curator of the castle.

From the square Roman tower, we looked far down on the two blue harbours of Fiume and Sushak, separated only by a spit of land and the small river. Eastwards the Croatian littoral ran past the big bare islands of Krk and Cres and Dalmatia, and behind it, gauzy grey, we could see the high Velebite mountains that lie between Zagreb and the coast. On the west there was the rocky Istrian shore curving southwards at Abbazia, an elegant but now deserted resort. The old man pointed out the route by which Charlemagne's generals had met the Croats in battle and after some reverses had checked them in Istria, so that they never came into Western Europe. He sketched the campaigns of the Francopans, of Marshal Marmont and Laval Nugent. He had none but local visitors for a long time and he was pleased to talk.

The chapel that Laval Nugent built lies above the dungeon of the Francopans. It is a big classical building but it and one of the Francopan towers has been badly damaged by war and vandalism. There was a stack of planks lying beside it and the old man told me that the Yugoslav government were going to spend large sums in restoring it. "Some young communists in the village said it should all be thrown into the sea," he remarked, "as a reminder of feudalism, but I told them that even the Russians respected old things. When the Finns could not pay their reparations in cash, they said, 'Then pay us in antiques.'"

A huge double-headed Austrian eagle in stone perched on a

coat-of-arms was lying on the ground. When the Italians came first they had brought a row of lorries to take anything valuable away but the village boys had anticipated them by pulling down the eagle and hiding it in the earth. Countess Nugent liked the Italians and so they had tied her in her chair and put a handkerchief in her mouth while the digging was going on. That was during d'Annunzio's raid. In this war she had been too old to interfere and the Italians had pulled the lids off Laval Nugent's marble sarcophagus and rummaged for gold, and they had smashed holes in all the other family vaults as well. After the fall of Italy a German general arrived at Trsat. "What barbarians the Italians are!" he had exclaimed and the Nugent bones were collected and the vaults re-sealed again. A modest vault, which the Italians had not bothered to break into, had the name JANE SHAW carved on it. "I wonder is she a relation of Bernard Shaw?" the old man said, and he told me that some time before the war the playwright had come to Fiume in a yacht and that he had stood on the bridge at Sushak and sung a song. "We all crowded round and laughed and were very pleased."

He brought out a big portfolio from the house and showed me photographs of the village boys grouped round the Austrian eagle in their best clothes after they had dug it up again with ceremony. Also there was a photograph of Countess Nugent talking to him on a seat. She had a mass of white hair and a cross, distinguished face. "She was very fond of reading Nietzsche," said the old man, "and knew every language but Croatian though she had lived among us for fifty years." She always called herself an Irishwoman. Her house was perpetually full of visitors, French and German and Italian and English sailors from the ships; it was only the Croats she did not like. When she grew old, she became very dirty and suspicious and would let nobody near her. Though she was stone blind she went down every day to eat in Fiume or Abbazia* and knew her way about the streets perfectly! She had not survived the war long. Her last words were "Wo ist mein Geld?" She had been a

---

* *Fiume*: Italian for the city of Rijeka. *Abbazia*: Italian for the town of Opatija.(Editors)

remarkable ascendancy type and the old man had learnt much of his history from her.

When we left the castle of Trsat, the church bells were ringing. One little chapel lay just below us, but as I came towards it the bell stopped and I saw that there was no one inside; it was bare and small and cool with a delicious scent from a vase of Madonna lilies. Outside there were two men lying on the grass on their faces. I think they had been ringing the bell in this deserted chapel of the Nugents simply to reinforce the sound from the belfry in the large church in the square towards which the crowds were streaming. Trsat village still has a feudal appearance in spite of the hammer and sickle and Communist slogans stencilled on the house walls; many of the people had the look of old retainers and their cottages were lined deferentially along the road to the castle. Their gardens were full of flowers and oleanders were already blossoming in empty petrol cans on their window sills.

The church of Trsat has been for centuries the focus of pilgrimages from all over Europe, and outside the door there is a cluster of beggars and a row of booths selling candles, sacred mementoes, pictures and a small book about the Blessed Virgin of Trsat written by a former priest of the parish. The story is well known but he writes with some charm and tells many details that I have not seen elsewhere.

In 1272, as is carved on an ancient archway through which a long flight of steps descends into Sushak, the house of the Blessed Virgin at Nazareth transferred itself to Trsat; in December three years later it left again. The first to notice the strange phenomenon were some men cutting wood early one morning in March. The Adriatic below them had stormed all night but all at once it had become peaceful and still and they heard a chime of silvery bells behind them in the wood and smelt the fragrance of spring flowers. They followed the bells and came upon a small house, shaped like a tiny church, and inside it a picture of the Virgin. They went straight and told the priest, who was ill. He seemed to be expecting them for he told them he had that night had a vision in which the Blessed Virgin had appeared to him and told him what had occurred. She explained how after her death the apostles had used her house as a church, and that was the reason for its tiny belfry. The priest recovered from his sickness and there was great excitement in the village. Count Francopan quickly took charge of the matter and sent down builders to make a fence to protect the house from cows and repair the damage that had been done in its voyage. Yet lest he be thought superstitious and trivially minded he sent a priest and two skilled engineers as a deputation to the Holy Land to bring back evidence. They took with them the precise measurements of the house in Trsat and when they got to Nazareth they had no difficulty in discovering the foundations of the house of the Virgin. They compared the two measurements and finding that they completely coincided, they brought back the happy news to Count Francopan. Soon afterwards some Franciscans were put in charge of the chapel.

That was the start of the great fame and huge concourses of people that came to the village every year. However, very soon in 1295 there was a sad rebuff for Trsat; one morning it was found that the Virgin's house had flown across the Adriatic to a village near Ancona. It did not stay there long but after several further flights it finally settled at Loreto, where it has remained ever since.

The great stream of pilgrims was diverted from Trsat and even the Croats travelled across the sea to Loreto. One day Pope Clement visited Loreto and saw a group of Croat peasants, wailing with tears in their eyes, "Come back to us Holy Mother and bring your little house!" The Pope was touched and to console them he sent a famous miracle-working picture of the Virgin, painted, it is said, by St Luke himself. In a very short time this picture attracted as many pilgrims as the house itself had formerly, and Trsat recovered its celebrity and has retained it ever since.

In the early eighteenth century it was decided in Rome that the Virgin of Trsat should be crowned, and there was a three days' ceremony of incredible pomp and magnificence at which a strip of gold was fixed to the Virgin's head and the picture paraded through the streets of Sushak and Fiume. Boys dressed in white sprinkled flowers before it, trumpets blew and cymbals clashed, guns from the ships in the

harbour roared salvoes and there were fireworks and torchlight processions in which all the civic dignitaries of the state played a part.
Unfortunately, the cardinal who was to have performed the ceremony
was detained by the plague, but there was a vast number of bishops
and monks, in particular Franciscans, for it was they who had charge
of the picture.

If one were to study the story of the Virgin's house and its wanderings against a background of mediaeval history, much that is perplexing
would become significant. Trsat may well, through the Franciscans,
have been a sort of bridgehead for the Catholic advance on the Byzantine and later the Moslem world, lying as it does on the frontier of Slav
and Latin cultures. When the Franciscans of Bosnia were driven out
by the Turks, many of them found refuge in the monastery at Trsat
and later, when they returned to Bosnia, they still seem to have kept
in touch with Trsat. The part played by Franciscans in Yugoslavia in
recent years has been perplexing and anything connected with their
former crusading days cannot fail to be of interest. In Western Europe
the story of the Virgin's house is treated more or less allegorically.
Aviators are under the special patronage of the Virgin of Trsat and
Loreto. In Ireland there is a small chapel at Baldonnel Aerodrome where
she is honoured.

During the war the Franciscans of Trsat supported the Ustashe, the
pro-Nazi Croats, who, led by the regicide Pavelitch, crusaded to elim-
inate or convert to Catholicism the two and a half million Serbian
Orthodox who lived in the newly created independent state of Croatia.
The Serbian Orthodox claimed that it resulted in the greatest religious
massacre in the history of Christendom, and the account of the discovery of 289 mass graves at the Ustashe concentration camp of Jasenovac in Croatia, published in The Irish Times, 1 September 1977, seemed
to bear this out.

At Trsat the guardian, Father Igncije, and three friars received minor
decorations from Pavelitch "for their long and selfless toil on behalf of
the Croatian people, especially at the time of the return of Sushak to
her mother, Croatia, in 1943." I do not know whether they were

punished for this, but though the church has "Long live Tito" written in huge letters across it there was no evidence that there had been any interference with the worship there. When I got inside the priest with his gold cape held back on either side by two small acolytes was walking up the aisle swinging his thurible towards the large crowds on either side. The church is almost like a picture gallery, and I was sorry that I had not come at a time when I could look at it more carefully. In front of me was a column on which was suspended a glass case containing a big stone and a picture of a ship, the *Ban Mazuranich*. While sailing from Havana in 1897 the ship had sprung a leak which would have sunk it, had not the stone fallen into the hole and miraculously stayed there. The captain, Bertini, a native of Trsat, had given the stone and the picture as a thank offering to the Virgin. There are many other pictures of ships through the church, of Austro-Hungarian merchantmen which had been saved at the last moment from imminent destruction in places as far apart as the Bristol Channel and the China Seas. In the back of the church which I was not able to visit is the Virgin's picture and many magnificent trophies, a silver candlestick presented by a Croat warrior to the Virgin of Trsat, who had nerved his arm to cut off a Turk's head, and a curious ornament presented by the wife of a Serbian king.

In Fiume and Sushak, as in all the other towns of Yugoslavia, the walls are covered with stencilled slogans and in shop windows and in the halls of public buildings printed exhortations to brotherhood, voluntary labour and socialism are displayed, yet I did not, as in Russia during a similar revolutionary period, see any posters deriding the Church or its practices. An Italian in Fiume told me that he believed that the Communists would try, as the Fascists had done with success, to exploit the Churches in their interest. They would make no direct attack on the Christian mythology but would hope that by tact and perseverance it might be assimilated to their beliefs. He told how Mussolini had adapted Christian phrases, practices and festivals, so that those whose Christianity was one of ritual observance found an easy passage into his fold. The Fascists had had their "pilgrimages," their "martyrs," their "Hierarchs." He told me how the King of Italy himself had gone on a pilgrimage to Mussolini's birthplace, and that there had been a Fascist festival of "Mothers' Day" on Christmas Day, which was by slow degrees to supplant it. In the same way the Christian festival had once supplanted the birthday of the Sun, which had been celebrated by Mithraists on December the 25th.

Yugoslav Communists are often angry and insulted when accused of attacking the Church, and it is certainly possible that the more ingenious of them may be unwilling that a spiritual machinery which was of undoubted use to the Fascists and Ustashe should be sabotaged without an attempt to run it in reverse. The Communists of Yugoslavia still keep Sunday and various Saints' Days, and foster the same cult of birthplaces, processions and martyrdoms that was once fostered by Mussolini and the Francopans before them.

(1947)

Maria Pasquinelli
and the Dissolution of the Ego

The story of Maria Pasquinelli, who aspired to be an Italian Joan of Arc, needs an introduction. After the First World War Italy had counted on receiving, as a reward for entering the war on the side of the Allies, the whole Adriatic littoral of what is now Yugoslavia, from Trieste to Budva. It had once been a part of the Austro-Hungarian Empire and the British government under Asquith and Grey had promised it to her by the Treaty of London. However, at the peace conference territorial changes were based on ethnic majorities and all Italy received at Versailles was Istria at the head of the Adriatic, Zara on the Dalmatian coast, a couple of islands and – after a brief period as a free city – the great port of Trieste.

It was undeniable that the inhabitants of Dalmatia were racially Croatian, but the Italian claim was based on history. Many of the beautiful cities of Dalmatia like Split (Spalato) dated from Roman times and owed much of their architectural beauty to their long dependence on the Republic of Venice. These little towns had a measure of self-government even when Venice or Hungary or Austria was the dominant power, and though their prosperity was based on commerce they had a cultural independence and creativity that was only inferior to the city states of Italy. Latin and Slav seldom mixed, but they had lived for the most part on friendly terms with each other.

After the fall of Mussolini and Italy's defeat, she lost almost all she had gained in 1918. She retained only Trieste and lost the large hinterland of Istria and the Quarnero˙, in which the small towns and cities such as Pola were mainly Italian, whereas the surrounding country was inhabited by a Slav majority.

Mussolini, casting his eyes across the Adriatic, had coveted the whole of Dalmazia Nostra. It was first d'Annunzio, and then he, who introduced the new passionate racism – the disease of the twentieth century – to Italy. Few countries were immune from it, least of all the small states which received their freedom at Versailles. Czech despised Slovak, Croat despised Serb, Germans despised almost everybody. As for the Italians, they scorned and attempted to Italianize the Croats and Slovenes within their borders and, when the war was lost, it was infinitely bitter to be subjected to those whom they regarded as their inferiors.

Maria Pasquinelli felt it to be her duty to stand out against this iniquity, even if she stood alone. She had such a lofty and articulate sense of Italian cultural superiority to all the Slavs that her trial caused almost as much of a sensation as she had wished˙˙.

When in 1947 she assassinated General de Winton at Pola, nobody could think of her as an ordinary murderess. It might be best to accept her at her own valuation, a symbolic figure who had slain another symbolic figure, so that the attention of the world might be drawn to the sufferings of her people. She compared herself to Jael and explained to the court that she had chosen General de Winton, of whom she spoke with respect, because it had not been practical to make her demonstration against one of the Big Four. It was they who were responsible for the decision by which Istria was handed over to Yugoslavia.

Everything she said in court had plainly been much rehearsed and much brooded over, but she revealed herself as a more human, less stagey figure than could be guessed from her written declaration. In that she says:

˙ Italian for the Kvarner Bay region.
˙˙ Pasquinelli died in 2013, at the age of 100. (Editors)

> At Pola, capital of Istria, wet with the blood of the martyred Sauro, I reconfirm the indissolubility of the chain which binds the motherland to the most Italian lands of Zara, Fiume, the Venezia Giulia*, our heroic bastions against Panslavism, which threatens all Western civilization. I rise in rebellion against the Big Four. In outrage to justice, humanity and political wisdom, they decided to wrench once more from the maternal bosom these sacred lands, condemning them to the experiences of a new Danzig or, with the most cold consciousness to our people, indomitably Italian, of death, deportation, exile.

Even here the careful reader will notice the absence of some expected flourishes. She makes no references to "the deadly menace of Communism." Hers was the fastidious arrogance of a demagogue, and, in her defence, she made a careful attempt to analyze her fears and antipathies. Her distrust of the Slavs was cultural, not political, and explicitly she says that Communism, as such, did not particularly frighten her. She knew, I suppose, that the Slavs of Istria – though for twenty years they had been goaded, tortured, proscribed, persecuted by Italian Fascism – were a domestic and home-loving people who would adopt one totalitarian creed only to protect themselves from another.

Most of the English who heard Maria Pasquinelli at Pola said in a tolerant way that she was "crackers." To most Italians, except those on the Left, she was what she meant to be, the symbol of the peoples' will to resistance. Giannini, a celebrated advocate, exalted her with evident sincerity as few women have been exalted before, claiming that "nobody would deny to her a superior morality." She is certainly a remarkable figure for which it is easier to find an Irish rather than an English equivalent. In the great democracies people are usually content to learn

---

* The Julian Alps. (Editors)

by post the details of their duty to their country, and very few have the opportunity of interpreting it in the intense and dramatic way which Pasquinelli chose. Her story is strange. She was a schoolteacher but, when the Italian armies were in retreat in Africa, she joined them, dressed as a man, and when at last she was identified and forced to withdraw, she passed from one dramatic form of self-sacrifice to another. At the time of Italy's collapse, she was in Split, working herself to death as a teacher in that cultural campaign by which Dalmatia was to be made Italian. She recognized that Dalmatia is more than 90 per cent Croatian but she moved in a world of sublime thoughts and believed that in offering to the Croats the unwelcome gift of Italian culture, she was conferring upon them something infinitely precious for which one day they would be grateful. "I could understand the beliefs of the young Croat men that the land was theirs and I admired them. But I never doubted for a moment the right of Italy to that territory. Dalmatia was Italian as was Pola." Of the Slovenes of Istria she also spoke, with a devastating charity:

> The Slav people express themselves according to their possibilities. They are a young nation, which has the merits and demerits of all young peoples. They believe in their dogmas to the point of fanaticism. The power of self-criticism, which is possessed by Italians and all older peoples, is not theirs... As I lived among Slavs I must admit, apart from their infinite cruelty, they are also infinitely generous, endowed with great capacities both of goodness and perfidy.

She said she had many moving proofs of generosity from Slovenes and recalls how once, when being put in prison in Split, a Croat woman sympathized with her with "infinite sweetness."

Maria Pasquinelli was fixed in her opinion that she and her people are more richly endowed with self-criticism than the Slavs. When the prosecutor asked if she was capable of tolerating other people's ideas, the reply came, prompt and enthusiastic, "Yes, the good ideas of other people!," but clearly she did not think that Slav resistance to Italian culture was a good idea.

She saw that Dalmatia, Croat or not, must be annexed to Italy:

> Violence is a harsh necessity to which one must be subject, if required by fatherland. I thought that in opposing Slovene advance I was also favouring the religious question, but I was not able to satisfy myself on this point which concerned me deeply. I hoped that in the infinite goodness of God, the question might be left open; maybe I have loved Italy more than I have loved my soul.

When Italy capitulated the Partisans came down from the mountains and occupied Split; Maria and the other Italians took refuge first in a school, then in a church. One hundred and six Italians, including the school supervisor, were killed and buried six kilometres from the town. Witnesses testified to the courage and resourcefulness with which Maria cheered and comforted her fellow fugitives. But the Partisans only held Split for seventeen days, for the Germans arrived. A handful of Italians holding out on the Marian hill were shelled by German Stukas; the remnant passed from Yugoslav hands into the captivity of their former ally.

We get an amazing picture of the confusion in Split, where four different armies contested for its possession. The Ustashe, the Croat Quislings, had hoped that with the defeat of the Italians and the Partisans Split would be theirs. The Germans taught them quickly that they were mistaken. But Maria had an obsession, which had nothing to do with contemporary politics – she wished above all to exhume the bodies of her martyred Italian comrades "who had written a last page in the tragic history of Italians in Dalmatia." First of all she appealed to the Ustashe commander, but he refused to dig more than the first trench where six slaughtered Ustashe were buried. Maria then appealed to the German commander, who allowed her to use the Sanitary Corps in which the Italian prisoners had been enrolled. The Italians had been buried eight kilometres from the town, for the thin Dalmatian soil only accommodates itself in places to mass burials. They marched there with spades and dug till their task was completed and they were faint with exhaustion. They worked with masks though the bodies had been buried for a month only. Maria identified many of the bodies and informed their relatives. Her further adventures till she arrived in Pola and slowly formed the plan for the assassination were described at length at her trial. It is easy, I think, to picture her desperation and horror when she learnt that that Italian culture, for whose extension down the Dalmatian coast she had worked so hard, was now to be withdrawn, even from the coastal towns of Istria where it had existed for over two thousand years. She recalls how in Pola the Italians wandered round the streets in consternation, crying "What are we to do? Where are we to go?," and how boatloads of many thousands sailed off from all the Istrian ports to unknown destinations. No doubt it was impossible for them to believe that the Yugoslavs would treat them any better than they themselves had been treated when Italy was dominant in the Quarnero. It was then that Maria's great gesture against the Big Four was planned and successfully accomplished.

In the Italian press its repercussions were wide enough, and Gianini as an orator surpassed himself. He quoted Montesquieu and Stendhal and Shakespeare, Rousseau and Bentham, to prove that only by such an act could a sensitive soul draw the attention of a callous, unreflecting world to so much human suffering: "In their egoism and their political compromises, the governments respond with a wall of silence and indifference to the huge human tragedy which is happening." He also quoted Sartre:

> There is something anguishing for each of us in the act of creating under compulsion an existence of which we are not any more masters and of ceasing to be ourselves and becoming people, tribe, fatherland, nation. This fragmentation and dissolution of the ego leads to anguish and explains the actions dictated by anguish.

In the court a careful and learned report by two psychologists was presented as evidence. With different emphasis it spoke, as Sartre had spoken through the mouth of Gianini, of the dissolution of the ego, but this process seemed to the psychologists in her case diseased and pathological. They discussed her endocrine imbalance and her suspicious, egotistical nature. By a crescendo of altruistic sublimations and self-projections, she had identified herself first on a personal level with her comrades, then with her province, then with her country. She was on the way to identifying herself with Western civilization. Yet the psychologists should surely have owned that these stages, except the last, which is at present only adumbrated in most minds, represent a normal, if reprehensible, course of development. It was the disaster which had befallen Istria which was abnormal. There is powerful evidence that to a vast majority of Italian nationalists, Maria is a heroine, not a pathological freak. The psychologists did not bring their argument to its proper conclusion, which would have brought all nationalism, American and British as well as Italian, into disrepute and cost them their jobs. For it follows that in the extension of our sympathies, or, as the psychologists say, the dissolution of our ego, there is a limit beyond which it is unwise to proceed. We are emotionally qualified to identify ourselves with large masses of men. Such an identification, unless it is, as with most men, perfunctory and shallow, will only lead to hopeless and futile acts of anguish. While Maria Pasquinelli remained on the level of comradeship, she was capable and kind; it was when she tried to see herself as Istria, Italy, Western Civilization, that she felt a challenge to which there was no response on the level of ordinary social intercourse. She could only make a wild gesture of despair.

On the national plane there is no clear way in which the enmity of Slav and Italian can be ended, for it has been inflamed by twenty years of Fascist oppression and a terrible Slav revenge. It is only on the plane of comradeship that reconciliation is possible. The makeshift comradeship of Communism provides a temporary appeasement. In Fiume and Trieste on May Day thousands of Italian workmen marched contentedly behind Slav banners and slogans in the Slovene and Croat tongues.

They have merged their differences certainly, but less than ever are they masters of the new existence which they have created under compulsion. Sartre would seem to suggest that men can be themselves and associate spontaneously with each other only by escaping from the wider, more abstract loyalties. Yet the comrades in the processions have accepted a loyalty more engrossing and more widely shared than those they abandoned. They are advancing amicably to a further stage in that dissolution of the ego which the psychologists deplored.

(1947, 1979)

The Russian Consul

On the night journey to Split, the other berth in my compartment was taken by a solid, youngish-looking man whom the wagon-lit attendant told me *sotto-voce* was the Russian Consul at Split. After we had shown our passports to the next official, the Russian told me that he had never met an Irishman before, though he had read about our agricultural problems in Engels. He was the first Russian I had seen after three weeks in Yugoslavia, though I had been told they would be ubiquitous, so we were both of us ready to be talkative. He discovered a catch in the window-frame which released a small table and in a remarkably short time he had it covered with bottle of wine and beer and mineral-water and two tumblers.

He disposed quickly of Engels and Ireland and then he asked: "What do they say of us in your country? Do they say we are savage illiterate mouzhiks?"

"No, not exactly that," I lied, "but they are convinced that you are trying to get control of Eastern Europe."

"They're always saying that but it's not us, it's the people in these countries themselves. In the old days democrats used to look for their models to England or America or France; nowadays Communists look to us as we are the only Communist nation. Is that not natural enough? As for the propaganda, look at this country! We have only fifteen representatives here, the British have about thirty. Look at the English reading-rooms and clubs and the British Council. Do you know in Belgrade there's a French, and an American and a Czech and a Polish and two British reading-rooms, but not a single Russian one? And look at the other towns too, Zagreb, Maribor, Dubrovnik and the rest!"

I knew he was right about Belgrade and Zagreb, but I also knew that English people would say that Russian influence travels through un-official channels and is applied through direct and sometimes violent measures. The Russians, they say, can dispense with reading rooms. But I had only started to mention this when the Consul began about American intervention in Turkey and Greece, which I had to counter with remarks about Russian penetration in Hungary. I realized we were launched on one of those barren newspaper arguments from which there is no exit but silence and ill-temper.

"You see," he said, "we have never forgotten that Churchill and the Western powers intervened against us after our Revolution in 1917; we know that they'd like to do it again now. Why should we trust them?"

I was not sure how to reply to this, because I had been in Trieste and had met many Yugoslave émigrés and their British sympathizers and I had heard the cry raised a score of times:

"England and America must fight Russia now, while she is weak; in ten years' time it will be too late."

I could only repeat to the Consul the platitude: "Because everybody knows that the next war will be the end of civilization," but I was not convinced myself. I had read its refutation in the eyes of the Triestan émigrés: "We must all die soon anyway, and if civilization dies with us our personal tragedy will be, if anything, less anguishing."

There are numbers of broken and frustrated people with no great love of life nor expectations from it, who look forward to Armageddon with an almost religious excitement. Communists, on the other hand, never developed a mystique about war as a cataclysm that purges and sanctifies and, at the worst, releases. That kind of thinking is a disease of the West. Communists only like wars which they win or profit by. It is the saving grace of materialism.

The Consul told me how much he and his family were longing to get back to Moscow. Split was nice enough – and he made a few defer-ential remarks about its antiquities – but it was not like home. His wife found Split women stand-offish and unfriendly. Though he had only been a year in Croatia, he spoke Croatian fluently, so similar is it to the Russian language. Yet he seemed to feel himself almost as much a foreigner in this country as I did. Croatia is honeycombed with ancient prejudices and idiosyncracies and a Soviet citizen, used to the size and shapelessness of Russia, soon looses patience. He finds himself constantly obliged to move circuitously around some venerable taboo.

The Consul's father had been an illiterate Moscow factory worker, and he spoke with immense pride of the campaign against "analphabetism." Soon there would be no illiterates left in the Russian army.

When I asked him about the devastated areas of the Ukraine he had the usual inhibitions. Sympathetic enquiries are always treated as attempts to spy out the nakedness of the land. He said quickly that in spite of Russia's vast sufferings she would in two years, because of her gigantic efforts, be stronger than ever before.

We spent a large part of the night talking like this, never entirely frank but always affable. The light was coming in under the blinds and the wine had been of the stimulating not the soporific kind. When I lay down in my berth, I knew I could not sleep so I tried to give some shape to the ideas left by his conversation and my experience of Russian influences in Zagreb and Belgrade.

The competition for cultural influences is one of the newest and nastiest features of international relationships and so far the Russians, preoccupied with economics, have played rather a small part in it. The Pan-Slavs were associated with reaction and the Communists have not yet abandoned their belief that genius is international. Yet there are signs in Slav countries that they might modify this creed in the interests of a reformed Panslavism. At the Zagreb fair in June, for instance, much honour was paid in the Soviet pavilion by means of busts and books, pictures and articles to the great Russian writers, even those who, like Dostoievsky, have been considered reactionaries.

Undoubtedly this Panslavism was inflamed by the German and Italian assault upon Slav culture; it might be still further stimulated by the cultural competitiveness of the Western democracies. When in the course of a friendly article in the *Manchester Guardian* on Yugoslavia Professor A.J.P. Taylor wrote quite accurately that Croatia had always had closer cultural ties with the West than with Russia, he was venomously attacked in the Moscow papers.

How can this Russian distrust be overcome? In their contacts with the West it is impossible for Russians to make those admissions of insufficiency or indebtedness which as individuals they will make so generously. I found circulating in Zagreb a well-written article on the corruption of the British press. It was only by accident that I discovered that the Russian writer had drawn most of his material without acknowledgement from a book by Wickham Stead. A comparable analysis by a Russian of the Russian papers would at present be impossible. I see only one way in which a breach might be made in the wall of Russian suspicion, and that is by demonstrating constantly that other communities can criticize themselves and flourish; also by emphasizing always the cultural inter-dependence of nations and the international character of genius. Communists in theory believe this too and opportunities for cultural collaboration in small ways might open up.

Unfortunately the Western powers in their official contacts are much concerned with prestige than with candour or real cultural reciprocity. There is a kind of self-advertisement that many British mistake for self-criticism. "We may be slow-witted," say writers like Mr Arthur Bryant, "but somehow we "muddle through" in the end, thanks to our glorious... etc," or again, "Maybe we attach too little importance to book-learning, too much to what we English call character..." Only very ingenuous foreigners mistake this for the real thing. Handed out by the British Council in liberal doses, it acts as an emetic or perhaps I should call it a virus, because it induces something akin to rabies in the sensitive foreigner who comes into contact with it.

Leaving all the prestige-business aside, an attempt should be made to show how extensive is the literature of criticism and revolt in Western countries and how closely inter-related and what deep roots Communism has in Western thought. It could be shown that Western revolutionary theory is still developing and that Communism is only one of its offshoots. In England, for example, Wells, Shaw, Russell, the Huxleys, Orwell and Koestler are the legitimate heirs of the revolutionaries.

Yet such ideas have made little headway. They were nor reflected in the collection of English books displayed by the British Council last June in Belgrade and Zagreb, nor in the small present of books given by UNO to Zagreb University. Typical of the nine or ten dozen presented, I found *The Life of Charlotte M. Yonge, The Later Life and Letters of Sir Henry Newbolt,* Vols II and VI of Ben Jonson's Plays and a mass of belles lettres by Alfred Austen, etc. The idea behind this choice was probably a kindly one. "The patient is in a nervous state; give bromides!" An alternative possibility would be that there was no idea at all.

At present there is little organized resistance to Western cultural propaganda. The British reading-rooms in Yugoslavia are always crowded, the exhibitions of British books had a huge attendance and a couple of Yugoslav ministers at the opening. A large shop in Ilica now stocks a big collection of British books, and the demand is not only for bromides. A professor of Zagreb University has just translated *The Years* by Virginia Wolfe: 5000 copies have been published and are likely to be sold. In the universities there are five or six times as many students of English as of the Russian language. All this does not suggest a severe censorship or a cultural subordination to Russia. Yet such a subordination is so constant a theme in American and English circles that it is impossible not to believe that it derives from pique that any other cultural influences besides their own should be admitted. The constant marching about of children with flags and songs is regarded as a direct import from the Soviets, but actually the embarrassed godfather of marching, singing, over-confident children was Baden-Powell. As for sport, English influence is still supreme with Futbalkup, Boksmech, Dirt-track, Fiskultur, Ping-Pong. Only the earnestness with which they are regarded comes from Russia, as does the enthusiasm for chess. (There are special chess-match excursion trains.)

I am sure that the strongest foreign cultural influence still comes directly or indirectly from Hollywood, and though an attempt has been

made to counter it with French, Russian and home-made films, it has
not been successful. A good Russian film like "Alexander Nevski" would
not even today draw as big a crowd as a million dollar American
production.

Russian example is no doubt responsible for the new State bookshops in Zagreb and Belgrade. There are a great many, and in structure
and display they are a vast improvement on what preceded them. The
books are largely political pamphlets, but there are foreign classics as
well. Dickens, of course, is the favourite English author, Upton Sinclair,
Steinbeck, etc, among Americans. Of the Russians the great writers
are all represented. A window in one shop was given entirely to
Lermontov.

The Zagreb Theatre, which is being very lavishly subsidised, is certainly not under exclusive Communist control. While I was there
Othello, as well as *A Midsummer Night's Dream*, was staged, a Molière,
an Ostrovski and two Croatian classics. In Fiume, Shaw's *Widowers'
Houses* was showing. Owing to the advent of a left-wing government,
the greatest of Yugoslav dramatists, Krleza, a revolutionary, has after
a generation of suppression come into his own. In three months his
chief play, *The Glembays*, has been staged more frequently than in the
previous two decades.

Unquestionably there will be an increase of Russian cultural influence, but it is as likely to be exercised through the Russian classics as
through their Soviet successors, and in view of the affinity of language,
and race it will be natural enough. Unless there is pressure from other
nations it will not inevitably be chauvinistic. Yugoslavia should be
regarded not as a cultural battlefield in which Russian influence must
at all costs be defeated, but as a meeting ground in which propaganda
might take a rest and friendly reciprocity begin.

After Ogulin the train passed through the Lika and I drew the blind
up cautiously to see, if I could, that savage country of massacre and
reprisal which Father Chok had described. The tiled houses were more
substantial than I had remembered but they were scattered in lonely
clusters around these forbidding mountains. Round each settlement

were maize fields and cow byres and well-tended lettuce beds. Here and there a settlement was scorched and roofless. These were the crimes of neighbours, not of enemy bombers, and that much the more horrifying.

The blind slipped from my hand with a snap and woke the Consul. We talked again till Split, where he was met by a lively and charming family. When he said goodbye the Consul added with warmth: "I do not see why two different systems cannot exist side by side in friendliness." In print this reads easy and meaningless; as he said it, it carried conviction. A sociable and inquisitive people, the Russians do not enjoy the isolation into which a conflict of principle has forced them.

(1947)

Some Encounters: Zagreb 1946

When the war was over and the Germans had withdrawn from Yugo-slavia, I went back to Zagreb and visited old friends. Among others were the Drashkovitches, Countess Manya and her brother Yuritsa. They were members of an old Croat landowning family, reduced, since the collapse of Austria-Hungary, to living quarters in an outer suburb near Mirogoj, the cemetery. I remember the tram to the cemetery had hooks on its rear end on which the bereaved could hang their wreaths.

When I got to the Drashkovitch apartment, I was sad to find only Manya. Yuritsa had died: he was always delicate and had succumbed to the inevitable deprivations of the war years. I knew they were short of sugar and as I had been keeping bees all through the war I several times sent cans of honey to him and other friends. They had all written gratefully back.

It was dark when I started back to the city centre and I found only one person waiting at the terminus. She was carrying a striped Serbian bag full of what I at first thought were flowers, but then I saw they were vegetable-marrow thinnings, tiny fruit with their flowers still on. She must have been to see a friend in the country. We could hear the screeching of the tram in the distance but it never came nearer.

I commented on this impatiently to her and very soon she found I was no Croat and broke into fluent English. "I love the English," she said, "it's almost a religion, and I went on loving them even after a Pen Club Conference I went to in Edinburgh with my husband, when we found they were just like everybody else only more fortunate. During the war it was a joy to us to hear the voices of fortunate, confident people on the wireless. I listen to them still... But look!" she suddenly interrupted herself, "I've remembered that after ten the trams finish three stops away from the terminus; we'll have to walk." So we walked.

As it was dark and I was unknown and our language not likely to be understood by passers-by, she began to explain how sad and disillusioning life had become for elderly idealists, as she described herself. "I have to keep reminding myself of all the wicked things that were done under Alexander and Stojadinovich and Pavelitch but it does not console me much. We expected nothing from them and had such great hopes from the Partisans. But everything is lies. We were given a wonderful Constitution but it's not observed." She told me things which I have often read in English papers but did not know how to interpret: how, in spite of *habeas corpus* regulations, people were arrested and detained for months without trial; how in the elections there is only one party. "If you choose to vote against it, there is a black box into which you can put your voting ball, but there is always somebody there at your heels explaining which box is which and the little ball makes a small noise as it drops."

I told her that friends of mine had assured me that whenever they had voted the room had been crowded and no single attendant could have managed to watch all those hundreds of darting hands and listen to the tiny noises.

"Most people are sure they are being watched all the same. Perhaps it is the Communists themselves who spread these rumours just to save themselves the trouble of spying. If people even think they are being spied on they are more likely to vote for the government. The worst spies though," she added, "are not the Communists, they are the ex-Ustashi. They have bad consciences for collaborating with the Germans and they hope to get back into favour by denouncing others."

"But would they be listened to?"

"It's hard to forget something you are told even if you don't believe it."

"Why," I asked, "are you not frightened of saying all this to a stranger?"

"Because I don't care what happens to me, and I think it might be a relief to those I am fond of if I am no longer here. My son is in Italy now and while I'm alive he worries what they may do to me because of him. You see, when the Ustashi came to Zagreb he joined Mihailovitch. My son Ivo never collaborated with Germans or Italians, whatever the other Chetniks (followers of the royalist, Mihailovitch) may have done, but he's best where he is... he works in a canteen for the Allied troops in Venice.

"My only other relation is my brother; he's a teacher and he's very generous to me. He gets a big ration, of course, as a Scientific Worker,* without his help I don't know how I'd manage. But I feel I'm a handicap to him because of Ivo, as well as a responsibility."

"Is your brother contented?"

"Well, he likes to appear contented and that's another reason why I'm only an embarrassment to him, because I'm one of the few people who knows he couldn't really be contented. My brother has always been good at deceiving himself. I asked him the other day why he wasn't finishing his book on Mazzini which he went on writing even under Pavelitch, and he said 'Paper rations.' But there's loads of paper, and though they say publication is free the government only gives out the rations for the books they like. They ask to see the manuscript first 'in order to estimate the quantity of paper required.' He doesn't even want to show his manuscript in case it isn't liked."

"But what could they do with him if it wasn't?"

"Well, I think he has a holy dread of the new Secretary of the school council, a young man who stalks about in front of them in high boots and lays down the law. The French master objected to being ordered about by an ignoramus in high boots and resigned, but my brother said: 'You see he fought like a lion in the Fifth Montenegrin Brigade at Nevesinje. Unquestionably he is sincere and has a gift of leadership, a

---

* This is copied from Soviet Russia, where every teacher is called 'Naoochni Rabotnik', 'Scientific Worker'. (H.B.)

revolution is going on and we need somebody outside our petty academic quarrels to get something done,' and so on and so on –"

"But aren't there always interfering fat-heads on school committees all over Europe?"

"Yes, but they're different," she said. "The French master can't get any work and is starving.

"You know, you mustn't think I'm a reactionary; when my husband and I went to the Pen Club Conference in Edinburgh ten or fifteen years ago, he went round lecturing about the way the Fascists were treating the Slovenes in Italy and he tried to get Galsworthy interested... and he fought against Fascism at home, too; he got up petitions for the release of imprisoned Communists under Alexander and Stojadinovich; he was always writing in the papers and then seeing his articles blacked out and feeling that he was under suspicion. He kept all those black strips and now they are all I have to prove what a fine revolutionary thinker he was. I burnt all the rest under Pavelitch."

"Did the Ustashi trouble you?"

"Not at first, though I think they must have been watching us in case we were in touch with my son who was with Mihailovitch and the Chetniks. But in spite of Ivo, our hearts were with the Partisans as soon as we heard reliably that some of the Chetniks had come to terms with the Italians. We started sending the Partisans bandages and blankets and iodine through the milkman's brother, and we said that we would join them ourselves if we could be of any use. We were never Communists. My husband used to say that Communism would be all right if practised by saints but that we are none of us saints. All the same, we thought that the Partisan movement was so incoherent it was necessary to accept the temporary leadership of a party with a positive policy and doctrine, and the Communists had that. So, when one day three Partisans drove up in a car and said, 'We've come to fetch you, get your things,' we were delighted. We got the three men to help us bury what we valued in the garden and we brought out the last of our stores and blankets and our wireless set and piled them in the car.

And do you know where they drove us to? The Sava Cesta prison. They were Ustashi dressed as Partisans and we had been denounced to them by a gardener we had dismissed. He had been using my carnations to make wreaths for the Ustashi and keeping the money.

"My husband and I were separated and I was put in with some Communist women. They were so sweet and good to me, as for the first three days you cannot get food from outside and you must eat prison food, which is awful, so they shared their food with me and were pleased to find an educated person with them. I was there for three months and it was not till I was let out that I learnt that my husband had died. When I got back home I found that there was a German general in my house, so I just went to the garden and found what I feared I would find, that the three men who had helped us dig in our treasures had come back immediately and taken them away. I had relations near Senj on the coast and I managed to get down to them... and I stayed there till the end of the war. It was peaceful enough and the Italians did not interfere with us. I came back to Zagreb soon after the liberation.

"I found that because a German had been living in my house the Partisans had confiscated half my furniture as German property, and allowed a Bosnian family to get into the ground floor and use what was left. The Bosnians expected me to be grateful for holding onto it and for paying a tiny rent. With difficulty I got enough of my furniture back to do up a couple of rooms but I never got compensation for what was seized.

"One of the first persons to pay a visit to the Bosnians was my gardener; he came when he thought I could not see him, but I did. Then I knew that it was he who had urged this family to take up my ground floor... I'm sure he was annoyed to see me upstairs; he wanted that for himself. He's probably thinking of some way to get me shut up again so that he can work the garden for himself for market.

"The Bosnians are no more Communist than he is; a good many of the Bosnian Ustashi came up here to Zagreb when they saw the time had come to change sides. They'd be too well known at home. The woman had no ideas in her head but lying on the sofa and eating cake and listening to the wireless. She's learnt a few catchwords by heart. She knows I'm a reactionary because I speak English and had a good education. Perhaps she knows about Ivo... She cut down the legs of my beautiful bureau so that the child would be able to do his lessons at it. They are making it very hard for me to get my garden back into order because they leave the gate open deliberately and let their chickens in. All my seeds get scratched up. When I complained she just looked at me and I thought she had not heard. It is that she is so primitive she can't think of anything nasty to say straight away. She went away and then came back and showed me a hotel label on an old suitcase of mine... a very magnificent turreted place in Stockholm where we had once stayed for a conference, and she said, 'Go back there then. We're not grand enough for you in Zagreb now.'"

"But you are not sorry that you and your husband were idealists, are you? What went wrong, do you think?"

"I'm tired of thinking but perhaps we hoped too much from our international conferences and delegations and reports. We were always having to conciliate some group so that they should not walk out. I remember how it was considered politic for us to sit quiet while an Italian woman delegate gave a talk on how slavery was being abolished in Abyssinia, because she had sensible views on something else. Conferences are always like that. When anyone was spontaneous and vehement, as H.G. Wells was at the Pen Club Conference at Dubrovnik, he was regarded as irresponsible. Our nice societies are dead now in any case, so what would it have mattered if they had smashed themselves up for the truth a few years earlier? If we had not compromised I would look back now on them with pride, not just disappointment. I don't think the opportunities we once had will ever come back. All the international societies in Yugoslavia for peace and freedom have been abolished or absorbed into official ones.

"A friend of mine argues that we are being punished now for our selfishness. We lived contentedly for so many years enjoying privileges and opportunities which others lacked. If the others are hostile and distrustful now, it's our own fault, she says. And we talked of how when a Moslem came to the Anglo-Yugoslav Club before the war, not a soul would talk to him. It was rather swanky then to be Anglophile; people felt they were being very democratic if they went to the club and read *The Illustrated London News* and they wanted to forget that some of us Croats are Moslems like the Indians.

"All the same I find the idea that we are just getting what we deserve a dangerous one, it's a typical masochistic Slav idea. Among my friends the most resigned to the disappearance of the leisured, educated classes were the lackadaisical ones who were quite satisfied to be on top before. My husband and I were never satisfied and we tried to justify our leisure by the use we made of it. I am not resigned to effacing myself now or thinking of myself as a piece of past history. When I was in prison with the Communist women and we were all on a level, they respected me and listened to me because I was better educated and had more ideas about how to make prison endurable. I could make even Communism work better than they could; I know more about it.

"Even now," she said emphatically, "I could play a part in our street committee, if I wasn't so worried by money problems and these people in my house. I know many of the people on our street committee are good and only treat the Marxist manuals as gospels because they have no ideas of their own and no experience of the interchange of ideas. I've no politics left now and no religion but I still have a few very simple notions, which these people find strange or frightening. I believe, for example, that we should be good to each other and put kind interpretations on each other's faults and failings, and not harsh ones. But these people have small vocabularies and not very flexible minds. They could not say anything like that without using Church words, and that, of course, would be out of the question."

"Why could you not say it though?" I asked.

"Because they've not even left me the privacy to think, and when one is dependent on others for charity, as I am now, it is not in very good taste to preach it. Why, I had to beg even these vegetables off someone else, in spite of my lovely garden."

She shook her basket of marrows at me mournfully and we drifted apart as we entered the well-lit street, in which the tram was moving towards us.

* * *

In Zagreb I found to my surprise that I was not shunned as a foreigner, whose company might be compromising. Many were glad to meet someone from beyond the sea, who would not be bored with the story of their extraordinary experiences and might listen to the new notions that these experiences sometimes generated. Their small world had just been turned upside-down and shaken and everything would have to be rearranged. One would have to be very cowed or stupid not to have ideas how this should be done. One would be eager to try them out on a stranger with an open mind.

I was buying some picture postcards in a bookshop, when I felt a small fat hand on my shoulder. I saw a man of about fifty, with sad eyes and an unshaven chin. "I saw you at the Marionette Show yesterday," he said, "did you like it?" "Well, I was rather far back," I said, "and..." "Well, I will explain then," he interrupted me. "There were three brothers and the youngest one was terribly stupid, but he had made great friends with a horse..." He told me the whole story of Ivanushka while I was choosing a card and then he said, "May I speak to you for ten minutes? I want your advice." "Well, I'm going to the post office," I said, "and you can come along if you like." He told me that he had had a shoe shop in Banja Luka but had run into debt, and his wife, who was a seamstress, had found the German Occupation so much on her nerves that she had become very neurotic. During the war he had though it might be a good idea to go with the Germans to work in Essen. But it hadn't been a good idea. What did I think he ought to do now. Was England or America a good place to be? But he did not wait for an answer. All this had been a way of making an opening for his ideas. They weren't very clear, but I think he wanted a broad band of neutral countries down the middle of Europe and thought we should discuss things much more. He hadn't, as I supposed, wanted to abuse the government or borrow money. We came to the post office and I shook hands with him warmly with a gentle outward pressure, but when I had got my *poste restante* letters and turned round, I found he was still beside me. He handed me a name, Stanko Peritch, and an address on a slip of paper. "This is who I am. I will write you my ideas. Give me your address please!" I don't remember how I got out of doing this but I did. He looked hurt and used to being hurt and, as he turned away, I realized he wasn't an *agent provocateur* or a government spy but what he said he was, a bankrupt shopkeeper with a neurotic wife. He was one of those people – it's not easy to detect them – who likes giving more than taking, and all he had to give was his life story.

There was still a row of shoeblacks on the pavement in Jelachich Trg but it was lunch-hour and I had to wait a bit for my turn. There was a dark-haired man without a hat with his shoe on the foot-rest. It was a good shoe and he was waving its fellow at the gaping old boots of the old man, who was bent forward doing the polishing. A woman was standing beside him and, as he talked, he swept us all three into his audience with gestures and glances. I had to ask him to start again and go slower if he expected me to catch up. "I was talking about his boots," he said. "His boots are bad, mine are good. That is wrong. We must share things. There is not enough "grouping" in Zagreb, we all act on our own. It is not fair that you should have a shabby coat like this," he tweaked at my overcoat sympathetically, "and I should have a smart one. That is wrong and we can only change it by meetings and discussions. We must do it through our 'syndikats'." He took his foot down off the stand and walked away briskly and buoyantly. Two or three of the words he used, like "*zajedno*," together, were almost wearisomely familiar, so frequently did one read them on the posters and in the speeches in the wall-gazettes, and it struck me that his altruism, though no doubt genuine, had a rather official character. "Was he

wanting you to support he Five Year Plan?" I asked the woman, "Yes,"
she said without enthusiasm. She was a sad, preoccupied person. She
told me her husband, a Serb, had been shot by the Ustashi and she had
been taken to Berlin, where she had typed in an office. She said she had
not enough to eat.

(1946)

Two Faces of Post-War Yugoslavia: Belgrade and Split

I

Belgrade

A long, glass-fronted restaurant is attached to a smart hotel in Belgrade. To enter it from the hotel you must go through the small telephone room, squeezing past half a dozen arm-chairs which stand on their heads, and a couple of hundred empty bottles. In Belgrade you can count on a traditional and copious dinner and supper, but breakfast has always been a vague and formless meal. Because of the shortage of milk and butter I decided to forget about old prejudices and improvise. I had beer and salami and a hunk of dark bread.

The hotel guests who wriggled in through the telephone room looked mostly like delegates to conferences; non-residents came through another door that lead onto the street. The two streams mingled incongruously and almost fused half-way down the room. There were lean, patriarchal peasants with big black moustaches, black sheepskin hats shaped like tea-cosies and embroidered brown felt coats. One of them at the table beside me had a basket in which something moved. He was talking to a hotel guest with a shrewd face and heavy jowls: the guest's wife, who was fat but elegant, was sorting a bunch of tea-roses. She went away for a moment and the old peasant thoughtfully picked up a rose and widened his buttonhole with a salami knife to

receive it. At four or five other tables there were other mixed groups
like this, and all over Belgrade you meet them. The patriarchs are usually perfectly at their ease and in no way abashed at the business deals,
the ladies and the tea-roses, the chromium and glass.

The impact of these curious collisions is muffled and uncertain. Is
it East meeting West, or science meeting superstition, or capitalism
meeting Communism? The names are in fact unimportant and easily
interchangeable. Town meeting country is perhaps the simplest way
of describing it. It was from the poorest and most tradition-bound parts
of Serbia and Montenegro that the principal emigration to Belgrade
came and still comes. And they influenced its politics with their inflexible loyalties. Village life had its rigid taboos and its stern punishment for their infraction. The payment of debts, the moral obligation
to your neighbours and kinsfolk ("brother" and "sister" are terms that
can be stretched to cover remote cousinship) were more binding and
sacred duties than in the West. Coming to the city, the villager had to
expand his narrow but exacting tribal code to meet the needs of a
complex, heterogeneous community. He brought with him his sense
of loyalty to persons rather than to principles and was often able to
extend this to include the whole Serbian people; more than that he
could not do. Yugoslavia remained an abstraction. His taut Serbian
patriotism was invincible in the battlefield but in the later tasks
of negotiation, compromise, co-operation, it snapped under the strain.
It was an exasperated Serb from Montenegro who shot Raditch, the
Croat leader, in the Parliament House and brought about in 1928 the
collapse of the first democratic Yugoslavia. Today, in federated Communist Yugoslavia, the Serbo-Croatian tension is relieved but other
tensions remain, and Belgrade is a city of extraordinary contrast and
incoherence.

There is less than ever left now of the old Turkish Belgrade. After
two appalling bombardments, streets and squares have vanished and
in some places you already find lawns and flowerbeds where they existed. Repairs are going on at an intense speed and much of the work
is being done by volunteer labour. In the main street some young men

and women, who looked like students, were working away with picks and shovels. Part of the King's Palace had gone and the remainder has been turned into a museum. By the time I reached the Irish friend with whom I was lunching (Betty Duncan from Dublin) the workmen were taking their mid-day rest. Some collapsed loosely into wheelbarrows, others lay face downward high up on the scaffolding. A tall old man was queuing outside a cafeteria with a big brown sheep under his arm.

Betty works in Radio Belgrade and had managed to bring up two sons, lively and strong and intelligent, through the terrible years of the Occupation. Like everybody else in Belgrade, she has suffered extraordinary things. When the Germans reached Belgrade, as a warning to the inhabitants they strung up the corpses of a dozen who resisted on lampposts in Terazia, the central square. Betty's Serbian husband Sava Popovitch said that it was their duty to go and see these corpses so that they could bear witness later to the crimes the Germans had committed. They were disappointed with themselves for feeling no particular emotion, the corpses just looked like dolls; her husband said, "There's German culture for you!" and they turned away. He moved on alone and at the same time a small woman, who had been beside them, scuttled across the street. When Betty went to join her husband it was a moment before she could see him. Then she saw him a hundred yards off. He was being marched away between the two Gestapo men to whom the little woman had borne her tale. Betty followed after him and discovered the prison to which he had been taken. Three days later Sava was let out and crawled home. He never recovered from the beating which he had been given: his kidneys had been injured and after a short time he died.

Children endure acknowledged horrors which they can describe in words quite as well as adults, and Betty's children did not seem at all warped in temperament by what they had seen. They had seen a lot. One day they were bathing in the Sava at the time when the Croats, incited by the Ustashi, were murdering the Orthodox: a wedding party came floating down the river towards them, the bride in her white dress, the bearded priest in his black robes, the bridegroom and a couple of friends. The huge bundle was corded round and skewered through with an iron prong. Another time it was a barrel of babies' heads.

In their school they were obliged to be precociously critical of their teachers, for some were more subservient to the Germans than others. I have never heard characters so patiently yet ruthlessly dissected; and it struck me that their comments on their elders were far more tolerant and imaginative than those of schoolboys usually are. They may find it hard to adapt themselves to a more normal life with its discreet taboos and veiled horrors.

I spent the afternoon in Kalemegdan, the lovely park which runs down to the confluence of the Sava and the Danube. On my way there I had to call in at the Press Bureau. As I climbed the stairs I heard shrill screams of agony approaching me. I went on rather apprehensively and round the next corner met a woman coming downstairs carrying a good-sized pig under her arm. I was not able to find out what she had been doing with it in the Press Bureau.

There is an old red-brick Turkish fort at the point of Kalemegdan and the remains of a Roman bath, for there was a Roman town here on the site of the old Celtic settlement of Singidunum. The museum beside it used to be principally devoted to trophies of the murdered King Alexander and had the atmosphere of a mortuary. There were photos and letters, favourite books and favourite thoughts, his bullet-pierced jacket and blood-stained shirt, Bibles, penwipers, trousers, swords. There was the car in which he and M. Barthou were murdered at Marseilles. I do not know if the Germans replaced them with their trophies. Now the rooms are full with mementoes of dead Partisans or National Heroes, the name by which the bravest were honoured. In addition there are excellent maps and plans explaining the development of the campaigns. There are small blurred news-sheets printed in the woods in 1942 and 1943 which have now become the great daily organs of Belgrade.

It was impossible not to admire the adept arrangement of the exhibition, but I could not see the emergence of new ideas or any reflection of the intellectual ferment in which the revolution had its rise. It seemed to be merely a skilful transference of sentiment and mythology from one kind of hero to the other. It was like any other national war museum and there was no trace in it of the Communist belief that all men, even Italians and Germans, are brothers divided only by ignorance, exploitation and mistrust. Nor was there an attempt to suggest the complex character of the struggle and the economic and military assistance of Britain and America. Such an enterprise would not have been possible in so small a space, but even a modest gesture in the direction of international thinking would have been encouraging. War is evidently not a good introduction to social revolution. Ideals that were vigorous and soaring begin to droop over the graves of dead heroes and too much attention is paid to the reflections of the physically brave.

The Americans have a display room in Prince Michael Street. The idea is to make it a window on the Western world for Yugoslavs with claustrophobia. Clearly they find some difficulty in knowing what to put in it that is both edifying and advantageous to themselves. It was closed when I passed, but I could see the windows. One was full of pictures of spring fashions from New York dressmakers, and in another was a big hand putting a vote into a ballot-box very secretively. The meaning of both these is clear but I was not sure of the intention of a large display and description of the Cathedral of Science (which is, I think, at Pittsburgh) in the third window. This building has a nave and transepts and a soaring Gothic spire, with many floors each devoted to a different science. Thus you could do mineralogy, say, in the belfry, gynaecology in the Chapter House. I think the idea behind the cathedral and its reproduction in Belgrade is that science is the religion of the modern world and can with a little ingenuity be fitted reverently into the framework of the old religions. A gentle reproach is conveyed at the crude iconoclasm of the Communists. The Americans do not realize that the Yugoslavs are a deeply serious people.

II

Split

If one were to make a study of Yugoslav problems, Split would be a pleasant and propitious place to choose as a headquarters. It is an ancient town proud of its tradition but not, like Dubrovnik, withdrawn self-consciously from the confusion of the present. ("We were a republic for centuries," say the citizens of Dubrovnik. "There is nothing now to get so excited about.") Ideas, influences, enthusiasms new and old, foreign and native, percolate freely at Split; fresh syntheses seem possible and daring experiments are made that do not usually lead to bloodshed.

Diocletian's Palace, into whose walls much of the modern town of Split has been skilfully fitted, is a good symbol of this adaptability. In the centre of the palace is the Roman peristyle round some of whose fluted columns a church was built by the Venetians. In front of the church used to stand Mestrovitch's huge bronze statue of Bishop Gregory of Nin, who preached there in the tenth century. He is a symbolic figure. It was Bishop Gregory who stood up for the rights of Croatian against Latin culture and won from the Pope the privilege for all Croats from the coast inwards to read the Mass in Slavonic rather than Latin. For a long time, by concessions such as these, a tolerable cultural relationship was established between the Croat and Latin peoples and it was possible for a Croat, without disloyalty to his race, to admit the great part that Rome and Venice had played in building up the cultural communities of the Dalmatian coast.

All this changed when the Fascists came to power. In 1919 d'Annunzio seized with his Arditi the Croatian island of Krk, which had been awarded by the Treaty of Rapallo to Yugoslavia. On Christmas Day 1920 a group of them stormed the church where Father Bonefachitch, now Bishop of Split, was preaching and commanded that henceforth Latin must be substituted for the Slavonic tongue. The man who attacked Father Bonefachitch was battered to death by the congregation and in the reprisals several people were killed, but Slavonic was never abandoned. The same campaign was carried through with greater success in Istria, which fell to the Italians. It had disastrous results all through the Dalmatian coast. Incensed by Mussolini's parrot cry "Dalmazia Nostra," Croat hooligans started to smash whatever reminded them of Venice. In the lovely little town of Trogir, for example, the Venetian lions that surmount the archways had their heads hammered off. Then the Fascists tried to win the sympathies of the Croat opposition to Belgrade by maintaining Pavelitch, the future Quisling of Croatia, in Italy and supporting him financially. But the art of Mestrovitch is the best reply that Yugoslavia ever offered to Italian bragging, for his genius proved that Croats could renew the sculptural beauties of the Dalmatian towns. When the Italians came to Split the statue of Gregory of Nin, the symbol of the successful struggle of the Slavs for cultural freedom, was removed from the peristlye. It was feared that it would be broken up for war material, but the Italian commander was not as barbarian as that; it was taken and stored in the basement of Mestrovitch's house outside Split.

Mestrovitch was at that time in America but his house was being looked after by an old friend of mine from Zagreb, Dr Milan Curcin; he was the editor of *Nova Evropa*, the best of the Central European journals. With the problems of Serbia and Croatia in mind, he had visited Ulster.

Mestrovitch's house lies on the northernmost side of the harbour. To reach it you must walk down the whole sea front with its venerable row of palm trees, and out for about a mile along a road lined with dusty ilex and poplars. The house stands high above the sea, approached by a long flight of steps that climb up three terraces to a long portico with eight Ionic columns. In front of the steps is a bronze woman playing a guitar in a big open space (where there were to have been lawns and flower-beds). She gazes out at the masts of a small fishing-vessel which was bombed close to the shore in the early days of the invasion. (Beside her are some huge wooden packing-cases containing sculpture which Mestrovitch has requested for exhibition in America.) Inside, the house suggests a sculpture gallery rather than the country villa for which Mestrovitch intended it. Maybe it is true that he intends to bequeath it to the town of Split. Three or four large rooms are filled with huge pieces of sculpture, many of them familiar from exhibition or repro-duction. Mestrovitch was working on two colossal wooden statues of Adam and Eve when the war broke out, and they soar in their unfin-ished state in the studio. The dining-room has a sort of recess at the end whose roof is supported by caryatids dressed in the costume of Mestrovitch's native village. Similar caryatids are on the War Memorial which he built at Avala near Belgrade. An outside studio is still being used by a pupil of Mestrovitch and in it I saw some recent sculpture of remarkable promise; a tombstone for a young man killed by Italian soldiers, a Roman wolf tearing at his breast; a wounded Partisan being carried away by the women of his village.

When the war broke out Mestrovitch returned to Zagreb to look after some work he had left there. Pavelitch tried to gain his support but failed and the sculptor was imprisoned for several weeks. Soon after that he escaped on the plea of a visit to the Biennial Exhibition at Venice, where Croatian work was to be exhibited under Italian aus-pices. He obtained through the Vatican a visa to Switzerland and never returned.

At the other end of the town lies the museum. It is one of the most charming I know. A great number of the Greek, Roman, Croatian and Venetian exhibits are displayed in a long cloister which extends round a garden full of mimosas and oleanders. Earliest are the graceful Greek tombstones from the islands, later the large and numerous urns and sarcophagi from Salona, a very large and prosperous Roman provincial town just north of Split which was destroyed by the Avars 1300 years ago. The pompous busts of the dignitaries of Salona and their wives and children, the elaborate scenes from Greek and Roman mythology and legend which are deeply carved on their tombs, recall the secure and self-satisfied life that must once have been lived on this barren shore. Their only enemies had been the Liburni and Illyrians. There is a fragment of a huge triumphal arch which celebrated the victory over these tribes, and their weapons are carved on it. There is the tomb of a Roman legionary and a door closed by massive handles to show that "He is gone" and above it the tokens of a soldier, medals and military badges, straps and ornaments. Later on come doves and lambs and other ambiguous symbols carved on the sarcophagi, which hinted to the initiate that the dead man was a Christian. Diocletian, the great persecutor of the Church, became a near neighbour, and there were many martyrs. It was not till the last days of Salona that the cross and specifically Christian symbols were openly displayed. All the sarcophagi have huge holes in their sides where they were plundered by the Avars at the fall of Salona. After the Avars came the Croats, and of the Croatian work before the arrival of the Venetians there are some elegant examples in altar-rails and arches; they are simple and graceful with interwoven tracery, not unlike Celtic work but without naturalistic or animal ornament. Finally comes the Venetian sculpture, rather brutal and grotesque.

The Yugoslav government has already done much for archaeology. A row of houses that masked the western wall and entrance to Diocletian's Palace has been pulled down and a large ethnographical museum is to be built at Split, similar to the magnificent museums at Zagreb and Belgrade. The new museum is going to be used for educational purposes; the study of their country and its past is to be included in the curriculum of schoolchildren. A memorandum on the new museum suggests that it will be used to illustrate the diverse currents of race and culture which have contributed to form the Dalmatian communities. There is evidence in the Yugoslav museums of great skill in the use of maps, diagrams, models, photographs; Russian influence will, perhaps, be strong but Russian museums are passing through that early crude phase when every exhibit must have a Marxist explanation, and if the new museum at Split develops on the generous lines indicated, it should do much to bring order and sanity into the cultural and emotional tangle of Dalmatia.

Yet one thing made me fear that the curators of the museum might have much silly chauvinism to fight. Outside the Belvedere Hotel I

found that the large eighteenth-century fountain had disappeared and
was nothing but a pile of rubble from which stone fragments of dragons'
jaws, snakes' heads and human limbs protruded. Enquiring, I was told
that it was ugly and had been built by Italians. Yet it was not as ugly as
much else that had been allowed to survive, and it was old enough to
illustrate the history of Split as well as any museum. I learnt that before
it had finally disappeared it had constantly been masked with planks
for processions and demonstrations, so that slowly the public had been
indoctrinated with the idea that it was an eyesore, unnecessary, an
obstacle to the march of progress. The same thing has been happening
to the statue of Ban Jelacic in the central square of Zagreb, who, with
his horse, disappears from time to time under more and more comprehensive extinguishers. Yet Jelacic was a great and patriotic Croat
nobleman who did much to revive the independent spirit of his countrymen, and scored a resounding triumph against the Hungarian oppressors. It is true he was betrayed by the Habsburgs whom he served,
but he is a splendid symbol of the Croatian will to resistance. By removing him the authorities will show that they are more frightened
of history than the Hungarians, who allowed him to stay there; and
that like small-minded Philistines they do not like or trust any greatness of character or intellect that has not been produced in their own
workshops.

A museum is a good index of the cultural problems of a country and
the chances for their solution. The tragedy of Fiume is illustrated poignantly in its museum. It is "closed for repairs" but a knock at the door
brings out a baffled, exasperated scholar with a three days' beard. All
around him in dumps on the floor lies the wreckage of history, once
thought glorious, now dishonourable. What is to be done with all these
photographs, busts, pictures, manuscripts, Austrian, Hungarian, Italian? In the lumber-room there are the double-headed Austrian eagles
taken from the town buildings, cameos of archduchesses, medals and
illuminated addresses and all the paraphernalia of the Habsburgs, covered in cobwebs. Sometimes, as in Torre Civica, the Italians sawed one
of the heads off a carved eagle and made him a lopsided Italian fowl,

but mostly they sent them here. Now a huge white marble bust of Victor Emmanuel has joined them. "The provinces of Italy to their newly recovered little sister Fiume and the Quarenero" is the inscription. There are multitudes of pictures and photographs of d'Annunzio with his sallow hairless face and jaunty green hat. Only the pictures of the Hungarian governors of Fiume have been left on the walls, both by the Italians and the Yugoslavs, whiskered self-confident noblemen covered with medals. What are the Yugoslavs to do? Only in country crafts were they permitted by their overlords to create anything worthy of a place in a museum.

I anticipate that the small nations of Europe will take a lead in the creation of folk-museums. In this the Yugoslavs are like ourselves in Ireland and have to look back for a purely native inspiration to distant periods of history and prehistory before their ancestors were enslaved: the modern Yugoslav, like the modern Irishman, must, now that he is free, acknowledge the rich cultural deposit left by the invader. Only by such generosity of spirit can the long years of human tragedy and loss be made good in the future.

(1948)

In Europe's Debatable Lands

1. Yugo-Slavia

The relations between Yugo-Slavia and her neighbours change rapidly. Looking over some notes of a visit I paid three months ago with a delegation, with which I was unofficially associated, from the National Peace Council under the leadership of Lord Boyd-Orr, I find that this particular mission, although it did what was required of it, has not much present relevance.

It is only our incidental experiences that still have interest. We were invited in order to testify to the falsity of the Cominform allegations, for it had been said in their press and on the wireless that Yugo-Slavia was making warlike preparations against her neighbours and had handed over bases to Britain and USA.

We were not, I suppose, expected to make any impression on the Cominform Press. It was thought we might do so on the domestic Communist in Britain, who felt that Yugo-Slavia was being used as a bridgehead for an Anglo-American assault on the Soviets. Whether we changed this view at all I don't know, but even if we had had no military experts with us, the facts were self-evident. We studied the allegations closely, and went to all the reputed British or American bases, except one, the island of Vis. We planned our own routes and timetables. We visited the Albanian, Bulgarian, Rumanian and Hungarian frontiers, the aerodrome of Nish, the Belgrade to Zagreb highway, the Kossovo Polje and the island of Korcula.

The assurances we received from the heads of the Orthodox, the Roman Catholic and the Moslem communities, as well as from Mr Moshe Pijade and many Yugo-Slav officials, convinced us of Yugo-Slavia's desire for peace. But more convincing still were our encounters with the ordinary people in the streets and cafés of provincial towns. We wandered where we liked, and those of us who could not speak Serbo-Croatian usually found some other common tongue. We met no one believing in preventative war, or any war.

Peasant Gaiety

When we got within fifteen miles of the border, a Yugo-Slav officer accompanied us, so that we should not be treated as spies, but nobody interfered with us. We spent several hours, for example, in Dmitro-vgrad˙ on the Bulgarian frontier. (Dimitrov has been made by the Bulgarians a posthumous hero of the Cominform so it is exasperating to them that the anti-Cominform Yugo-Slavs dissent from this view of him, and still think it an honour for this little border town to bear his name.)

In a café there we found some refugees from Bulgaria. One, who called himself "a stomatologist," had jumped off a boat in the Danube and swum ashore. Like many others he had secured a job in the town. It was a feast day of the Blessed Virgin, but the dancing, which usually took place in front of the now locked church, had been transferred to the market square. From a balcony overlooking it in the new Dom Kultura, a sort of civil center, we looked down on a mass of shifting colours as the country people, mostly Bulgarians, in their gorgeous clothes whirled round in the kolo, the national dance.

The town has a population of only 2,500 but the hall in the *dom* had

---

˙The district around Dmitrovgrad and Pirot, now in Eastern Serbia and not far from the Bulgarian capital, had been a continuous source of tension between Bulgaria and first Serbia, then Yugoslavia, since the Serbo-Bulgarian War in 1885. (Editors)

room for fully a quarter of them. There is a library there, largely Bulgarian and not oppressively "tendentious," and several recreation rooms. The rather anaemic murals of idealized peasants and the effective frieze of country scenes, moulded in cement, were the work of a couple of local artists.

These frontier journeys took us through the regions where racial minorities exist. Today Bulgarians, Albanians, Macedonians, and the others have what they never had before, encouragement to publish in their own languages and cultivate their own traditions, as far as these can be fitted into the rigid Marxist framework. I saw a number of their literary quarterlies, in which the extremes of internationalism and parochialism meet and try to mingle. The experiment, a not unusual one in many western countries, can seldom have been tried in such difficult circumstances.

Frontier Delilahs

But we had to do our duty by the Cominform charges. The Orient Express passes through. Dimitrovgrad is on the way to Sofia and Istanbul, so the frontier post outside the town has some importance. Two soldiers came out to meet us from a customs shed of white-washed mud, on which an old dog sat upon some firewood. One of the soldiers was the hero of a recent frontier episode, which he recited with much pride. He had been, according to the practice of the railway, in the habit of travelling with the express across the frontier to the next station in Bulgaria, Dragoman, and back again to Dimitrovgrad. It was a reciprocal arrangement. But after the Cominform resolution the Bulgarian officials on the train had started to bully him, taunting him with Yugo-Slav treachery*. Once they had pushed him off the train.

Another time they had said: "Curse your Serbian mother" (a terrible oath it would appear) and flung his red star away. There must have been

---

* The context here is the Tito-Stalin split of 1948. (Editors)

a Bulgarian soldier traveling on the express too, but it was not until after that it occurred to me to wonder how he fared when the train crossed into Yugo-Slav territory, so this delicate issue was never raised. Now neither Bulgarian nor Yugo-Slav soldiers pass the frontier with the express.

There were stories of aimless but provocative shootings across the border and of Russian officers clearly seen mixing with the Bulgarians. So too at the other frontiers. At the Rumanian frontier post, near Bela Crkva, below the Carpathians, an officer produced from the guard room a large log book, in which every "incident" since the "Resolution" was carefully dated and recorded. The most startling of these had happened three weeks before. A party of schoolchildren on an outing had been paddling in the boundary river and had unwittingly crossed into Rumania. They had been arrested and no word had yet been heard of them. Further back in the log book the officer blushingly drew our attention to another entry. The Rumanians had one day, by means of female fascinators, tried to entice the Yugo-Slavs on the opposite bank to neglect their duties. In vain.

Stalin Eclipsed

What is the significance of this continuous series of incidents, each one of which might be inflated into an act justifying war? Are they really inspired from a higher quarter, as the Yugo-Slavs appear to think? I do not believe it. Closed frontiers are a source of provocation in themselves. The guards have infinite leisure on their hands to imagine they are being insulted and to think of ingenious retaliations. The uniformed peasants, whom they see moving about on the opposite bank, are probably of the same stock as themselves, but they become mysterious and sinister through being unapproachable. Their gestures, their shouts, their laughter are all put down conscientiously in the logbook. It is not necessary for the Russians to manufacture hatred and suspicion. They grow of their own accord.

Some of us expected to find that the rupture with the Cominform would have led to a retreat from Marxism, but there was no sign of this. On the contrary, Marx and Lenin have grown in stature as Stalin has shrunk. Similarly, after the Reformation the authority of the Bible grew as the authority of the Pope dwindled. When we suggested to Mr. Moshe Pijade, one of the great figures of the Government, that the sacred books of Marx and Engels had lost some of their significance he drubbed us severely.

Yet, in practice, there are signs of a much greater freedom and flexibility. The professor in Marx has become more important than the prophet, and professors can be criticised.

After the supreme blasphemy of rejecting Stalin had been committed, "theological" Communism, as the Yugo-Slavs call it, has been severely shaken. In two directions the effects are apparent; there is a drive towards decentralisation. Belgrade has taken over all the prestige of Moscow, but has shared it out with Skopje, Zagreb, Cetinje, and the other republican capitals. Stalin has shrunk but Tito has not, I think, appreciably swollen. In civic buildings, where portraits of the two once hung side by side, Stalin has been replaced by unglamorous figures, provincial secretaries and presidents. There are far fewer slogans, banners, processions, neon-lit exhortations. There is more criticism and reflection. The breach with the Cominform has had another notable effect. The difficulties of meeting and talking with foreigners are now slight. It is possible for a citizen to invite them freely to his home and to chat with them in the street or in hotels. Unless there is some special reason for constraint, it does not exist.

Hunger, Pride

Some people saw a happy augury for the future in the Yugo-Slav hostility to their neighbours. We did not all feel this. The kind of peace that is based on an equilibrium between several sharp antagonisms is never reliable. Yugo-Slavia's alienation from Russia might bring her into the Western camp, but such an alignment would be based on strategy, not on sympathy. It would be precarious and unreal.

The Yugo-Slavs are, on the whole, proud of their desperate isolation. The world, they say, is divided into East, West and Yugo-Slavia. The longer they can keep their independence uncompromised the better it will be for everyone. At the worst they can now offer a forum where capitalist and Communist can meet without constraint or hostile intentions.

There is now one thing that obsesses their minds, far more than the fear of war. They are desperately hungry and dread a famine. Not for political reasons, but for Christian reasons everything possible should be done to bring them relief.

2. Dubrovnik and Cavtat

I went to Dubrovnik in a captured German aircraft, on whose dark walls some Canadian soldiers had scribbled their names and addresses. I had bought a large map so as to trace our passage over the mountains of Bosnia and Herzegovina, but I found that it was only by kneeling on the floor, with my elbows on the seat, that I could catch an occasional glimpse of a mountain.

The aeroplane pitched and rolled. The small windows were mostly of opaque glass and only one or two had clear centers. When I gave it up in despair a soldier promptly picked up the map and started a lively description of his experiences in the Partisan war. The passengers all left their seats and crouched round him, peering though the portholes for the landmarks he described. We swirled over the peninsula of Pelleshatz. I thought I caught a glimpse of the Mestrovic Mausoleum on the promontory of Cavtat, and then the aircraft came down in a field 18 miles north of Dubrovnik.

It is the only flat space on that rocky coast, and a poor aerodrome at that, a swampy piece of land without concrete runways. It did not need an expert to see that neither Yugo-Slavs nor Americans were converting it for military purposes. A cottage on the highway above served as an air terminus. It was draped with a big banner, on which was written "Long Live the Ninth Chess Olympiad of Dubrovnik."

Peasant Grace

A group of people crouched over the papers reading the latest chess result, for chess is to the Slav what dog-racing is to the Dubliner. I soon learned that Yugo-Slavia was leading over the other sixteen competitors. As we were talking a girl, in the dark Dalmatian costume, wearing a large straw hat on one side, came gracefully down the hillside, leading a mule whose two panniers were full of purple grapes. She passed by gravely smiling, like a figure on a frieze, while we offered to buy some of her grapes. "No, they're for the chess players" she said, and all our pleading was in vain. The bus arrived, and as we sped along the lovely road the driver, in reply to a questions of mine about the Olympiad, replied: "Oh, no, the Russians didn't turn up. They only come when they're sure of winning."

I do not think that even the Cominform had declared that Dubrovnik was an American base but we were encouraged to go there, not only because it is the port for Korcula, but so that we should see how peacefully and happily the Yugo-Slavs were entertaining themselves. In addition to the chess there was a literary congress, with delegates from many countries. The Dubrovnik Festival was also in progress, with musical entertainments every night and plays by Ragusan authors of the fifteenth and sixteenth centuries. (The old name for Dubrovnik was Ragusa). There were several exhibitions, historical and marine. For a small seaside town, this does not seem bad.

Madame Comrade

I searched the 200 pages of the beautiful Festival Book to discover any reference to Marshal Tito or Communism. There was none. Nor did I see in the streets the red stars, slogans and banners which usually decorate a Communist festival. Dubrovnik is the most conservative and urbane district of Yugo-Slavia. Its citizens naturally shun what is crude, and their Communism is polished and polite. I was told that it was a long time before they could accustom themselves to saying "Comrade." They said "Mr. Comrade" and "Madame Comrade."

Although Dubrovnik was occupied by the Italians it was never, like the north Dalmatian coast, annexed to Italy. It belonged to Pavelitch's Croatia, but Pavelitch was never seen there. So the Italians did not, as in Split, make efforts to Italianise the place. (Actually there were only about ten Italian residents.) All that they did was to remove the Mestrovic stone carving of King Peter of Yugo-Slavia from the town walls and in other ways destroy traces of the old Serb and Yugo-Slav kingdoms.

The Italian garrison adapted themselves quickly to the pleasant life of the town. They did not bully, and as they were short of wine they sold their revolvers and equipment. After the fall of Mussolini they were replaced by Germans, and everything changed. I do not believe there is any spot in the world where nature and art combine in such loveliness as at Dubrovnik. The old city, inside the town walls, is undamaged – the Rector's Palace, the Mint, the churches, monasteries and old town houses are treated with reverence. Dubrovnik is being preserved as a museum of Dalmatian history.

It is too early to expect complete objectivity, for the Croatian contribution is over-emphasized while the influence of Venice is insufficiently stressed. But this is an inevitable reaction from the exaggerated claims of Italy. Scarcely 1% of the population was Italian before the war, but in the University of Padua, I once saw a students' hall decorated with frescoes of half a dozen Dalmatian towns, represented as outposts of Italy. Mussolini was constantly declaiming about "Dalmazia nostra," and every time he declaimed some Croat patriots would destroy an emblem of Venetian rule in some Dalmatian town.

Great European

The Lion of St. Mark over a town gate would lose a head or a tail, or an Italian fountain would be mutilated. That was before the war. Now there is no more declamation or destruction, but a certain evasiveness is still evident in the potted history of the guide books.

The town itself is the cool grey colour of the Dalmatian rocks, but outside the ramparts there seem to be more flowers than stones. Cascades of purple bougainvillea cover the walls and every kind of exotic shrub flourishes in the gardens. The caper plant, already shedding its long pale flowers, grows from crevices in the walls. There are pale blue plumbagos, giant heaths, lemon-coloured daturas.

The naval yacht, which was to take us to Korcula, was delayed so we spent the afternoon on a visit to Cavtat. Mestrovic's Mausoleum was built in memory of our members of the Racic family, wealthy and cultured ship owners, who died of influenza in 1918, and the monument is considered one of Mestrovic's masterpieces. The sculptor is still in America to which he escaped from Pavelitch's Croatia; his house at Split, which he built for the display of his sculptures, is empty. Another large collection of his works preserved by an old friend at Zagreb awaits his return. He is eagerly expected in his native land, and I believe there is a chance that he will return before long.

Few artists have ever exercised so great an influence on their country as Mestrovic. He was a Croat, an ardent Yugo-Slav, and a great European. He and his friends believed that the whole of humanity is one spiritual family, but he was no shallow internationalist. He wrote: "I knew that it was my duty to do whatever I could to sow a few seeds on the wasted soil of my own country." That is the way people thought in the new countries of Europe after the First World War.

On the way to the Mausoleum we were hailed by a purposeful old woman with a large key. She insisted on showing us over the private gallery of the 19th century painter, Vukotitch, a revered native of Cavtat. Some Yugo-Slavs who came with us stood entranced in front

of the glossy academy portraits, identifying the son who went to the
Argentine and Mrs. De Bont's brother, and so on. Eventually the high
priestess of the shrine became bored with their enthusiasm and we
escaped. This corner of Dalmatia has its own small local gods who dwarf
the stature of the national heroes. Neither King Alexander nor Pavelitch
was ever regarded with favour here, and it is going to take Tito all his
time to make an impression.

Fragrant Land

When we got back to Dubrovnik three naval officers were waiting for
us, drinking wine on the terrace under the olive trees. The journey to
Korcula takes six hours, but although it was nearly 10 p.m. we decided
to start at once and sleep on board the naval yacht. The vessel was built
for comfort rather than combat, and we guessed that its builders must
have had in mind some Austrian archduke, who would hover importantly on the fringes of battle. There were four berths, and the rest of
the party reposed in the chairs and settees in the saloon.

We were comfortable enough on board, but at early dawn I went on
deck to watch the grey coast Korcula. We went the whole length of the
island, and as we came closer I caught the unmistakable fragrance of
Dalmatia. It is a smell of myrtle and juniper and rosemary, and all the
evergreen shrubs which grow on thin rocky soil. It seems to be sealed
into their hard dry leaves and does not vary with the season.

Now and again we passed a small sea port of high grey houses with
tiles of mottled umber. The windows in the lower storey are always
small, for they keep their stores and wine there in cool dark rooms.
Above, the large windows of the bedrooms have green wooden shutters. We went so close to the coast that we could see the early risers
looking after their vines. At times, the coastal islands are so bare that
it is hard to see what reward there can be for building that network of
small stone walls to protect a few tufts of grass in a waste of grey rock.

When at last we landed at Vela Luka, the town was already fully
awake. Some of us did the routine job of visiting the Harbour Master

and seeing his records of the incoming vessels and their cargo. As usual, we found him perplexed, but polite. An odd Italian trading boat had come, but when we enquired about Americans he simply laughed.

Quick Wits

We were followed by an interested crowd, chiefly of young people. Why is there such a disproportionate number of the young in Yugo-Slav towns? Perhaps it is because the war destroyed so many of their elders. I have seen as high a figure given as 3,000,000 dead out of a population of 16,000,000[*].

The children and young people of Korcula are mostly fair-haired, unlike the Serbs, with fine features and quick wits. They are well dressed and if we had not known it from other sources, it would have been hard to guess that they were under-nourished. I escaped from the crowd down a side street and saw an old man leaning against a leather shop. "Have you ever seen any Americans on the island?" I asked him after a chat. "Yes, a bunch of them," he replied promptly. "When was this?" "They are here now!" he said conspiratorially and beckoned me to follow him.

We went up one of the narrow staircase streets with which the island is honeycombed. At the top the old man drew me behind the shelter of a Venetian fountain. From the terrace we looked down over the sunlit quay and saw John Lawrence and a couple of our party talking to some fishermen. "There" hissed my guide triumphantly. Pointing to the group, he said proudly, like a naturalist who has added a rare butterfly to his collection, "Americans."

---

[*] To date, the most reliable estimate of total Yugoslavs killed during the Second World War is approximately one million (separate studies by Bogoljub Kočovic and Vladimir Žerjavić). (Editors)

3. On Korcula

When we got a chance we visited the schools wherever we went. We did this partly from curiosity (we had a British Professor of Education with us), but partly because a school is an admirable centre of gossip. There are children there from all surrounding districts. If an American had been seen in this village or that, some child would be ready to chatter about him, for Yugo-Slav children are seldom tongue-tied.

The class at Vela Luka on Korcula was no exception. We broke in without shame, totally disorganizing the lesson, which a plump, pleasant young woman was conducting. John Lawrence stood by her desk and told the children why we had come. "So have you seen any Americans?" he ended. "No" they cried all together, but as this answer seemed so bleak the livelier ones tried to embroider it. "Yes, yes" one small boy waved his hand furiously. "I've seen Americans." "Oh have you? Where? Tell us." "In Africa."

It appeared that during the war he had been moved to the Yugo-Slav camp on the Suez Canal. Then another boy, with a black eye waved his arm too. "Yes, yes, I've seen Americans." "Oh where?" "On the films." He was the school jester and there was a roar of laughter at this. One of his school mates explained that he had got his black eye because he had visited an American film called "Gentleman Jim" and had started to behave like one of its heroes. We seemed to be following this particular film round Yugo-Slavia, in Montenegro, Macedonia and in Croatia. "Dzentleman Dzim" was on all the hoardings, corrupting the young Marxists with his flagrantly bourgeois ethic.

War Paradox

Korcula had a fairly peaceful history during the war. It became a refuge for the Jews, who had fled from the Nazi persecutions in Zagreb, and the Italians, who were in command there, had treated them with relative kindness. The Italians hoped to annex the greater part of the Dalmatian coast. Because of this, their relations with the Croats, who formed 98% of its population and yet were supposed to be allies of the Axis Powers, were often uneasy. Although Pavelitch, the "Leader" of Croatia, had offered the throne of Croatia to the Italian Duke of Aosta and agreed to cede to Italy much of the Croatian coast, most of the Croats were furiously resentful. The result of this was that the Italians frequently favoured the Serbs, who were their enemies, against their allies, the Croats. When the Croatian Ustashe (the followers of Pavelitch) had started on the extermination of the Serbian Orthodox in Croatia and Bosnia, the Italians had sometimes intervened on the side of the Serbs. This throws some light on the complicated story of Mihailovitch*, whose commander on the Dalmatian coast was given a state funeral by the Italians, his avowed enemies.

There were small regional wars going on, in which, as in whist drives, the partners were changed. It was warm and lovely when we sailed back from Vela Luka to the town of Korcula, the capital. The dolphins played around the boat, and once a flying fish landed among the deck chairs. There was a staff officer on board, whose job it seemed to be to watch in some obscure way over the crew. He was dignified, and one of us tried to thaw him out with jokes through the interpreter. "You're the spy, I suppose?" was the first well-meant joke, but it didn't translate at all well. In frigid tones, the officers replied that "he only served his country and did his duty, as any British sailor would." There was a click of heels and he vanished, with the interpreter after him interpreting madly. That was not the last British joke that misfired. They went on being made with wonderful perseverance.

Departed Glory

Korcula is one of those enchanting medieval cities in miniature, whose survival is hard to understand. A period of great prosperity must have been followed abruptly by centuries of stagnation. Just enough energy

---

* See note on Mihailović on page 125. (Editors)

remained to keep the noble palaces, archways and churches from crumbling away, but nobody had replaced anything or destroyed what was useless. Near the Cathedral there was a huge pile of recent rubble, in which the heads and legs of Venetian lions could be distinguished. But the inhabitants were not responsible for this vandalism. It was the result of two British bombs.

The future of these beautiful islands is not rosy. Their prosperity coincided with the prosperity of Venice, when each island was a stepping stone on the southward and eastward path of a great maritime power, a store-house or port of call, which gave access to the interior. But apart from such a little fishing and some special crops such as the rosemary of Hvar and the pyrethrum (for flea-powder) of Mljet, they have few means of subsistence. There is no water in Korcula, and it has to be stored in tanks or brought from the mainland in barrels. There is a large hotel being built outside the town and, perhaps, it is as holiday resorts that Korcula and the other islands will survive.

As we walked back to the boat we met, facing the sea, a large white wall, on which successive occupants of Korcula had stencilled their slogans. There was a scar on the plaster, where a blunt human head, that must have been Mussolini's had peeled away. Under it a few letters of "Duce, Duce," were discernible. Fading away below it was a slogan that had been superannuated, rather than repudiated: "While Tito fights, the King gets married." And another, which I noted gratefully, was fading also. It read: "It is the duty of every honest man to unmask traitors."

Wall News

When I got back on board I hunted round for the wall news. It has always seemed to me one of the customs of Communist life most worthy of imitation. Three years ago they could be found in cafés and schools, and in railway stations and barbers' shops. They were often lively and revealing. But the wall news in the yacht was hidden by a pile of packing-cases, in front of which sailors were playing chess. The sheet was full of stereotyped platitudes about duty. I contrasted it unfavourably with the wall news I had seen on a less ostentatious passenger boat. There had been a long poem about the crew, which I spent a happy half-hour putting into English to amuse the captain. It had begun:

> The little Rab goes on its way,
> Though seas be calm or tossing,
> While comrade Janko cleans the decks,
> And Captain does the bossing.
> While Bozho Baltich cooks the meals,
> And Antun waits at table,
> The passengers sit round and eat
> As much as they are able...

And so on, through all the members of the crew. There were also in that wall news many obscure private jokes and the usual exhortations to co-operation. It was not very original, but clearly it was an attempt to give expression to the friendliness that must grow up between men who work together. A Dalmatian who was with us told me that the wall news, like so many other importations from Soviet Russia, was falling into disfavour. So too were the voluntary labour corps and the discussion groups, which every citizen was supposed to attend. None was bad in itself; indeed, voluntary labour corps are said to have been first advocated by "A.E." and adopted and applied by a friend and admirer of his in Bulgaria (though I note that Sean O'Casey denies "A.E.'s" authorship). The idea has its good points, but in its application there had been much petty tyranny. Still, the compulsion was not as irresistible as its opponents have claimed.

Pay in Kind

One morning I was in a café in Dubrovnik listening to six strangers rejoicing over the abandonment of this intolerable burden of pseudo-voluntary labour. One of them suddenly asked: "Which of you has ever done any?" It turned out that one of them three years before had spent three weeks helping with the harvest on an abandoned German farm in Slavonia. He had been given a pair of boots for the work, and he said: "Yes, I must admit it was one of the best holidays I have ever had. And at my job it would have taken me a fortnight to earn the pair of boots."

The others admitted that they had never been obliged to go on one of the voluntary labour shifts at all, not even once in four years. The excuses had been various: old age, illness, or that they could not be spared from their jobs and so on.

The Croats, who have been for centuries a subject and insubordinate people, have always grumbled with such ingenuity that it is impossible for the foreign visitor to discover what are the genuine grievances and what are not. This is particularly unfortunate today, when it is obvious that real hardships abound.

4. Montenegro

Geographically, Montenegro begins at the Dalmatian coast town of Hercegnovi, though all round the Bay of Cotor, which lies south of it, the people are chiefly Catholic Croats. There used to be a big emigration from these parts to America. We were reminded of this by a yellow bus which met us on the outskirts of Hercegnovi. On it in large letters was inscribed, "School Bus. The Gift of the Montenegrins of California to Their Brothers." It is known locally as "schoolbus," and is a proof of the friendship between the Yugo-Slavs of America and the home country which politics has not yet destroyed.

We stopped at the large Boka Hotels, in which ten years ago all the members of the British colony of Yugo-Slavia were detained before they started on their two months' journey through Italy to Britain. In the garden we found a large table laid out for a meal. We were met among the palm trees and the bougainvilleas by the President of the Odbor, or local council of Hercegnovi, and by the Finance Minister of Montenegro. He is a big affable fellow, who was given a curious recommendation to me by a middle-class friend in Belgrade: "Yes, he's an honest man, he was always a Communist, not just a post-war opportunist." There was also Canon Lukavich, a Catholic priest, who was also the local historian and a scholar of repute. The President of the Odbor had spent a long period of the war in Dachau. He had been elected to the presidency on his return. He seemed an able, thoughtful man, with a smattering of foreign languages.

Vendetta's End

After the meal, John Lawrence and I, because we could talk with them in Serbo-Croatian, went for a drive with the Finance Minister and Canon Lukavich. On the Canon's advice, we stopped at several places. One was the Orthodox Monastery of Sveti Sava, where a fine collection of silver reliquaries and fifteenth-century MSS still survives. Later, we stopped at Risan, where an amateurish excavation of the old Roman town was being conducted by the local art master. We parted from the Canon on arriving at his parish in Cotor. He was an amiable and intelligent old man; he had taken no part in the fighting, but had organized help in food and comforts for the Partisans. In recognition of this he wore a Partisan medal and had a small post in the Montenegrin Cabinet.

I do not know of any other place like the lovely Bay of Cotor and its little towns, Cotor, Dobrota, Perast, Risan. These have huge palaces, where Venetian merchants once launched travelling vessels to the East from the quays at the end of their gardens. They have all, except Tivat, the naval base, been dead for centuries, and today they seemed more dead than ever. At the entrance to one town we saw a sign: "Go slow. Blind People." Another town seemed full of cripples. Budva has hospitals and a hostel for the writers and journalists of Montenegro. The whole coast is becoming a place for convalescence, repose and recreation. Its prosperous, aggressive past is gone beyond recall.

I knew this district fifteen years ago. In the mountains above Cotor I attended the last *izmerenje* or reconciliation ceremony to take place in Yugoslavia. It was Easter, and the two families to be reconciled were the Bauks and the Orloviches, who had a vendetta because of a murder committed six years before. The murderer, a slim city clerk, had sheepishly gone through the ceremony of being adopted into the family of the Bauks. He had had to creep down a long lane formed by a hundred Bauks, confronted by a hundred Orloviches, all in their splendid Montenegrin clothes.

At the end of the lane he had been raised to his feet and embraced by the brother of the murdered man. Then there had been mutual embracing between all the Bauks and all the Orloviches. After an address by the priest the complicated ritual had ended in a banquet in the churchyard, at which the Orloviches waited upon the Bauks. It was a moving ceremony, but the life was even then going out of it. One or two of the gorgeous Montenegrins exchanged *sotto voce* sarcasms in American slang. There was a journalist present, but a cine-camera operator who should have arrived missed his bus, and the murderer had only the traditional humiliations to endure.

Palace Beauties

The long, winding road up Mount Lovcen took us to Cetinje. We ended the evening in the hotel at a big table from which we looked down the hall, on some fifty young holiday-makers dancing a kolo and singing a strange litany, of which I could only pick out a fragment of the refrain:

> *O, Central Committee, we reject the lies, the slanders of the Cominform!*
> *Where were you, Anna Pauker,*
> *When Tito was defying the enemies of our people?*

These prosaic words, when sung, had a gay and exotic effect. While we listened an archaeologist from Sarajevo took his place beside me. I found we had a mutual friend, an archaeologist in Ireland, to whom we sent a joint postcard. He was supervising a new archaeological survey conducted by the Montenegrin Government.

The Palace at Cetinje, which we visited the next day, contains sumptuous but not tasteful furniture, and rooms full of weapons. There are many photographs of nineteenth-century royalties, for the handsome princesses all made great alliances. Upstairs are the relics and pictures of the great Montenegrin poet Prince Njegosh. A member of the Petrovich dynasty, a huge, dark fellow, with a startling resemblance to the portrait of one of his ancestors, hovered round us politely. Apparently he still lives in the palace.

There is a monastery near the palace. While we were exploring its library, the Curator exclaimed: "Do you know the bishop is in town today – I expect he'd like to see you." Soon afterwards we were chatting with the Metropolitan Arsenije in a small, book-lined room. He was a fresh-faced old man, with a grey beard cut like a spade; and we found him jovial and talkative. He is a great dignitary of the Orthodox church. He was acting Patriarch for a time, and was thought to be a likely successor to the later Patriarch Gavrillo.

Gestapo's Choice

He answered our questions briskly. "No, religion was taught in the churches only now. In theory it could be taught in the schools, too, but..." He gave a gesture which we had seen often before and whose meaning we understood. Conditions varied from place to place; there was a real conflict between Christianity and Communism, but, on the whole, it was being waged with less ferocity than might have been expected.

He talked to us more freely about the days of the war. In 1940, as Vicar to the Patriarch, he had received a deputation of three English Bishops whose names he could not remember. (Stuart Morris, who was with us, was of the opinion that he was referring to the visit of the Bishops of Chichester and Gibraltar.) They had come to discuss the possibility of a closer union between the Church of England and the Orthodox Church.

The discussion had been friendly, but conclusive and non-political.

The Gestapo heard of it when the Germans had reached Belgrade, and it aroused their deepest suspicions. So Arsenije found himself at the Gestapo headquarters in a room with two doors. "That way to freedom. It depends on you which you leave by." Then he sternly asked what the English Bishops had discussed. Arsenije at last convinced the officer that they had been debating exclusively doctrinal differences, "One of our principal causes of disagreement is the doctrine of the Real Presence."

"And did you come to an agreement about it in the end?" the Gestapo man asked searchingly.

"No, I'm afraid we did not succeed," Arsenije had sighed.

"You didn't? Hooray!" Here Arsenije, the narrator, jumped out of his chair, mimicking the Gestapo man's delighted exclamation. With a smile he led Arsenije to the door for freedom.

The Metropolitan said that the Germans had reproached him for giving a Christian burial to the Communist Partisans. He then explained to them that every Serb of Montenegrin [origin] was an Orthodox Christian until he signed a written declaration to the contrary. "I'd give them all Christian burial, if I was asked," added Arsenije.

He had been in Croatia before moving to Montenegro; and we asked him what difficulties existed now in a mixed religious community. Was the *Ne Temere* Decree a source of bitterness?

Exiled Bishops

We asked him about the Ustashe massacres and the compulsory conversion campaign. He had been in Croatia after the liberation, and gave us a horrifying account of the devastated villages and wrecked churches he had seen. There had been, he said, 240,000 compulsory converts and half a million people had been massacred[*]. We asked him about the Stepinac trial. He did not answer directly, but said instead, with conviction, that the conversion campaign could have been stopped, if

---

[*] See note on page 178. (Editors)

the Roman Catholic Bishops in Conclave had at the beginning issued a proclamation denouncing it.

I asked him about Pavelitch's establishment of a Croatian Orthodox Church, after the murder and exile of all the Serbian Bishops in Croatia and Bosnia. It has been explained by Archbishop Stepinac's champions as a sincere attempt to stop the massacres. A Russian émigré bishop, Germogen, had been appointed head of the artificially constructed Church in place of the imprisoned Dositej in Zagreb, and an unfrocked Orthodox priest, Mifka, had taken the place of the murdered Bishop of Sarajevo.

I had heard about Germogen previously. Before the war he had lived in retirement in Yugo-Slavia until the Albanian Government desired to form an autocephalous Orthodox Church which, according to Orthodox tenets, is impossible. The Albanians wished to consecrate as Patriarch an Albanian bishop, but could find no other bishop to carry out this sacrilegious task, so they sent for Germogen with an aeroplane and twenty thousand dinars. Germogen had complied. He had performed the act of consecration, and then returned to do penance in the monastery of Hopovo, which he had left only to become the head of Pavelitch's Orthodox Church.

Mr. President

"But our problem was Mifka," said Arsenije: "just before the liberation we had a meeting of our bishops and the question came up, what in the world are we to do with Mifka? And I said to them 'Don't worry. We won't have to do anything, the Partisans will cut off his head.' And sure enough they did."

Before we left we were told that the President of Montenegro would like to see us. For half an hour or so we sat at a long table opposite a row of Ministers, some of whose faces were familiar to us from their portraits in Montenegrin hotels and cafés. As usual, there was an awkward beginning and a friendly, sociable end. One of the Ministers spoke English, and questions and answers flashed backwards and forwards.

First we disposed of the business of Anglo-American military aid and then we talked of schools and theatres, the management of factories, decentralization of control, the food situation, and the minorities. It would be out of place to touch here on these vast and complicated subjects. I can only say that any question we asked was freely answered and no one made light of difficulties and failures.

5. Macedonia

Slav endurance is a wonderful thing. At one extreme there is the most civilized patience in the world, at the other end, the most abject submissiveness. We chiefly met the patience. To carry out our programme we had many times to change our plans, but we never met with irritability.

Mrs Vilfan, whose husband was one of the delegates from Yugo-Slavia at Lake Success, and our other Yugo-Slav companion, Petar Knezhevich, were telephone-minded, so that whatever place we chose to visit we found there a reception committee. When we reached Skopje at 2 a.m. there was still a tired secretary drowsing over a banquet of roast pork and grapes; two Ministers of the Macedonian Government had been waiting for some hours and had gone to bed. It was friendly and flattering but at 2 a.m. bed is better than banquets.

Our three chauffeurs, Rade, Yanko and Pero, were the chief sufferers from our vagaries, for often we had to keep them driving for hours on end. Once at midnight in Kossovo Polje, the great plain where the Serbs had fought their last battle against the Turk in the 14th century, Rade turned quietly into the roadside, and went to sleep. The other two cars drew alongside and waited twenty minutes. Only the passengers were wakeful, listening to the snores of the chauffeurs and the distant barking of dogs. After a time all three awoke simultaneously and soon we were off again.

Not Etiquette

From Skopje after our usual investigations, we travelled towards the Albanian frontier. On the road we passed the local train on its way to Tetovo. It was going at about ten miles an hour. The little engine had something like a fire screen on top of its funnel. In a truck behind there was an oddly domestic looking assortment of objects like bellows, shovels, scuttles and watering cans. But most remarkable of all was the train itself, for out of every window on the running board, on the roof, passengers were crowding and the rear was brought up by a flat, sideless tray, on which there gravely squatted forty Albanians in white skull caps. My companion, Joseph Lauwreys, had a camera, and when we were a couple of hundred yards past the train he slipped it on and jumped on to the embankment. The others also stopped, and the train puffed slowly past us to the clicking of cameras and delighted English exclamations.

It was not until we had started again that we realized from the grim faces of the chauffeurs and that we had been guilty of a breach of good taste. "Why did you take that photo?" Rade asked Joseph. "Oh, because I thought it would make a nice picture."

"It is a nice picture to see a lot of poor people crowded and uncomfortable?" Joseph made desperate efforts at appeasement. He talked of the crowds on the London underground and he added, "We went to see the old as well as the new that is replacing it. It is your fight against poverty that we admire."

"And why so?" Rade pursued inexorably. "It is riches we are fighting against, not poverty."

We plunged deeper and deeper into misunderstanding. But when we left abstractions behind, we seemed to leave our disagreements with them. Rade, like other country Serbs, had the gift of saying simple things so that they did not seem banal. When we sounded him about Russia and the Cominform, he said, "There are good Serbs and bad Serbs, good Russians and bad Russians, good English and bad English. I do not prefer one nation to another. I like good people."

Simple Faith

He said this without a hint of smugness. It had been the same that night on Kossovo Polje, when Pero, looking at the stars, advanced some theological arguments which would have sounded trite, even in the gas-lit days of Bishop Herber; but here, in these strange, lonely surroundings, they had an appealing freshness.

"Why Pero, you must be a believer," Yanko laughed.

"Yes, I am," Pero said easily.

There is little talk about religion in Communist Yugo-Slavia, but, if you hear someone speak openly about God, or immortality, it is a real voice talking, not a routine echo of something obligatory. There are few political implications or overtones. Rade did not seem to have been troubled one way or the other by the religious conflict in which Yugo-Slavia was plunged. I asked him if he was Catholic or *pravoslav* (Orthodox). "I am *pravoslav*, of course, anyone who is not a *pravoslav* is not a Serb."

We noticed in all Yugo-Slav drivers a callousness which has nothing to do with the decay of religion, but much to do with the rapid mechanisation of a simple people. When bullock-carts or pedestrians came in the way of our cars, they were driven remorselessly into the ditch, and when we protested, we were made to feel unmodern.

On the road to Tetovo, in a village where the tobacco leaves hung in racks outside the cottages and the maize straw was stacked in the branches of pine trees, we met a touching funeral procession.

A child's coffin, covered with a Bosnian carpet, was borne on a wagon pulled by two oxen wreathed in flowers. The priest, walking ahead with a platter of bread and wine, was preceded by a man bearing a wooden cross with a circlet of marigolds where the shafts intersected.

Dickensian

The busiest shop in Tetovo was the large, new bookshop. I do not think it possible to exaggerate the significance of the rapid growth of literacy in Yugo-Slavia. Where will it lead to? In England, in late Victorian times, there were great Presslords ready to take advantage of the newly-won literacy of the masses. They captured their public by studying its tastes, but the contents of Macedonian bookshops are painfully austere, with few concessions to frivolity or crime or sex, or even light entertainment. Reading is still the pursuit of the earnest, the priggish, the ambitious.

There has been a big purge of the Marxist manuals since the split with the Cominform, and the gap is filled with the books on electrification, viticulture, political speeches and translations from the classics. A small crowd gathered round us in the bookshop, led by a lively Macedonian boy. We were asking for the poems of a Skopje professor whom we had met in the morning, but the boy said: "No, don't read that, it's childish. Read *Veliki Ochekivanja.*" I puzzled over this: "Big waiting?" Then he brought the book. It was *Great Expectations,* by Charles Dickens.

How will literacy be used in this backward Republic, from which Alexander once set out to conquer the world? Almost anything might happen. A friend, a theatrical producer from Zagreb, who was transferred to Skopje, was astounded at the contrast between the enthusiasm of the unsophisticated Macedonian audiences and the blasé destructive scepticism of his native town. As the Marxists relax their grip on culture – and this seems inevitable – will Hollywood step in? The bookshops now enjoy more prestige than the cinemas but a closer intimacy with America will alter the balance.

Toleration

One of our tyres was always puncturing, and to the ensuing delays I owed several curious conversations in remote places. In a Serbian Village I talked to a peasant with a German name. He pulled out of his pocket a crumpled photograph of a son whom he had lost in the war and also an official notice in German describing the youth's death on the field of honour. It was signed by the commanding officer and stamped with a swastika seal. There was also a neat map of Central Bosnia with an arrow showing the spot where the young soldier had died.

I wondered at the innocence of the old father, at the perfection of the Nazi charity machine, at the wisdom of the Yugo-Slavs in tolerating among them this unsophisticated old traitor. The son must, I think, have been fighting in the Prinz Eugen Brigade, which was composed of Yugo-Slavs of German descent or sympathies.

Another time, at midnight, a peasant overtook us with a wagon load of grapes. He shouted at us in German. He had been taken to do farm work in the Luneberge Heide. The farmers had treated him well. "Gute Leute" (good people), he had said, "Gute Leute." There must be many Serbian peasants who never in their life-time sort out the extraordinary mixture of experiences which they have undergone.

Humour

Once or twice Yanko diversified our night drives with sport. In the plain of Leskovac the car started to leap from side to side of the road for fifty yards. There was a sudden bump, a squeal of pain, and the vehicle stopped. He got out with a smile of triumph, and picked up a big hare which he had been chasing. That was our longest drive.

A little later we began once more to bounce from side to side. I listened for the squeal, but instead we heard the horn of the car behind. We stopped and Pero came up. "Yanko is going to sleep. Mr Knezhevich is going to sit beside him as he talks more than you do."

I changed over to the other car, but soon Pero began to fall asleep. So he opened the window beside him and kept his head stuck out. "It keeps me awake," he said, "if the wind blows my eyelids open."

We reached the city at 4 a.m. A wag, who was less drowsy than the rest of us, played a cruel prank when we arrived. He got out first and roused us up. "Quick," he said "the Minister of Finance is upstairs. He has been waiting for us for hours with grapes and roast pork."

6. Croatia

The massacre of the Serbian Orthodox in 1941 was one of the most terrible events in the history of Christendom. In 1943 the exiled Orthodox Church in America published an account of it, *The Martyrdom of the Serbs*. The book stated that in its cruelty and in the number of its victims this massacre of Serbs by Croats far surpassed anything that happened in the French and Russian Revolutions. Although the book was sponsored by the Archbishop of New York and had contributions from General Mihailovitch and the heads of the Orthodox Church, it is now almost forgotten. The facts it contains are too painful and disturbing for journalism, and the time for a serious historical study has scarcely arrived.

When I was in Zagreb, I found that one of the most important of all the documents relating to this period had never been published in Yugo-Slavia, far less translated into English. It was a long letter, dated November 1941, from Archbishop Stepinac to Pavelitch, the quisling leader of Croatia, protesting against the barbarities of the campaign of compulsory conversion to the Catholic faith which Pavelitch had begun. The letter contains extracts from the memoranda of four other bishops.

Counter-Denials

I spent a couple of days in Zagreb translating it and some other documents, and published them in *The Church of Ireland Gazette*[*]. The authenticity of this letter is beyond a doubt. Why has neither faction used it in the bitter controversy about Archbishop Stepinac? I think the reason is that one party has hotly denied that the compulsory conversion campaign ever developed. The other party has asserted

---

[*] See "The Compulsory Conversion Campaign: I-III" on page 177. (Editors)

equally emphatically that Mgr. Stepinac backed the campaign unreservedly. This letter gives lie to both parties.

The regions in which the massacres and conversions took place are
not easily accessible to the ordinary visitor. While I was still with our
group, I only once, by accident, found myself in a village which had
suffered from them. Something had gone wrong with our car in the
middle of a flat northern plain and I had walked on until I came to a
broad village street in which the large cottages each stood in its own
field, like a farmhouse. It was dinner-time and the street was empty,
except for a few long wooden carts laden with maize and driven by a
peasant. I was overtaken by a man dressed like a clerk. He asked me if
I was looking for someone. I asked if he could show me the Orthodox
priest's house. When we reached the door the priest came out in his
shirt-sleeves. His beard was grizzled, his clerical clothes stained and
worn. After taking me across to the church, the priest shut the door
and assured himself that he could not be overheard. He then began to
tell me of the miserable state of the Orthodox Church under Communism, no money, no rights, and the people afraid to come to worship.
He asked me had I seen the carts full of maize going by. "Yes, I had."

"They are requisitioned by the Government. The peasants are raging
about it," he explained. He said that he had been imprisoned by the
Germans in Belgrade for more than a year. The church had been locked,
except for a short time when a Catholic priest from Djakovo had taken
services. "He was a good man," said my informant. Most of the people
of the Orthodox faith, it seems, had run away from the village. Those
that remained had to be converted, but their conversions by the kindly
priest were purely nominal to save their lives; he did not plague them
to give up their beliefs and traditions, as they were plagued in other
places.

"It was far worse round Nashitse, to the north of us," said the Orthodox cleric. "Often they were massacred even after they were converted." He would like to have gone on talking, but I was afraid I might
delay the others, so I had to leave. I was later to find that he was true
to type and that the Orthodox bishops had a more conciliatory spirit

that the average parish priest, both towards the Communist Government and towards the Catholic hierarchy of Croatia – or perhaps, they were more diplomatic in expressing themselves.

A few days later in Zagreb, when I was by myself, I drove from Krizhevtsi, where the Greek Catholic Church has its headquarters, to Bjelovar, and to several other villages nearby. I chose the route from the maps and arranged where to stop. I was glad to have a Communist, Miss Jovanovitch, with me, because otherwise I might have found myself under suspicion. She was helpful and intelligent, and understood that I should sometimes wish to pay my calls alone.

Hunted Out

To chose one of my many encounters, when I was at Narta (in East Croatia) we found the Orthodox priest, Father George, at home, a jolly friendly fellow, with a red face and white skullcap. He said he had only been there since the previous priest had been hunted out into Bosnia in 1941, and had died here, and the whole village had been compulsorily converted. He (the new priest) had come from Serbia, but when he got there first the Communist organizers blamed him for the slow progress their propaganda was making in the village. He was then imprisoned for a year. "But now I'm back again," he said cheerfully, "and they don't interfere with me, and I can usually get the village council to do what I want."

He took us into the church which adjoined his garden. After the village had been converted the church had been adopted to Roman Catholic usage. This meant the removal of the icons and the iconostasis, the large screen which divides the Sanctuary from the body of the church. He showed me the newly-erected iconostasis, a temporary affair of brown paper and laths. He had attached to it several icons that had been badly battered, but was being restored, and he told me that he was doing it out of his own funds.

"I gave 20,000 dinars myself," he said. "I've only a wife to keep, and I can afford it. The villagers can't."

"How many come to church on Sunday?" I asked him.

"Oh, none," he said, surprised at the naiveté of my question. This raised a number of other questions but I could only ask the crudest, "Where do you get your money from then?"

"Well, they are not frightened to come on Feast Days, so I make a bit then on candles and other things like that. I managed to collect about 1,200 dinars a month."

"Do you get something from the State, then?" I asked in surprise for these sums are very small. Foreigners can spend as much on a hotel meal.

"Nothing. I am allowed to charge 200 dinars for baptisms, 300 for marriages, but the peasants can't usually afford it, and I don't ask them. Then we have to give about 200 dinars to maintain the Bishop of Zagreb."

He took us to his house through his well-kept garden with its rows of aubergines and cabbages, and green and red paprikas. He told us that he had 12 acres. Inside the house he led us to a long bare room with a big table, which looked as if it was used for vestry meetings. Out came the inevitable bottle of silvovitsa brewed not from plums but from his own black currents. He started a good-humoured attack on Miss Jovanovitch: "I have nothing against the Communists as such," he said to her, "but we Christians ought to be much better Communists than you are. We say that if a man has two shirts, he should give one to his brother. Did Karl Marx ever say that? And, do you know," he added, "there is a great deal more graft now than there used to be. In the old days the Secretary of the Odbor (the village council) took at least fifteen years to save enough to build himself a house, and the present fellow's done it in a year and a half."

This was the first time I had met with such free speech, but he obviously knew what he was about. No perfunctory tribute to the regime could have done it so much credit in my eyes as the free candidness of Father George's criticism.

Free Speech

The only Christian leader whom I met in Yugoslavia, who seemed to accept the new order with something more than resignation was the Evangelical pastor of Zagreb, Dr. Edgar Popp. There are historical reasons for this. Until nearly a century ago, Protestants were barely tolerated in Croatia. As late as 1820 Protestants were still, by imperial edict, forbidden to settle in the frontier zones. A little while previously the authorities had driven out the Quaker Kukfuss. Even under the Yugo-Slav state there had been some prejudice against them because of their foreign affiliations. (They are called the German Evangelical Church).

At the time of the German occupation, Zagreb was full of Protestants. Bishop Popp, Edgar Popp's father, found his congregation much increased and a serious problem facing him. It was too hard for him to solve. He did not manage to prevent his church from being implicated in the campaign against the Orthodox, since the forced converts were given the choice of four religious communities into which they might be received, the Roman and Greek Catholic, the Evangelical and the Moslem.

I learnt that Edgar Popp's father had for humanitarian reasons received in Zagreb 420 "nominal" converts; their names had been entered in a book, but they had not been baptized. Because of the pressure of his German and German-Yugoslav congregation, the bishop had been inveigled step by step into the quisling camp and had accepted from Pavelitch an Order "with star" for "sincere collaboration with the Croatian Government." When the partisans reached Zagreb, he was executed.

Dr Popp was not at home when I called first at the offices of the Evangelical Church, so I went to the picture gallery at the end of the street. It was built before the war by the sculptor, Mestrovic, but had never been used for its intended purpose. Pavelitch, who favoured the Moslems against the Orthodox, had, on his arrival, changed it into a mosque and added two minarets, which have only just been pulled down. An exhibition of "Zagreb under Pavelitch" was being held.

The walls were covered with posters acclaiming Hitler and denouncing Serbs and Jews, and public notices about the execution of those who had resisted Pavelitch. I recall, in particular, the death sentence on the cook at the Esplanade Hotel, who had harboured an enemy of the State.

When Dr. Popp returned he was wheeling a new bicycle and was loaded with parcels. He had been to the station to receive goods from Protestants in America. The bicycle was to help him on his calls in his wide and scattered parish.

He was a vigorous, cheerful young man. His community, which once had 400,000 members, had shrunk a lot with the death, deportation or flight of many German Yugo-Slavs who had favoured Pavelitch. The remnant could not be considered an alien minority. I think the Communists were following the policy of King Alexander and all authoritarian governments who are confronted by hostile groups. It is their practice to support the smaller against the larger one. Because of his policy the bulk of the Croats consistently opposed the monarchy, while the Protestants in Croatia were more favourable to it.

(1951)

Trieste

Has opportunist diplomacy ever had such devastating exposure as over the question of Trieste?

A Free State was established after the war in an attempt to reconcile the Yugoslav ally and the Italian enemy. The task was difficult and in a few years the occupiers wearied of waiting for the dove of peace to walk into the neat hutch they had prepared for it.

The Italians were well-bred and sociable, the Slovenes surly and suspicious, and, as it became clear that Italy was more friendly than Yugoslavia to the Western democracies, there was some relief felt, I think, among the Anglo-Saxon intruders when Italy was suddenly promised Trieste. At last they could go home.

But before the promise could be carried out, the situation changed.

Tito quarrelled with Moscow and became no longer an ex-friend enemy, but an ex-enemy friend. He had to be encouraged so Trieste was not handed over.

And then recently another change. Extremists threatened to get control in Italy and the Italian government declared that their collapsing prestige must at all costs be bolstered up by the recovery of Trieste.

The Western Allies decided to take the risk and Mrs Clare Luce, the American ambassador in Rome, is said to have prophesied that Tito would make a fuss but come to heel in the end.

Was there ever so false a prophecy! There is a wild chauvinistic screeching from Rome and Belgrade, there are threats and riots. Will the curtain go up on an Italian Trieste as promised, or has it struck a second time? Behind the scenes one can hear the frantic shifting of furniture and the stage is, I hope, being set for an altered programme, but what a way to do it!

In the meantime not quite so many stones are flying through the windows of Anglo-American cultural institutes in Belgrade but a lively fire has opened on their associated offices in Rome (one sad aspect of the government patronage and publicity for the arts is that the arts have lost their old international prestige. Shakespeare and Dante have to climb down from Mount Olympus in order to become commercial travellers and whipping boys fro rival Foreign Offices).

What is to happen?

Obviously in her present vengeful and chauvinistic mood, Italy cannot be given Trieste. Under the pretext of anti-Communist measures the large Slovene minority would be crushed or forcibly Italianized. Reprisals would be taken in the Yugoslav-controlled Zone B and that would lead to further Italian territorial demands. Signor Pella's prestige would have to be fed with pound after pound of Slovene flesh.

Obviously the only possibly policy is to give the Free State a longer and fairer trial.

It is objected that there is something artificial about its autonomy and it is true of course that it has not had a long history of freedom like the Hanseatic States, but its Italianita, despite all the braying, and rioting and flag waving, is equally artificial.

Trieste owes its size and importance to a Rhineland baron, who conceived the idea of expanding a small Slovene fishing village into a great port for Austro-Hungarian commerce. Italians poured in from outside to fill an empty shell reared by Teutons and Magyars in a Slav countryside.

The Triestini are, and in their less excitable moments will admit to being, a Mischvolk.

Of course there was a Roman Tergeste, but that has as much bearing on the situation today as Roman Verulam or Roman London.

There was never a Venetian Trieste. Indeed to escape the suffocating embrace of Venice the little medieval port flung herself into the arms of the Habsburgs.

When I was last in Trieste I found there was a small but sturdy and serious group of Triestini who believed in the Free State and its power to develop organically if it could be nursed through this terrible epoch of reprisal and counter-reprisal.

In the 1952 elections this party polled 22 per cent of the votes.

Not very many, you will say, till you remember that the two annexation parties have powerful states at their back while the occupying powers are scrupulously neutral.

Of the twenty-odd newspapers of Trieste, *Trieste Sera*, the organ of the Independentists, was perhaps the poorest of the lot, crippled for office space and only able to appear twice a week.

What can one hope for?

I do not feel justified in recommending the pure milk of pacifism but only a rather adulterated kind.

The occupying troops obviously cannot at present be withdrawn. Yet something could be done to support the only party of reason and reconciliation.

Can we not urge publicity, propaganda, research on behalf of this struggling group, which would like to be the mediators between Slav and Latin, between the culture of revolution and the culture of tradition?

If reason were restored to her throne in Italy, from which she has so often ruled the world, she might welcome such a state, where Slav and Italian enjoy equal rights. Yugoslavia might be ready to enlarge the frontiers of the little state with the adjoining regions whose inhabitants now under Yugoslav rule have the same mixed inheritance as the Triestini.

Is this all a fantasy? When we consider the terrible alternative we can reject no peaceful plan because it is difficult and likely to be slow in fulfilment.

(1953)

Endnote: Zone A, including the city, was held by the Italians, with popular support, under UN protection as the "Free Territory of Trieste" between 1947 and 1954. Zone B, to the south, came under the control of Yugoslavia. Border issues were finally settled with the Treaty of Orisino in 1975. (Antony Farrell, The Lilliput Press)

Yugoslavia Today

There have been three good books on Yugoslavia in the past few weeks; an autobiography by King Peter II, a travel record by a Swedish writer, M. Sommelius, and lastly this work of Mr Tennyson.[*]

Alone of the three writers, the King was personally involved in the great catastrophe that swept away a still medieval kingdom and left a question mark in its place, while M. Sommelius brought a poetic vision and a certain Nordic honesty to the study of this enigma upon the Adriatic. Mr Tennyson brings a Quaker seriousness and cheerful matter-of-fact optimism (but I am not certain whether, as organizer of various international Quaker undertakings, he was acting as a Friend or as a Friend of the Friends).

To me Mr Tennyson's book is the most congenial of the three. Without being a professional middle-of-the-road man, he is beautifully objective, or let us say, rather, that he observes other roads in Yugoslavia besides that which runs between Communism and democracy. The Marxists and their opponents are only indirectly involved in many of the sad crises and conflicts that are inevitable when an ancient people is pushed by circumstances from medievalism to modernity.

Consider the sad dilemma of many Moslem women today. The Communist law prohibiting the veil has been supported by the religious leaders, the Hodjas and Immams, who declare that its origin is

---

[*] Hallam Tennyson, *Tito Lifts the Curtain, The Story of Yugoslavia Today.* (Editors)

not in religion but in custom. Yet the tradition is strongly cherished and many a Moslem wife sits indoors all day, terrified to walk out of doors unveiled lest she infuriate her husband, or to walk out veiled lest she be prosecuted by the police.

There are many bad old customs, which, like the veiling of women, have been handed down reverently from generation to generation. Only the dynamite of some crude revolutionary philosophy will abolish them, yet one is not obliged to commend the liberating violence, but rather to deplore the strange impotence of the humane and educated, who acknowledge the necessity of reform, but leave its execution to bandits or bureaucrats. If the Hodjas acknowledged that the veil should be abolished why did they leave it to the infidel to enforce the abolition?

Mr Tennyson has certainly no illusion about the tact of the new Communist evangelists, but he is touched by their simple zeal. His enthusiasm for the old Macedonian dances worried his Communist friend in Macedonia who expressed himself like this:

> We must be modern. We have to put the nix on dervishes, witches, beggars, ballad singers and these here long festivals up in the hills. Maybe they was useful in the olden days... But today they waste the precious time when the farmers ought to be improving their livestock and their agriculture... You won't write only 'bout them dances, will you, comrade? You won't forget the pottery and the tobacco refinery and the fruit packing plant and the hydro-electric station?

Despite his admiration for the dances Mr Tennyson recognizes the sincerity of this lament, for in many villages where Orthodox, Catholics and Moslems were present together there were as many as 200 holidays in the year excluding Sundays.

Mr Tennyson declares that in Yugoslavia he would "as a believer in God and party politics" have been no more than "a second-class citizen with limited rights" but he considers that in a country, where new things are happening every day, the individual and his decisions may have an importance that they lack in a land like Britain, where the individual's rights have long been assured and democracy rolls along effortlessly on traditional rails.

Justifiably he plays down the influence of doctrinaire Marxism in contemporary Yugoslavia. "Materialism," he says, "for the average Marxist boils down to no more than a vague feeling that this is the only word we are likely to know and therefore we had better make the most of it." It is probable that, even without the breach with Moscow, Yugoslav Marxism would have had to adapt itself to many strong regional and cultural idiosyncrasies. Mr Tennyson is doing a good work for peace, when he shows that the way of dogma, which the Yugoslav Communists have built against the Christian world, has many gaps in it and is not at all formidable to the sincere explorer.

(1955)

Tito's Marxist Heretic

Most of the heroes of history have had enthusiastic communities behind them, giving them moral support when they fail, looking after
their posthumous glory when they succeed. Milovan Djilas is one of
the exceptions.*

As a former Vice-President of Yugoslavia, he is too deeply implicated
in Communism and probably too proud to qualify for the laurels that
the West bestows on those who defy the Marxists in their citadels.

He cannot be represented as crusading for anything much except free
speech and yet that is too vague a cause to be glamorous. Yet he thought
it worth going to prison for, and this book with its unemotional account
of his boyhood in Montenegro does much to explain his decision.

It is a sober account of a small society intoxicated alternately by
religious, racial and political passions, and rarely have these violent
disorders been chronicled with so little bias by one so intimately involved. Montenegro, to which the poet prince Nejegosh gave the name
Land Without Justice, was famous for its crusading heroes, their epic
deeds and independent personalities.

There can have been few countries where the distinction between
peasant and aristocrat was so slight. It was a democracy achieved by
levelling up rather than by levelling down, and the humblest was able
to behave with the eccentric freedom of an eighteenth-century English

---

* Milovan Djilas, *Land Without Justice* (1958). (Editors)

nobleman. It was a moderately united land while the Turks were still there to focus upon themselves the concentrated ferocity of the Christians, but in Djilas' boyhood the Cross finally triumphed over the Crescent.

Alas, it was a political and not a moral victory. Barbarous cruelties were practised on the defeated Moslems. Those who restrained themselves from murder looted. Djilas saw one of his uncles forcing a Moslem child to squeeze through the narrow window of a mosque and bring him the carpet, another uncle specialized in Moslem chickens, Djilas' mother acquired a load of wheat. By the time he grew up there were few savage disillusionments for which this young Montenegrin was unprepared.

Very soon the Montenegrins were at war with themselves, for some wished for incorporation in Yugoslavia, others wanted their independence and their king. Young Djilas observed with loving but candid eyes how his family and friends were swayed first by one loyalty, then by another, and finally came to be guided by self-interest alone.

His father was a slightly modernized descendent of a long line of peasant warriors who had won deathless glory in fighting against Turks and Austrians. He had scruples and hesitations unknown to his ancestors, and sometimes felt embarrassment when engaged on a crusade. Once vengeance was being taken on the villagers of Rovchi, who were reluctant to be incorporated in Yugoslavia: "There were many routine things to be done, the women had to have cats sewn up in their skirts and the cats had to be whipped, old men had to carry young soldiers pick-a-back across the river and much else." The elder Djilas, as he stood beside the cannon that was demolishing the village, began to falter.

What had these villagers done to deserve this? Had he not once like them been a supporter of the king; was he not really in his heart a supporter still? Suddenly reassurance came to him. He remembered that some men who had stolen his bull, Spot, had probably come from Rovchi. Now he felt comforted.

After every volley of the cannon he cried out: "Ha! My bull, Spot! Ha!" Montenegrin justice was vindicated.

It is difficult to praise as it deserves this book, which is a picture of a primitive society in violent collision with the sophistication of the West. The new ideas that fly like sparks from an anvil under the furious impact of the modern world do not always seem to us very new at all. Sometimes chapters end with weighty reflections that are in themselves as trite as cracker-mottoes.

Yet recently quarried from experience, they seem to have a vigour and dynamism lacking in our most venerated truisms. The book has been translated by an anonymous American professor. I like his version, though the narrative remains rather rugged and uncouth and patently translated. He does not waste time searching for smooth English equivalents. The English *mot juste* is often a dreary veteran, while those Montenegrin kinsmen of our platitudes are still fresh and lively.

The injustices and squalors of which Djilas writes often do not seem to belong to any time or nation. *Homo Homini lupus* is his theme. He narrates how in the First World War a young Czech doctor joyously came over to their side, confident of a welcome from his brother Slavs, and how one of these brother Slavs, a neighbour of Djilas, blew his brains out to get his watch.

He remembers the small shabby incidents that chroniclers of epic deeds usually forget. "The Montenegrins," he recalls, "pitied the Serbs rather than helped them," during the great Serbian retreat to the sea. He cannot forget the tiny piece of bacon that his mother gave to the starving Serbian soldier and the big slabs that were stored away for the family in the attic.

His nostalgia is not for the past but for that imagined world that we create when we are young, in which the injustices of the actual world are redressed. For as we grow older even that visionary world ceases to be credible.

"Old Montenegro," writes Djilas, "faded away with its men and customs, while the new order failed to bring peace and liberty even to those who hoped for these and fought for them."

This book is full of gloomy prognostications and yet is fundamentally cheerful. Djilas has, I think, the sort of mind that in a more prosperous community might have been strongly introverted and might have harvested misery out of disillusionment and intellectual frustration. But it would be hard to be an introvert in Montenegro, where thinking has little status except as a dim prelude to violent action.

Djilas chronicles the poverty and disorder of his native land with a tenderness of feeling that sometimes seems to run counter to his indignation. It is clear that he loves Montenegro almost as much as he loves truth, and that he has never been affected by that weariness of living on which genuine pessimism must be founded.

(1958)

Return to Hellas

When I was young, but not young enough, I walked through the Peloponnese with a mule. It took, I think, thirteen hours from Andritsaena to the ferry across the Alphaeus. I had never enjoyed anything so much, but I felt very angry that my education had been back to front. Here was the jam at last after I had stuffed myself to repletion with dry bread. Had I known of all this before, the fragrance of myrtle and mule droppings, the memory of roast sucking-pig and retsina, would have reconciled me to knowledge, which till then had flowed in a contrary direction to my curiosity. Why, for instance, had I never grasped that the cistus, on which the mule trampled, that showy nurseryman's plant with pink flowers and dark sticky leaves (catalogue price 7s. 6d.), was a commonplace to Herodotus. The Greeks, he said, made incense from it by combing the beards of billy-goats. Why did I never guess that in a meadow at Olympia, ringed with asphodel and narcissus, the Hermes of Praxiteles would shed like the scab of an old wound its frowsy kinship with a plaster cast in the Science Buildings at Charterhouse?

Travel to Greece is now so easy and cheap that only a very unenterprising or underprivileged boy or girl would study *The Agamemnon* without going to Mycenae, or the Persian Wars without a visit to Salamis. But the more ambitious examinees will not go by mule now. The mules and the muleteers are still there, but, just as the peasant costumes of the Balkans are moving from the backs of peasants to the tourist shops, so, though more deliberately, the mules are shifting away from nature towards art, towards those unnatural animals which carry giggling metropolitans across the Gap of Dunloe, insulated from the present by a strict tabu upon tourists with cars.

Indeed, one might say that everything is too easy now, information too accessible, and in a different way the Greek world has got out of focus again. We now know more than the average Greek knew about the development of his pots and trade routes, his dialect and his racial descent. The scholar's approach is no longer humanist but clinical. I have heard of a French doctor who failed to recognize an old acquaint-ance till he had seen his bottom, which he had treated for boils. "Ah, mon comrade, c'est toi!" he exclaimed, as he embraced him. This back-side intimacy with Greece is now the only kind of which we dare boast.

Is it because too many banalities have been uttered about "the Greek spirit" that the scholar now buries his head in potsherds and paradigms? As we boarded our plane in the early fifties with twenty-eight other middle-aged unprofessional phil-Hellenes, we knew well how banal we were. Yet we were conscious of our power. It is for us that a trunk-road sweeps between Helicon and Parnassus and that six thousand new bedrooms (bathrooms attached) and thirty-three new hotels have been decreed. From now on the mariner, as he rounds Cape Sunium, will not see the Temple of Poseidon, as Byron saw it, lonely and aban-doned, but flanked by a Tourist Pavilion and a Hilton Hotel. An avenue lined with cypress and eucalyptus leads right up to the tumulus at Marathon, so that the front bumpers of our charabanc could actually graze the green sod beneath which 192 Greek warriors were laid.

Well, and why not? The Greeks, a vulgar and gregarious people, loved tours and tourists and international gatherings and painted each garment of the Caryatids a different colour. The Temple of Poseidon once was more expensively gorgeous with gold and ivory than the lounge of the Hilton Hotel, not yet completed, will ever be. The flutings of its Doric columns were red and yellow; its present admired colour is the work of time, which turns all our bones to apricot and ivory.

Obviously group travel by chartered plane is revolutionizing Hel-lenic travel and, to judge by our experience, the first revolutionaries are conscious of what they are doing and doing it well. On our Wings Tour in less than a fortnight we saw more of the Greek world than Strabo and Pausanias could have seen in five times the time; collectively we could have compiled a patchy but not contemptible epilogue about its flora and fauna and surviving antiquities. For sophisticated travellers it used to be a point of honour to dodge their compatriots, except those in embassies, but we found through our companions an enlargement of our senses. X saw and shared the eagle resting on a rock at Cameirus, the vultures gliding over the Doric Code of Laws at Gortyna, two hoopoes and stonechat. Y observed how as we went southward the pink anemones faded and gave place to white, the golden camomiles of Crete replaced the white ones of Rhodes, the lemons grew smaller. Z identified for us Ithaca and Delos and the mouth of the Acheron. Above the clouds and below, our perambulating city-state was well governed by two intelligent and amiable archons and those who had no special knowledge to share cemented its solidarity with maps and aspirins, field-glasses and Penguins. It was only on the subject of Ancient Greece that I observed a competitiveness that was not shown about the best seats on the plane, the best beds in the hotel. I attribute this to compulsory classics, which fester like an abscess under the skin of so many middle-aged men. A century ago it could erupt in parliament or the Law Courts, when rolling periods were decorated with quotations. A generation ago it could still exude through the competition page of the *Saturday Westminster*, when a poem by Herrick would be "neatly rendered" into Alcaics. But now, except for conferring Honorary Degrees in a witty way, what public use can one make of it all? If it does not earn you a salary, it is often just a focus of irritation. When at Marathon Mrs N. mused, as she pointed at Mount Parnes, "I love to think of Xenophon sitting on a throne up there and watching the battle," there was a febrile pounce from two middle-aged public schoolmen. "Xerxes!" gasped the first. "Salamis!" chided the second. "A spur of Mount Aegaleos," said a third, a near-professional, in a competitively uncompetitive murmur, thereby winning trick, game and rubber. After that Mrs N. kept all her loving thoughts about antiquity to herself.

Nobody wants to hear about what we saw in Greece and its islands,
for now they are so accessible that everyone can see them for himself.
So I shall confine myself to two digressions, expounding two out-of-
date heresies in terms of Attica, the Argolid, Rhodes and Crete.

First, there is the question of Mrs N. and cannibalism among amateur and professional phil-Hellenes, who, except on cruises and bus-
tours and chartered planes, at conferences and in common rooms, are
a scattered and insignificant community. Ethel Smyth, in an admirable
Greek travel-book (not un-scholarly but anti-scholarly), indicates that
archaeologists are even bigger prigs than classical scholars. "Most
workers," she writes, "perhaps most humans, are prone to secret jealousy, but for undisguised scorn of all other workers in his own field of
business, commend me to the archaeologist." And she describes a
meeting between "two frigid and lordly ones of the orthodox type"
who were looking down their noses at each other but ran together like
twin dewdrops in implied disdain of a third, who was unorthodox. "His
buoyancy of spirit was greatly against him."

One explanation of this might be that archaeology is now largely
financed by the public and not by private wealth or voluntary subscription. The paid professional, slightly askew to reality, is sheltered from
the freezing indifference which unsubsidized enthusiasm would meet
from 99 per cent of his fellow citizens. A century ago Mrs N.'s eager
little advances might have meant a 5s. subscription to a struggling
archaeology society. Now she is probably paying the state more than
this towards the discovery of the past, but her enforced benevolence
is hidden even from herself in the labyrinth of the budget. It does not
have to be solicited or gratefully acknowledged.

Great reappraisals are often chaotic, experimental and vulnerable
to ridicule. They are seldom conducted in the trim laboratories where
reputations are nursed. At Mycenae and Cnossos one cannot forget that
the great archaeological revolutions of recent times were carried
through by amateurs in the teeth of bitter professional opposition.
Schliemann, Evans and Ventris all had "buoyancy of spirit." Now the
"Treasure of Priam," which Schliemann had presented to the German

nation, has disappeared, removed by the Russians. But who knows or cares? The apathy of the average man, which the amateur tried to ruffle, is not so burdensome to the professional.

It was inevitable that nationalism should creep in with state-supported archaeology, and its ravages could be observed in Greece. It was obvious that the superb excavations at Cameiros and Lindos in Rhodes caused acute schizophrenia in many scholarly Greeks. If you ask who carried them out, they will say in a rapid undertone: "The Italians had that privilege," and then will explain how no proper report of the work done has yet been published and so no one knows how many treasures were transported to Italy. Yet no one can deny that these graceful columns, these ranks of tombs and votive monuments, woven out of fragments of imagination and cement, are highly magnetic and that it is not only the spirit which they enrich. One is told that the money brought in by tourists, added to that which is sent home by emigrants, is more important to Greece than all her exports of olives and oranges. Even so, there are certain debts which one ought to be excused from acknowledging. Go for instance to the most ambitious of all the Italian restorations on Rhodes, the Palace of the Grand Master of the Knights of St John. Though its medievalism is more convincing in the twilight, there is a dollar-compelling majesty about its mighty walls, clad in roses and bougainvillea, its vast courtyards and lordly stairways. Inside you must crawl crab-wise round the saloons, because the floors are covered with rich Byzantine mosaics. You may hear a whisper that the Italian governor of the Dodecanese (the guide-books call him "the tyrant de Vecchi") looted them from the island of Cos to decorate the palace for himself, that he walked across them without even carpet slippers and that the Muse of History is mocked by his bathrooms and his alabaster lifts. Yet the Greeks are a thrifty as well as a proud people. The tyrant's palace will remain. But so too will the long Italian inscription in the hall-way which reveals that Rhodes was once one of the fairest jewels in the Fascist crown and that, reviving its ancient glories, the Italians were trying to revive also the patronage which Hadrian and others had once bestowed on the subject Hellenes. The marble

plaque relates how Cesare Maria de Vecchi, Conte di, etc., in the reign
of Victor Emmanuel II, King of Italy, King of Albania, Emperor of Abyssinia, etc., under the leadership of Benito Mussolini, etc., did cause
to be reconstructed, etc., in defence of the Law and Faith of Rome, etc.

There is a notion that archaeology is a grave, objective science and
that it can accept the patronage of governments without being defiled.
But in fact it is neutral coloured and highly absorbent and can be dyed
black or brown or red with the greatest of ease. Because of Schliemann
and the Aryan theory Mycenae was dyed brown during the German
occupation and the names of Göring, Goebbels and Himmler and scores
of officers of the *Panzerdivisionen* were written in the visitors' book at
La Belle Hélène, once Schliemann's headquarters. The offending page
was torn out, possibly because "learning being above politics" Greek
scholars had signed their names beside Himmler's. Himmler, like Mussolini, was an ardent patron of archaeology, believing that confirmation
of his Aryan theories lay beneath the sod. Many of the frigid and lordly
ones believed that they could smile at his views and accept his subsidies. Distinguished German scholars went to Norway for Himmler to
excavate under the aegis of Vidkun Quisling. Was learning advanced
by what they discovered? We carry the past about with us in its entirety
and nothing is gained if to illuminate what is remote we must wear
blinkers to blot out the present. It is possible that German and Italian
leaders deliberately switched the searchlight of scholarship onto ancient times, so that the darkness which veiled their own manoeuvres
might be deepened.

Aristotle, now over eighty, an assistant of Professor Wace, spends
much of his time sunning himself outside the Belle Hélène. He loves
to talk of the Professor, of Mrs Wace and Miss Helen and of all that
happened since they left. Wave after wave of foreign warriors visited
Mycenae, but the Nazi officers surpassed all the others by their ability
to quote long passages of Homer by heart; after them came the English
and the Italians; at the bottom the Americans.

Does this mean some affinity between Himmler and Homer? I think
that all it signifies is that when a state is sufficiently vast, its wartime

needs are so varied that all but impossible people can accept a portion
of its policy with a portion of their minds. It is a matter of bringing
matching pieces together. Many who in cruder days would have had
to be expensively court-martialled or imprisoned can be drafted to
some zone of co-operation which does not offend their consciences.
Dedicated to departmental virtue, they feed the hungry and homeless,
they diffuse culture. Everybody contributes according to his gifts.
While unfastidious Germans were sent to exterminate and enslave
the peoples of eastern Europe, a polished and humane élite, who played
French cricket with the kids in their billets and made small safe *Witze*
about Göring's medals, were sent to charm the Channel Islanders. In
Ireland it was well known that our cultural gauleiter was to be a competent Celtic archaeologist, who, though a German, had been till just
before the outbreak of the war Director of our National Museum. It is
not, therefore, surprising that genuine Homeric scholars have appeared
at Mycenae with Himmler, flattering themselves that they were di-
verting him temporarily from his wickedness to the patronage of
learning. Possibly, as the Supreme Commander of the SS and the
Gestapo bent over a shaft grave, some irresponsible amateur may have
been tempted for liberty's sake to push him in and crack his skull open
with an inscribed stele (*c.* 1550 BC). Then he will have recollected that
"scholarship is above politics" and that one should do nothing that
would discredit archaeology and check the flow of subsidies to
research.

In small communities on the Greek model, self-deception was not
so easy as now. There were few humane or learned sideshows in which
dissenters could bury their scruples, so there was an abundance of
uninhibited traitors. At Marathon there was an Athenian traitor with
the Persian fleet and another signalling to it from Pentelicus.

Surely Greek art and letters owed their crystalline clarity in part
to this small-scale simplicity. Traitors were traitors and there were no
multiple loyalties to muddy the mind. Could one say that in the city-
state men could not escape from each other except by open succession?
The constant friction and fusion of diverse personalities in a confined

space caused some creative combustion and sparked off explosions of genius, which could not have happened in those large loose federations, which the Greeks despised.

Here I am in the middle of my second digression. If my explanation sounded nonsensical, why has no better one been offered for the prodigious flowering of genius in the city states? Why has no sociologist given them the same attention that he gives to more trivial and nebulous problems – the effects of television on the sex-life of miners, the devaluation of the piano as an index of social prestige and so on? Are they scared of the professors, who have been oddly fallacious in their assessments? The great Hellenizers of a generation ago (I mean those who believed that the Greeks offered to students "a message" and not merely some interesting linguistic and ethnological puzzles), Zimmern, Murray, Lowes Dickinson, were all deluded by their enthusiasm for the League of Nations and that "wider citizenship" in which the old Greek ideals were to be merged. They buried the city-state honourably but the epitaphs they wrote are so odd that surely the corpse ought to be exhumed for more detailed analysis?

Lowes Dickenson considered that "the good citizen" of the Greek type could now only survive on the county council level, concerning himself with sewage and parks. More aspiring men would be liberated by the administrative machinery of a huge multiracial state for wider, freer speculations and experiences. Zimmern thought that "the state in these days of large-scale government does not expose its citizens to the daily falsehoods and hypocrisies which seem inevitable in the life of the smaller groupings of men and women." Writing in the year that Hitler was elected president of a small dining-club in Munich, he said that Germany, "her population relieved from military duty and available for productive tasks, has the advantage over the most ideal construction of ancient Greece." With all this Gilbert Murray would surely have agreed. With Nazism, Stalinism, and McCarthyism just ahead, could they have been more wrong?

The small Greek community has had many strange and fruitful reincarnations in free principalities, republics, cities. Today when all the sober orthodoxies are harnessed to apocalyptic beliefs of the most bizarre character, the Decay of the State, the Conversion of Russia, the final triumph of Communism or Democracy or Mahomet or the White or Black Races, I see nothing grotesque in believing that in some unforeseeable society of the future the function of a man and a citizen will again converge.

Who knows how? When it first happened it was an accident. It seems that many millennia ago Poseidon shook the Aegean continent into scattered fragments and imposed upon Greek exuberance a consistently small and sober pattern, which appeared to later Greek thinkers to be that best suited to man's social and intellectual development. Poor external communications helped to train the ancient cities in social self-sufficiency. They managed to be self-centred without being parochial. Their limitations, which appear to us so crippling, proved to them a blessing. Aristotle, reflecting on the greatness of Athens, declared that a large state was as absurd as a ship two furlongs long, that men should know the characters of their fellow-citizens if they were to judge them. "A nation" was a barbarous conception. "Who could be the herald of such an unwieldy multitude except a stentor?" To the Greeks there was nothing paradoxical in the association of great men with small communities.

It was an extraordinary phenomenon. In a few small cities on the rocky promontory and islands of the Aegean all our arts and sciences were founded in a few generations. Then followed centuries of imperial and feudal stagnation. Was the explanation racial? No, for the Greeks were mongrels. It concerns the nature of man. If Aristotle was wrong, what better interpretation of this marvel can sociology offer?

At the moment even if it was admitted that the small community was the best nursery for genius and freedom, everything is against it. Ancient Greek liberty was as precarious as it was lovely and it is doubtful if any modern Greek would accept it. How many blessings descend on those who are content with less! The Italians, even the tyrant de Vecchi, were extremely indulgent to Rhodes, so that liberty would not now be half so dear to the Rhodians if it were not sweetened with many fiscal concessions. For example, they get their sugar for 5 drachmas the kilo, while the Cretans, with whose affections no wealthy foreigner has tampered, have to pay 10 drachmas at least.

And apart from the question of groceries, there is that of security, so that in fact few sensible men believe that it is wise for small peoples to wish for independence. It has long been so. Mahaffy, the Provost of TCD, loved freedom and was an ardent phil-Hellene. Describing very readably his travels in Greece with Oscar Wilde, he faced squarely certain ambiguities in his concern for liberty, which as an Irish impe-rialist he could not dodge. He thought that, when England occupied Malta and the Ionian Islands, she should have taken Sicily and Southern Greece as well.

> What precious results [he wrote] might have been gained for these countries themselves and for Europe at large! While our invalids and sybarites would have spread wealth and refinement through the beautiful uplands of Sicily, our route to India would have lain through Greece... Greek art and antiquities would have become the household property of good society, instead of being seen only by a few privileged people to the great disgust of their envious neighbours.

Except that they would have disagreed as to whose invalids should refine the Sicilians, the tyrant de Vecchi would have fully understood this point of view which still survives in many respectable bosoms. I felt it stir in my own, when at Corinth our guide told how she had taken round a party of English journalists concerned about Cyprus. She spoke of the monuments they had seen, the banquets they had eaten, the contacts, the camaraderie and "the greater mutual understanding" that had ensued.

"Softening-up process!" interjected one of my fellow-travellers.

"Brain-washing!" said a second.

A third was more explicit: "I think you were cheating. You were using your beautiful country to influence a political decision."

I felt neutral, for it is the Greek intention to bring Cyprus directly under the Athens Government, as Crete is. No doubt that is what the Cypriots want, but I cannot suppress my conviction that Hellenic liberty was the discovery of small pig-headed communities, which resisted assimilation to larger ones at the price of security. It was almost a definition of liberty that it should be insecure. Groceries or no groceries, it might be easier for Cyprus to extricate herself from the bored clutches of an alien than from the tender and suffocating embraces of Mother Greece.

Certainly Mother Greece loves Crete in a very possessive way. Though we never heard sedition preached there, there is a constant grumbling about taxes and jobs. As regards jobs, it was odd that the admirable guide, who showed us Cnossos and Phaestus as well as Rhodes, was an Athenian. Are there no unemployed intellectuals in the land of Kazantzakis, whom I believe to be a major European novelist? And was the tourist policeman who sat beside the guide an Athenian too? It was his job to go ahead of us and refine the Cretans. Once when we stopped in a village for a drink he dashed into the café first and we found him engaged in a fiery battle with the proprietor and his waiters. We begged for our drinks, but Greek had met Greek and they had no time for us. The policeman was telling them that they should have clean shirts on and a black tie for the tourists, and the waiters were roaring back, "Why didn't you phone us from Iraklion and warn us you were coming?" The policemen stamped his foot and said, "Can't you understand that you have to have clean shirts for the *whole* of the tourist season?" The monstrous absurdity of this left the waiters speechless, and we managed to order our drinks.

As a civilizing influence would Mahaffy have been pleased with us? In his day, when an unrefined people was to be refined by an imperial one, the patient had to be put in some sort of political strait-jacket and culture had to be pumped in by resident expatriates. But now refinement comes by plane and train and bus from every land of the west. Such progress has been made in the canning and sweetening of culture that huge concentrated doses, capable of neutralizing the toughest insularities, the most obstinate regional idiosyncrasies, can be dumped anywhere by anyone, and they will be greedily absorbed. Culture vibrates through the air and croons and quivers on celluloid. When we landed in Crete we heard a voice warbling in our own tongue from the charabanc that had come to meet our plane: "I guess I'll have to dream the rest!" it managed to say before we extinguished it. At Cnossos and Mallia the chauffeur remained with his discs in the charabanc and the warbling would start up again, transporting him to distant lands and remote experiences more effectively than we, the raw unsweetened products of those lands, could ever do. In fact he did not like Anglo-Saxons in the flesh and when we passed the American air-base near Mallia he wrinkled up his nose to illustrate how aloof the Americans were. Pointing at the rocket-site, he said: "They make Crete very important place; we all get blown up in next war. Greek Government want to be important, Cretymen not." Cretans and Anglo-Saxons meet each other like shadows beyond the Styx. We saw an American airman looking at Minoan pots; a patch on the back of his tunic five times the size of the Phaestos disk was embroidered with a map of Crete, the word IRAK-LION and many letters and numbers, as though he had come to Crete in the mail-bag. The travels recorded on his spine had left no imprint on his face, which was amazingly blank.

In Rhodes at the lower end of the Street of the Knights, we met a crowd of German soldiers dashing with tanks under an ancient archway. Under their Nazi helmets black Greek eyes were sparkling. They straggled back twice and dashed through again, then a third time *da capo*. There was a tourist policeman there, but we were too middle-aged to need his reassurance that there was no cause for alarm. In fact David Niven and Gregory Peck and a host of cameramen and supers and secretaries were at work on their film in the huge and sprawling Hotel Miramare on the road to Cameirus. In an annexe was a publicity department daily sending out advance notices to Arizona and Malaya. A couple of million pounds was to be spent on the film, and a half of this, we were told, would be spent in Rhodes. In a few months the film will rise like a rocket and encircle the globe, and before the last vibration

of this mighty effort of the human imagination has died down enough
gold will have been stirred round to rebuild the Colossus of Rhodes ten
times over.

But here we have to ask how far we have damaged the intimate
relationship between a creative mind and its milieu by distending almost limitlessly the field of vision and hearing, dulling the impact of
experience on our senses by exposing them incessantly to titillations
from afar? Rhodes is a suitable place in which to ask this question,
because it was to Cleobulus, the Rhodian sage, that the Greeks attributed the famous maxim *mēden agan* or Nothing to Excess. In the lounge
of the Miramare did I only fancy that the film-folk passing by were
practising some kind of intellectual levitation and only made contact
with Rhodes through the soles of their alpagatas? They had the con-
stipated look of men who have consumed more irrelevant experience
that they can digest. In the corner a man was chalking up the names
of horses on a blackboard. As he wrote, the mimosas seemed to wilt
and the skies to become grey. We were at Aintree. We had to wait at a
table with picture papers on it and for ten minutes we were transported
to Paris and New York and some provincial town, I think, Leeds. And
this is happening to most of us the whole time. Impressions from far
away as soft as snowflakes are choking up the channels of perception,
making sharp corners into curves, generalizing what is particular,
reducing everything to a boundless colourless uniformity. There is now
no escape from *agan*.

The Age of the Parasites, which runs concurrently with the Age of
the Satellites beyond the Oder, may last longer than the Age of the
City-State did, but it cannot last forever. Whatever their inward affinities, the Parasites and Satellites daily prophesy for each other inevitable dissolution. And indeed it seems that sooner or later these great
commensal communities, consolidated by fear and greed, will disintegrate. Giant states are only suitable for dwarfs. Full-sized humans
cannot be fed on abstractions and build a society with others, whose
existence can only be deduced from statistics, from digests of opinions
and mechanical projections of voices and profiles. An idea, which is to

travel far by modern means, must like an air-passenger's luggage be meagre. That is why small thoughts and personalities, which would have met with a rejoinder of their own size in the agora at Cameirus in 300 BC, ripple round the world unchallenged.

And in fact all these engines of refinement, which are supposed to spray the wilderness with culture, always slip into reverse and operate as suction pumps. Those men who are susceptible to external influence are drawn away to the cities leaving the torpid and incurious behind. For various reasons no one minds this much. Our chauffeur in Crete was proud that they had had no civil war there comparable to that on the mainland and very little Communism. "You see," he said, "we have our family wars. That is enough." And he explained that his stay-at-home relations with a full-time vendetta on their hands, ramifying through distant cousins and unrelated namesakes, had no time for international politics. In Rhodes sophistication has settled in one corner like currants in a badly cooked cake, leaving the interior ignorant and primitive. I walked round a grave-yard in the village of Archangel and it seemed to me that the peasants, their school-teachers and their priests must be as poor and illiterate as in the days of Cleobulus. The names of the dead are roughly scratched with a nail in cement slabs fringed with bathroom tiles. In the phrase *Enthade Keitai* (Here Lies), I read on various tombs, "keite, kite, keetai, kitai." One would not find so much misspelling on the memorial slabs which the Italians unearthed in the ancient Rhodian cities.

These peasants are the sediment which half a dozen infusions of foreign culture have failed to dilute. Sophisticated foreigners in revolt from their age find a certain sweetness in their mummified traditions. There is an epicene pleasure in watching others believe things which we no longer believe ourselves. Lawrence Durrell, whose book on Rhodes is so subtle and observant, sternly censures the village poet because he only half believed in the efficacy of the sacred pool at Soroni, in which two old nuns, wading about in nightdresses, were immersing the village idiot. For the poet's scepticism he blames "the village schoolmaster and lawyer, those heirs to the vague radicalism and agnosticism, which is poisoning the whole source of our culture."

Mary Renault, in her charming novel about Theseus, also recoils in this odd direction from what she calls "the levelling fashions of the day" and "the standards of Admass," and tries to make credible those stories about Crete and Minos, of which the Greeks themselves were sceptical.

Nostalgia for lost innocence is an affliction of the over-civilized from which country intellectuals are immune. All the best verse about bean rows and simple sacrifices to rustic gods was inspired by the roar of Oxford Street or the Roman Forum. Such sentiments were alien to the Hellenes, a half-rustic people, vaguely radical, vaguely agnostic, who rose to glory and laid the foundations of our culture by extricating themselves from primitive superstition and outworn political forms.

We have locked the Hellenes in a museum because the small communities in which they thrive seem to belong irrevocably to the past. Though our eyes have rested on the lavatory seat of the Queen of Cnossus, and our local branch of the Town and Counties Bank is a close replica of the Temple of Zeus at Aegina, the Greeks themselves are more irrelevant to us than they used to be. Only a very young undergraduate would dare to take Aristotle seriously and to ask whether in ancient Rhodes a citizen could realize his faculties more fully than we can, whether fewer talents were wasted, fewer brains distorted. Few would speculate whether there was less *Angst* and ulcers among its painters and writers than among the gifted artists at the Hotel Miramare. Yet these questions are as pertinent to human society as those which sociologists normally ask.

I think we can acknowledge squalor and slavery and spasms of barbarism, and yet say that, when Lindos and Cameiros were thriving cities, the Rhodians had some precious gift of reconciling disparate things which we have lost. Society was closely knit without curtailment of variety. Ideas were freshly minted from experience, curiosity moved freely and truth was not yet imprisoned in quotation marks.

The temples often combined the functions of city-churches and municipal galleries and archives. Religion adapted itself to the vaguely agnostic trends of the time. Pindar, whose ode to the Rhodian boxer, Diagoras, was preserved in letters of gold in the Temple of Athene at Lindos, was very devout but he had, like many others, manufactured his own beliefs, discarding discreditable stories of the gods, even when, as often, these were the most ancient and traditional. In the temples the integrity and independence of the artist were fanatically respected, if one is to believe the old story of Protogenes and his picture of the Satyr – and why should one not believe it? He had painted a partridge on a pillar beside his satyr, so lifelike that all the partridge-breeders of Rhodes (they still breed them there) had brought in their pet partridges to cluck at it. Protogenes considered that this showed such disrespect to the Satyr, his masterpiece, and so vulgar a misunderstanding of art, that he had asked permission of the temple authorities to paint out his partridge. Permission was granted.

Later, of course, Rhodes against her will became involved in the gigantic imperial designs of the successors of Alexander and, in the homeland of Cleobulus, the Colossus, that great ebullition of excess, was erected. It lasted only fifty years, crashing in the earthquake of 227 BC. The Rhodians lived among the fragments for nine centuries, then a Jew from Syria bought them for boiling down. There were, we are told, nine hundred camel-loads to be carried away.

If in some man-made earthquake our colossal enterprises were to collapse today, it would be as hard to tidy up after them, nor does disaster seem to curb the appetite for excess. On the other hand, these enterprises, as their social sterility becomes apparent, may slowly cease to dominate our imaginations. They may yield priority to the study of human relations, at which both in their theory and in its practical application, the Greeks so enormously surpassed us.

(1961)

The Final Solution

The First Phase

When you talk to people about the Eichmann trial, 90 per cent of them (and in Ireland 95 per cent) will say, with some parade of originality: "Personally, I think it a great pity to rake it all up now. What an opportunity it would have been for the Jews to make a generous gesture!"

There are even eminent Jews like Martin Buber and Gollancz, who, for more complex reasons, disapproved of the trial. Yet if one were to investigate, one would find that a large proportion of these vicariously magnanimous people had at the beginning been sceptical about the extermination camps. What we are asking the Israelis to forgive and forget is not so much Auschwitz and the rest as our own former indifference and incredulity.

I remember, when the film of liberation of Belsen was shown in Kilkenny after the war, it was considered in very bad taste. Someone wrote to the local paper complaining that the pleasant wholesome film which preceded it (about cowboys or married love) had been spoilt for him by this morbid intrusion of horror propaganda. He suggested that the film director had gathered together a crowd of starving Indians to impersonate the Belsen inmates. No one contradicted him, and the same paper printed a letter complaining, "As regards the cigarette situation, Kilkenny is a regular Belsen," together with an announcement that a man had won a prize at a local fancy dress ball as the Beast of Belsen.

In fact, whether you believed it or not, the whole affair was utterly beyond our imaginations. We had to treat it as either a lie or a joke. And this was happening all over Europe. Yet Belsen was one of a score of similar camps and genocide and deportations were practised by no means only on the Jews or by the Germans. They had become quite respectable and might at last have reached ourselves. Himmler was intending to transfer eight and a half million Dutch to East Poland but, because of stomach cramp, was advised by Kersten, his doctor, to postpone this exhausting enterprise. What had Himmler had in mind for *us*?

The most effective criticism of the Eichmann trial which I have read is by Hannah Arendt and was published this spring in five long instalments in the *New Yorker*. She blames Ben Gurion for staging the trial as a pageant of horror to floodlight an epoch and the long torment of an ancient people. It was really the trial of a man, and that was how the three very scrupulous judges insisted on treating it, but they were constantly forced to admit evidence that had no conceivable bearing on Eichmann. He had had nothing, for example, to do with the killing of the Eastern Jews, for this had been a military responsibility and did not require the services of an expert negotiator like Eichmann. Yet when some eloquent survivor of the heroic battles in Poland or Estonia pleaded to be heard, it was very difficult to cut him short.

The trial was undoubtedly a muddle and hard to justify legally, yet Dr Arendt concedes that it had some very notable results. Unprecedented things happened in West Germany as soon as it was known that the trial was impending and that a fresh crop of war criminals were likely to be named in Jerusalem. Baer, the commandant of Auschwitz, was arrested, as were a dozen or more of Eichmann's and Himmler's closest associates who had been quietly working as foresters, printers, lawyers, without even troubling to assume false names. It is true they are being given only small sentences for enormous offences, but at least the reproach of sheltering them was removed from West Germany.

Also the trial disclosed an extraordinary amount of fascinating facts not only about Jews and Germans but about all Europeans and about twentieth-century man.

What was most terrifying about Eichmann was that he was not terrifying at all. Had there been no social cataclysm he might have lived out his days in some quiet German town as the local agent for an oil company. He was immensely ordinary and it was, in Dr Arendt's view, an unfortunate outcome of the Jerusalem trial that he has been presented so stagily as one of the Monsters of All Time. He had had his early schooling in the YMCA. He was and remained an excellent and devoted husband and father, and a loyal and conscientious employee. He had a great sense of propriety. When a young policeman in Jerusalem lent him *Lolita* to entertain him in prison, he returned it coldly after a glance or two: "A most distasteful book!" He was in no sense a sadist rejoicing in the mass exterminations which he organized. Physical violence made him sick as it did Himmler, who used to shake the nerves of firing squads with his compassionate sighs. The prosecution tried to make out that he had once beaten a Jewish boy to death but there was no real evidence and the charge was dropped.

He spoke of himself continually as "an idealist" and in the sense that he was not vindictive or particularly greedy, and that he was more concerned with principles than most people are, the word could be applied to him. He said that he had always liked Jews and wished them no harm, and that his mother had Jewish relations. Like all genteel Nazis he strongly disapproved of the coarse Jew-baiting in which vulgarians like Julius Streicher, editor of *Der Stürmer*, indulged.

He went to his death with dignity, refusing the black hood and saying at the foot of the gallows: "After a short while, gentlemen, we shall all meet again. Such is the fate of all men. Long live Germany! Long live Argentina! Long live Austria! I shall not forget them." As exit-lines rather clichéd perhaps but respectable. As an agent of evil he was unutterably banal.

Was he a demoniacal anticipation of the Organization Man, that phenomenon of our mechanical civilization that is troubling American sociologists? He had certain traits that suggested this. He was extremely well-adjusted, he was wonderful on committees, knowing the right people to approach and the right "public image" to present. With the minimum of friction and hysteria he manoeuvred his Jews on to the conveyer belt that bore them to destruction. Their co-operation was, he said, the "corner-stone" of his work. He wanted to make things as "palatable" for them as possible, and to be "fair to both sides."

It is this aspect of the Jewish tragedy that is hardest to grasp, despite the abundant evidence from every land. The Jews have always had their Gideons and Solomons. If so brilliant a people, practised in survival both by fighting and by diplomacy, could be manoeuvred into collaboration, no people in the world is safe.

It happened by stages. Acting on principle, but adapting it gradually to altered circumstances, millions of respectable and women, by no means all of them Germans, became accomplices in mass-murder and received right up to the end a measure of "understanding" from their victims. The Jews, like their persecutors, had the Organization Man's fatal respect for orderliness. They had in 1935 mostly welcomed the Nuremberg Laws, because they seemed to regularize a chaotic situation and guarantee them certain limited rights. They co-operated therefore. Then these rights no longer protected them and they were advised to emigrate. Again they co-operated. The war started, frontiers closed, voluntary emigration became impossible. But new lands were available in Poland and forced evacuation – it was called "Resettlement" – became necessary. They co-operated. Finally the fourth stage, the *Endlösung* or Final Solution, was reached. By that time they had lost the art of resisting. Jewish policemen rounded them up, Jewish technicians built gas chambers, extracted gold teeth, dug graves. Jews dug them up again to destroy traces of crime and then were exterminated themselves.

But even this degree of co-operation had its apologists. For example, Chief Rabbi Baeck of Berlin, the leader of the Jewish community and a cultivated sensitive man, believed that Jewish policemen would be "more gentle and helpful" and "make the ordeal easier." And he thought that the deported should not be told the truth since "living in the expectation of gassing could only be the harder."

This was not true.

The Organization Man

Eichmann himself moved only by degrees towards the Final Solution. He never exceeded his orders or treated them cynically. To him "resettlement," till the Final Solution had been decreed by Hitler in August 1941, had always meant simply resettlement. He had studied the possibilities of Madagascar and of Nisko in Poland and he was, until the end, a great admirer of the Zionists, considering them "idealists" like himself. They were allowed great freedom of movement and were excused wearing yellow stars. He had read "the basic books," Herzl's *Der Jüdenstaat* and Böhm's *History of Zionism*; he had learnt a little Hebrew and had accepted an invitation from some Zionists to visit Palestine.

It was in Vienna, 1938 to 1939, that Eichmann, in the interests of the emigration of the Jews, perfected his system of co-operation, which he was later to use again and again for their extermination. It attracted the attention of his superiors; he was made an officer and later rose to the rank of Lieutenant-Colonel. Luck had favoured him at the start. In Vienna he found, as he was to find elsewhere, that the local Nazis had in an excess of zeal imprisoned all the leading Jews. Eichmann promptly let them out and formed them into a Jewish Council and asked them to advise him. After their experiences they were naturally very eager to leave Austria and here was Eichmann ready to help them. He got the head of the Jewish community, Dr Löwenheiz, to write down his "basic ideas" on emigration and he put Rabbi Murmelstein in charge of the Viennese scheme. Even humble Jews who knew him in those days say he was very friendly, called them "Mister" and asked them to take a seat. He worked out a plan by which the rich Jews were able to furnish money for the poor Jews to emigrate. To help "resettlement" he set aside little plots round the city, where the future settlers could practice agriculture. I think the twenty or so members of the Kagran Gruppe who came to Ireland before the war (see *The Children of Drancy*, p.197)* may have been lent the small swampy patch of land near Vienna which they tried to cultivate, on Eichmann's orders.

He was a wonderful organizer and negotiator and the Jews, at first, had reason to be pleased with him. If they wished to emigrate, they had had to fill in endless forms and stand in queues at different offices. There were officials to be bribed and insults and humiliations to be endured. Complicated inventories of property and effects had to be made out. Eichmann changed all this by assembling all the necessary offices in the one building and delegating to the Jewish Council the job of collecting in an orderly way all the data about funds and goods and furniture.

The Jews now swept rapidly through the offices, going in at one door full of problems and coming out at the other, stateless and propertyless, but with only one problem: how to get out of Austria. But here again Eichmann was at hand to help them. He had sent Jewish functionaries abroad to collect the Vorzeigegeld**, which they needed for their visas, from some Jewish Relief Society. It all ended for him triumphantly. In eight months more than twice as many Jews left Austria as left Germany in the corresponding period, and in eighteen months half the Jewish population had gone. Once in a fit of impatience at some temporary delays he had slapped Dr Löwenheiz in the face. He apologized to him in front of his staff (he was very conscious that with his commission he had become a gentleman), but he reproached himself with his rudeness to the end of his days.

If we accept that he was genuinely attached to his Jewish "helpers" we get closer to the horrible complexities of human life. Is one to laugh or cry at the story of Commercial Councillor Berthold Storfer? Abandoning his post on the Viennese Jewish Council, which guaranteed

---

* H.B., 1990.
** *Vorzeigegeld*: payment for documents and authorisations of various sorts.

him immunity from deportation, Storfer had gone into hiding. The Gestapo had ferreted him out and sent him to Auschwitz and he had persuaded the commandant to send a telegram to Eichmann appealing for his help. I have regretfully to abridge Eichmann's fascinating account of what happened then.

> I said to myself, "OK. This man has always behaved well. I'll go there myself." So off I went to Auschwitz and found Storfer in one of the labour gangs. He told me all his grief and sorrow and I said to him, "Ja, mein lieber guter Storfer, we certainly got it! What rotten luck! But what a silly thing to do to bolt, when you didn't need to! No one can be got out, once he's put in. That's Reichsführer's orders and I can't help you." Then I asked him how he was and he said he couldn't he be let off the work – it was heavy work.

Eichmann went to the commandant but was told that everyone had to work.

> So I said, "OK. I'll make out a chit saying that Storfer has to keep the gravel paths in order with a broom (there were little gravel paths there), and that he has the right to sit down with his broom on one of the benches. Will that be all right, Dr Storfer?" He shook hands and was very pleased and then he was given the broom and sat down on the bench.
>
> It was a great inner joy to me that I could at last see the man with whom I had worked for so many long years and that we could speak with each other.

Thus it happened that, through Eichmann's intervention, Dr Storfer was able to muse on a bench with his broom for six weeks before he was incinerated. This story of Eichmann and his feelings surely has the ring of truth in it.

At his trial everyone must have hoped that Eichmann would

stammer and lie and contradict himself, but he never really felt guilty or fully understood what had happened. He had been completely integrated into a criminal society so that the demands it made on him in the name of duty could not be recognized as crime. One could no more shame him than one could convince a faithful old family butler that he was "a lackey of the bourgeois" and "a traitor to his class." Just like the old butler, Eichmann always called his Nazi employers by their formal titles even after they had been hanged. For him Himmler was always "Der Reichsführer."

The lessons Eichmann learnt in Austria he applied in every other country where a Jewish Council could be established. He told them how many Jews were needed to fill the trains and the Councils made out the lists of deportees, tabulating their property so that it could be easily collected and arranging for them to board the trains. Then when all the smaller people had been gathered and taken away, the Council itself was deported and their property confiscated. They were sent to Theresienstadt, a Czech town from which the Czechs had been evicted. Privileged Jews stayed there "till overcrowding made thinning out necessary." It was an entirely self-supporting community. There was a resident Jewish hangman.

In three or four countries it was impossible to form a Jewish Council. In Belgium, for instance, all the prominent Jews who would have been appointed to it had fled before the Occupation, and there was no routine way of registering the 5000 Belgian Jews who remained. The result was that not one of them was deported.

In Holland, by contrast, appalling disaster fell upon the Jews. There was a very strong Dutch Nazi party, and the proud Dutch Jews long established there were confident that it was only the immigrants that the Nazis would dare to attack. A Jewish Council or Joodsche Raad was formed to list and assemble the deportees and Jewish police were enlisted to help the Dutch police in rounding them up. The Dutch themselves were brave and kind and as many as 25,000 Jews survived in hiding. But three-quarters of all the Jews living in Holland were killed.

The Dreams Collapse

The Nazis discovered that all the states of Europe, except Italy and two small ones (Bulgaria and Denmark), would under pressure accommodate themselves to their racial programme. Save in Romania and the East, one cannot attribute this to anti-Semitism. It is surely an aspect of modern war. As our mechanical weapons multiply, our powers of moral resistance, as though superannuated, become feebler and feebler. When the Maginot Line collapsed it looked for a time as though Eichmann could do what he liked with the French. The French prefer to forget this or there would today be some great monument at the Gare d'Austerlitz to one of the most sickening crimes in which they have ever been implicated. I wrote of this in *The Children of Drancy*.

François Mauriac has told how one grey August morning in 1942 his wife had seen crowds of children packed into cattle wagons at the station. There were 4051 of them between the ages of two and fifteen. They had been seized with their parents in July and kept for four days without food at the Vélodrôme d'Hiver. Then their parents were moved to Auschwitz and the children were to follow but there were transport difficulties and they were detained for ten days in the camp at Drancy, north of Paris. Compassionate policemen handled them and sad little stories are told by neighbours who heard the children crying every night across the camp. There was a little girl with a bleeding ear who had not been quick enough in removing her earrings when the children and their bags and parcels were being inspected for valuables.

Such stories seem obscene, for has one a right to witness such things and survive? Bus-drivers, engine-drivers and porters were all deeply moved but a dozen trainloads of children rolled on across France and Germany and Poland. No one stopped them. At the end of August the children were incinerated.

Mauriac wrote that the an era had ended for him that day at the Gare d'Austerlitz. The dream of a happy future to be attained through science and enlightenment, which the thinkers of the eighteenth century had conceived, had dissolved forever. Some era certainly should have ended there but which and how? The Nazis who ordered the deportation of the children, the Vichy government which sanctioned it (the authorization came from Laval), were hostile to the dreams of the Enlightenment. On the other hand the Danes, who alone resisted the Nazi racial policy on principle, are often scolded for their prosy devotion to the Age of Reason. The issue is by no means clear.

It was in Hungary that Eichmann achieved his most spectacular successes, and it was here too that he demonstrated most clearly that he was not a monster but merely the well-adjusted child of a monstrous age.

The Hungarians had first of all in 1941 been too impetuous, hurling some thousands of foreign Jews into occupied Russia before the Germans had camps and extermination facilities prepared for them. They had had to take them back into Hungary and kill them themselves.

The next year they had been equally unco-operative, for though the Hungarian government had agreed to the deportation of a further 300,000 refugee Jews, they would not surrender their own 500,000 native Jews, even though Eichmann explained that it would be too costly to set up the elaborate machinery of evacuation for one category of Jew alone. On grounds of economy the purge was postponed for two years. But in March 1944 the Germans occupied Hungary because, with the Red Army approaching through the Carpathians, they feared that Hungary might sue for a separate peace. It is surprising that at such a moment they should have bothered with "the liquidation of the Jewish problems," but they did. The problem had by now become colossal. Including converted Jews, there were now about 950,000 to be evacuated. The Russians were approaching and everybody knew by now that evacuation meant murder. The Zionists, more realistic than the others, had publicized the truth to the world, and the world was aghast.

But Eichmann knew that his moment had come. He arrived in Budapest with a large staff of typists and ten officials and he summoned his experts from all the occupied countries. He had expected difficulties but in fact, as he was later to recall, everything went "like a dream";

the Hungarian police were co-operative and the government friendly and helpful, and most astonishing of all, he had gathered his Jewish Council together in a fortnight and had persuaded a prominent Jewish Privy Councillor, Dr Stern, to act as president. Never before had there been so great an exchange of small courtesies between the murderers and their victims. Typewriters and pictures were wanted to furnish the new office and the transport offices. Herr Novak, who was musical, wanted a piano. Original Watteaus came and eight pianos. Novak laughingly returned seven. "Gentlemen! Gentlemen! I'm not opening a piano store. I merely want to play the piano." Eichmann himself visited the Jewish library and the Jewish museum and had constant meetings with Zionists. Even at this stage he appeared to have persuaded himself and others that he wished "to be fair to both sides." It was all temporary, he explained.

The vast enterprise, so often repeated, seemed now to be working of its own momentum. There had been conferences in Vienna with the officials of the German State Railways and a new branch line was constructed so that the freight cars could come within a few yards of the crematoria. The personnel at the gas chambers had been quadrupled, so that it was possible to kill about 10,000 every day. Messrs Krupp had their representatives there to salvage able-bodied Jews for their Auschwitz fuse factory. The Reichsbank, the army, the Foreign Office, the mint, industry, everything was geared to the smooth fulfilment of the Führer's tremendous dream.

In two months 147 trains carried 434,351 Jews to Auschwitz, yet by good organization the gas chambers were just able to cope with this vast and sudden influx. In the East the Russians were still advancing but even the German generals could not clear the lines for their retreating armies. They were choked with freight cars carrying Jews.

Yet Eichmann had difficulties. They came not from the Jews, but from one of the SS officials in his own entourage. He had offended against all that Eichmann held most dear, for was not the motto of the SS, "MY HONOUR IS MY LOYALTY"? Dr Becher, now a prosperous merchant in Bremen, was secretly sabotaging the Führer's dream and Himmler was behind him. Now that the war was going badly it had seemed to Himmler more politic and more profitable to sell Jews to relief committees than to kill them. The compassion of the Allies could be turned into trucks and food and arms for their destruction. But of course the idealists, the Führer and Eichmann, must not know. To mollify Eichmann, just in case he should hear of it, Dr Becher gave him a chaffuer-driven amphibious car. Meanwhile, he was able to sell 1684 Jews for 1000 dollars each and had prospects of 20 million Swiss francs from the American Joint Distribution Committee. On behalf of Himmler he had taken over some vast Hungarian-Jewish factories for aeroplanes and bicycles and in return had given the panic-stricken owners free passage to Portugal and some foreign currency.

To Eichmann, when he heard of it, this was all "Schweinerei" and gross betrayal of the Hungarians who were paying the cost per capita for the deportation and extermination of the Jews and were entitled by agreement to inherit all their property. He was beside himself.

Every day the Russians drew nearer and Hungarians and Germans became progressively more "moderate" in their views. At last Admiral Horthy, the head of the government, stopped all further deportations and arrangements were made for dismantling the gas chambers. Only Eichmann remained loyal to his Führer and in June 1944 by a clever ruse he got the better of Horthy and, illegally, sent one last transport of 1500 to Auschwitz.

After that Auschwitz was closed and even Eichmann had to realize that "ideals" must be abandoned. The tottering Reich was in need of labour. Eichmann promised 50,000 able-bodied Jews and Jewesses, but there were no trains to take them, so in November 1944 he made them walk. The nature of these "dead marches" need not be described.

When on 13 February 1945 Hungary capitulated to the British army, less than 160,000 out of nearly a million Hungarian Jews remained alive.

Grounds for Hope

Is decency that is unarmed quite helpless in a modern war? I would like to hurry on to the proof that it is not. But the evidence for the other side is still far from complete.

When northern Greece was occupied by the Germans, Eichmann sent two trusted officials to Salonika in February 1943. There were 55,000 Jews there, many of whom had lived in Greece for centuries. Eichmann's two colleagues met with wonderful co-operation from the German military governor, Dr Marten, and soon were able to persuade Chief Rabbi Koretz to gather a Jewish Council. All the Jews were quickly concentrated near the railway station, and within two months the entire community, except the staff of the Council and a few others, had been evacuated to Auschwitz. Dr Marten and the Nazis met with great "understanding" from the Greeks, and soon after the war he returned there to run a travel agency. He was arrested in 1959 and sentenced to twenty-five years' imprisonment, but as it was feared that his detention might injure the Graeco-German tobacco trade he was immediately released. He now lives in West Germany; he is loyal to his old colleagues and always ready to bear false witness on their behalf. He tried to help Eichmann by testifying that he had saved 20,000 Salonika Jews. This surprised Eichmann considerably as he had never been there.

The Romanians showed even more "understanding" than the Greeks. Antonescu, the dictator, had, on joining the Axis, initiated such enthusiastic and ill-organized massacres of Jews that Eichmann himself urged the Foreign Office to intervene. The Romanians were proposing to dump 110,000 Jews across the river Bug in German-occupied Russia, where there were as yet no proper facilities for orderly extermination. They had invaded Russia too and begun vast pogroms there, killing 60,000 Jews in Odessa alone. Of their own native Jews they had killed 270,000 without German help, but in such a scandalous and disorderly way, sometimes exposing them on meat-hooks in butchers' shops, that Eichmann decided he must direct the final operations himself. To do this he had to rearrange his entire schedule, for Jewish problems were being settled from west to east and Romanian Jews would normally not have engaged his attention till much later. He persuaded the German railroads to organize transport for a further 200,000 Jews to the extermination camp at Lublin; all was prepared when he learnt that Antonescu had let him down and his labour was for nothing.

No Jews were to be sent to Lublin. Antonescu had hit upon an idea, later to be copied by Himmler in Budapest. He had found that by emigrating Jews to Palestine he could collect thirteen dollars a head from foreign relief committees. Overnight he became a Zionist.

All over Europe people sheltered Jews. Many met anonymous deaths on their behalf and the Jews themselves, in scattered groups, particularly in Poland, fought back courageously. But most men need the stimulus of publicity for their heroism, and courage can be sapped by censoring every evidence of it. The Jewish fighters in the East got neither aid nor recognition from the Allies and the fact that they existed is now an embarrassment to be forgotten, even by the Jews themselves. Terrible reprisals were taken on the whole Jewish community for any act of resistance, so the Jewish Councils, believing that death could be avoided by diplomacy, surrendered their more militant members first for deportation.

As for the Germans, the names of only three German heroes recurred at the Jerusalem trial. There was the Lutheran, Propst Grüber, the Catholic, Dompropst Lichtenberg, and Sergeant Anton Schmidt, the last two of whom were executed. There was no mention of the "Inner Emigration," those who claimed that they were best able to modify the Nazi movement by taking part in it. Dr Globke, for instance, Under-Secretary of State in the West German Chancery, was once, in his Nazi days, able to defend insulted Czech womanhood. They had been obliged to show nude photographs of themselves before marriage to a German soldier could be licensed. Dr Globke signed a new decree permitting them to wear bathing dresses. He has never had the gratitude that he thinks he deserves.

Miss Arendt believes that by exaggerating the blackness of Eichmann the Jerusalem court managed to bleach the dirty grey background against which he worked. Every social institution was implicated in crime. One instance of this should suffice. Like Krupps and I.G. Farben and many other large firms, Siemens Schückert, the engineers of the Shannon Scheme, set up factories at Auschwitz and Lublin for the employment of slave labour, paying the SS four to six marks a head for them at Ravensbruck. The intention of the camp authorities was to kill by toil. We do not know the figures for Siemens, but Raul Hilberg in *The Destruction of European Jews* says that about 25,000 out of 35,000 who worked for one of the I.G. Farben plants, died.

Yet one can end this record hopefully. One does not, in fact, have to be as tactful as Dr Globke or as business-like as Messrs Siemen and the Greeks in order to survive and win respect. Proof of this comes from three countries. The Italians and Bulgarians passed anti-Jewish laws but ceaselessly sabotaged them, whereas the Danes resolutely refused to take any part whatever in the campaign against the Jews. The story of Danish resistance cannot be told too often since it proves that a helpless defeated people can, by non-violent action, defend its integrity better than many a powerful military state. The government threatened to resign rather than legalize any measures against the Jews, immigrant or native. If the wearing of the yellow star were enforced, the King would be the first to wear it. The Germans accepted this decision until August 1943, when orders came from Hitler himself that all the Jews in Denmark were to be deported.

What happened then was astonishing. The German officials, who had lived for some years in Denmark, were themselves infected by the spirit of resistance and even the Jews took heart and courage. The German military commander refused to put troops at the disposal of Dr Best, the German governor, and Best himself showed an amazing lack of zeal. Seeking for a compromise he went to Berlin and secured a promise that all the Jews in Denmark would be sent to the camp for "privileged Jews" in Theresienstadt.

It was privately arranged that they were to be arrested on 1 October and put on board the ships, which were waiting for them. But a German shipping agent warned the Danish government, and the government warned the leading Jews, who spread the news through the synagogues. All withdrew to hiding-places prepared for them in Danish homes. When the German police called, they found only 477 Jews out of 7800 at home. Shortly afterwards the Danes used their fishing fleet to transfer them to Sweden and paid the cost of transport (about 100 dollars a head) themselves.

In Bulgaria, as in Denmark, the German officials took their colour from their surroundings. The ambassador and his police attaché advised the Foreign Office that the situation was hopeless. The Bulgarians were showing no "understanding" at all. The Jews next caught the contagion of "non-co-operation" and when in 1943 Eichmann's agent, Dannecker, arrived in Sofia, he totally failed to form a Jewish Council. He could not even make contact with the chief Rabbi, who was being sheltered by the Metropolitan, Stephan. Not a single native Jew was deported from Bulgaria*.

The example of Denmark and Bulgaria shows that unanimous disapproval, openly expressed, still has power and that in a small country the art of non-co-operation should be studied more than any other branch of civil defence.

Can one argue that in small countries, where anonymity is difficult, the Organization Man cannot operate freely? Either he does not exist, as in simple Bulgaria, or his mechanism is fully understood, as in sophisticated Denmark. Croats, Greeks and Romanians do not fit too well into this pattern, and it is easier to diagnose the vast apathy of the great bourgeois states. Science is partly to blame. Every invention produces a counter-invention and, to match the speed of communication, there are devices for not-knowing which our ancestors never dreamt of. The

---

* However, the Bulgarian authorities did agree to the deportation of Jews on their occupied territories (Yugoslav or "Serbian" Macedonia, and Southern Thrace), who were thus rounded up by Bulgarian officials and deported to Treblinka. (Editors)

press and the radio have superseded oral communications and are much easier to control and the committee habit helps by endlessly deferring and delegating. And, of course, the specialist has his sound-proof bolt-hole.

If one were to choose the three most murderous affabilities of the twentieth century, what would they be? I would give first place to: "I'm a simple gas-fitter (engine-driver, dentist, nuclear physicist). I do my job and mind my own business."

Less obvious, perhaps, is: "I felt so sorry about Einstein (or poor Miss Cohen)." This enables amiable people to swallow their indignation by mincing it up into mouthfuls.

And finally, of course: "Why rake it all up again? It only makes bad blood."

(1962)

Rebecca West In Yugoslavia

I am glad that this famous book (1941) has been reissued.* Emotional, digressive, highly subjective, it will always puzzle and infuriate the professional historian, yet in no other way could Rebecca West have recreated so perfectly a vanished era, as well as a country and a people, which have been changed beyond recognition. When she made her journey round Yugoslavia in the late thirties, the glow of hope and excitement that had gilded the years after the First World War had not faded. Though the League of Nations was dead, the PEN Club dowdy and the *Wandervogel* sinister, those who have lived through that springtime can never forget it. Miss West writes of the ecstasies of the newly liberated peoples:

> They were all like young men stretching themselves at the open window in the early morning after long sleep. To eat in public places in these countries, to walk in their public gardens, was to fill the nostrils with the smell of happiness. Nothing so fair has happened in all history as this liberation of peoples, who during centuries of oppression had never forgotten their own souls.

---

* Rebecca West, *Black Lamb and Grey Falcon.* (Editors)

All the succession states, the Irish Free State included, had been carved out of one or more powerful empires, and each one was confident that the genius of the land and its ancient culture could assimilate all those of their fellow citizens whose traditions were different.

The fact that the alien soul could be captivated was not a delusion. Just as Ireland owed much of its cultural nationalism to men of English and Anglo-Irish descent, so it was that the submerged culture of all the Slav subjects of the German, Austrian and Russian empires had first been roused by foreigners, like Johann Herder, a Prussian, and the Catholic Bishop Strossmayer of Djakovo, an Austrian. Miss West devotes several pages to this far-seeing and generous patron of Croats and Serbs. These men were all humanists and the arrogant racialism to which their teachings sometimes seemed to lead would have appalled them.

Soon after Miss West returned home all these once young and happy peoples had been engulfed in the Nazi empire. To what extent were they themselves to blame? This is a question that Miss West frequently asks. Like Thucydides, she tells much of her story in dialogue, real people making unreal speeches to each other, long, shapely and logical. Croat talks to Serb, Orthodox to Catholic, Christian to Moslem, and her husband, whom I remember as articulate and intelligent but not given to page-long monologues, draws suitable conclusions.

As it seems to me that they are usually right, I do not quarrel with this artform. We are kept in touch with reality by Gerda, their German travelling-companion who is agonizingly true to life. Arrogant and stupid, she is like an early blueprint of a Belsen wardress.

In the twenties, the small self-governing state, forging anew its cultural identity, had seemed the only answer to imperialism, Communism and international capitalism, yet hardly any small people were ready to grant to others the liberty they claimed for themselves. Instead they toadied to the big ones and despised each other. Arthur Griffith's book, *The Resurrection of Hungary, A Parallel for Ireland*, was ominous, for Hungary, defending her culture against the Austrians, trampled on all the small peoples, Serbs, Croats, Slovaks (Griffith calls them "the

Slav hordes"), that came within her power. To quote Miss West: "Kossuth declared he would suppress the Croatian language by the sword and introduced an electoral bill that omitted the name of Croatia and described her departments as Hungarian counties."

Miss West, who once told me she is Irish by birth, writes elsewhere (thirty years ago, remember): "The nationalism of Ireland and Hungary have always been intense but Hungary has always been industrially ambitious and resolute both in maintaining a feudal land system and in opposing the alien within her frontiers, while Ireland, though she desires to annihilate Ulster, wishes to be a peasant state with industries well within manageable proportions."

As for the Croat-Serb tensions, it is Henry Andrews, who brings a long dialogue to a conclusion:

> "Is it not the tragedy of the situation here," suggested my husband to Valetta, "that you Croats are for the first time discovering that your religion and your race run counter to one another and that you are able to evade that discovery by putting the blame on the constitution of Yugoslavia? The Croats, like all Slavs, are a democratic and speculative people. You lived for long under the Habsburgs, whom you could blame for everything... Now the Habsburgs are swept away you should see the Roman Catholic Church as it is; not at all democratic, not at all in favour of speculative thought... You should proceed to the difficult task of deciding whether you can reconcile yourself to this bias of the Church for the sake of the spiritual benefits it confers on you. But you are postponing this task by letting the Church throw the blame for all its suppressions of free speech and free press on Belgrade."

I am sorry that Miss West, who used Valetta, a mutual friend, as a spokesman for the Croats, overlooks his colleague Dr Milan Curcin, the editor of *Nova Evropa*, a man of much greater stature. A Serb, living in Croatia and a convinced Yugoslav, he saw his country's racial and

religious problems against a European background. A PEN Club enthusiast in the challenging days of H.G. Wells, he came to Ireland from the
Edinburgh Conference to harvest impressions that he could use in
Croatia ("the Ulster of Yugoslavia"). He wanted to come back, when
the Conference was in Dublin, but Yugoslavia was in disgrace here at
that time and I could not get an invitation for him.

In her epilogue Rebecca West tells magnificently of Yugoslavia's
epic resistance to Hitler. Though its army was overwhelmed after three
days, guerrilla war burst out spontaneously in the mountains and
played a noble part in Hitler's defeat.

Yet it was those first three days that electrified Europe. "The news
that Hitler had been defied by Yugoslavia travelled like sunshine over
the countries that he had devoured and humiliated, promising Spring."

It is on this note that the book ends. With all its faults it is surely a
memorable work, and after more than thirty years has lost nothing of
its freshness and vigour.

(1977)

A Three-Day Nation: Alexei Gierowski and Carpatho-Russia

I've always been a nationalist and believed that small nations have been less likely to be corrupt than large ones; and the fact that most of the small nations that were born or revived in the early twenties have appeared to be mediocre or commonplace or ended disastrously in 1945 has not utterly disillusioned me. AE was always reminding us that Attica was no larger than Tipperary and Athens no bigger than Clonmel, and yet he would have argued, if he had not died disillusioned in Bournemouth, that the one million of Athens produced Pericles and Socrates and that the two hundred million of the USA produced President Reagan.

Now I know that is a phoney argument; it is not size that dwarfs us but some cosmic malady which attacks even quite small communities. When I was in the USA I was captivated by the single-minded dedication of an elderly Russian called Alexei Gierowski. He had spent all his life campaigning for the freedom of his native country, Carpatho-Russia, and when I first met him in the sixties the game was up. Carpatho-Russia, which had been ruled by Czechs, Slovaks and Hungarians, had been swallowed by the Soviet Union in 1945, after less than a week of the freedom that Gierowski had secured for it*.

---

* Carpatho-Russia (also known as Carpatho-Ukraine, Sub-Carpathian Ruthenia, and at least half a dozen other names) is a region in the Carpathians. Its territory, as

It was natural that in New York, that city of a hundred races, I should want to meet a Russian with whom I could walk and talk. But how I came across Alexei Gierowski I cannot recall. He had only one fault, which was shared by all the Russians I knew. He liked walking and he like talking, but his Russian was so much better than my Russian that it was torture for him to harness his natural flow of speech to my understanding. And so we spoke English as we walked, sometimes round Central Park, sometimes round Karl Schurtz, or in cold weather in his flat on Beekman Place.

How much talent New York has sheltered! How much it has extinguished! It has been an honour but also a tragedy to be the chief English-speaking recipient, still alive, of Gierowski's knowledge and wisdom. He gave me, as they came out monthly, copies of all the issues of the journal he edited in Newark, New Jersey, *Svobodnoye Slovo (Free Word)*. I have some seventy issues and I believe that only about ten are missing. I know the difficulties that faced him in New York. Sometimes, when he told a story about what happened to him there, I asked him to write it down. (This was wise as it is now thirty years ago and I would certainly have forgotten it.)

It seems to me that his little fatherland vanished from a combination of all the ingredients which, in doses variously compounded, have afflicted all our countries: race, religion, language, and the political use that can be made of them. Carpatho-Russia was, until 1914, a tiny territory on the eastern frontier of Austria-Hungary. Its basic population was Russian, as was Galicia to the north and Bukovina to the south. The Austro-Hungarian Empire was composed of many small distinct

---

understood in the Orthodox Christian tradition, is currently divided between Slovakia, Ukraine, Poland, Hungary and Romania. Whilst previously Russian Orthodox, its people (often known as Ruthenians or Rusyns, traditionally speaking Eastern Slavonic dialects) are now predominantly Eastern Catholic. More generally, the Eastern Slavonic world (sometimes called "Rus") has four traditonal branches: Russians (once known as Great Russians), Ukranians (once known as Little Russians), Belarussians (or White Russians), and the stateless Carpatho-Russians.

peoples, mainly Slavs, and several religions: Roman Catholic, Orthodox, Protestant and Uniat. There were frequent rebellions, but the
people with which she found it hardest to deal were the Russian Orthodox who lived along her eastern frontier. Behind this frontier stretched
the Russian Empire, prone to consider herself the patron and protector
of most of the Slavs and of all the Russians beyond her borders, her
kindred and co-religionists.

Austria-Hungary, whose fate was sealed at Sarajevo, had been like
a well-organized household: the Austrians had been the landlords, the
Hungarians the stewards; the Czechs had been the butlers and house-
keepers; Croats, Romanians, Serbs and Wallachians were the outdoor
staff. The Carpatho-Russians were not considered to have a country at
all. They were foresters and gamekeepers on the estates of Hungarian
barons and Czech bankers on holiday in ski-resorts in the Carpathians.
Yet there were, in fact, upper-class and middle-class Carpatho-Russians, Russian-speaking and proud to be the countrymen of Tolstoy
and Pushkin. Many of them had found it intolerable to be patronized
by the Czechs and deprived of the rights of self-government that President Wilson had granted them in 1919. They emigrated in vast numbers
to the United States and it was there that a flourishing movement for
independence began. Its leader was my friend Gierowski.

There was a reason why both Austria-Hungary and Czechoslovakia
insisted that Carpatho-Russia was Ukrainian, not Russian (they called
it Carpatho-Ukraine), and Catholic, not Orthodox. The western neighbours of both Czarist and Soviet Russia hoped that in a successful war
the Ukraine, the richest province of Russia, would fall to them. When
war broke out in 1914 a leading Austro-Hungarian general called Count
Szepticki, who was also a Catholic archbishop, wrote a memorandum
about it. He maintained that the Ukraine should be assimilated to
Austria-Hungary when their armies had successfully conquered it. This
scheme fell into the hands of the Russians who published it in Moscow
and Petrograd.

Gierowski, a Russian who was never subject either to the Czar or
to Stalin, recounted this scheme from the standpoint of Carpatho-Rus-

sia, his native land, which had struggled vainly for independence from both the Austrians and the Czechs.

At the end of the war, almost unobserved, Carpatho-Russia was taken over by the Soviet Union. Gierowski's struggle for himself and his people to be Russian, not Ukrainian, Orthodox, not Catholic or Uniat, democratic, not Communist, probably failed; but how could one tell without going to see? I decided to go and wrote to the USSR Embassy in London. I was sent about fifty coloured pictures of Carpatho-Russia. Gierowski, who by now was dead, had never thought of telling me what I might have guessed, that it was very beautiful. Its beauty is of the marketable kind; one photograph shows some well-dressed people having dinner by candlelight (the electricity only shines at the cash desk) in a cave in the Carpathian mountains. I don't believe the waiters in their black dinner-jackets speak either Lemkovsky or Boekovsky (the Carpatho-Russian dialects spoken by Gierowski's parents), or Ukrainian or ordinary Russian, but probably some tourist language – English, French or German. After seeing that picture I never wanted to go there.

The new nations born in 1919 out of the three dissolved empires lasted till Adolf Hitler shattered them twenty-one years later. By the Treaty of Versailles not only was their freedom and independence guaranteed but, as very few were peopled by a single homogenous race, the dominant races pledged to give a measure of independence to all those smaller peoples whose language and culture were different. But these pledges were seldom observed.

Thus in Czechoslovakia the Czechs were pledged to give a measure of independence to the two million Sudeten Germans on its western frontiers. The Czechs failed to do this, so Hitler was able to appear as a deliverer when he invaded Czechoslovakia and assimilated the Sudeten Germans to Germany. A similar pledge had been given to the Carpatho-Russians who peopled the easternmost prong of Czechoslovakia that extends into the Russian Ukraine.

It is of this small country that I am writing. Its history is complicated, for just as the human body is composed of a multitude of complex cells, so every section of a section is multi-cellular. Alexei Gierowski was a member of the Russian Orthodox Church, whose dogma he never questioned. Though I don't share his beliefs, I do not find it theatrical to think of him as a soldier of Christ who was always fighting for the truth. But he is different from those hymn-book heroes who battle against the powers of evil in the valley of Jehosophat. He fought real people – editors, bishops, ambassadors – and real lies in real places: America, Hungary and, most passionately, in his native land Carpatho-Russia.

He was not self-righteous about himself or his Church, but he found inspiration and entertainment in ecclesiastical wickedness, and though he must have been over eighty when we met, he often laughed in a happy youthful way when he related some particularly monstrous story. He shared my belief that the ecumenists are on the wrong track. What is most likely to unite us is not the spectacle of a pope embracing a patriarch or a heretical archbishop, or the return of St Andrew's skull to Petras or some holy keepsake from Byzantium to Rome. We have to venture out from the well-kept museum of symbols on to the junk-heap of cast-off clothes, broken crockery and maggoty corpses which is history. We all know, inside ourselves, what love is or should be; it is hate, corruption and hypocrisy that we need to see objectively from outside, to poke at, dissect and analyze. They are the same everywhere. It is in small everyday occurrences that we reveal what we are like. All Gierowski's stories are full of elaborate and fascinating detail.

I will [not] follow him around with a gazetteer and an encyclopaedia explaining him. I will plunge into the middle.

We were walking in a small grove of trees in front of the Museum of Natural History on the West Side, which my grandchildren were exploring.

"What I can't understand," I said, "is why the Orthodox of Carpatho-Russia should have been under the protection of Belgrade and why Bishop Dositheus, a Serb, should have been their diocesan bishop? Carpatho-Russia is in Czechoslovakia, not Yugoslavia."

"That happened after 1919, when Carpatho-Russia was taken away from Austria-Hungary and then federated with Czechoslovakia, and Sremski-Karlovac – the site of the Orthodox See – was at that time also taken from Austria-Hungary but given to Yugoslavia. The Czechs found it intolerable that subjects of theirs – and that is what they considered the Carpatho-Russians – should be in the diocese of a foreign bishop, and they were as obstructive as they could be. By the Treaty of St Germain Carpatho-Russia was entitled to the same autonomy that Slovenia enjoyed, but the Czechs cheated us of it and played every possible trick to deprive us of our Russian nationality and our Orthodox faith, to which we had adhered for centuries. Like the Austrians and Hungarians before them, they wished to sever our link with Russia and represented us to everybody as Ukrainians and Uniats."

"Yes, that explains Smyllie's book," I said. "When he was editor of *The Irish Times* he wrote a book called *Carpathian Nights*, quite good but all seen through the eyes of his Czech guides. To him, all the Carpatho-Russians were Ukrainian."

"Well, you've seen our people here in America," Gierowski said, "and you know they speak Russian and mostly worship in the Orthodox churches. And you know our Carpatho-Russian monthly here, and you know that it is all printed in Russian: verse, prose, everything. We are able to keep it going because ours is the most vigorous of the Orthodox communities in the USA; we have been emigrating here for years, trying to escape first from the Austrians and Hungarians and then from the Czechs. There was constant pressure to make us Uniats. I've told you, haven't I, how when I was a boy there was a policeman always in a back pew, watching to see that the priest introduced the "filioque" clause. It was only in America that we could call ourselves what we really were."

"Yes, but Dositheus was a Serb, not a Carpatho-Russian. How did you like having him as bishop?"

"We always had our own bishop, as I said, from Sremski Karlovac.

We accepted him gladly, and he lived for four years in Ize, our holy city, because the Serbs had always acknowledged our faith and our nationality. He became my friend and when I was arrested by the Czechs an expelled from my own country, the Serbs accepted me. They made me legal adviser on Carpatho-Russian affairs to the Holy Synod in Belgrade. I knew Dositheus well long before he became the Metropolitan of Croatia. He was always striving for unity among the Orthodox, since he considered it the only way in which we could survive."

"I thought," I interrupted, "that your great strength was that you are not closely united, that the Patriarch in Constantinople is only *primus inter pares* and had only spiritual authority."

"That is our strength, certainly, but in desperate times like ours it can be a weakness also. Dositheus saw what was coming and it was his dream to strengthen the Serbian Orthodox by uniting us with the Bulgarian Church. King Alexander listened to him and sent him and me to Sofia. He had a good pretext. There had been an earthquake in Bulgaria, and to relieve its victims Dositheus was entrusted with several million dinars."

"But you were a Carpatho-Russian."

"Yes, that's why I was sent. If the king sent a Yugoslav official, he would have committed himself and there was some opposition to the idea. But we nearly brought it off. We met the Bulgarian Patriarch of Sofia as well as the prime minister and afterward it was agreed that we should have alternating patriarchs. When the present one, who was old, died, he would be succeeded by a young man who would prepare the way, and after him there would be a Serb, who would be ready for the union of our two countries and our two Churches."

"But what about the King of Bulgaria?"

"Oh, he wouldn't have been a difficulty. He's just a German. We've got rid of a king before now. We sent him to Rumania after the Turkish-Russian war. That is what we'd do again, but of course we'll have to get Macedonian support."

"But aren't they very hostile to Serbia?"

"Yes, because the Serbs occupied the greater part of Macedonia. But the prime minister was a Macedonian and he put me in touch with their leader who was from Skopje. I had plenty of friends in Bulgaria who had been educated with me at the University of Czernowitz. He showed me the house where he had been born and where his brother, a Yugoslav citizen, still lived. It was one of those century-old houses with plenty of windows. To the Macedonians it seemed a friendly solution of their problems. We would all call ourselves quite accurately Yugoslavs – Southern Slavs – and the Bulgarian and Macedonian languages would rank with Serb and Slovene as variants of our mother-tongue.

"So Dositheus and I returned to Belgrade full of hope. But King Alexander, who had encouraged us, looked depressed. "We'll have to take account of our allies," he said, and I knew he was thinking of Czechs and French and the Little Entente. Yugoslavia would have been menacingly large. Then Dositheus went to the foreign minister who had been educated in France and, being half-Jewish, had a cosmopolitan outlook and an amazingly varied career. The minister received him courteously, listened to all he said and replied not a word. He said a polite good-bye. And that was all. The dream was over."

"It would have made the Orthodox Church overwhelmingly large in Yugoslavia," I said, "but would the patriarch in Constantinople have agreed to the abolition of the Bulgarian patriarchate?"

"Oh, the poor patriarch!" he exclaimed. "He'd have hated it. But he couldn't have done anything. You know, in 1919 there were 700,000 Christians in Istanbul, but by that time there were only about 50,000. The rest had been chased out by the Turks in 1926. He was helpless. When the Czechs wanted his blessing on a newly created Czech patriarch – which the vast majority of the Orthodox, being Carpatho-Russian and looking to the Serbs for their patriarch, did not want – they secured his assent with a large sum of money. He's not a free agent. The Turks are thinking now of driving a main road right through the Phanar, the Christian district of Constantinople and seat of the patriarchate, and it would not even be necessary to bribe him. He had to make all those ecumenical gestures in the press, but they mean nothing at all."

"Did the Yugoslav patriarch agree with Dositheus' plan for Bulgaria?"

"Oh, entirely. He is very old, as I mentioned. In about 1934 he made Dositheus the first metropolitan of Croatia. When it had been a province of Austria-Hungary, the Habsburgs had never allowed one there, even though a quarter of the population was Orthodox. Archbishop Bauer and his successor Stepinac resented it deeply, though there was a Catholic bishop in Belgrade, where only one per cent of the people was Catholic. I told Dositheus, "Look out! They'll give you a dog's life," but he replied, "I must do what I'm told." I saw him year later and he told me that stones had been thrown through his window and he was often insulted in the street. Women shouted after him "Yarats!," which means "billy-goat," because of his beard. They bleated after him and spat. At that time, of course, because his efforts to unite the Bulgarian and Yugoslav Churches had been frustrated by the French and Czechs, the Macedonians were in revolt. They would have been pacified by such a union – they were midway culturally, as you know, between Serbs and Bulgars. This gave Pavelitch his opportunity. He had a choice of Macedonian terrorists at his disposal for the assassination of King Alexander, which he had planned with the help of Italians and Hungarians: there was an Ustashe training camp at Yanka Puszta in Hungary. The plan was for Pavelitch to arrange the assassination in France, while Artukovitch went to London, so as to be ready to act there, if the Paris plan failed. It didn't fail."

All this had been common knowledge in Yugoslavia for years, but it had come to me in a newspaper wrapping, which Gierowski was able to peel off.

"One day after Pavelitch and Artukovitch had come to power with Nazi help and had started on the destruction of the Orthodox Church, I had a dream here in New York. I saw Dositheus stand before me, very pale and erect. He said nothing and then disappeared."

"You were just worrying about him," I said – for what I like best about Gierowski is a certain prosy factuality. I did not like him to look for supernatural reasons for his everyday solicitude and common sense.

"Yes, I was worrying, so I went to Konstantin Fotich, the Yugoslav ambassador in Washington. He advised me to write for news of Dositheus to Dr Tibor Pataky, a Protestant in the Hungarian government, who had relations in Carpatho-Russia and a strong sympathy for the Orthodox. I wrote twice but got no reply. However, the next time I was visiting the embassy I nearly collided with a stranger, who was just leaving Fotich's study. "Stop!" Fotich called out to him, "Here's the very man who needs you." The stranger proved to be a Viennese Jewish doctor, who recoiled from me at first, like all the people who have escaped from Hitler's Reich. He suddenly warmed to me when Fotich mentioned Dositheus. The Serbs, he said, had done their best for him and made him the doctor in the gaol when the Nazis reached Belgrade so he need never be seen in the street. One day, while he was there, two SS men brought in the Metropolitan Dositheus, breathing heavily and covered with bruises. "We found him," the SS men said, "in gaol in nothing but his underwear, but as we were told he was a Serbian bishop we brought him to Belgrade." I sent him straight off to Dr Zhivk-hovitch's nursing home, but then I had to escape to Greece myself so that is the last I saw of him."

"Didn't you hear anymore?" I asked Gierowski.

"Well, I wrote to the Metropolitan Joseph, the *locum tenens* for the patriarch, who had been imprisoned in Dachau because of his resistance to the Nazis, and he told me that he had visited Dositheus in the nursing home. His memory had gone, and though they had been old school-fellows he could not recognize Joseph. But some time before he died he recovered himself briefly and told how he had been beaten in the streets in Zagreb and how the women had been the worst. When I heard this, I remembered how concerned he always was about the subjection of women in Yugoslavia."

"Is it possible that Stepinac and the other Catholic bishops knew nothing of the assault of Dositheus?"

"Of course he knew!" Gierowski snapped back.

"I can understand – sort of – why Stepinac and the other Catholic bishops held their tongues, but why were the Serbian Orthodox themselves so silent about a religious massacre of such vast size and significance? They might feel that whatever they said in Yugoslavia would be given a Communist slant, so had better be left unsaid, but once they got to England and America they were free. Why wasn't this broadcast twenty years ago?"

"You don't understand the situation here. I once went to *The New York Times* about an editorial which I knew to be false and the editorial-writer just said, "Yes, I know it's a lie but we just can't afford to say what really happened.""

"I suppose they were frightened they'd lose advertisements. I was told that one page in *The New York Times* might cost $7,000."

"Oh, that wouldn't be the reason. Most of the big firms like Macy's are Jewish and wouldn't mind. It's just that even *The New York Times* couldn't risk being boycotted. The only paper that dared to write about the massacres was the Protestant paper *The Churchman*, which Guy Shipley edited, and you know what happened to me when I wrote in it about Dositheus, and at another time about Stepinac?"

He had told me, but I asked him to write out his experiences in his own words.

I was an employee of the Berlitz School of Languages for seven years. I started with writing an Italian self-teacher. After I had completed about half of it, I became a teacher of Russian. In addition to giving Russian lessons I wrote the Berlitz self-teacher and a Russian grammar.

The Berlitz School no longer belongs to the Berlitz family, but is a joint-stock company. The majority of shares belonged to a Mr Strumpen-Darrie, who had his office in the school and was the "commander-in-chief." He was German-born, a Bavarian and a devout Roman Catholic. He went every day to church across the street, St Patrick's Cathedral, where he prayed on his knees with a rosary in his hands. His wife, the former Miss Darrie, was British-born, educated in Catholic boarding-schools in England and France. She was a fanatical Roman Catholic. And so was their son, who was born in the United States and educated in Jesuit schools...

Mr Strumpen-Darrie had his office in the school. Then there was a gentleman who had married Strumpen-Darrie's daughter. He had been a Protestant but converted in order to marry a Strumpen-Darrie. Mrs Strumpen-Darrie had no room of her own, but she was there every day and meddled in everything. It was a family affair: four Strumpen-Darries...

It was after the last war that I joined the school. Most of the several hundred students were veterans and the government paid for them. There were about forty classrooms on one floor in Rockefeller Center. No doubt a big business...

Strumpen-Darrie often called me just for the purpose of chatting about European politics. He was very much impressed by the fact that I spoke German like a real German and that I even spoke his Bavarian dialect. I went to school in Innsbruck, where the same dialect is spoken. He was not less impressed by my knowledge of so many languages. He appointed me head of the Slavonic Department...

Everything was okay until 1952 when I wrote an article about the Stepinac case. My friend Dr Leiper, assistant secretary of the World Council of Churches, sent copies to several Protestant magazines. The article was published by *The Churchman*. One day Mrs Strumpen-Darrie came into my room, pale and furious, and showing me my article, yelled, "How did you dare write this? It cannot be true."

"You never heard about the Inquisition?"

"Yes, but it was five hundred years ago."

"I'm sorry, but it happened again."

"How did you dare attack the Pope? He is a saint!"

"I don't think he is a saint. What I wrote about him is true."

Mrs Strumpen-Darrie became hysterical. Her husband sent her to Florida for a rest, invited me to his room and said,

"I want you to know what I think about the matter. You have the right to write anything you want. You can be against anything, but you have to be pro-Berlitz. And I know you are pro-Berlitz. We need you." He told me again what he had already told me many times, that he never had in his school anyone who knew so many languages, and was so useful in many ways...

Several weeks passed and Mrs Strumpen-Darrie showed up again at the school. A few months later old Strumpen-Darrie had a heart attack in the school and died there.

Her son became commander-in-chief. I knew he would fire me, but he wanted me to go by myself to make me lose my unemployment insurance, so I stayed. There was a lot of manoeuvring on his part to make me go. Among other things, I was transferred to the bookkeeping department, and it turned out I was able to do my work better than my predecessor. The head of the department, Mr Liebermann, was astonished and sometimes gave me some calculations of his to look over to be sure he had made no mistakes.

He came to my room one day, closed the door, locked it and said, "I would like to know why our boss hates you so. I heard you wrote something. What did you write?"

When I told him about the article, he said he would like to read it and was astonished when I told him I had a copy in a drawer of my desk. I gave it to him, he went to the door to be sure it was locked, and then sat down and read it very attentively. When he had finished he said with a deep sigh, "It is terrible. I understand you had to write it."

Then he said that young Strumpen-Darrie wanted to get rid of me and had told him weeks ago to persuade me to leave. I told him to tell young Strumpen that he had to fire me, that I would not leave by myself.

Weeks passed until one day Liebermann came into my room very abashed and said that the chief had ordered him to tell me that I was fired. It was a few days before Easter and it was clear why he did it just then, because he had been told by his Jesuit confessor that it would be a mortal sin not to do it now before Easter.

Gierowski also showed me the introduction that Archbishop Leonty had written for his book and asked me to go around to various publishers with him. I thought the most likely might be some Boston firm like the Beacon Press, with its Unitarian associations. Together we went to others which had New York representatives but an expression of indescribable weariness came over their faces. The public was tired of atrocities and all that, said one of them. They had just turned down a book from somebody who had escaped Belsen, "No, Ravensbruck it was, I think. Absolutely ghastly! But people know it all."

I had brought *The Martyrdom of the Serbs* with me but I saw that even the gruesome illustrations – the Serbian mayor with his brain extracted and the other with his head laid beside him – had lost all power to shock. I was not in the least shocked by them myself. We never succeeded in interesting anyone. There had been a great surfeit of wartime books. Readers' minds had been sated with horrors. There were the Nazis, the Communists, the Fascists, and people did not want to hear that Christians like themselves could be guilty too.

Gierowski's hopes were low, as he had been in the USA for twenty years or more before I knew him and his views had got him into trouble. Sometimes he was supposed to be a Communist, because Archbishop Stepinac, whom he condemned, had had a celebrated trial before a Communist court in Yugoslavia. Sometimes, as he had strongly anti-Czech views, he was supposed to be a supporter of Henlein, the leader of the Nazi anti-Czech faction in Sudetenland, whose activities brought about the collapse of Czechoslovakia. For this last he was pursued by the FBI and had to appeal to Milan Hodza, former President of Czechoslovakia; the letter which Hodza wrote him in reply was to provide a rough map and to say that Gierowski was by heredity, as well as by ability and deep conviction, a Carpatho-Russian leader, and that

Carpatho-Russia's educated classes speak Russian and the peasantry speak a dialect that is more like Russian than Ukrainian. Though it is an impoverished and mountainous country with few resources, it is of great "geopolitical significance."

Gierowski himself had total confidence in his own opinions, which were based on ancient loyalties. I have never penetrated far into the mysteries of Orthodoxy or felt any urge to adopt it, but I acclimatized myself to see it through Gierowski's eyes.

I have always thought that compared with the question of how we behave, what we believe is of little importance. But where race or region is roughly identified with religion (as in Ireland), behaviour takes second place. Different views of the message of Jesus Christ attract bombs from different quarters.

It is a strange story that Gierowski tells. Is it about "a faraway country" and "people of whom we know nothing," to use Chamberlain's phrase, or is it about Man in the twentieth century?

(1990)

Endnote: This was Hubert Butler's last written work. It is of a piece with "Peter's Window," his essay on Russia in *Escape from the Anthill*, sharing its lapidary discursiveness and focus on an individual, a shard of ancient Europe exiled among the "hundred races" of New York and retrieved from the flotsam of history. In it many of Butler's interests converge: the fate of small nations, the struggle between Orthodoxy and Catholicism in the Balkans, the workings of history, the interrogation of self, the concern for home and hearth, the "small everyday occurrences" that "reveal what we are like." These voices – Gierowski's, Guzelimian's, Butler's – are the stuff, and conscience, of our century. (Antony Farrell, The Lilliput Press)

Afterwords

A Well-Meaning Slap

Vuk Perišić

Hubert Butler was different. He wrote about highly sensitive and controversial political and historical themes, though he did not actually care about history and politics *eo ipso*. That is not of course to say that he ignored them, but the focus of his interest is always on individuals and their ethics, whether the ethics of an anonymous citizen whose ethics are tested by circumstances of war and life in an occupied country, or those of a notorious protagonist who determines those very same circumstances – producing new, mutilated ethics and devouring the fates of thousands, of millions.

While the behaviour of a helpless citizen can be justified, as Butler does when discussing the hypothetical Nazi invasion of Ireland ("The Invader Wore Slippers"), "great" protagonists have the ability to choose.

Butler is the child of the Irish historical experience which he lived through with both emotional empathy and intellectual reflection. He knew practically everything about the ethical abyss that can be opened by religious and state-building struggles. His intellectual and moral perception was even stronger thanks to his being a sincere believer, a Christian devoted to Christian ethics, in the best sense of those terms. One could not find an intellectually and morally honest liberal, socialist or atheist who would remain indifferent to the beauty of the ethical imagination with which Hubert Butler lived and wrote.

Today, in a new cycle of conflicts between modernity and diehard clericalism and sectarianism, Butler's consistency in viewing people through the prism of his faith may appear naïve, but it is also the greatest value of Butler's ethics as it reminds us of human essentials.

Butler was an old-fashioned kind of intellectual. He was born in 1900. He was sceptical about phenomena that we see today as inseparable parts of modern culture. He was sentimental about ancient Greece, with the enduring love of all intellectuals of his era who did not resist the temptation to see the Hellenic polis as a utopia of sorts calling out. So his essay "Return to Hellas" is full of ironical observations about modern tourism, commercialization of culture, intellectual snobbery, and even about the movie industry. (During his stay on Rhodes *The Guns of Navarone* was being produced, a *blockbuster* from an era, 1962, when the term did not yet exist). Intellectuals of Butler's stamp did not take movies seriously and could not have imagined a time when TV series would become a new and relevant artistic form.

This is the very insight Butler gives us into one-time, forgotten insights. His essay from 1937 ("In Dalmatia"), where he says that people who like "life that is simple and unspoilt must go now before Dalmatia becomes a second Côte d'Azure," has the effect of a time machine. This game of different temporal perspectives has a rare cognitive quality and compels us to ask ourselves: has Dalmatia since become a Côte d'Azure, should it become one, is it a pity that it still has never become one and, most importantly, what was the scent of Dalmatia like almost eighty years ago?

His essays do not just give insight into past events, but also into the past perceptions of those events. They are not just the story of one era, but of the self-perception of that era as well. Butler's essays are a kind of time-capsule, and their moral attitude has an everlasting, timeless quality.

He says without hesitation that he had "always been a nationalist and believed that small nations have been less likely to be corrupt than large ones." His own Irish nationalism – about which he was critical – was an inclusive one, a great conciliation of Protestant and Catholic, a great open framework from which all kinds of pluralities could freely coexist.

In Butler's time intellectuals cherished the sense of duty towards the community in which they found themselves, where they attempted to appease that duty with the individual freedom which, consciously or unconsciously, directed their whole ethical and intellectual being. Doubt that such a reconciliation is possible is their legacy to us.

Butler does not negate the significance and value of national culture, a phenomenon that today is a symbol for provincialism, but reminds us that it is condemned to disaster if it is not open to other particular cultures. In this, it is easy to spot the influence of old and forgotten Giuseppe Mazzini's utopia of Europe as a union of free nations that are communities of free citizens: nations that relate to each other with empathy. Who could better empathize with other nationalisms than a nationalist himself? Is this kind of "nationalism" really nationalism? It surely is not the same kind of nationalism that awoke in Eastern Europe in 1991 – in the year of Butler's death – and sought to liquidate all forms of empathy, offering nothing but kitsch and cheap sentimentality.

Such a man, such a writer, but also a nationalist and believer, with a feeling of responsibility towards his community and full of understanding towards alien beliefs and communities, remained permanently astounded by one episode of the Second World War, an episode that was marginal but unique in it horror: the so-called Independent State of Croatia.

It is significant that it was not the large-scale massacres at the centre of his attention, but the compulsory conversion of the Orthodox population trapped in the territory of the Quisling creation. In Butler's Ireland Protestants and Catholics hated, insulted and killed each other. Or they tolerated each other, or tolerated the duty to be tolerant. The better among them did not pay attention to the denomination of their neighbours, or even recognized the beauty of plurality. But they never tried to convert each other. Not by force or on a large scale, anyway. It should be said that in the time of the Great Famine of the 1840s Protestant missionaries plied the starving peasants of the West of Ireland with soup and Bibles, and their own interpretation of the Bible; and

Butler says that in this attempt at conversion they were well-meaning. But Irish Catholics remember that attempt with disgust – and as unforgivable.

The only alternative to conversion in the NDH (the Croatian acronym for the Independent State of Croatia) was death. Conversion was often fraudulent, and was not in itself a guarantee for survival. In spite of all that, the Catholic Church saw a convenient opportunity to increase its flock. This became the intellectual and ethical obsession of Hubert Butler, to which he would always return. Only a nationalist and believer like him – an empathetic nationalist and believer – could fully comprehend the horror of the compulsory conversion engineered by the Ustaše regime. Croatian nationalists would very gladly forget this horror, or diminish its significance, or would rejoice in it in the darkness of their innermost feelings. Serb nationalists would magnify it above all conceivable limits, would enjoy the hatred produced by this magnification, and would make impossible any rational understanding. A-national atheists do not possess the necessary sensibility for comprehending the essence of compulsory conversion and its intimate drama. Only such a Protestant from Kilkenny could do this, who was most happy in his own orchard, beside his own beehives. During the war he sent honey from neutral Ireland to his friends in occupied Zagreb.

In a certain way the factual and moral lessons regarding the Ustaše conversion campaign, which Butler tried to announce to the world, are secondary. What is most valuable is the *emotion* with which he wrote about it, especially his disbelief when he discovered that one archbishop had written an idiotic ode to a notorious criminal. He several times cited verses from Šarić's "Ode to the Poglavnik," as if trying to assure himself that such a thing really happened.

Stepinac, however – a central figure in *Balkan Essays* – belongs among those great protagonists who had the ability to make a choice. He was a brave man faced with two evils. If he had confronted the greater evil, and become a martyr in 1941 instead of 1946, he would indeed be a great saint–the Croatian Dietrich Bonhoeffer.

It goes without saying that Butler was uninterested in "taking sides" in the conflict between Serbian and Croatian narratives. (In contrast to Rebecca West). It seems that neither of these nationalisms can stand truth and objectivity any more than the other. Therefore this book will be nauseating to both. Or they will perhaps minutely search for minor details to try and prove that he was really "on our side." But they are hostages of their own narratives and proof that every meaningful book is quixotic.

Butler in one place says that he has "sympathy with the man who gave his son a good slap so that he would remember having seen a salamander." His essays should have the effect of a good slap to the Croatian public. Or more precisely, to anyone who has the slightest national or sentimental doubts about that marginal, horrible episode of the Second World War which abducted and tried to disfigure the name of Croatia–but which was neither independent, a state, nor Croatia.

Translated, from the Croatian, by Jacob Agee.

Vuk Perišić is the editor of the Croatian edition of this book, Balkanski eseji, *translated by Srđan and Hana Dvornik, and published simutaneously by Fraktura, Zaprešić, in September 2016.*

On Hubert Butler

Joseph Brodsky

In less than six years our criminal century will be over, and the United Nations will no doubt appoint a commission to estimate the loss of life owing to political violence in the past hundred years. The estimate will be rough; perhaps it will also be negligible in view of the year 2000's global census. Still, it may run up to a hundred million in Europe alone.

One can choose to be sanguine about this simply by citing survivors' lack of alternative *vis-à-vis* the past, or the majority's *vis-à-vis* the minority. The grip of this sort of ethics gets tighter and tighter with every next headline. So ours seems to be an odd time for Hubert Butler's book of essays. However, no other time thus far has turned out to be congenial.

Which is to say, for most of Hubert Butler's life, since he was born in 1900; which is to say, also, for most of this century, since the first collection of his essays was published by a small press in his native Ireland only in 1985, five years before his death in January 1991.

He lived a much longer life than most of these essays' subjects. However, before he gained this advantage, he was their contemporary, and it is the contemporary of victims inexorably growing into the contemporary of villains – for the latter tend to outlast the former – that you find in these pages.

Small wonder that Hubert Butler shows an extraordinarily keen eye and ear for every shade and whisper of demagoguery. The events he happened to witness left him no choice if he wanted to retain his sanity and self-esteem. Apparently, this desire in him was stronger than in the bulk of his compatriots and those of his generation elsewhere. One can put this down to the particularity of his family background, which went back to the twelfth century, but that would amount to extolling the Irish aristocracy. Given Butler's own views on the subject, that route should be avoided. But Ireland is partly the reason, and one can safely paraphrase here Wystan Auden's line on William Butler Yeats – "Mad Ireland hurt you into poetry." All we have to do is replace "poetry" with "essays" and we'll have our man.

For all its extraordinary beauty, Butler's island is an extremely divided place. Because of its size, loyalties and animosities there get incestuously tangled and hurtful; in a place so small, it's hard to miss a target. And the divisions themselves, be they political (into unionists and nationalists) or religious (into Catholics and Protestants) are all articulated in English and equally oblivious of the Commandment: Thou Shalt Not Kill.

"Mad" is perhaps a bit too strong. Schizophrenic is a better word. Ireland indeed could be likened to a brain dissatisfied with the body it belongs to and craving autonomy. The body's enemy is therefore this brain's friend. This sort of predisposition can be easily exploited, as it was in Hubert Butler's lifetime, and still is, resulting now and then in bad dreams and very strange mental bedfellows.

Also, because the place is relatively rich in history, evocation of it is nearly relentless. Uncertainty always seeks to provide itself with a pedigree of casuality, and Ireland's politicians for the better part of the century indeed could qualify as parvenus of uncertainty. Given the almost vengeful Irish mastery of the English language, the level of public rhetoric is as high as it is venomous. Small wonder that a word translated into a deed often results in spilled blood.

Smaller wonder still that someone who grew up in such a mental climate and ventured into the large world eastward would find its weather, in the thirties and fourties especially, quite familiar, although a good deal more frightening. That, however, would have to do with the size of the place and with the masses falling prey left and right to the divisive rhetoric of rectifying history's mistakes, not with its substance. That also had to do with the physical existence of strange bedfellows exploiting that rhetoric and overtaking those places and masses. Indeed, what the thirty-year-old Butler saw in the Balkans and in Russia must have felt to him like the Irish brain's dream coming nightmarishly true.

History makes no mistakes because it has no purpose – that much Hubert Butler must have known by that time if only because at Oxford he read the Greek and Roman classics. In any case, the dishonesty, self-deception and self-aggrandizement of those evoking history to pull the trigger didn't escape him, nor did their utter humanness. His knowledge of Russian (he is the best English translator of Chekhov's *The Cherry Orchard*, among other things) and of Serbo-Croatian, not to mention his French and his German, helped him along the line, no doubt, enormously. The detection of humanness in those whose words and deeds obscure it is, however, his own feat. On the other hand, this must have been easier for him, an Irishman, since schizophrenic uncertainty is humanness' integral part.

Yet observed by Hubert Butler as well as not, the large world kept at turning his contemporaries into victims, mounting up data for that would-be UN commission. No single man could stop this, certainly not an Irish gentleman living in his ancestral house and translating Russian novels. His sense of impotence must have been overwhelming, but not unique. This was the time for the armies, which were slowly and inevitably piling up a lot of similar data in the process. Those upon whom their roofs were not falling and under whose feet the earth didn't burn had to take the long view, and that's what Hubert Butler presumably did.

He was, one imagines, a man of phlegmatic disposition, fond now and then of quoting Horace, and the distinctly Horatian equipoise that marks his writing wasn't a posture. As early as the age of fourteen he resolved to live where he was born, and for all his languages and travel he stuck to this resolution to the end of his days. Which is to say, he knew his place on this earth, and this was what enabled him to provide us with a unique commodity: a perspective which is steady.

In this perspective the world as it emerged from the Second World War, the world where to all intents and purposes the just cause seems to have prevailed, didn't appear entirely attractive. At least, it didn't appear to Hubert Butler to be the subject for his automatic embrace. For one thing, the rhetoric of division, instead of dying in the flames of war, has emerged from them as the physical reality of divided Europe. Living in its better part, Hubert Butler now and then would notice in the crowd of cheerful survivors the familiar faces of those who disminished that crowd substantially.

He registered his observations, and you'll find some of them in this book. Made where they were made, *i.e.* in the Irish press, they caused a substantial stir, since they concerned the role played by the Catholic Church in wartime. Made when they were made, *i.e.* in the fifties, when the free world's chief nemesis was Communism, opposed by the Catholic Church, they seemed as well to recall that the old adage "my enemy's enemy is my friend" still can be played to the gallery with reasonable success.

Make no mistake, Hubert Butler was no Nazi-hunter or Protestant crusader against the Vatican: he was a dishonesty hunter. He just happened to know Serbo-Croatian better than the gentlemen in the Roman curia, and was more aware of the bloody record of some of the Croatian prelates retained by Rome for an otherwise worthy cause. But then he happened to know several things better than others did, apart from languages. Small wonder that he came to regard the post-war world's ethics as "dirty-grey."

For modern readers, Hubert Butler's most valuable insights would be no doubt those that have to do with *Mitteleuropa*. He knew the reality first hand, and in its worst period at that. Which is to say that our understanding of its present conditions logically stands to benefit from what Hubert Butler depicted half a century ago. A man of immense learning, he was interested in this borderline zone, with its fusion of Latin and Slavic cultures, presumably because he sensed in their interplay the future of European civilisation. Born where he was, he couldn't help being concerned with the fate of Christendom, whose natural son he was.

It's too bad that he wasn't listened to earlier. And it's too bad that he is not with us now, although he would feel badly dismayed and impotent once more. On the other hand, he might have again taken the long view. Still, this book is here, and it should help you cut through the verbiage and mental garbage of the trigger-happy swine whose faces you no doubt will be able to espy in any future crowd of cheerful survivors.

Amsterdam, September 1994

This essay was the epilogue to In The Land of Nod, *Butler's fourth collection of essays, published posthumously by The Lilliput Press in 1996.*

Appendix

The Stepinac Case

Editors' Notes

*The following detailed and controversial correspondence and journalism
appeared in both the Irish and British press, including* The Irish Times
(Ireland's most historic newspaper), The Standard *(later* The Catholic
Standard, *the foremost Irish Catholic newspaper at the time), and the left-
wing* New Statesman *in Britain. All the pieces here – accompanied by the
correspondence to which Butler is responding, as well as other relevant articles and reviews – were preserved in a large scrapbook maintained by Butler
in the 1940s and 1950s.*

Butler's main direct Irish antagonist is Cornelius O'Leary, the Editor of
The Standard, *who frequently cites the book on Stepinac by the Foreign
Editor of* The Standard, *Count O'Brien* (Archbishop Stepinac: The Man
and His Case, *London, 1947); but further correspondence by the noted
English Catholic writers Graham Greene, Evelyn Waugh and Micheal de la
Bédoyère (Editor of the* Catholic Herald *in Britain), as well as by the Yugo-
slav journalist M.J. Sudjic and the Dutch journalist Kees van Hoek, is also
included in this scrapbook (though not below).*

*Apart from "The Pope's Plea" – which illustrates Butler's early interest in
the fate of the Churches under the Nazi regime, and so sets the context for his
subsequent Croatian reflections – all these pieces deal directly with the trial*

and imprisonment of Archbishop Stepinac, and/or generally with the col-
laborationism of the Catholic Church apropos the Quisling Pavelić regime
of the NDH, and its German and Italian patrons.

The controversy was kicked off in earnest by Butler's talk on RTÉ radio
in September 1947, just after his first post-war visit to Yugoslavia. Butler
describes the talk in "The Sub-Prefect Should Have Held His Tongue."

Given the somewhat rival prominence of The Standard *and* The Irish
Times *– to say nothing of the audience for the original RTÉ broadcast – all*
this constituted a highly-charged and widely-diffused public political con-
troversy with marked interdenominational overtones. After all, not long
afterwards, in May 1949, over 100,000 people would gather in the centre
of Dublin to protest at the treatment of both Cardinal Mindszenty in Hun-
gary and Archbishop Stepinac in Yugoslavia – until then, one of the largest
demonstrations ever to have taken place in the city.

Butler's Notes

In the aforementioned scrapbook, Butler wrote the following marginalia:

> Count O'Brien of Thomond was foreign editor of *The Stand-*
> *ard*; he now holds a professional post in the USA. He is Aus-
> trian, remotely of Irish extraction. He was editor of the
> Viennese clerical paper the *Reichspost*. He arrived in Ireland
> after this war and was almost immediately naturalised. In
> his sympathies I would say he is a follower of Schuschnigg.
> (Perhaps I am wrong in saying he was the editor – possibly
> he was only on the staff. He is a man of some culture and
> capacity.)

> ~

> Mr Van Hoek is a Dutch journalist who arrived in Ireland
> before the war and was attached to the Catholic *Irish Inde-*
> *pendent*. At the end of the war he did not return to Holland

but became naturalised. He is a Catholic; his political sympathies are very obscure; and his appointment as foreign commentator of [the] Protestant *Irish Times* surprised many.

The Pope's Plea

To the Editor of The Irish Times

Your correspondent, "Veritas," is right in suggesting that there were many strong opponents of the Nazi régime in Germany. For example, in 1932, 42,000 Germans courageously and openly supported the pacifist, Ossietzky, when he was imprisoned for his long campaign against the Nazis. "Veritas" is, however, wrong in supposing that the Confessional Church was fighting anything but an ecclesiastic battle against the régime. This was most painstakingly explained by Dr. Wurm himself, by his colleague, Dr. Meiser, Bishop of Bavaria, and, very recently and emphatically, by Pastor Niemöller.

It is, therefore, misleading of "Veritas" to say that Dr. Wurm denounced "the practices of the Hitler régime." What were, in fact, the practices to which he took exception? In 1933 he and Dr. Meiser complained of an illegality in the appointment of the Reichsbishop and other irregularities. In April, 1934, he resisted with courage the attempt to get him removed from his bishopric. In September, Dr. Meiser, preaching in Munich, bravely defended Dr. Wurm against a false charge of having used public money for purposes other than those of the Church. Dr. Meiser concluded with an affirmation of his allegiance to the Führer and the Third Reich. They remembered Hitler in their prayers every day, he said. "The struggle was not political, but ecclesiastical." The congregation departed singing the Horst Wessel Lied*. Dr. Wurm also applauded the great work of the Führer in creating in the

---

* *The Horst Wessel Lied:* the Nazi Party anthem. (Editors)

Church, as elsewhere, a really united people, and declared he was ready to forward it. Where were the "strong denunciations" to which "Veritas" refers?

It would be very wrong to disparage the courage of the German bishops in fighting their corner, but the insidious nature of National Socialism will be misunderstood if we forget how many otherwise excellent men were at least partially deluded by it.

To quote Mr. Seton-Watson's book recent and admirable book on Eastern Europe:—

"While the Gestapo tortured and murdered Austrian democrats, socialists and Jews, Cardinal Innitzer had the Swastika flown from the graceful spire of St. Stephen's Cathedral, and the Archbishop of Canterbury (now Lord Lang) read in the House of Lords a letter received from a friend in Vienna describing how wonderful the New Order was."

The Irish Times, 4 September 1945

A Primate's Trial

To the Editor of The Irish Times

All Christians will deplore the ruthless sentence on the Primate of Croatia and will admire his courage. Yet your leader writer and Mr. Randolph Churchill in his rather shallow article go gravely wrong in suggesting that the issue is one between Christianity and godless Communism. This is an absurd and dangerous over-simplification.

During the war an official bulletin was published in London on behalf of Mihailovitch, called "Yugo-Slavia at War." The writer accused Stepinac and other prominent Catholic prelates of collaboration. For example, he asserted that Mgr. Sharitch, Archbishop of Bosnia, published under his own name in a Zagreb paper a poem hailing the quisling Pavelitch as "the sun of Croatia." True or false, these and many other charges came from monarchist and Christian sources.

There is at least confirmation that Mgr. Stepinac associated with the enemies of the Yugo-Slav State. His secretary, Colonel Lisak, leaving the court under death sentence, cried out: "Long live independent Croatia!" The Archbishop admitted that he had been photographed with members of the quisling Government. I think it is clear that he gave a qualified, but useful, support for a long time to the invader. He had been educated at a German-Hungarian college at Rome, and by temper and training he was probably more attracted by Austrian than by Serbian culture. He must, too, have been influenced by the moral support which the Primate of Austria, Cardinal Innitzer, gave to the Nazis.

The savagery of the verdict is the result less of Marxist intrigue than of that religious bitterness to which before now many good men have fallen victim. The Croats call their land with some reason the Ulster of Yugo-Slavia. When in 1936 the Premier, Dr. Stojadinovitch, a Serb and later a collaborationist, first introduced the concordat with Rome, he was excommunicated by the Orthodox Church. In the mind of the layman, the concordat was associated with a simultaneous commercial treaty with Fascist Italy for guns, rolling stock and aircraft. When at the same time the Patriarch died from poisoning, Catholic complicity was suspected, and the funeral became a demonstration against the Government and the Catholic Church. The Orthodox Bishop, Simeon, was struck down by a policeman and taken to hospital. Reuter's correspondent, Mr. Harrison, who witnessed and reported the incident, was forced to leave the country.

Surely there is enough inflammable matter here to account for an inhuman sentence without bringing in Communism? The Serb is naturally kindly and democratic. He would like to live in the light of the old saying, *"Brat je mio koje vere bio"* – "He is my brother whatever his faith." Yet he is deeply suspicious of interference from outside, and, apart from what has happened since, the problems which he inherited from Italy and Austria-Hungary in 1918 were sufficient to try the tempers of a people more experienced in self-government than his.

I suggest that it is hysterical and premature to present the tragic

Zagreb verdict as a Russian gesture of defiance against Christianity and the Western world.

The Irish Times, 12 October 1946

The Real Issue

To the Editor of The Irish Times

Your leading article on "The Real Issue" seems to me rather disingenuous, and perilously close to war-mongering.

A week ago your London correspondent examined the evidence for the charge against Mgr. Stepinac, and declared that it was fairly convincing, and did not justify that the Yugo-Slav Government should be condemned out of hand for the conviction. Today you plunge into passionate condemnation. Have you re-examined the evidence – or what has happened in the meantime?

The principle evidence for collaboration should be easy enough to test, since it is based chiefly on photographs and circulars of the Archbishop, published in the Press under the occupation. Do you now claim that these were forgeries? The Vatican does not appear to claim this. The *Osservatore Romano* has countered by issuing two photographs of the Archbishop attending a military parade with representatives of Tito and the Soviets. This is tantamount to saying that he associated himself impartially with the *de facto* Government, however much he disapproved of it.

You admit (as it were, under your breath) that "a case could be made against the Archbishop in respect of collaboration." But what else was the trial about? We can afford from here to be outraged and self-righteous at the bitterness with which these trials are conducted. We have not suffered. We have no right to judge the Archbishop, but have we a right to judge his assailants either? There is much to be said for unswerving pacifism in a Christian clergyman, but your apology for an opportunist collaboration would be rejected with scorn by Irishmen or Englishmen faced with a similar situation.

Our ignorance of the background of the trial is colossal. If I am to believe the figures published by the South Yugo-Slav Committee in London, close on a million Yugo-Slavs were massacred by Germans and Croat separatists, thrown alive into pits in the Velebit Mountains, forced at Novi Sad at the bayonet point beneath the frozen Danube*, and just plain massacred at Jasenovac. If our public bodies had made any protest against these crimes, I believe that their denunciations of the Zagreb trials might have been heard with some attention. Now they can only damage Mgr. Stepinac and increase the bitterness that already exists between the countries that lie under Russian and Anglo-Saxon influence.

I am confident that Mgr. Stepinac in no way countenanced these barbarities, and, indeed, offered such protests as were within his power. Yet the mere fact that he associated, in the slightest degree and under whatever constraint, with Pavelitch, the regicide, and the instigator of these crimes, will have damned him in the eyes of millions of Yugo-Slavs, Christian and Moslem as well as Communist. However unjust this may be, it could not be otherwise.

As for Communism, Professor Seton-Watson, an expert to whom that State owes more than to any other Englishman, was certainly aware that Tito was a Communist when he wrote the following of the Partisan Movement: "The suggestion that it is a skilfully camouflaged Communist conspiracy is simply ludicrous to those who know the personnel of the movement. It is a movement for a new way of life, social and economic, as well as political, and the federal idea upon which it is based offers a way of escape from the old internecine racial quarrels towards a wider confederation of free Balkan peoples."

That, to my thinking, is rather a rosy view of the matter, but which of us is in a position to speak with greater authority?

---

* This massacre was, in fact, perpetrated by Hungarian fascists alone. (Editors)

Your theory, propounded the day after Hersey's report, that the "real issue" is now between the soulless and mechanical civilisation of the Kremlin and the Christianity of the victors of Hiroshima is surely rather naïve. I do not believe we are as soulful as all that, or that there are lacking in the Slav countries men of goodwill, who appreciate the Christian virtues of mercy and forgiveness, but use different labels for them.

I believe that if an appeal was made on behalf of Mgr. Stepinac and his colleagues in less truculent terms than his champions have adopted here, it would have wide support in Ireland, and might not altogether fail of its effect in Yugo-Slavia. Whatever their political beliefs, Yugo-Slavs are as quick to respond to generous impulses as to unfair denunciations.

The Irish Times, 3 November 1946

Trial of Archbishop Stepinac

To the Editor of The Irish Times

The Independent State of Croatia was never recognised by our Irish Government or by any country that was not allied with Germany. Therefore, those who sat in its Parliament had no status with us except as rebels from the officially recognised Government of Yugo-Slavia, which had its representative in our capital. Archbishop Stepinac associated himself with this Parliament.

The laws of our country and his are equally binding on laymen and cleric alike. The penalty for treason in both countries is death, though appeals for mercy are frequently heard.

Many of us, who believe that Archbishop Stepinac committed an offence which in few countries, in time of war, escapes punishment, would like to see him restored to liberty. The tone of two recent correspondents would, on the contrary, suggest that they are not so interested in his being mercifully treated if this mercy is not extorted by threats and accompanied by the humiliation of Marshal Tito and his régime. How can we avoid the suspicion that this unfortunate man is being used to demonstrate that the higher clergy are in some way above the law? Though he was closely watched while he remained, he was given the opportunity to withdraw from Yugo-Slavia, like the other more deeply compromised bishops, and Marshal Tito has made it clear that the trial could have been avoided by his removal. Who would question the great courage of Mgr. Stepinac in remaining, whether his motives are ecclesiastical or patriotic? It seems all the greater when we reflect that, for the second time in his life, in full knowledge of the usual consequences, he withdrew his allegiance from the State to which he pledged it. He was born a subject of Austro-Hungary and was a conscript in her army till, with many other spirited Croats, he deserted to the Yugo-Slav Army. Yet neither courage nor humanitarian acts, such as Count O'Brien has recorded, have any bearing on the question of treason.

Let us grant this contention of Mr. de la Bedoyère and Mr. van Hoek that Archbishop Stepinac was an "ardent Croat patriot" and a separatist, who owed no loyalty to the Yugo-Slav State, though, in fact, he never avowed these views till Pavelitch made such an avowal possible and almost obligatory. How are separatists usually treated in time of war? Croatia was once a province of Austro-Hungary. Count O'Brien will recall that his countrymen did not tolerate Croat separatists any more readily in 1914-1918 than did Marshal Tito's Government in 1946 and the years before. He will remember the mass-graves in the hills above Sarajevo and elsewhere, where country people, shot in reprisal, were buried. M. de la Bédoyère, too, can reflect how the Breton separatists were treated in 1945; Mr. van Hoek knows well that the Indonesians, who looked for freedom from the Japanese, were not championed in the Dutch press or pulpit. Here in Ireland we remember the fate of the separatists of 1916. A confusion most harmful to the Archbishop and to clear-thinking is being made, and made deliberately, between mercy and justice.

Count O'Brien seems to think that everyone who disagrees with him has evil intentions. I know nothing about M. Sudjic, but I cannot see anything sinister in his visit to a public meeting in Westminster or in his adherence to the recognised Government of his country. He was, it is true, like everyone else in Yugo-Slavia, formerly the subject of a monarchy and is now a republican. A similar choice had to be made by Austrians in 1918, but very few, I believe, stayed with Otto when the throne was lost.

Some years ago I read M. Sudjic's book on Yugo-Slavia (in the "Europe Under the Nazis" series, Lindsay Drummond, 1942). In view of the date and place of publication and of internal evidence, I assume that he wrote as a supporter of Michailovitch, before the breach had occurred with the partisans, whose battles M. Sudjic also records in this book. His views, therefore, unless he was allowed unusual licence by the monarchist Government, cannot have been displeasing to him.

I can today find nothing in this book inconsistent with what he has written in *The Irish Times*, and there is no evidence of a sudden *volte-face* on his part. On pages 98 and 99, he makes the now familiar charges against Mgr. Stepinac and the Catholic hierarchy in Yugo-Slavia. The only distinction is that he believed then that, though Pavelitch had been received by the Pope, "the policy of the Catholic Church in Croatia was in direct opposition to that of the Holy See." The cleavage in the resistance movement was already imminent, and he sees in it great danger to his country. In spite of his praise of the Partisans, I can find no mention of Tito, who clearly merely renewed charges, accepted by all free Yugo-Slavs many years before. When the cleavage became irreparable, M. Sudjic was forced, like the British Government, to choose a side. What grounds has Count O'Brien for supposing that he made his choice from sordid motives?

Count O'Brien puts "evidence," like "Tito" and "Marshals," in sarcastic inverted commas, but, in fact, so far from seeing the evidence refuted, we have scarcely been allowed to see it at all. There was an outburst in Press and Dáil because *The Irish Times* quoted a modest portion of it. It is not surprising, therefore, that, apart from the Taoi-seach's dignified statement, what has been said has very little relation to the facts. In the Dáil, Mr. Norton made a moving appeal on behalf of "the aged Primate of Yugo-Slavia." The Primate was, in fact, 43 when his country was invaded. To the majority he is less a man of flesh and blood than a mascot in the anti-Bolshevik campaign. The Press has scarcely allowed him to speak for himself. The vital circular, which M. de la Bédoyère regards as genuine and innocuous, has been quoted only by his enemies. The editor of one paper has commended the suggestion of one of his readers that photographs of the Archbishop, with short and suitable legends, should be printed and freely circulated. Yet the truth is seldom short or suitable. It is not by picture-postcards, but by accurate knowledge and the desire for it, that a democracy can be armed and educated to resist Communism.

M. Sudjic has done us a service in drawing attention to Mgr. Shar-itch, and forcing from Count O'Brien some reluctant admissions about this remarkable prelate, well known before the war for his attempts to stir up hatred between Catholic and Orthodox, and his quarrel with the Franciscan Order, which was so deeply loved in Herzegovina. Surely he and those like him must bear some blame for the discredit into which Christianity may have fallen in parts of Yugo-Slavia? It can so rarely happen that an archbishop writes odes of praise to a convicted assassin (the least, but most spectacular, of Mgr. Sharitch's offences) that we shall be misunderstood by those who are not Christians if we make no comment. Yet Count O'Brien is undismayed; he merely says that another poet wrote a more bombastic poem still and was not pun-ished, and that M. Sudjic has exposed himself again as a fraud by saying that one of the poems was written in December, and not in April!

Your correspondents take these things so easily in their stride that it is hard not to wonder what they would have said or not said if they had happened nearer home. Yet there can be no doubt how the mass of Englishmen would have reacted if an English bishop, at the time when England was hard pressed, had written an ode to Mosley and

William Joyce (more reputable men than Pavelitch). If the bishop and his friends were later unkindly treated, few would take this as evidence of religious persecution.

The three writers converge on their goal by oddly different routes. For example, Count O'Brien repudiates the suggestion that Mgr. Stepinac could have appropriated an Orthodox monastery for Trappist monks. Mr. van Hoek justifies the appropriation as natural in the circumstances.

Count O'Brien has written elsewhere that the Archbishop "firmly believed in an Allied victory." Mr. van Hoek says that he was the spokesman of the Croat nation, and that the Croat people, from the start, did not resist the Axis invasion.

Count O'Brien thinks the circular sent out by the Archbishop so incriminating that it can only have originated in M. Sudjic's scheming brain. M. de la Bédoyère, on the other hand, has read it in full, and now explains it to us. He accepts it as "a long expression of gratitude to God for the acquired independence of his own people, etc."

I am afraid that, whatever the Archbishop intended, the simpler members of his flock will have interpreted the circular as M. Sudjic has done. When Mgr. Stepinac appeals to his clergy "to aid in the great task of protecting the Independent State of Croatia," he may have been thinking of spiritual adversaries, but as the State was being violently assailed at the time, his clergy could be excused for thinking he meant the Allied armies. When he expresses his deep conviction that he will get "the fullest support and understanding in their work" from the Quisling Government, M. de la Bédoyère says that this applies to "religious faith" only. Yet the idea that men can be understanding and helpful about religious faith and in other respects despicable assassins is a very subtle one, which the ordinary country Croat must have found difficult to entertain, and I do not believe he succeeded. I am sure that he thought the Archbishop meant them to give Pavelitch "the fullest support in *his* work" in return for what he had given them in *theirs*; and Pavelitch himself undoubtedly expected his *quid pro quo*.

I have written more harshly than I feel about Archbishop Stepinac.

Anybody who has seen the photographs of this unhappy man, who was exploited for propaganda purposes by Croats, Germans and Italians in turn at banquets and parades and birthday thanksgivings, and was forced to receive medals for ugly services he had probably never rendered, could not feel ill-will against him. His rôle may have been of his own choosing, but clearly he hated it. He made many protests and denunciations, but the executions continued unabated. He was powerless to prevent the publication of Sharitch's poems even in his own diocese. His clergy disobeyed him, for how else is it possible to explain that mass of forced conversions against which he protested too late to save either the converted or those who converted them from the vengeance of the returning Yugo-Slavs?

It is impossible not to feel pity for him and to believe that, if he committed treason, he did so in all sincerity. His sentence for an educated and sensitive man is a horrible one, if he is not amnestied.

The word "treason" does not carry reproach in Ireland, so why are we reluctant to use it? When Casement, who was knighted by the British Government for his humanitarian work in Africa, was tried, his friends in Ireland appealed for clemency. They sincerely wished him to be alive and free, and so they did not, I have been told, try to justify his actions, even where they sympathised with them. They tried to see the point of view of his accusers, who were fighting for their lives against those with whom he had allied himself. They failed, but I believe they came nearer to success than the Archbishop's champions will with abuse.

This is a very long letter, but you have given space to those who have taken an opposite point of view. A few years ago nothing was too good to say of the Yugo-Slavs, who resisted the Nazis longer and more vigorously than any other small nation. Today it is another story – but they are the same people.

The Irish Times, 3 December 1946

Archbishop Stepinac (I)

I have been sent a marked copy of *The Standard* containing references to me. I assume I am permitted to answer and that my answer will be printed in full. I do not know how to reply to the charge of being a "leftist intellectual," except by calling your commentator a "rightist emotional," yet this jargon seems to me rude, inaccurate and unhelpful.

I am satisfied that my interpretation of the Zagreb trial was a correct one, and that the Primate of Yugoslavia, in good faith, made a grave error of judgement at a time when such errors have terrible consequences and are terribly requited. Without question, he favoured the Croat Separatists, and I have not seen any refutation of the charge that he counselled his clergy to accept them, too. Archbishops have been known before to make such mistakes.

At the time of the last Home Rule Bill, our Protestant Primate, Dr. Crozier, supported the Ulster rebels, appeared on public platforms with Carson, and seemed almost to lend his sanction to a civil war. He believed, incorrectly, that Home Rule meant Rome Rule, and that his co-religionists would be persecuted. He had, at the time, great influence over them and over the course of events. Intelligent Irish Protestants would, today, admit that, in his views and in his actions, he was wrong. Had there been a civil war as in Yugoslavia, resulting in thousands of deaths and widespread devastation and bitterness, his opponents might easily, in the moment of victory, have taken some action against him which they would later regret. Retribution in Eastern Europe, for a number of reasons, is apt to be more violent than here.

The *Osservatore Romano*, the Vatican organ, published two photographs of the Archbishop attending a military parade in September, 1945, with representatives of Marshal Tito and of the Soviets. The prosecutors submitted similar photographs of the Archbishop attending such functions when Pavelich was the ruler of Croatia. It is not necessary to believe that the Archbishop accepted Pavelich with cordiality, but accept him he did. He, no doubt, did many humanitarian acts, yet he made no public protest against the dismemberment of the Yugoslav State. Try to picture the feelings of a Serb at even the most perfunctory association of the head of the Catholic Church in Yugoslavia with this man Pavelich. He had been condemned to death in his absence both by Yugoslav and by French courts for complicity in the murder of the King of Yugoslavia; his acknowledged aim was to break up the Yugoslav State with the help of the foreigner and to convert the Orthodox Christians of Croatia to Catholicism by force. The severe sentence on the Archbishop is surely tragic and unwise, but after a civil war by no means extraordinary.

There are many points in the trial which require elucidation. Many of the charges seem unjust. Yet, if Mgr. Stepinac alone is right, why did Father Martincic, the Provincial of the Franciscan Order, speak against him at the trial? Why did Mgr. Rittig, the Rector of St. Mark's, the chief church in Zagreb, accept office under Tito? And if they did so in bad faith, why have they not been excommunicated by name? It is very difficult for us, without close acquaintance with the facts, to pass judgement from here.

We should certainly try to do something to get the sentence on the Archbishop reconsidered, but I am confident that ferocious denunciations of the trial and the Communists will have the opposite effect, if any. Such denunciations have been hurled against the Soviets authorities for nearly thirty years, but only recently has the position of the clergy there been improved. This improvement has certainly not resulted from the denunciations. Russia was never more capable of ignoring them.

There has for long in Yugoslavia been a keen interest in Ireland, which attained its independence at the same time. Sometimes Yugoslavs came over to see for themselves; for example, Dr. Curcin, the editor of the Liberal Zagreb paper, *Nova Evropa*, came over to examine the Ulster question, which he thought had a close bearing on the problems of Croatia. Other students followed him, and lectures were given on Ireland in Yugoslavia.

It would be a pity if friendly relations between two small countries, with similar histories, should now be interrupted. The Christian doctrine that we should forgive our enemies is understood in Yugoslavia as in Ireland. If there is a serious intention to help Mgr. Stepinac, I suggest that an appeal for clemency should be sent, which showed some understanding of the heroic struggle of the Serbs and their terrible sufferings. In Ireland we are able to appreciate the savage animosities that arise from insurrection and civil war, and I do not think it becoming in us to be too didactic. Our county councils passed no votes of condemnation at the appalling massacres of Jasenovac or Novi Sad, horrors such as we in Ireland have not experienced since the days of Cromwell. An appeal for Christian charity, conveyed without self-righteousness, would, I believe, get the support of all men of goodwill in Ireland, and might not altogether fail in its effect in Yugoslavia.

Obviously Yugoslavia is now in the Russian orbit of influence, just as Ireland is in the British orbit. Yet both countries cherish their independence and do not like to be reminded of its present limitations. A sure way to affront Yugoslav opinion and make it intractable to outside influence is to treat their State as a satellite of Russia. Mgr. Stepinac's champions in this country may be good Christians, but they are bad diplomatists.

The Standard, 8 November 1946

Not a Red Whitewasher

Mr. Cornelius O'Leary's courteous criticism of my radio-broadcast requires an answer. I don't think if I had been, as he claims, a Red whitewasher I would have repeated with approval Count Sforza's statement that the second greatest danger to Europe is Bolshevism. I believe him as sincerly in this as when he said that the first danger is "fear of Bolshevism." Perhaps I should say that Sforza wrote this during the Fascist dictatorship in Italy, which, like national socialism, owed its rise to the systematic exploitation by the dictators of this widespread fear. Sforza, in his book, explains that the Bolshevik menace in north Italy was never serious and had been already averted by ordinary means, when Mussolini, the ex-socialist and ex-atheist, took up the hue-and-cry for his own ends. Sforza was foreign Minister, then as now, and can speak with authority.

Mr. O'Leary complains of understatement and omissions on my part. I did not emphasise the sufferings, deserved and undeserved, which the opponents of the present regime are enduring because these have already been widely published. I felt that some counterclaims were necessary, if a balanced picture of the situation was to be had.

When I was in Yugoslavia, no one interfered with me or thrust on me unwanted propaganda. I formed my opinions, as best I could, chiefly from what I heard and read in the streets and newspapers. I spent three days in the University Library of Zagreb studying the papers of the occupation period. You get a reader's ticket at the desk as in Dublin and walk in.

I found there much confirmation of the outspoken collaboration with Nazis, Fascists and Quislings; in which many leaders of public opinion in Croatia had indulged. To take a small instance from among the laymen, I saw published in several papers the appeal which M. Machek made to his followers in the Croatian Peasant Party to lay down their arms. The appeal was in oddly abject terms. I know that many of them, thereupon, aided the invader in disarming those Yugoslavs who had decided to fight on. In no country are these things forgotten or forgiven. Machek's testimony against the present Government was, a week or two ago, given much publicity in Ireland, but surely it cannot be thought impartial.

I checked up on various other declarations and photographs, which have been repudiated as fakes over here and which compromise leading personalities. I found them accurately reproduced and can furnish dates. But each of the legations has a press-attaché, with easy access to the old newspaper files in Zagreb or Belgrade, and these Yugoslav claims could mostly through them have been authenticated or rebutted, if accurate information had been desired. I am sure that a little more courage in facing the truth, even when it is unpalatable, would not harm us. No doubt, Yugoslav officials often tell lies,—are they the only ones?—but they would be more likely to tell the truth if they were believed when they told it. They might also be more ready to listen to our justifiable reproaches.

Mr. O'Leary says that I would not be allowed to speak enthusiastically about Ireland on Radio Belgrade. He may be right, but if I am ever able or allowed to return there I shall put this to the test. I certainly never claimed that freedom of expression, as we know it here, exists in Yugoslavia. It does not and never has. It is a delicate plant and Yugoslavia is an even more stormy land than ours.

The Standard, 3 October 1947

Proof to Editor

(Butler's handwritten note in the margin of these galleys reads as follows: "Proofs were sent me [by *The Standard*] to correct and I was told I would be allowed to reply freely. However, [the] letter was never published. In the end my solicitor secured the publication of the shorter letter 'Archbishop Stepinac'"[II]. See page 555).

I would have replied before to your very strange article of October 10, but I judged that if you intended to allow me to answer you would not have made so many statements that were easy to refute. For example you put into inverted commas and attributed to me some stupid and provocative phrases about Mgr. Stepinac, "traitor," "collaborator with the enemy," and said that I called him the driving force behind the forced conversions. I said none of these things in my letters nor in my broadcasts as you can verify for yourself.

Other things that you say have a more than personal and temporary significance. You claim that I was not telling the truth when I said that I had studied the papers of the occupation period in Zagreb, and found confirmation there of many of the documents, which have here been repudiated as false.

Both as a scholar and a lover of the truth I cannot ignore this. You conclude by saying: "The case of Mr. Butler is now definitely closed." I do not think it is. I have not till now had time to make translations of some of the documents to which I referred, but I send them to you now with the request that you will authenticate them yourself, which is easily done, as I will show. Then I will be grateful if you will tell your readers the result.

Before I went last summer to Zagreb, where thirteen years ago I held for a couple of years a scholarship from the School of Slavonic Studies, I made an examination of the large collection of documents dealing with the Churches under the occupation published by the Yugoslav Government in 1946. I will refer to them by the first word of their Croatian title *Dokumenti*. A large part of these were photostats of the signed depositions of witnesses or of letters from prominent people in the church or the Quisling state, which I will call by its Croatian nickname NDH. I saw no way of verifying these because forgery and moral pressure are not easy for a foreigner to detect.

But, in addition to these, there are about 500 newspaper extracts, some photographed, some merely quoted. They are all dated. It seemed to me a difficult thing to fake so many newspapers that had circulated five years before, because as well as the immense labour of editing and printing, it would be necessary to suppress all the genuine copies. Most of the papers were church papers and must have reached Italy, with which Croatia was, at that time, closely associated and possibly even the Vatican. The task of substituting the counterfeit for the genuine would be an impossible one. Therefore, I felt, even before I went to Zagreb, that either a transparent hoax had been perpetuated or the extracts were genuine.

In Zagreb I went to the University Library and searched the newspapers of 1941-45 for some dozen of the more striking passages. You calculate that either I read Serbo-Croatian at the rate of six pages to the minute or am a liar. I have never met that kind of arithmetic outside "Alice in Wonderland" and do not know how to reply. I read slowly and carefully and a large part of the time I spent just waiting. The assistants, at first very obliging, became a bit weary and suspicious as they brought volume after volume. It was the most shameful period of their history I was investigating.

I found all the references correctly quoted and therefore felt justified in believing that the newspaper extracts in *Dokumenti* were genuine. I would be grateful, though, if you would get confirmation of those which I attach or refer to here. As an editor you can surely ask this of the press attaché of any legation. There is one, for example, in the British Consulate at Zagreb. The iron curtain that hides these facts from us is of our own making.

Count O'Brien declares in his book that all the evidence has been "carefully sifted" but either he has not examined *Dokumenti* with which he claims familiarity or there was a very large hole in his sieve. He indignantly denied in *The Irish Times* and *The Standard* the reality of the Primate's April circular to his clergy at the time of the German invasion (*Dokumenti*, p.296). He denied that Archbishop Sharitch's "Ode to Pavelitch" appeared on Christmas Day, even though the photostat (*Dokumenti*, p.367) has an ornamental border of Christmas candles and silver bells. He denied that the Primate had ever applied to Pavelitch for the transfer of the Orthodox monastery of Orahovica to Trappist monks (*Dokumenti*, p.120).

Why did Count O'Brien deny all these things? Some would say that he was taking a chance, confident that in such a cause nobody but a Communist could be so impious as to criticise him and that few in Ireland would be qualified to do so. I am ready to believe, more charitably, that he is a very slovenly investigator, and this is borne out by many small, meaningless errors. For example, Orahovica appears in his book as Grahovica and he publishes there a rather fuller text of the Archbishop's speech of defence than the "full text" published in *The Catholic Herald*. There are new remarks about Mihailovitch and

Palestine and Catholic hospitals, etc., and it looks as though, as in ancient MSS, the marginal comments of pious scribes are creeping into the text. For this he must share the blame with the stupid intolerance of the Communist Party, not Pavelitch, which did not publish an authoritative version of this very able speech.

Yet there are omissions in his book, which it is hard to attribute to mere carelessness. There are long quotations from sermons, and private conversations which no one can verify, but the April circular, though no one now denies it, is not even mentioned. I am told there was a "paper shortage" (this, too, in Yugoslavia is the stock excuse for suppressing awkward information). Surely a single sentence acknowledging a vital fact which he had denied would not have exhausted the paper supplies?

As for the monastery, the Archbishop admitted in his defence the very fact which Count O'Brien denies, justifying the transfer among other reasons on the grounds that it had been Catholic in past history. Since most of the ancient ecclesiastical buildings of Western Europe were once Catholic, Count O'Brien did well to suppress the Archbishop's reasoning in *The Irish Times*. It is the same argument which recurs through the papers of NDH. The forced conversions were not real conversions, but simply a "return to the faith of their fathers" (who had lived 250 years before!).

In one respect I agree with *The Standard*. What happened in Yugoslavia cannot be dismissed as unimportant because it occurred far away and long ago among a savage people. The Croats have as high a civilisation as our own and there is a deep significance for every one in this violent clash between two different philosophies, a material and a spiritual one. The Yugoslav Communists are our brothers and what happens to them is our concern but is it our duty to take the mote out of our brother's even before we attend to our own? What virtue is there in denying that the Christian Churches of Croatia departed very far from the spirit of Christ's teaching and of its great Croatian interpreter, Bishop Strossmayer?

How was it, for example, that Archbishop Sharitch was allowed to become and to stay a spiritual leader? This strange person applauded the persecution of the Jews, and compared Pavelitch, who was, next to Himmler and Streicher, perhaps the vilest of the war criminals, to Leonidas. His poems are hard to translate but here is one of the 22 verses of the Xmas Ode:

> Dr. Ante Pavelitch, the dear name,
> Croatia has in him a blessing from heaven,
> May He, the King of Heaven,
> Always accompany thee,
> Our golden leader!

In the opening verse he tells how, before the war, he embraced Pavelitch in St. Peter's at Rome and in an article in May, 1941 (*Dokumenti*, p. 28) he describes a tour he made as a subject of the old Yugoslavia: "I was with our Ustashe (the Croat Quislings) in America, North and South, and we prayed [to] the Almighty for the Poglavnik, Dr. Ante Pavelitch, that He might of His mercy lead him to a free Croatia! And lo, the good God heard the cry of our hearts. We praise Thee, o God, we acknowledge Thee to be the Lord!" Count O'Brien asserts that Archbishop Sharitch was abnormal, but does this excuse his cruelty? Does it excuse the men who endured him as spiritual leader for so many years?

There were many brave and good men in Yugoslavia, but you debase the currency of praise by overpraising these who were neither better nor worse than anybody else. In justice to the unrecognised heroes I hope you will print Mgr. Stepinac's April circular and allow your readers to judge for themselves whether the diplomat is not more evident in it than the saint. Does his attitude to NDH strike you, as it strikes Count O'Brien, as aloof and censorious? He had known Pavelitch's record for years and had stood by the bier of the murdered king. How could he have seen God's Handiwork in Pavelitch's advent in the Nazi train?

There is that terrible sentence, which no sophistry can explain away, "knowing as we do the men who today guide the destinies of the Croatian people, we are deeply convinced that our work will meet with full understanding and help." There is the solemn *Te Deum* to be arranged "after consultation with the government authorities." Perhaps you will say that he had to rejoice at the liberation of Croatia from an intolerable servitude to Yugoslavia, but Count O'Brien tells us on page 9 on his book that the Primate wished for an independent Yugoslav State and that by August, 1939 Croatia already had "a large measure of autonomy."

We have been greatly misled in Ireland as to the extent and importance of the campaign of compulsory conversion. Since the days of Cromwell nothing like it has happened in Europe. The Orthodox clergy have no doubt that this had the support of many Catholic Church leaders and some of the newspaper records, which I attach, confirm this. Father Ilja Chok, a leading Orthodox priest of Zagreb, put the number of those converted or massacred because of their religion as high as 800,000. Father Chok is no bigot. He told me that his own life had been saved by the intervention of a Catholic priest, Father Mimica of Shtikada. I found later a deposition from a clerk of the ecclesiastical court bearing out the truth of what Father Chok told me of his own experiences at Shtikada (*Dokumenti*, 144).

Count O'Brien in his book (p.14) declares that "the Catholic Church as a whole, all her bishops and the overwhelming majority of her priests, led by the Archbishop of Zagreb, made this evil plan impossible." He mentions (p.7) that Bishop Shimrak, "the editor of the leading Catholic daily," was an intimate friend of his own for nearly 20 years and also a great admirer of Mgr. Stepinac.

This is how Dr. Shimrak wrote of the conversion campaign in his Diocesan Magazine. Verify it for yourself:

The regulation about the conversions from the Orthodox Church in Srjem, Slavonia and Bosnia:

Special church councils must be established immediately to assist the priest in all his duties, not only in regard to the organisation of conversion, but also to the creation of parishes for the converts. Every priest must have before his eyes that historic days have come for our mission.

Now we must put into practice that which we have spoken of in theory through the centuries. In the matter of conversion, we have done very little up to this, simply because we were irresolute and dreaded the small reproaches and censure of men. Every great task has its opponents, but we must not be downcast on that account, because it is a question of a holy union, the salvation of souls and the eternal glory of the Lord Christ. Our work is legal in the light of the ruling of the Holy See... Also in the light of the ruling of the Holy Congregation of Cardinals for the Eastern Church... And finally in the light of the circular sent by the government of NDH, July 30, 1941, whose intention it is that the Orthodox should be converted to the Catholic faith.

Dr Janko Shimrak, Apostolic Administrator
Diocesan Magazine of *Krizhevtsi*,
No. 2, 1942, pp. 10-11
(*Dokumenti*, p.340).

Count O'Brien has seen this passage and justifies his previous statement by saying: "Dr Shimrak was not yet a bishop then." A curious explanation, if you think it over.

But, even if it is true that Mgr. Shimrak was not honoured with a bishopric till after he had given the conversion scheme a trial, there were other bishops, Dr. Aksamovitch, of Djakovo, for example. I attach a translation of a leaflet, "Friendly Advice" (*Dokumenti*, p.55), issued by his diocesan printing house. *Dokumenti* p.105 shows a photograph of a form of application for conversion by the diocese of Banja Luka. I also show for your consideration an account of a very polite visit paid by the Bishop of Banja Luka and his secretary to a prominent Orthodox tradesman in his diocese. (*Dokumenti*, p.106.)

It rings to me true, though I base my case, not on the signed depositions but on the newspaper extracts, which you can verify. I have translated also a passage from *The Catholic Weekly*, which proves that the conversions were not, except in particular instances, formal only, a refuge from persecution offered to the Orthodox by kindly priests. (*Dokumenti*, 118.)

Here, too, are accounts of an actual ceremony of conversion of 400 at Kamensko, and of two telegrams of greetings sent to Mgr. Stepinac in the name of several thousand new converts. (*Dokumenti*, p.93).

Here is a further newspaper record of the conversion of 2,300 Orthodox Serbs of a village in northern Yugoslavia by a Franciscan Friar, Fr. Sidunije Scholtz. You will see that it says that Fr. Scholtz had been at work instructing them in the Faith for a long time before. Not unnaturally there is no newspaper description of his methods. Yet to convert 2,300 all at once is such a remarkable feat that remarkable methods must have been used. Perhaps you will not altogether disbelieve the deposition of the schoolmaster of Balenitse, describing how Fr. Scholtz did these things. Well, the Orthodox priest was first dragged from his house, and then his nose was cut off, and then... but you can guess the rest. (Dok. p.94 and 96.) The murder was confirmed by Fr. Vitas, Orthodox priest of Nabrdja.

It is true that it was repeatedly urged that conversions must be voluntary and a special form had sometimes to be signed by converts to that effect. But the word "voluntary" was not pedantically interpreted, as you will see from an article on "Conversions" in *The Catholic Weekly* (*Dokumenti*, 96). It begins: "*Ad amplexandam fidem catholicam nemo invitus cogatur,*" but ends, "Catholic believers (often in practice, we identify the idea of Catholic and Croat), are politically and socially in a markedly superior position to the adherents of other faiths and flocks. By conversion the convert assures himself various things which he might otherwise forfeit." The author is the Rev. Dr. Chedomil Chekada.

I need scarcely say that there were hundreds of good priests who loathed this bullying, but we are doing no honour to them by whitewashing those who acquiesced in it.

M. de la Bédoyère, the Editor of *The Catholic Herald*, was asked in *The Irish Times* what priests had been punished for their part in these conversions. He replied that he was very busy and had no time to waste on newspaper controversy.

It is clear that what the higher clergy in Yugoslavia came to dislike about the conversions was the physical cruelty and scandal. Had the pressure been more oblique they could have overlooked it, as Count O'Brien overlooked Mgr. Shimrak's indiscretions. Catholics in Ireland have a good record of tolerance to others, better, perhaps, than we Irish Protestants. I do [not] think they will forgive those who try to win their sympathy for bigotry and bullying.

I hope that I have not seemed to write with an anti-Catholic bias. Protestants have had fits of candour about the behaviour of Protestant churches in time of war, but perhaps this has been fairly easy, where foreign countries are concerned, as there is no strong feeling of solidarity between the disparate branches of the reformed faith. The Dean of Chichester has published a full account of the ecstatic welcome given to Hitler by the leaders of the Evangelical Church in Austria. There were not many Protestants in Yugoslavia but they may well have been influenced by what happened in Vienna, and their Church, with the Moslems, was one of the four invited to gather forced converts for the Orthodox (Dokumenti, p.107).

You confuse the issue by saying that many of the leading Communists were former Fascists and that most Yugoslav trials are political not moral. This may well be so, and if I was defending Communism or even interested in it, it would be relevant. But I am not, I am interested in Christianity and I want to know what went wrong, so that these vile things happened with the blessing and connivance of Christians and their ministers.

About Communism I know very little and cannot suggest whether the intolerance and suffering that is widespread in Yugoslavia is to be traced to Communist ideals themselves or to the failure to live up to those ideals or to the aftermath of the war and the civil war. In those wars nearly two million people*, more than half the population of Ireland, were killed and the country was invaded by seven nations. If you are correct in saying that the country is today largely led by opportunists, who do not believe in Communism, some weight should be given to the last two possible explanations.

I believe that our best defence against Communism lies in truthfulness and self-criticism, our worst in hypocrisy and pious lies.

(Response to *The Standard*, unpublished proof, late 1947 or early 1948)

Mr H. Butler
and Archibishop Stepinac

(Addendum to "Proof to Editor" on page 540)

(Butler's handwritten note in the margin of these galleys reads as follows: "Proofs were sent me but this was sent as a covering letter and not intended to be printed.")

I enclose a translation of Mgr. Stepinac's circular to his clergy at the time of the German invasion of Yugoslavia and the establishment of the puppet Croatian State. I do not think you will wish to print it but, as it is a full justification of my attitude, I am owed an explanation of your silence about it. No honest man can ignore the effect that this circular must have had in inflaming the passions of the Croat Quislings. The Archbishop had, just before the invasion, appealed for loyalty and prayers for the young King of Yugoslavia. In this later circular there

---

* See note on page 421. (Editors)

is not one word about toleration or mercy for his defeated Yugoslav countrymen, Serbian, Orthodox, Christian, Jewish, who were soon to be shot, gassed and evicted in their hundreds of thousands.

Your foreign editor, Count O'Brien, in *The Irish Times* of November 1946, and also in *The Standard*, denied the authenticity of this circular, though this was easily tested. He also asserted that the Primate was a loyal Yugoslav. I prefer to think that Count O'Brien is an incompetent investigator rather than that he was trying to falsify the facts. When I saw him at your office he no longer repudiated the circular, but he asked me to believe he did not print it or even refer to it in his book on the Primate because of "paper shortage." I cannot believe, in view of your lengthy statements about myself, that *The Standard* also is short of paper. Is there some other reason for your silence about the circular or must I believe that you are frightened of the truth?

There is a photostat of the Archbishop's circular on page 296 of *Dokumenti* from which Count O'Brien, who presumably knows Croatian, can correct this version made out of reach of reference books, if you decide to print it.

You are aware I am sure that Pavelitch, Leader or *Poglavnik* of the Independent State of Croatia, in whose honour the Archbishop decreed *Te Deums* and asked for prayers and devoted service, was one of the vilest of the war criminals and the contriver of the late King of Yugoslavia's assassination.

I believe that by truthfulness and self-criticism Christians can make some headway against Communism but none at all by hypocrisy and pious lies.

As I am making a study of the Christian crisis in Yugoslavia and its repercussions abroad, your attitude is of great interest to me. Your paper is, I believe, an Irish paper, and I trust that you will interest yourself personally in the matter and not delegate it to your Foreign Editor, who does not understand our people. When the facts are known—and they will be known—our kindly Irish priesthood will repudiate angrily any sympathy for the vile things that have been done in the name of Christ in Croatia.

The First April Circular

But faithful to God and to the Church, our Croatia will not only play its part in promoting the supernatural good of our people but it will also establish the firmest foundations and the healthy development of the national values and of the freedom and stability of the State. The Church, which already for two thousand years has watched the seething history of the world, is an everlasting witness of how *"regnum de gente in gentem transfertur propter injustitas et injurias et contumelias et diversos dolos,"* "How the kingdoms pass from one people to another because of injustice and wrong and shame and diverse defeats" (Crkv 10.8.) Therefore, we must regard it as our eternal duty that in these fateful hours in the history of the Croatian people we may inspire our whole national being with a deep regard for eternity. We must everywhere demonstrate and teach that our holy pride and our national exultation in building the foundation of the young State of Croatia is inspired with the fear of God and the love of God's laws and commandments because it is only upon God's laws and not upon the lying principles of this world that the Croatian state can be built upon firm foundations.

Answer therefore readily to this my appeal for an intensified effort for the protection and promotion of the independent state of Croatia.

Knowing as we do the men who today guide the destinies of the Croatian people we are deeply convinced that our work will meet with full understanding and help. We believe and expect that in the resurrection of the Croatian state the Church will be able to exercise in full freedom the indisputable principles of eternal truth and justice. It will observe the words of the epistle *"verbum Dei non est alligatum"*: "The word of God is not bound" (II Tim. 2.9.); and it will consider it its holy duty "opportune, importune, arguere, increpare,

obsecrare in omni patientia et doctrina": "Be instant in season, out of season; reprove, rebuke, exhort, with all long-suf-
fering and teaching" (II Tim. 4.2). So will it work and such
priceless assistance will it give in the hard task of raising up
our beloved Fatherland and the Croatian state.

God grant that it will be so and that it shall be so, I appeal
to you, reverend brotherhood of the clergy, that you do not
cease to urge trust in prayer upon the faithful, but that yet
more, you yourselves at the altar of God, raise your hands to
the "Father of lights, from Whom comes every good gift and
every perfect boon" (James I. 17), that He may fill the Poglavnik of the state of Croatia with a spirit of wisdom so that
he may accomplish his exalted and responsible service to the
glory of God and the salvation of the people, in justice and
truth; that the Croatian people may be a people of God given
to Christ and His Church which was founded upon the Rock
of Peter! If perchance, in the eyes of the world, prayer is
deemed a thing of small account, we regard it as the most
important thing in life, because if the Lord guard not the city,
vain is the task of him that guards it (Ps. 12.1). [*Butler's inserted
note here:* This appears to be a wrong reference, no doubt a
misprint—H.B.]

The Church of God has never spent itself in phrases, but
neither has it ever renounced that steadfast task of building
the foundation of a happy future for the individual, the people and the State. Act in such a spirit even now, reverend
brothers, and fulfil your duty towards the young independent
state of Croatia.

In connection with this, I announce that on Sunday, the
fourth of May, a solemn *Te Deum* will be held in all the parish
churches to which the local clergy are to call the district
authorities and all the faithful. I hope that it will be possible
to hold these ceremonies at that time. But where, on account
of difficulties of communication, it cannot be done on that

date, the service is to be held on the first free day. As regards
the Cathedral Church of Zagreb, I will arrange a date after
consultation with the Government authorities.

ALOYSIUS, Archbishop
Zagreb, 28 April 1941

Archbishop of Zagreb's Circular
(*Nedjalja* [*Sunday*], 29 April 1941)

*On the occasion of the re-establishment of the Independent State
of Croatia, His Excellency Dr. Aloysius Stepinac, Archbishop of
Zagreb and Metropolitan of Croatia, issued the following circular:*

The Archbishop to the Reverend Clergy of the Archbishopric
of Zagreb:

Reverend Brothers, there is not one among you who in these
last days has not been a witness of the momentous happenings in the life of the Croatian people among whom we work
as witnesses of Christ's gospel. These events have brought
our people in reach of an ideal long dreamed of and desired.
These are hours in which no longer does the tongue speak
but the blood with its mysterious attachment to the soil, in
which we saw the light of God and with the people from
whom we are sprung. Is it necessary to declare that even in
our veins the blood has flowed more vigorously and in our
breast, the heart has beat more strongly? No intelligent man
can judge us for that and no honest man can take it amiss,
because the love of our native land has been written by the
finger of God in His ordinances and on our hearts.

And who can condemn us, if even we, as spiritual pastors,
make our contribution to the national joy and pride, when,

full of deep emotion and warm gratitude, we turn to Almighty God. Because, howsoever confused the web of these fateful days has been, however many heterogeneous factors have affected the course of events, yet it is easy to distinguish the Hand of God in the work. "A *Domino factum est istud et est mirable in oculis nostris.*" "The Lord has done it and our eyes are full of wonder" (Psalm 117, 23).

But while I address you today from this ancient house in the shadow of this ancient fane, the witness of our Croatian history, I do not speak to you only as a son of the Croatian people, but much more as a representative of the Holy Church. I speak to you as a representative of that divine institution, which rose up in the wing of Eternity and whose fulfilment is in Eternity in a quite special sense of the word. As a representative of that Church, which is "firmamentum et columna veritatis"—"the foundation and the column of Truth" (I. Timothy 3.15), and which never feared, even upon my lips, to speak the truth when it was needful, even though, alas, its voice often remained the voice of one crying in the wilderness.

Therefore, speaking to you as a representative of the Church and a pastor of souls, I pray you and beseech you that with all your strength you strive and work so that our Croatia may be a land of God, because only so will it be able to accomplish the two great problems which, as a state, it must perform for the benefit of its citizens.

Loyal to God and to the Holy Church of Christ our Croatia will perform this exalted mission, which an earthly fatherland must accomplish to promote the spiritual good of its people. Loyal to God and the Church it will show that it believes that the ultimate goal of every human striving is eternity where lies our true eternal fatherland. Esteeming and guarding the values of faith and morals it will show that it believes that our earthly land is only then our true mother when it leads us by the hand and teaches us to give to God that which is God's and that it is only then the true guardian of our life when it instructs our steps which lead to the heights and when it appeases the tumult in the soul, which God has created for Himself.

(Response to *The Standard*, apparent further addendum to the previous proof, unpublished, late 1947 or early 1948)

Steps to Communism

In your friendly notice of my talk to the Rotary Club, I am reported as quoting a Yugoslav priest: "If Catholics were as enthusiastic about Catholicity as Communists were about Communism, it would be more than possible to fight the Red Terror."

This is not quite what he or I said. He knew me to be a Protestant and he thought that the doctrinal differences in Yugoslavia, which are very bitter, had opened the way to materialism. He said that if we Christians could put into the practice of Christian brotherhood the same enthusiasm and energy that Communists put into the practice of their beliefs, we need not fear them.

Drogheda Argus, 6 December 1947

Archbishop Stepinac (II)

To the Editor of The Standard

I regret that on the score of length you have finally decided against printing the reply which I wrote some months ago to your commentator's very lengthy and very inaccurate statement of my views.

I enclosed with my letter translations of a number of dated

newspaper extracts, principally from the church papers of the occupation period in Zagreb and I asked you to verify them for yourself
through the Press Attache of any foreign legation in Yugoslavia, a
simple and necessary proceeding if your desire for the truth is genuine.
Have you yet done so?

I know that any competent Slavonic scholar would bear out my
conclusions. Yet if they are proved wrong I shall write to your paper
and withdraw them. Surely such an offer should be reciprocated by you?

I think there can be few parallels in European history for the religious massacres in Croatia in 1941 and '42 or for the lack of moral courage which Christians have shown in admitting them with honesty.
They followed inevitably, though certainly not designedly, on that
campaign of compulsory conversion to which far too many of the clergy
gave their assent. One of the most outspoken advocates of the campaign
was that very Mgr. Shimrak whom Count O'Brien mentions with such
approval in his booklet on Mgr. Stepinac. I sent you an extract from his
diocesan magazine and documentary proof of all the other statements
which I made. How did it come about that these horrible crimes were
committed in the name of Christ? Till we admit the damage that was
done, all our efforts to repair it will be useless. Because Communists
often tell lies, why should Christians?

You will say that if these things had happened on so vast a scale,
dissimulation would have been impossible. I refer you to the great
Catholic historian, Lord Acton. Writing a generation ago on the massacre of St Bartholomew's Eve, he said (page 149), that till 150 years
previously that great crime was defended by many. After that it had
been lied about. The victims of this massacre were 7,000, the victims
in Croatia were many times that number, yet unlike the Huguenots,
they had almost no advocates outside their own country.

After describing the false versions of the Huguenot massacres,
which had been published by responsible scholars, Lord Acton concludes his essay with this fine sentence: "Such things will cease to be
written, when men perceive that truth is the only merit that gives
dignity and worth to history."

From the Editor of The Standard:

The reply to which Mr. Butler refers ran to about four columns. We offered to give him an opportunity of defending his point of view within a reasonable compass. In his letter above, his point seems to be that "religious massacres" were carried out in Croatia in 1941 and 1942, that there was a campaign of compulsory conversions backed by the Church, notably by Mgr. Shimrak (made Bishop of Krizhevtzi by the Holy See in May, 1942). On October 5, 1946, Pope Pius XII had these words in his speech to the Sacred Roman Rota "in reply to a request of the Yugoslav Legation to the Holy See on the movement of conversions, in which the said Legation expressly recognised that neither the Holy See nor the Catholic Hierarchy in Croatia had had any part." Practically every Bishop in the Catholic world has publicly declared that the charges brought forward at the "trial" of Archbishop Stepinac were either falsifications, distortions or malicious misrepresentations of the facts. Neither Cardinal Griffin nor Cardinal Spellman have been challenged by Tito's men in London or New York. Does Mr. Butler hold that the Pope and Bishops were lying?

The Standard, 4 June 1948

Forced Confessions

To the Editor of The Irish Times

Governments often tell lies; so it seems a pity to question their veracity when it is easily tested.

In your leading article today you hint that Mgr. Cule's confession at the Yugo-Slav trials was extorted by threats. This seems an unkind aspersion on his courage and truthfulness.

Katolichki Tjednik (*The Catholic Weekly*) is one of the principal Yugo-Slav newspapers. It is almost certainly filed in the Vatican Library and elsewhere abroad, so that the reference which I translate from it is easily verified. No. 42, Page 6, October 18th, 1942:

> Then the bishop thanked the Italian army, and particularly the regimental band, for its participation. He thanked the Croatian Government authorities, the civil and military associations, and the Ustasha Youth battalion, whom he called "the hope and pride of our future." Continuing, he said: "It is my task to be as accommodating as we can be to the Government authorities, and I wish loyally to collaborate in the work of the Independent State of Croatia, which the Poglavnik (i.e., Pavelitch) created." (Clapping and enthusiastic cheers. "Po-glav-nik!") His motto is: "I came to work and not to command." *Non ministrari sed ministrare.* Not to be served, but to serve. That is a motto which every Catholic bishop should take to himself.

If the Yugo-Slav Government falsified this newspaper extract, which I have not myself tried to verify, I think they should be exposed. It would then be possible to talk of forced confessions.

The Irish Times, 22 July 1948

Prison Interview
with Archbishop Stepinac

Is it possible for the partisans of peace to play a more positive, more authoritative part today? Have we not a right to be encouraged by the invitation that recently came from Yugoslavia to the National Peace Council?

A deputation was asked to tour the country so that they could later publicly refute the Cominform charges that Yugoslavia had aggressive intentions against her Cominform neighbours and was allowing the

Americans and British to fortify bases against them. Was not this proof that, in the eyes of one Communist country at least, the testimony of a small, unofficial body with a reputation for impartiality still has importance?

I was allowed to accompany the deputation and, after it had left Yugoslavia, I tried to get more data about the problem of Mgr. Stepinac, which I have studied for some years and which has been a cause of such friction and misunderstanding between East and West.

I visited him in Lepoglava and also many of those who could give me first-hand evidence; many priests and bishops, and also M. Vimpulsek, the President of the Court which condemned the Archbishop. I talked with M. Vimpulsek for nearly two hours. He answered all my questions freely and made a suggestion which seemed to me of far-reaching significance.

"We are ready to let all the evidence be investigated," he said; "why should not some impartial body in a neutral country like Switzerland re-examine the evidence and report on it?" He did not suggest that such a body should have any powers, juridical or otherwise, which did not simply derive from their own scrupulous effort and reputation for integrity. But such powers, often, even in the modern world, can inspire respect.

Anyone who studies the Stepinac case quickly becomes aware that it is not a simple one, and that much of the intense bitterness which it has caused and is causing, derives from the foolish claim advanced by both sides that it is simple.

In the background of the trial there is one of the most terrible massacres that the world has ever seen, in which 500,000 Orthodox Christians were slaughtered. It was accompanied by a Conversion campaign in which 250,000 Orthodox Christians were forced into the Catholic Church.*

All this happened in 1941 when Mgr. Stepinac was Primate of the

---

* See note on page 178. (Editors)

Roman Catholic Church in Yugoslavia. If you read the literature issued by the Orthodox Church, both from England and America, during the war, and also that published by the Monarchist Government in exile, it is obvious that its leaders concurred with the present Communist view that the whole Roman hierarchy of Yugoslavia were implicated, sometimes by their active complicity, sometimes by their silence, in the great conversion campaign.

Perhaps they exaggerate this complicity; it is hard to judge... but all I want to emphasize is that the dispute is by no means one in which Communists and Christians are ranged on opposite sides of a barrier, though that is the way we are asked to view it most often. A body which could prove to the world—and it would be very easy to prove—that this barrier does not exist, would be doing a great service to peace.

It is obvious that such a body would press, where possible, for the release of political prisoners, whether the captives were Communist or Christian and, without in any way condoning or minimising any offences of which the Archbishop may have been guilty, they would see little profit in his continued imprisonment.

A paradoxical situation has arisen in which the best way to secure the release of the Archbishop is to force upon public opinion the knowledge that he is not guiltless.

There is no doubt that, if the Vatican, in response to the pressure of public opinion, were to remove Mgr. Stepinac from the Archbishopric of Zagreb, on whatever grounds it chose, he would be released. Tito has said as much. And were this to happen, one source of international friction, at least, would be removed.

The Stepinac case is a relatively easy one, since the material is all readily accessible. There are other more difficult issues which could be treated. What about the Bulgarian pastors?

I believe there are millions of people in Europe who would be favourably impressed if an impartial searchlight was focussed on their case, if the behaviour of the British and American officials and the Secret Service was scrutinised as carefully as the actions of the Bulgarian Government.

It has never been done. The Bulgarians are retained in prison as a gesture against the foreign attempt to use the clergy for political ends.

Would not our Intelligence Services have been neglecting their duties if they had not tried to use them so? And are not we neglecting ours when we allow our people to get away with it?

Of course, I am not defending the action of the Bulgarian Government, but I think it would not so readily resort to force and slander against those it, perhaps unreasonably, mistrusted if it knew that anywhere in the world there was a body ready to examine their difficulties without national or political partisanship and to strive for a peaceful solution.

Another problem would be that of the Greek children. I have never seen any careful and authoritative report on this which did not show signs of bias.

Of course, it would be outside the scope of such a body to brand criminals, expose lies, far less to appease or find excuses for aggression. Its purpose would be to attain a degree of scientific impartiality in the analysis of these complex problems far beyond the reach of the ordinary international conference.

But it will be said there is no such thing as an impartial analysis. You must have some guiding principle.

Well, the analysis would be made in the light of our unshakable conviction that, in these intricate problems, not only force, but the mere hint of force fuddles the brain and saps the confidence. This is not sentiment, but sense.

This note (possibly written by Butler) followed the above article:

Monseigneur Aloysius Stepinac, Archbishop of Zagreb and Roman Catholic Primate of Yugoslavia, was tried in Zagreb from September 30 to October 8, 1946, on charges of collaboration with the enemy and anti-national activities during the occupation. Mgr. Stepinac pleaded "not guilty," declared that his conscience was clear and announced that he would not reply to any questions put by the prosecution.

Found guilty on all charges, Mgr. Stepinac was sentenced to 16 years hard labour, loss of civic rights for a further five years and a confiscation of his property.

The Vatican described the trial as "essentially political" and there was great indignation amongst Roman Catholics throughout the world.

Within the last month it has been suggested that Mgr. Stepinac would be released if the Vatican would remove him from the Archbishopric of Zagreb.

Peace News, 1950-51

Cardinal Stepinac

The Yugoslav government has recently forbidden Cardinal Stepinac to give interviews to journalists on the ground that, he, a convicted war criminal, is abusing his freedom in order to undermine the government's authority.

Though he is out of prison and living quietly in his native village of Krasitch, he is as much a focus of angry and conflicting emotions as before. The Cardinal's hat does not appear to have been sent with any pacific intentions and was perhaps the principal cause of the Yugoslav breach with the Vatican and the revival of accusations about the terrible compulsory conversion campaign of 1941.

Depressingly, no serious attempt has been made to piece together impartially the true facts though the campaign is more richly documented than any former sectarian crusade.

In the Zagreb papers of the period one can see the exact extent of the support that was given to the crusade by the Catholic hierarchy.

Roughly speaking one may say that the bishops were enthusiastic about the Quisling Pavelitch himself and saw in his advent to power an admirable opportunity of extending the domain of the Catholic

Church but were horrified when they found by what brutal methods the campaign was to be conducted. It was then too late for them to withdraw their support. No one was excommunicated and I do not think that the official Orthodox claim that 250,000 were forcibly coerced into the Catholic Church can be far off the truth.

Why have not the ordinary Christians of Europe demanded an enquiry into these horrors? Why has it been left to the Communists to prosecute and the Vatican to defend? It concerns us all. Hitherto, because the West is frightened of helping Communism we have been slow in demanding the truth, but our fears have helped no one.

Had there been a Christian demand for an investigation, I believe that Mgr. Stepinac would have been quietly withdrawn by the Vatican from Yugoslavia. He would never have become a prisoner, he would never have become a Cardinal. There would have been one storm centre the less in our turbulent world.

Peace News, 24 April 1953

Tito and Stepinac

To the editor of the New Statesman:

As an Irish Protestant I would like to assure Mr. Waugh that there can be no analogy between the Ustashe and the Sinn Feiners. In 1916, as in previous revolts, many of the leaders were Protestants and there was no shadow of bigotry against the "schismatics." It is true that we have a small organisation here now, which, like the Ustashe, wishes to take strong measures against schism, but it wears an Italian name, Maria Duce, and is alien in spirit to the Irish.

I cannot understand how the intimate and, for the most part, joyous association of the Catholic Hierarchy in Yugoslavia with Pavelic and his plans for the suppression of the Orthodox Church in Croatia and its two million adherents can be for a moment in doubt. Apart from the voluminous evidence of the Orthodox Church itself, published in England and America in 1942 and 1943, there is the large source-book of dated newspaper cuttings, photographs, etc., published in Yugoslavia in 1946. It is easy to check these extracts by reference to the papers themselves in the newspaper library at Zagreb University. I spent many days in 1947 and again in 1950 verifying the more incredible of these clerical utterances. I could not believe that Archbishop Sharic had really published a poem comparing Pavelic to Leonidas and applauding his measures against the Serbs and Jews. But he did. He published it not only in his own church paper in Sarajevo but also in *Novo Hrvatska* of Zagreb on Christmas Day, 1941. He is now writing for Pavelic's paper in Buenos Aires, very flatteringly of Mgr. Stepinac.

If Mr. Derrick has a friend with a knowledge of Serbo-Croatian, he will be able to find out all that he wants to know (and perhaps more) about Bishop Cule of Mostar, and Bishop Aksamovic (his middle phase), in the pages of Catholic journals of the Occupation period. I can give him the references.

None of this must be taken to imply that Mgr. Stepinac's trial was fair. On the evidence of the printed record of the trial I expect it was not, because his own speech of defence and that of his two counsels were omitted and I believe have never been published in Yugoslavia. Yet this has no relevance to the separate issue of Catholic bigotry in 1941 except in so far as that bigotry provided a notable pattern for later persecution.

New Statesman, January-February 1953

Index of Names